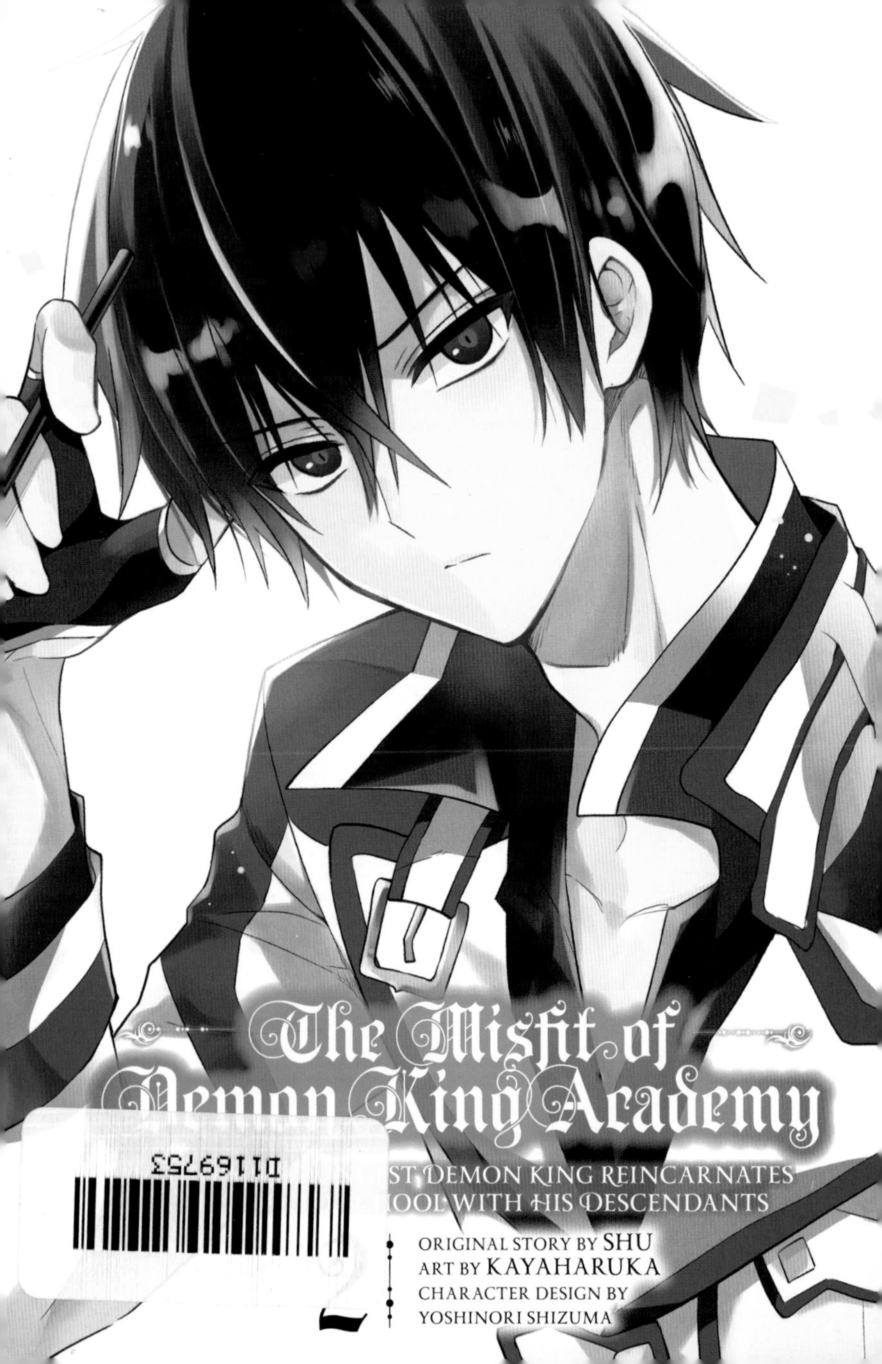
The Misfit of Demon King Academy
...ST DEMON KING REINCARNATES
...OOL WITH HIS DESCENDANTS
ORIGINAL STORY BY SHU
ART BY KAYAHARUKA
CHARACTER DESIGN BY
YOSHINORI SHIZUMA
1
D1169753

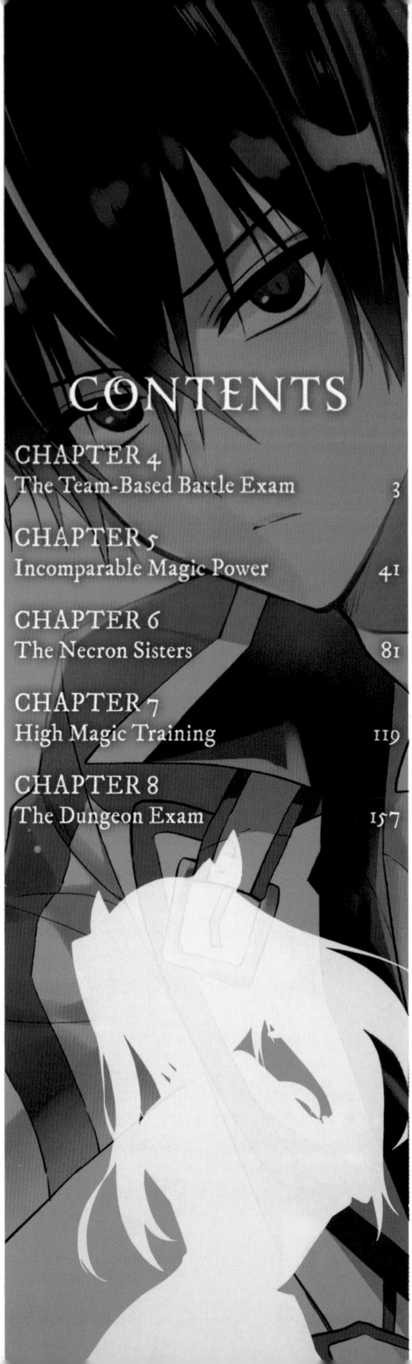

CONTENTS

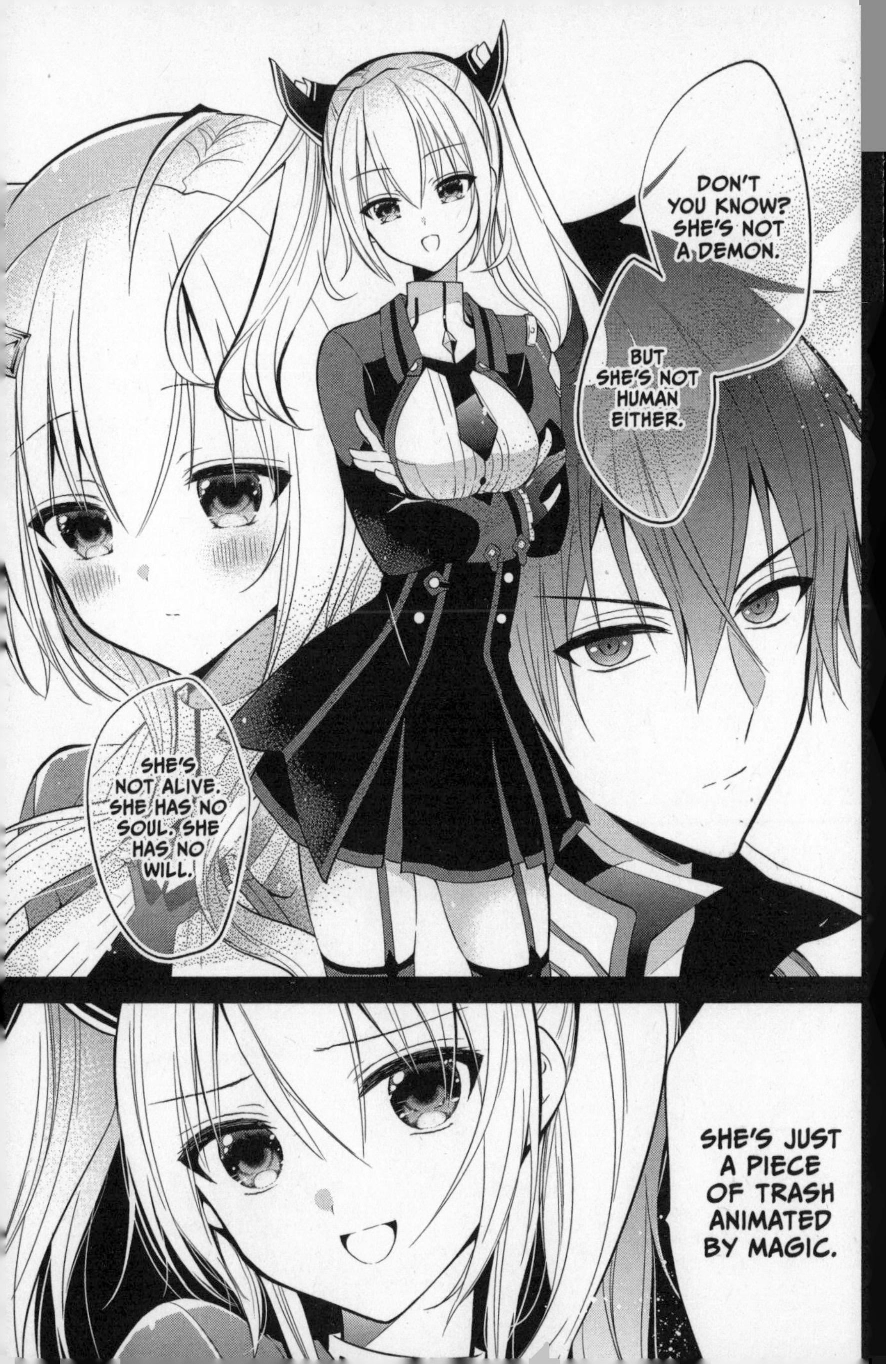
DON'T YOU KNOW? SHE'S NOT A DEMON.
BUT SHE'S NOT HUMAN EITHER.
SHE'S NOT ALIVE. SHE HAS NO SOUL. SHE HAS NO WILL.
SHE'S JUST A PIECE OF TRASH ANIMATED BY MAGIC.

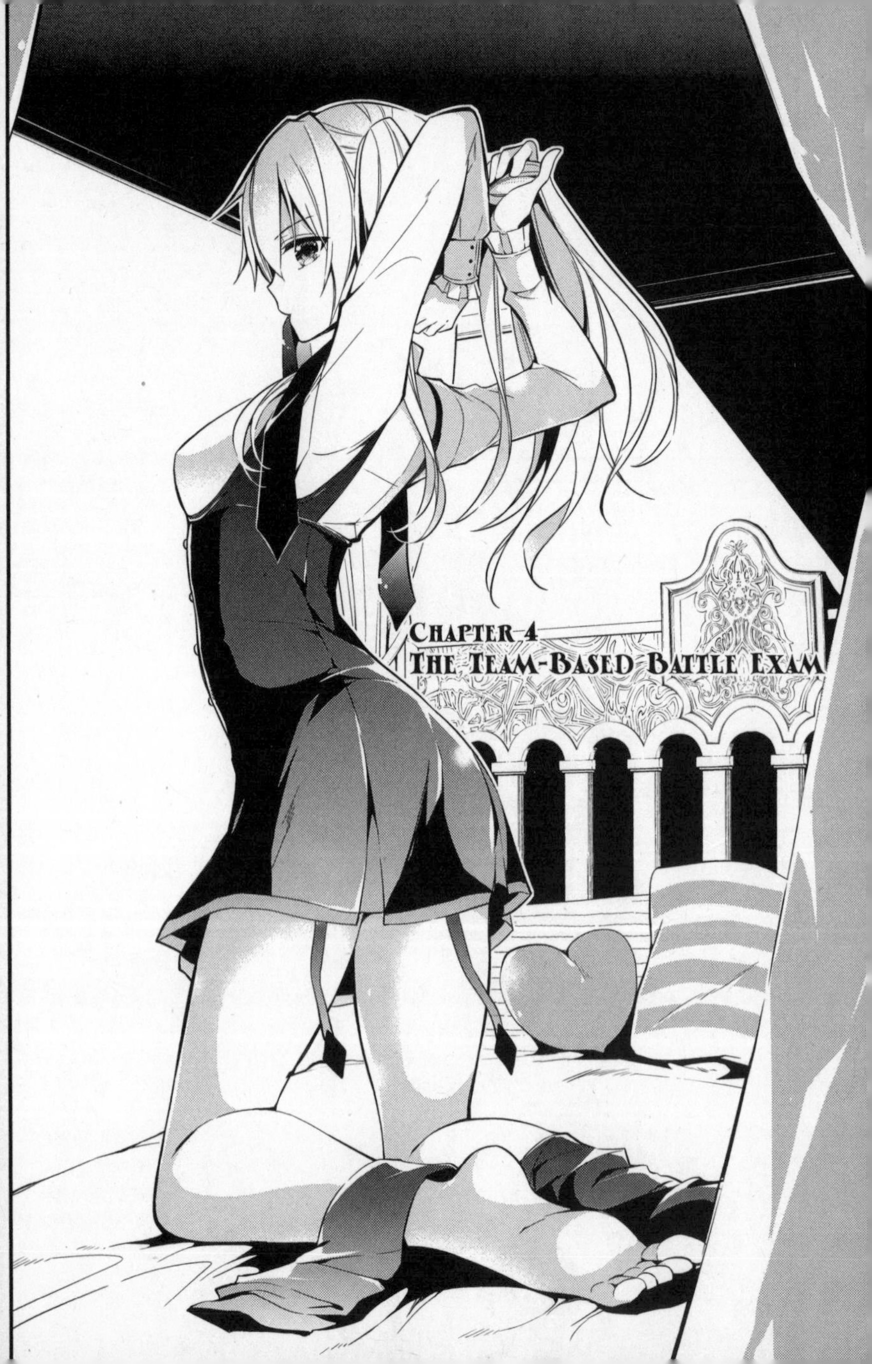
Chapter 4
The Team-Based Battle Exam

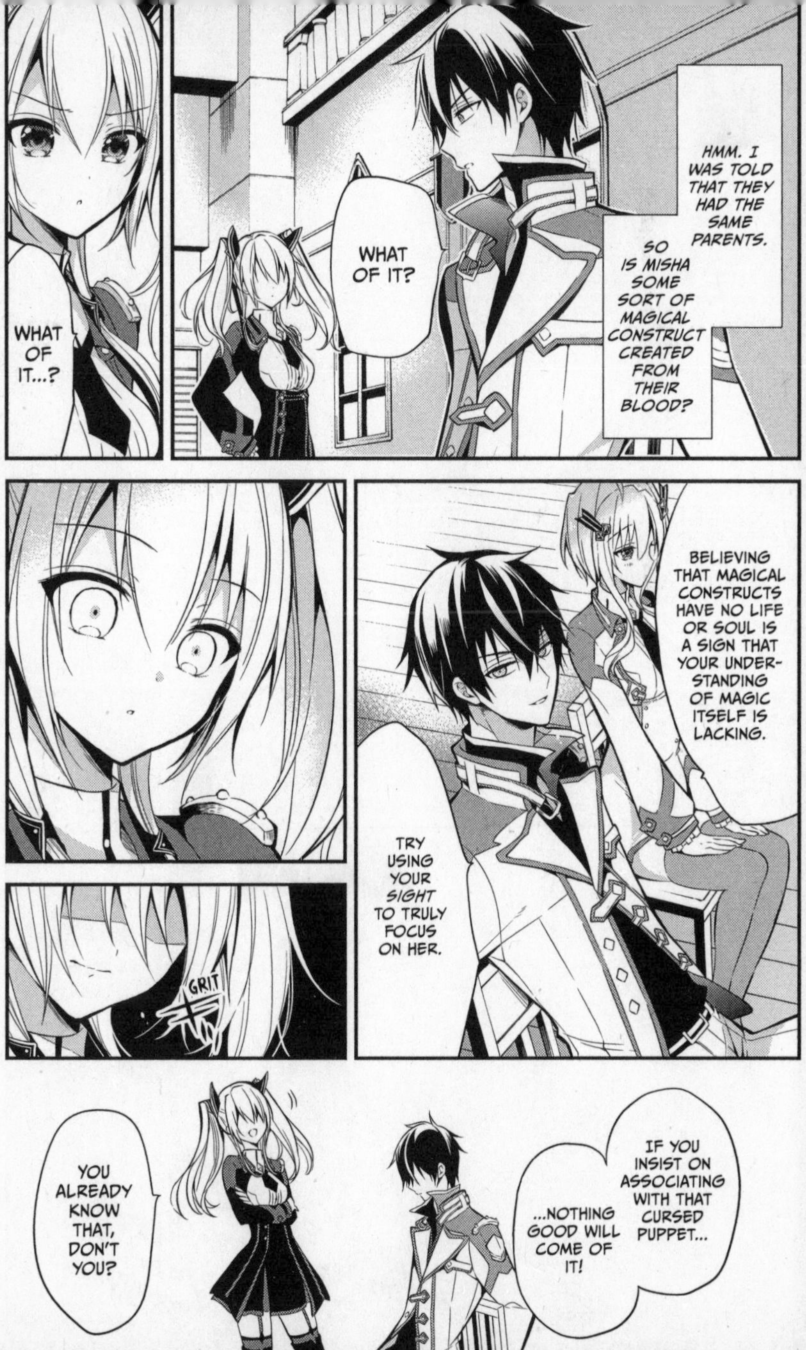
HMM. I WAS TOLD THAT THEY HAD THE SAME PARENTS.
SO IS MISHA SOME SORT OF MAGICAL CONSTRUCT CREATED FROM THEIR BLOOD?
WHAT OF IT?
WHAT OF IT...?
BELIEVING THAT MAGICAL CONSTRUCTS HAVE NO LIFE OR SOUL IS A SIGN THAT YOUR UNDER-STANDING OF MAGIC ITSELF IS LACKING.
TRY USING YOUR SIGHT TO TRULY FOCUS ON HER.
GRIT
IF YOU INSIST ON ASSOCIATING WITH THAT CURSED PUPPET...
...NOTHING GOOD WILL COME OF IT!
YOU ALREADY KNOW THAT, DON'T YOU?

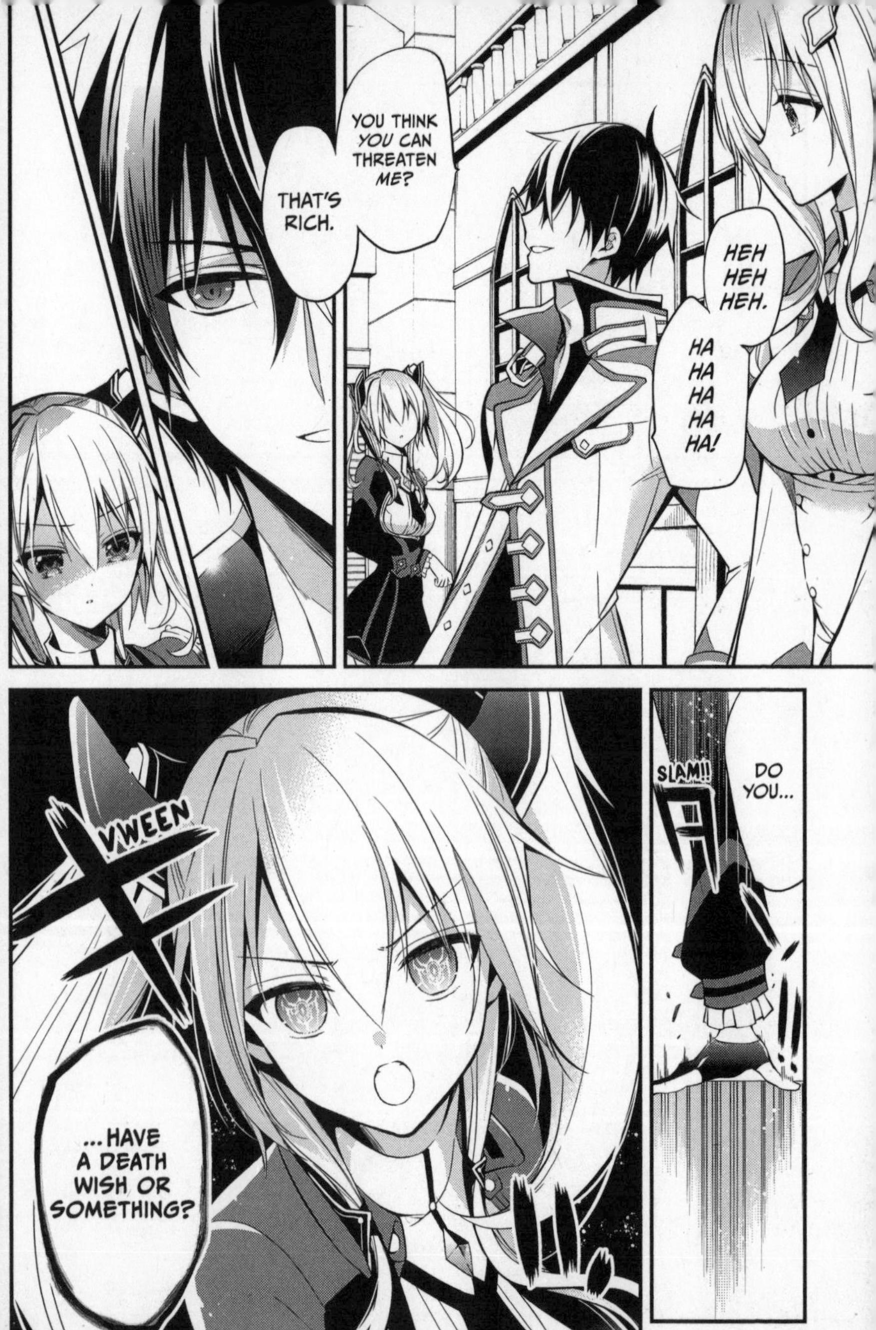
HEH HEH HEH.
HA HA HA HA HA!
YOU THINK YOU CAN THREATEN ME?
THAT'S RICH.
DO YOU...
SLAM!!
VWEEN
...HAVE A DEATH WISH OR SOMETHING?

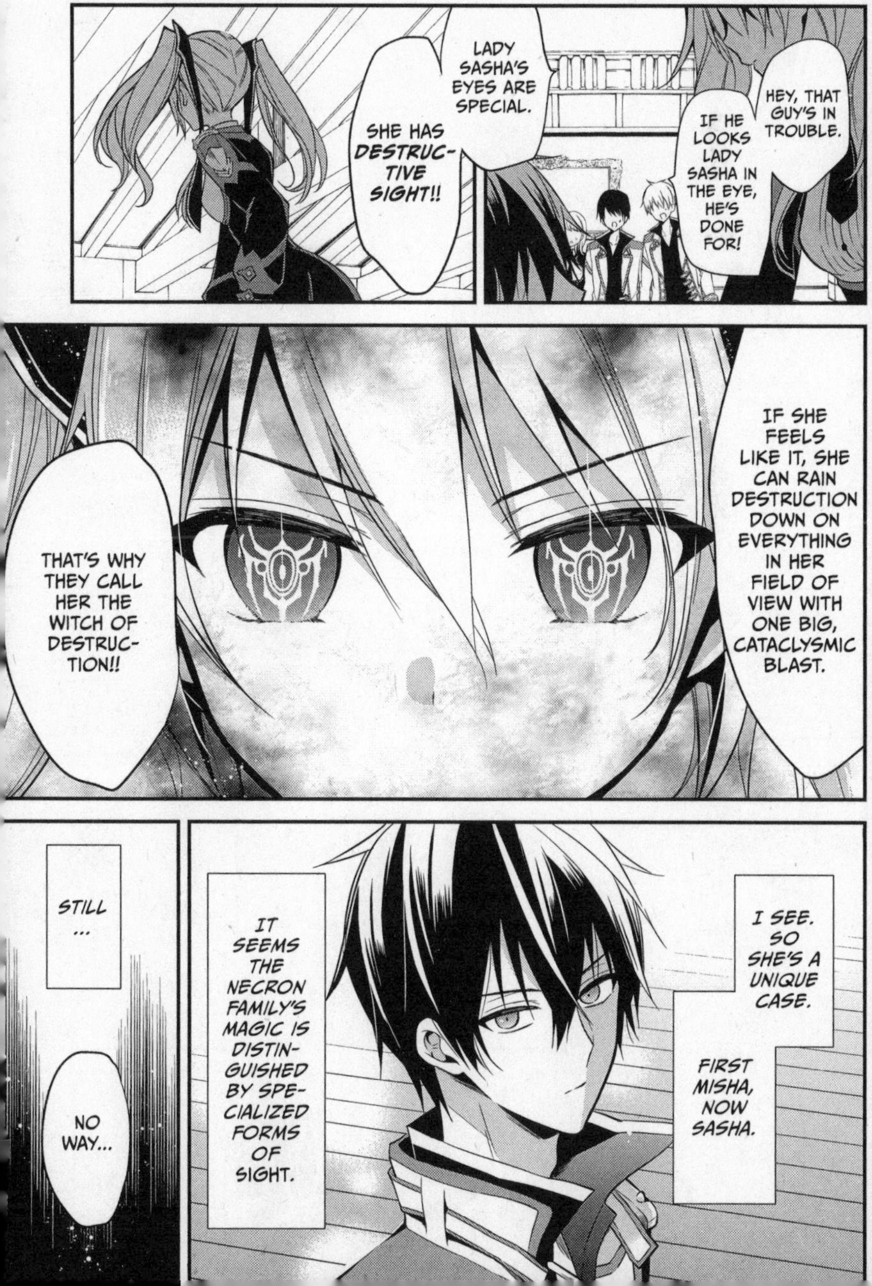
HEY, THAT GUY'S IN TROUBLE.
IF HE LOOKS LADY SASHA IN THE EYE, HE'S DONE FOR!
LADY SASHA'S EYES ARE SPECIAL.
SHE HAS DESTRUC-TIVE SIGHT!!
IF SHE FEELS LIKE IT, SHE CAN RAIN DESTRUCTION DOWN ON EVERYTHING IN HER FIELD OF VIEW WITH ONE BIG, CATACLYSMIC BLAST.
THAT'S WHY THEY CALL HER THE WITCH OF DESTRUC-TION!!
I SEE. SO SHE'S A UNIQUE CASE.
FIRST MISHA, NOW SASHA.
IT SEEMS THE NECRON FAMILY'S MAGIC IS DISTIN-GUISHED BY SPE-CIALIZED FORMS OF SIGHT.
STILL ...
NO WAY...

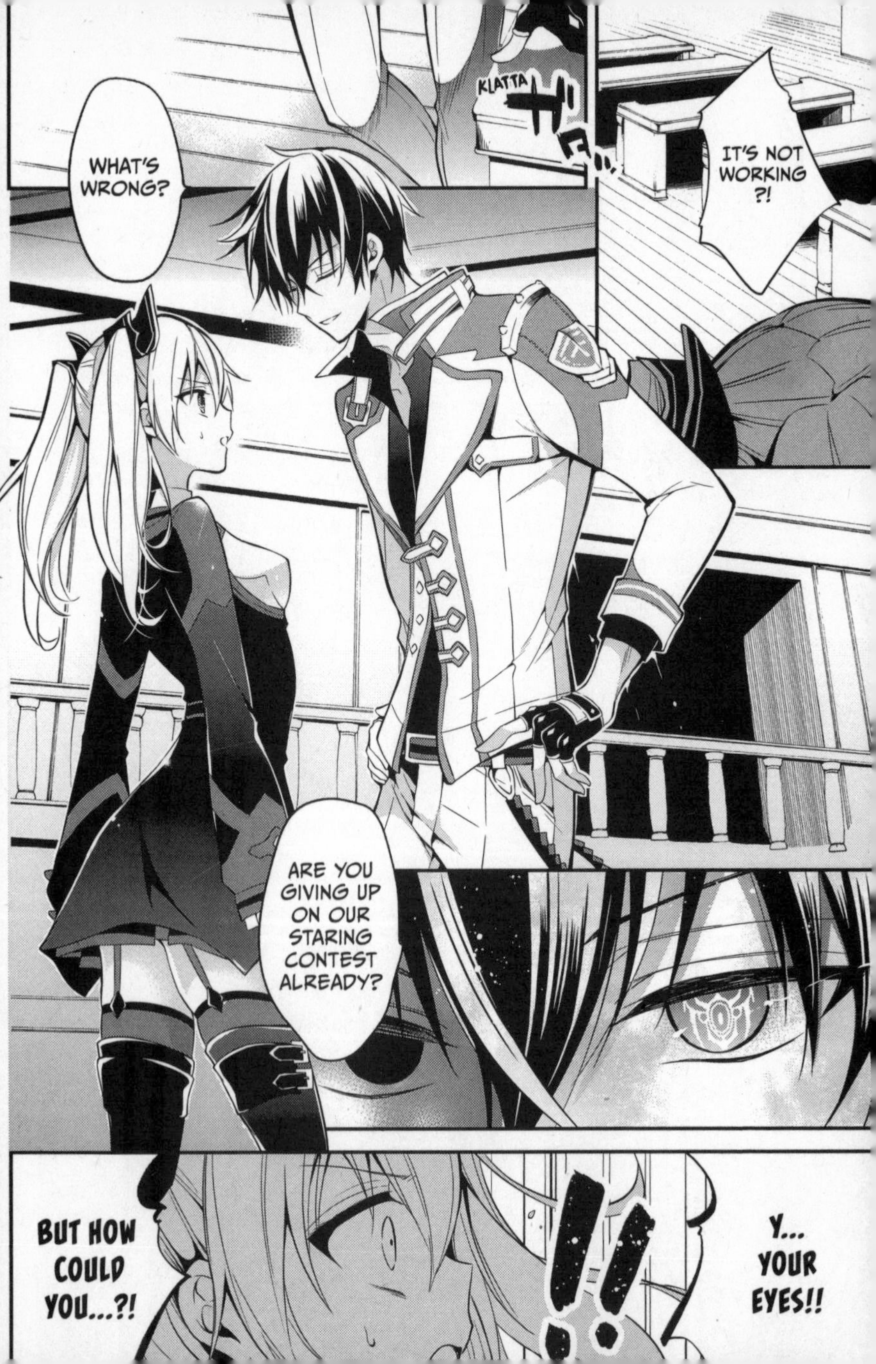
IT'S NOT WORKING ?!
KLATTA
WHAT'S WRONG?
ARE YOU GIVING UP ON OUR STARING CONTEST ALREADY?
Y... YOUR EYES!!
BUT HOW COULD YOU...?!

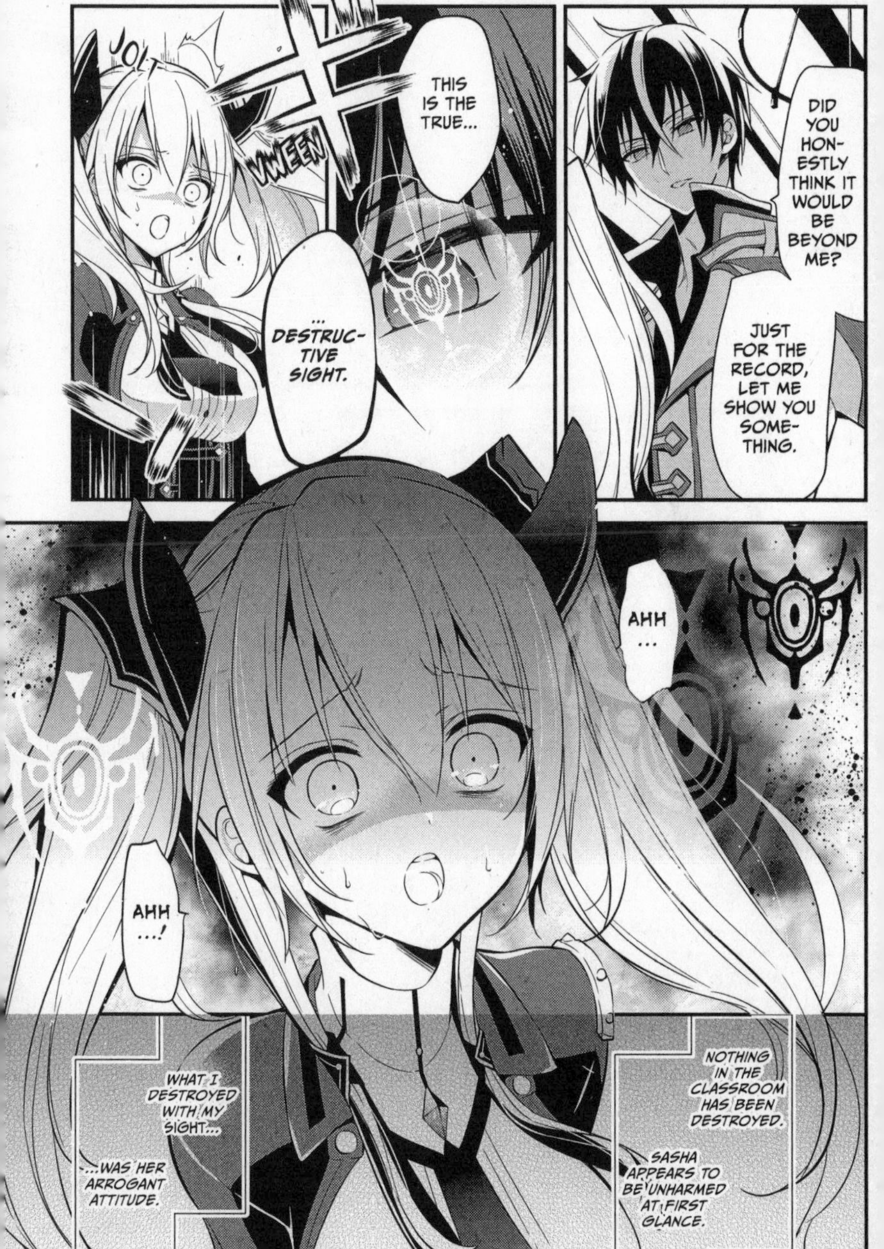
DID YOU HON-ESTLY THINK IT WOULD BE BEYOND ME?
JUST FOR THE RECORD, LET ME SHOW YOU SOME-THING.
THIS IS THE TRUE...
...DESTRUC-TIVE SIGHT.
JOLT
VWEEN
AHH...
AHH...!
NOTHING IN THE CLASSROOM HAS BEEN DESTROYED.
SASHA APPEARS TO BE UNHARMED AT FIRST GLANCE.
WHAT I DESTROYED WITH MY SIGHT...
...WAS HER ARROGANT ATTITUDE.

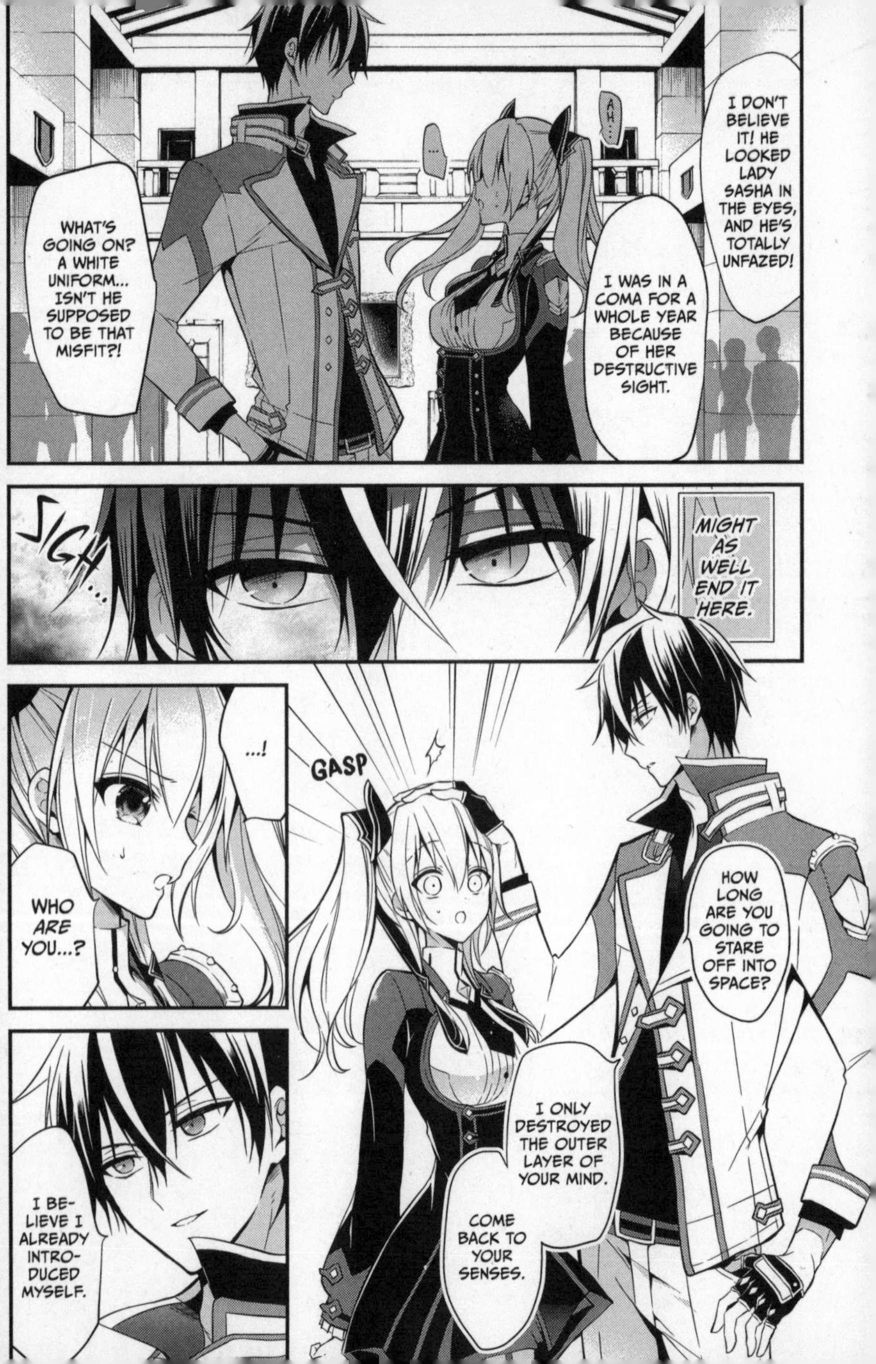
I DON'T BELIEVE IT! HE LOOKED LADY SASHA IN THE EYES, AND HE'S TOTALLY UNFAZED!
I WAS IN A COMA FOR A WHOLE YEAR BECAUSE OF HER DESTRUCTIVE SIGHT.
AH...
...
WHAT'S GOING ON? A WHITE UNIFORM... ISN'T HE SUPPOSED TO BE THAT MISFIT?!
MIGHT AS WELL END IT HERE.
SIGH...
GASP
HOW LONG ARE YOU GOING TO STARE OFF INTO SPACE?
I ONLY DESTROYED THE OUTER LAYER OF YOUR MIND.
COME BACK TO YOUR SENSES.
...!
WHO ARE YOU...?
I BE-LIEVE I ALREADY INTRO-DUCED MYSELF.

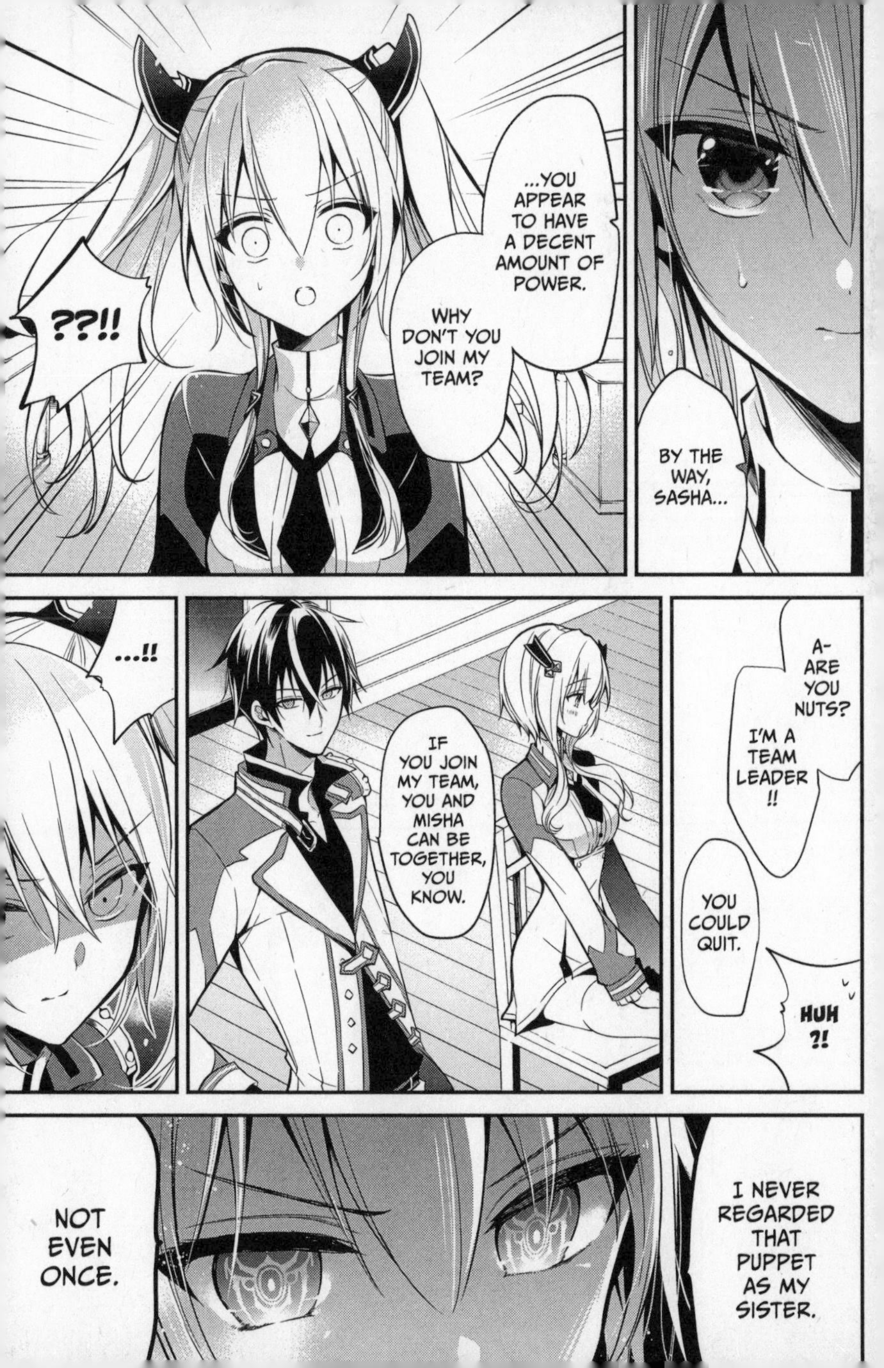
BY THE WAY, SASHA...
...YOU APPEAR TO HAVE A DECENT AMOUNT OF POWER.
WHY DON'T YOU JOIN MY TEAM?
??!!
A-ARE YOU NUTS?
I'M A TEAM LEADER!!
YOU COULD QUIT.
HUH?!
IF YOU JOIN MY TEAM, YOU AND MISHA CAN BE TOGETHER, YOU KNOW.
...!!
I NEVER REGARDED THAT PUPPET AS MY SISTER.
NOT EVEN ONCE.

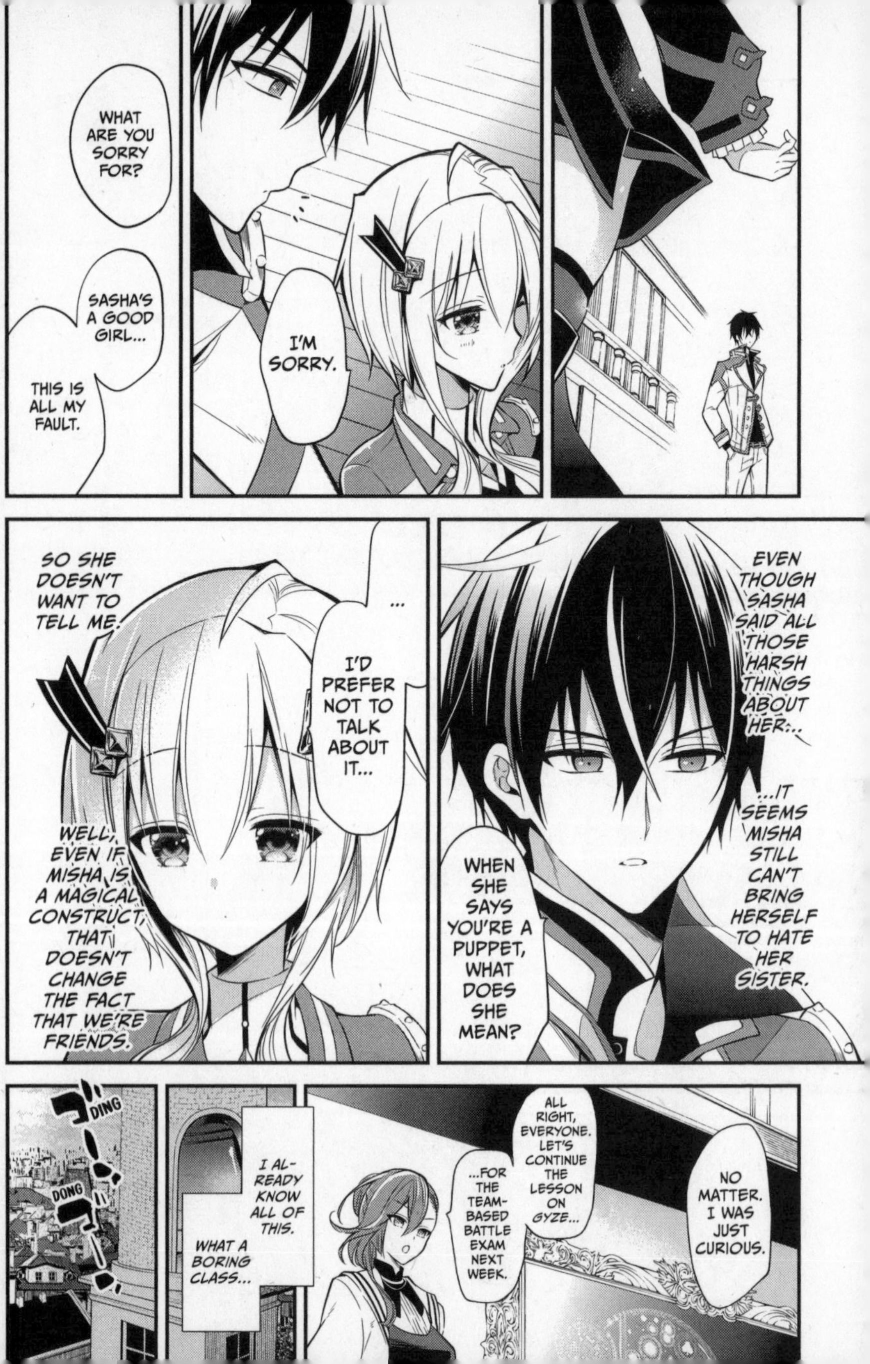
I'M SORRY.
WHAT ARE YOU SORRY FOR?
SASHA'S A GOOD GIRL... THIS IS ALL MY FAULT.
EVEN THOUGH SASHA SAID ALL THOSE HARSH THINGS ABOUT HER...
...IT SEEMS MISHA STILL CAN'T BRING HERSELF TO HATE HER SISTER.
WHEN SHE SAYS YOU'RE A PUPPET, WHAT DOES SHE MEAN?
...
I'D PREFER NOT TO TALK ABOUT IT...
SO SHE DOESN'T WANT TO TELL ME.
WELL, EVEN IF MISHA IS A MAGICAL CONSTRUCT, THAT DOESN'T CHANGE THE FACT THAT WE'RE FRIENDS.
NO MATTER. I WAS JUST CURIOUS.
ALL RIGHT, EVERYONE. LET'S CONTINUE THE LESSON ON GYZE...
...FOR THE TEAM-BASED BATTLE EXAM NEXT WEEK.
I AL-READY KNOW ALL OF THIS.
WHAT A BORING CLASS...
DING
DONG

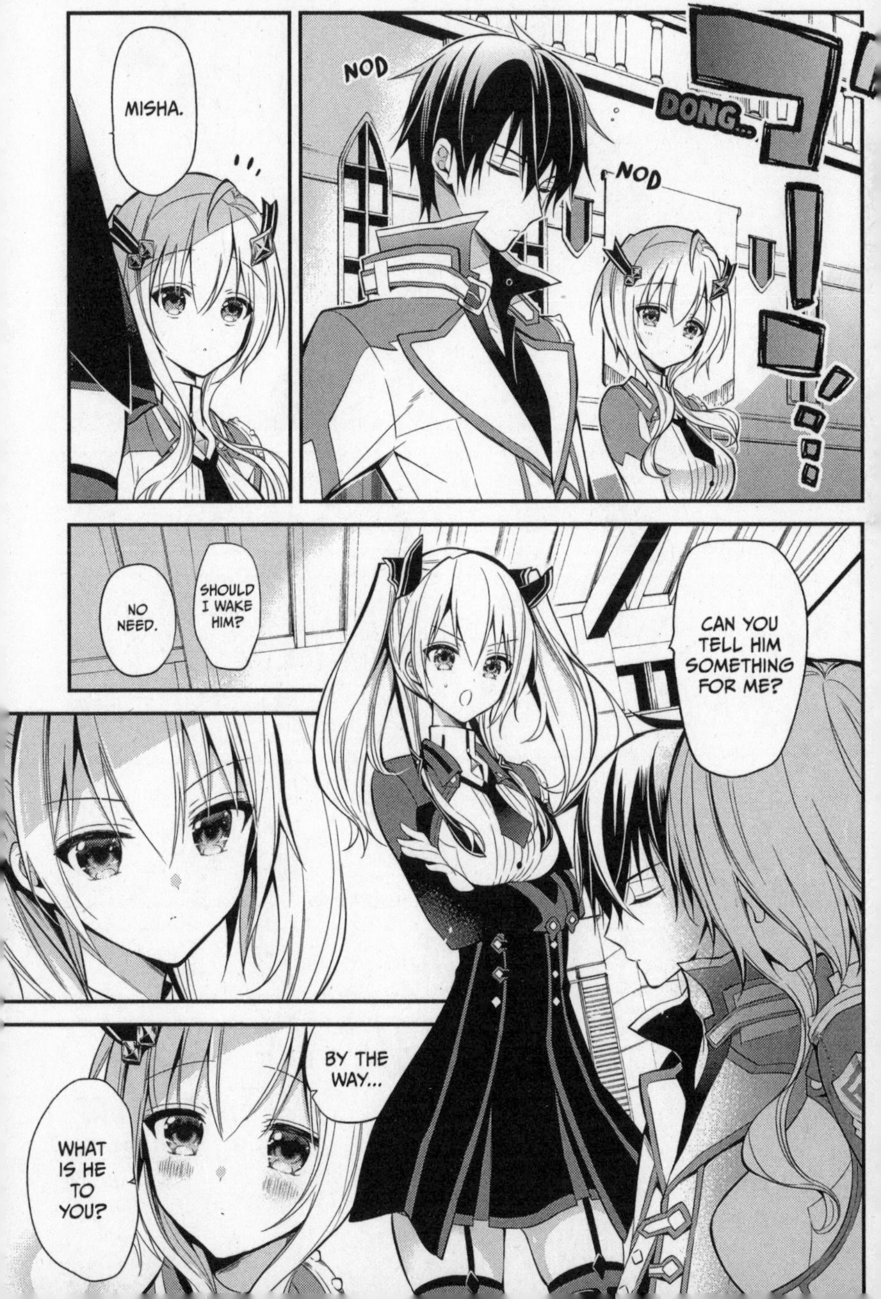
DONG...
NOD
NOD
MISHA.
SHOULD I WAKE HIM?
NO NEED.
CAN YOU TELL HIM SOMETHING FOR ME?
BY THE WAY...
WHAT IS HE TO YOU?

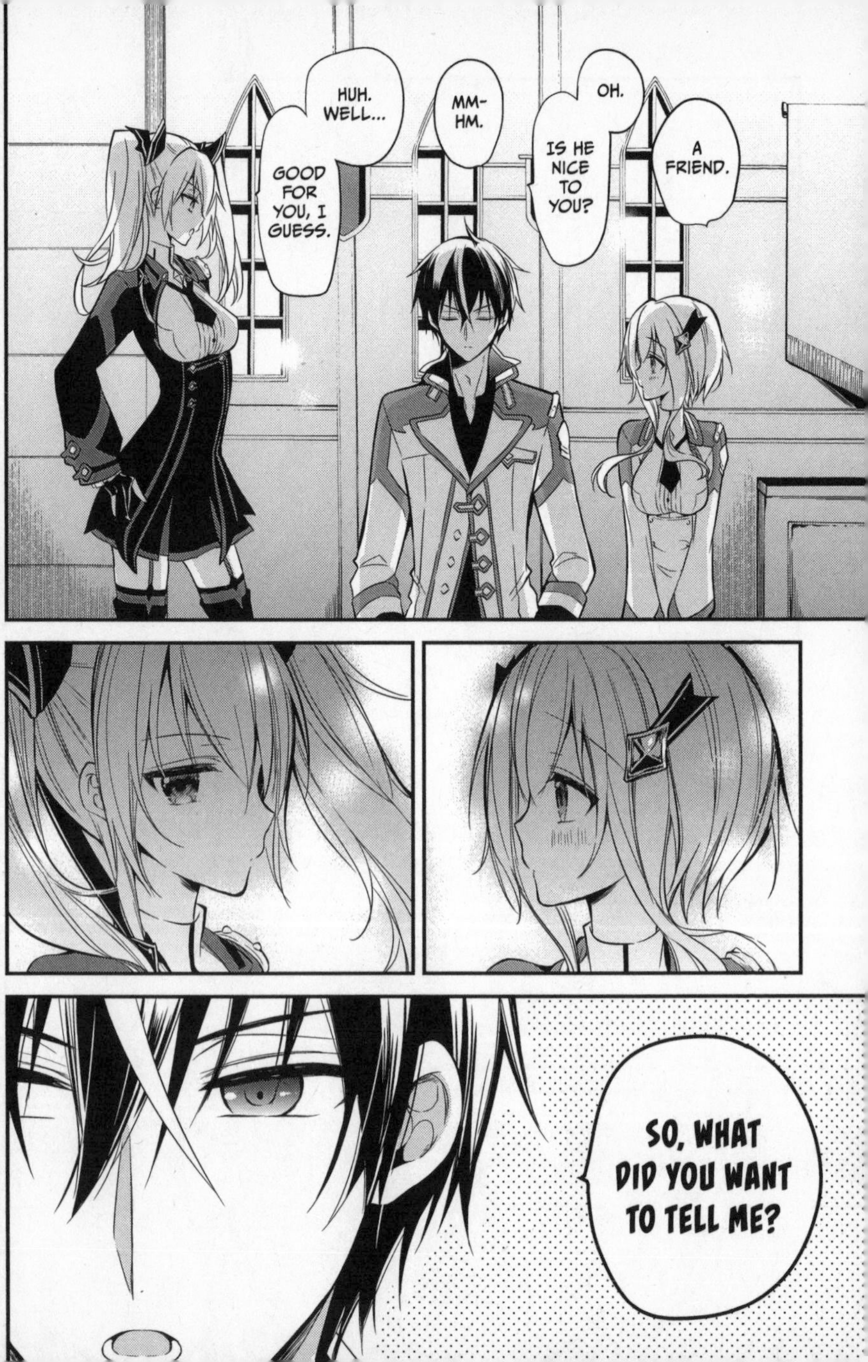
A FRIEND.
OH.
IS HE NICE TO YOU?
MM-HM.
HUH. WELL...
GOOD FOR YOU, I GUESS.
SO, WHAT DID YOU WANT TO TELL ME?

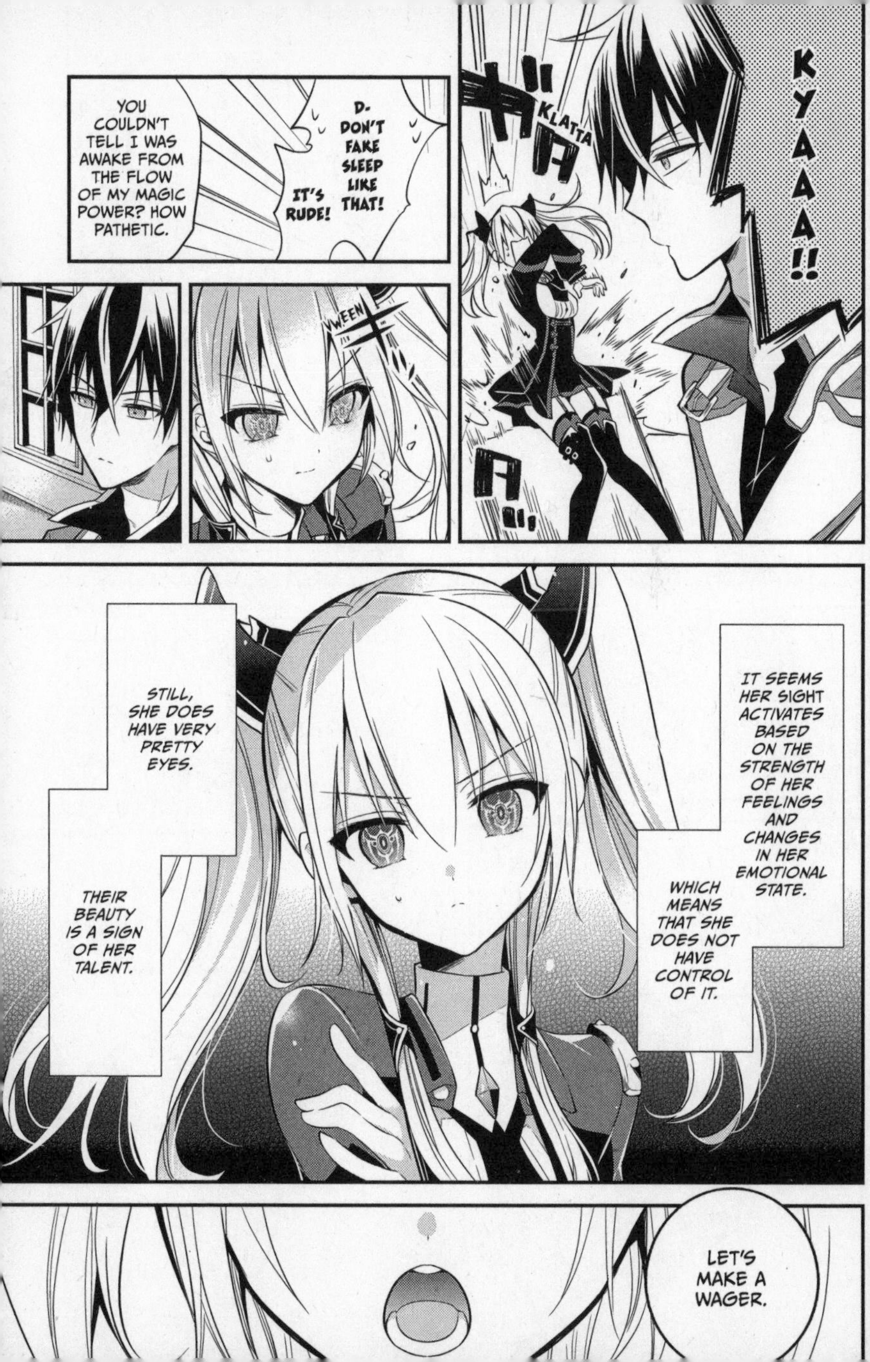
KYAAA!!
KLATTA
D-DON'T FAKE SLEEP LIKE THAT!
IT'S RUDE!
YOU COULDN'T TELL I WAS AWAKE FROM THE FLOW OF MY MAGIC POWER? HOW PATHETIC.
VWEEN
IT SEEMS HER SIGHT ACTIVATES BASED ON THE STRENGTH OF HER FEELINGS AND CHANGES IN HER EMOTIONAL STATE.
WHICH MEANS THAT SHE DOES NOT HAVE CONTROL OF IT.
STILL, SHE DOES HAVE VERY PRETTY EYES.
THEIR BEAUTY IS A SIGN OF HER TALENT.
LET'S MAKE A WAGER.

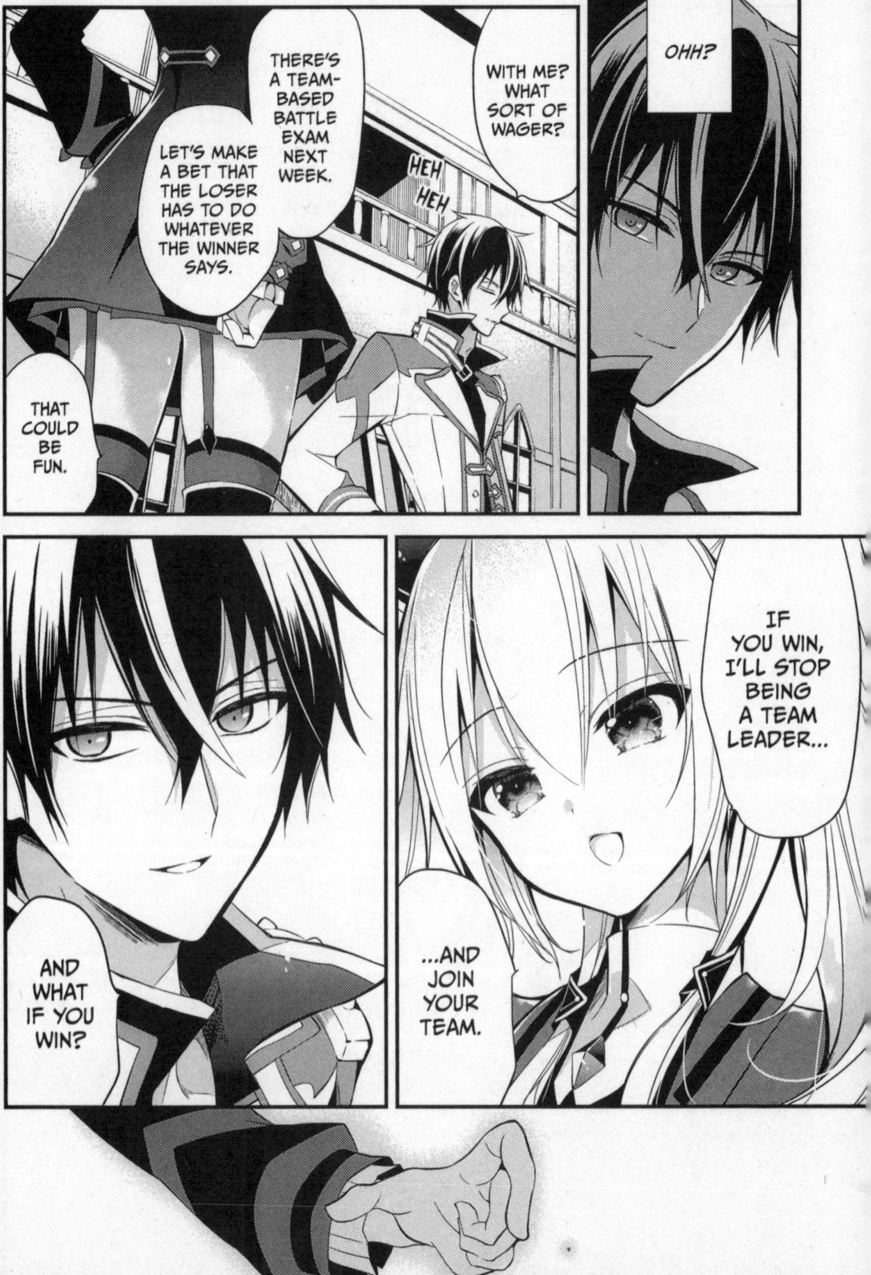
OHH?
WITH ME? WHAT SORT OF WAGER?
HEH HEH
THERE'S A TEAM-BASED BATTLE EXAM NEXT WEEK.
LET'S MAKE A BET THAT THE LOSER HAS TO DO WHATEVER THE WINNER SAYS.
THAT COULD BE FUN.
IF YOU WIN, I'LL STOP BEING A TEAM LEADER...
...AND JOIN YOUR TEAM.
AND WHAT IF YOU WIN?

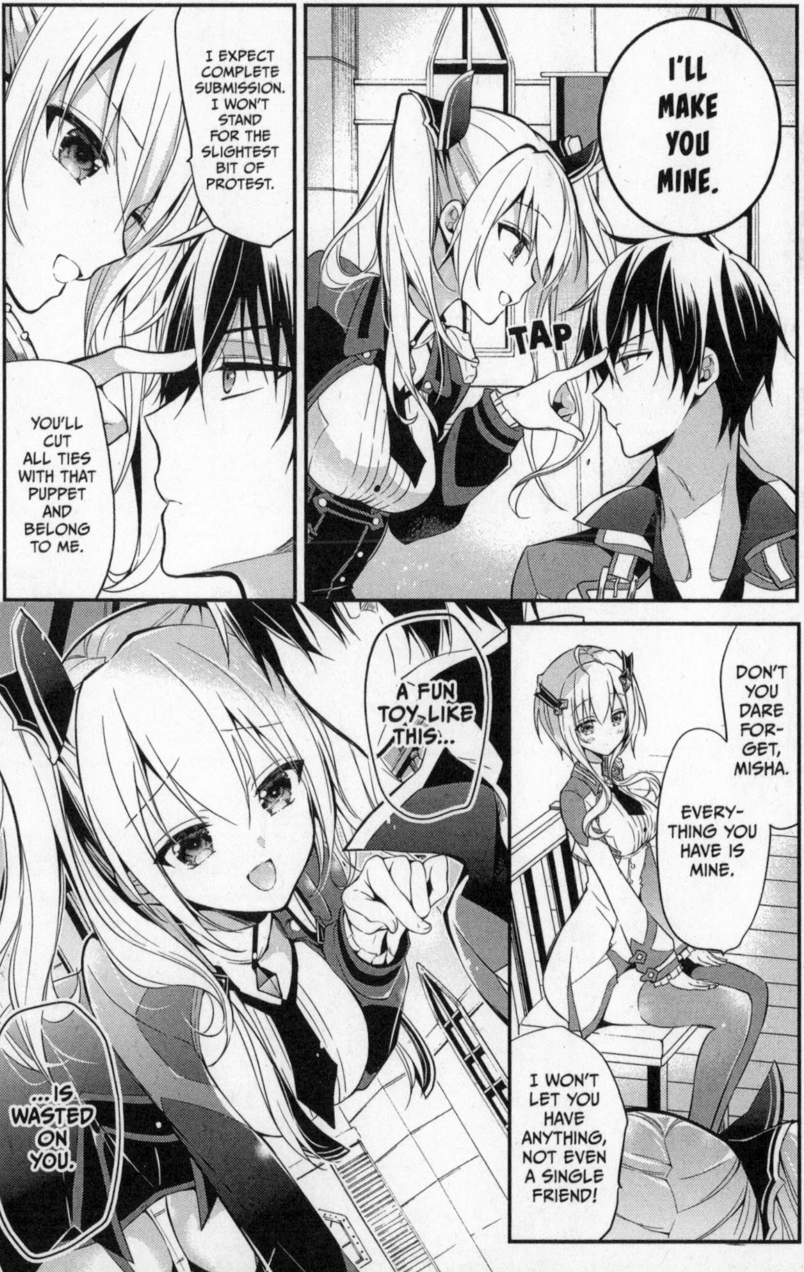
I'LL MAKE YOU MINE.
TAP
I EXPECT COMPLETE SUBMISSION. I WON'T STAND FOR THE SLIGHTEST BIT OF PROTEST.
YOU'LL CUT ALL TIES WITH THAT PUPPET AND BELONG TO ME.
DON'T YOU DARE FOR-GET, MISHA.
EVERY-THING YOU HAVE IS MINE.
I WON'T LET YOU HAVE ANYTHING, NOT EVEN A SINGLE FRIEND!
A FUN TOY LIKE THIS...
...IS WASTED ON YOU.

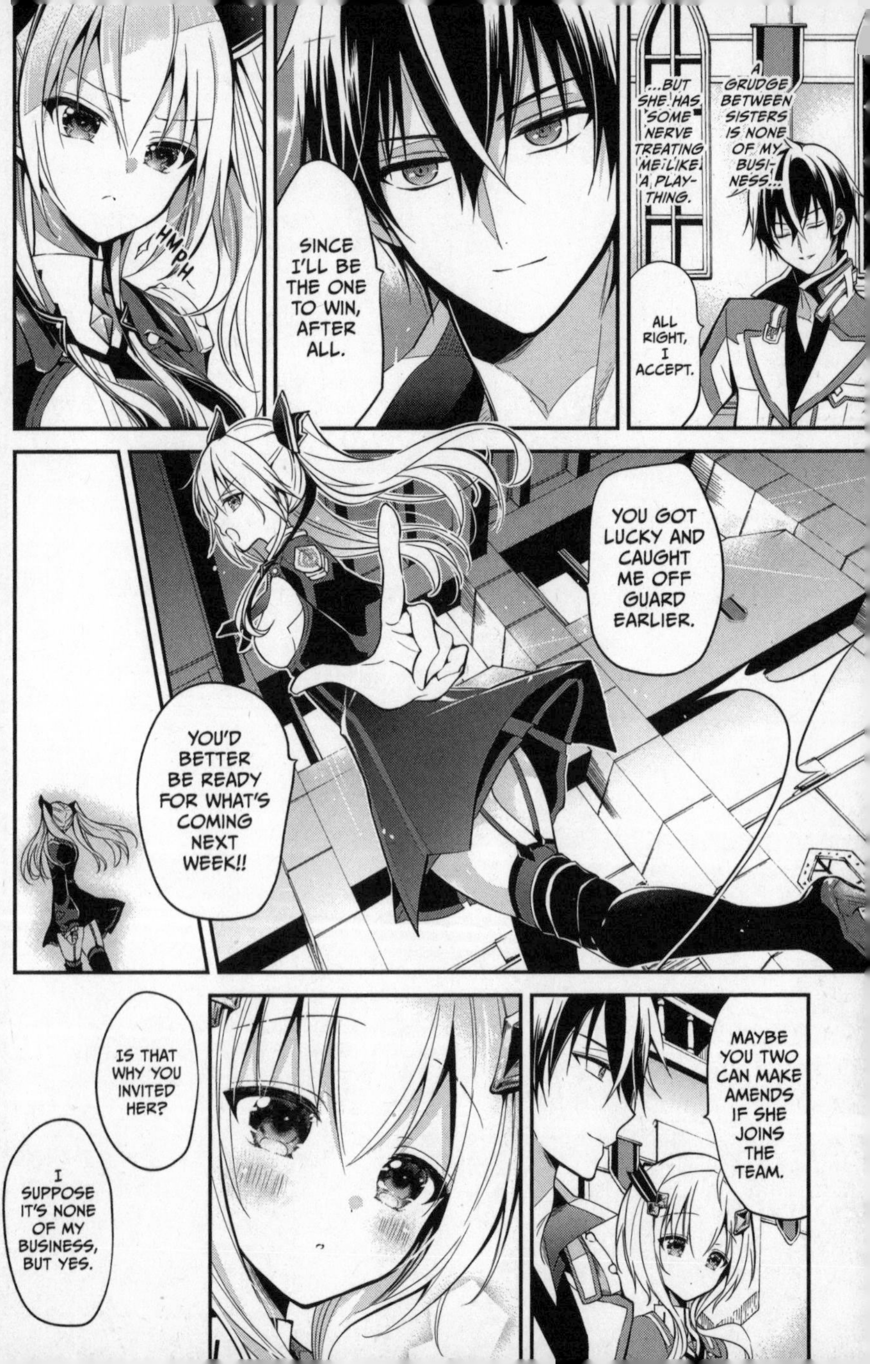

A GRUDGE BETWEEN SISTERS IS NONE OF MY BUSINESS...
...BUT SHE HAS SOME NERVE TREATING ME LIKE A PLAYTHING.
ALL RIGHT, I ACCEPT.
SINCE I'LL BE THE ONE TO WIN, AFTER ALL.
HMPH
YOU GOT LUCKY AND CAUGHT ME OFF GUARD EARLIER.
YOU'D BETTER BE READY FOR WHAT'S COMING NEXT WEEK!!
MAYBE YOU TWO CAN MAKE AMENDS IF SHE JOINS THE TEAM.
IS THAT WHY YOU INVITED HER?
I SUPPOSE IT'S NONE OF MY BUSINESS, BUT YES.

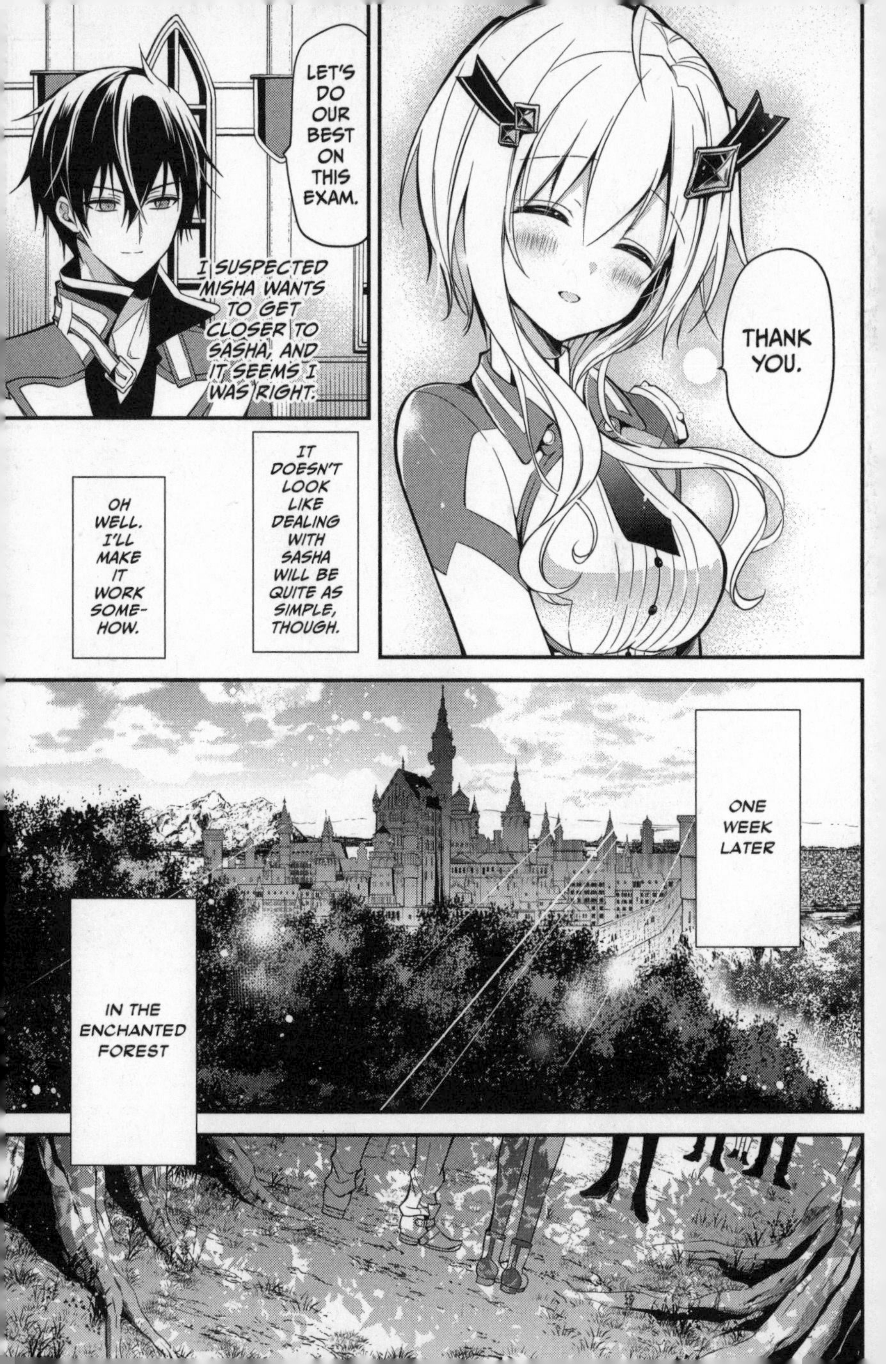
THANK YOU.
LET'S DO OUR BEST ON THIS EXAM.
I SUSPECTED MISHA WANTS TO GET CLOSER TO SASHA, AND IT SEEMS I WAS RIGHT.
IT DOESN'T LOOK LIKE DEALING WITH SASHA WILL BE QUITE AS SIMPLE, THOUGH.
OH WELL. I'LL MAKE IT WORK SOME-HOW.
ONE WEEK LATER
IN THE ENCHANTED FOREST

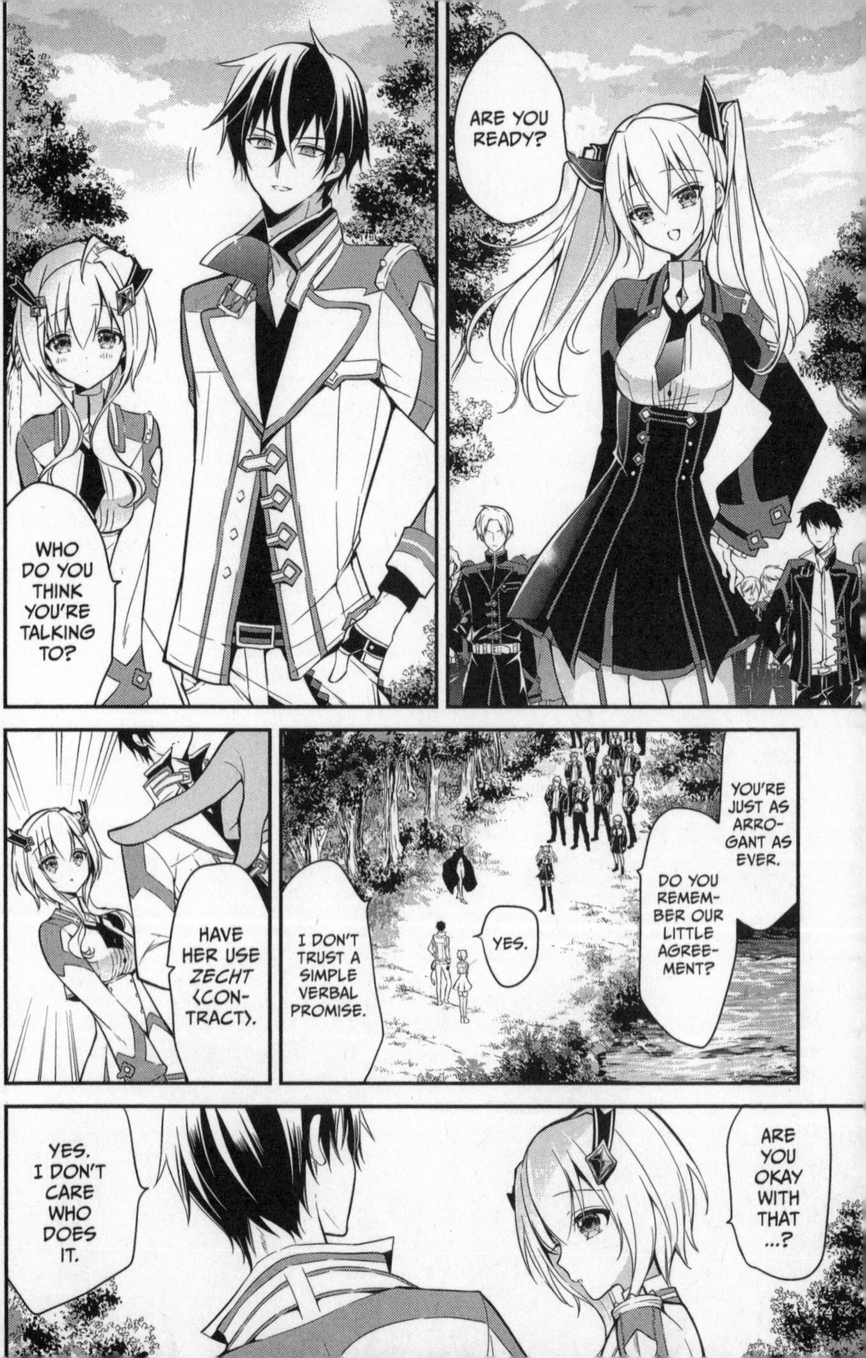
ARE YOU READY?
WHO DO YOU THINK YOU'RE TALKING TO?
YOU'RE JUST AS ARROGANT AS EVER.
DO YOU REMEMBER OUR LITTLE AGREEMENT?
YES.
I DON'T TRUST A SIMPLE VERBAL PROMISE.
HAVE HER USE ZECHT <CONTRACT>.
ARE YOU OKAY WITH THAT ...?
YES. I DON'T CARE WHO DOES IT.

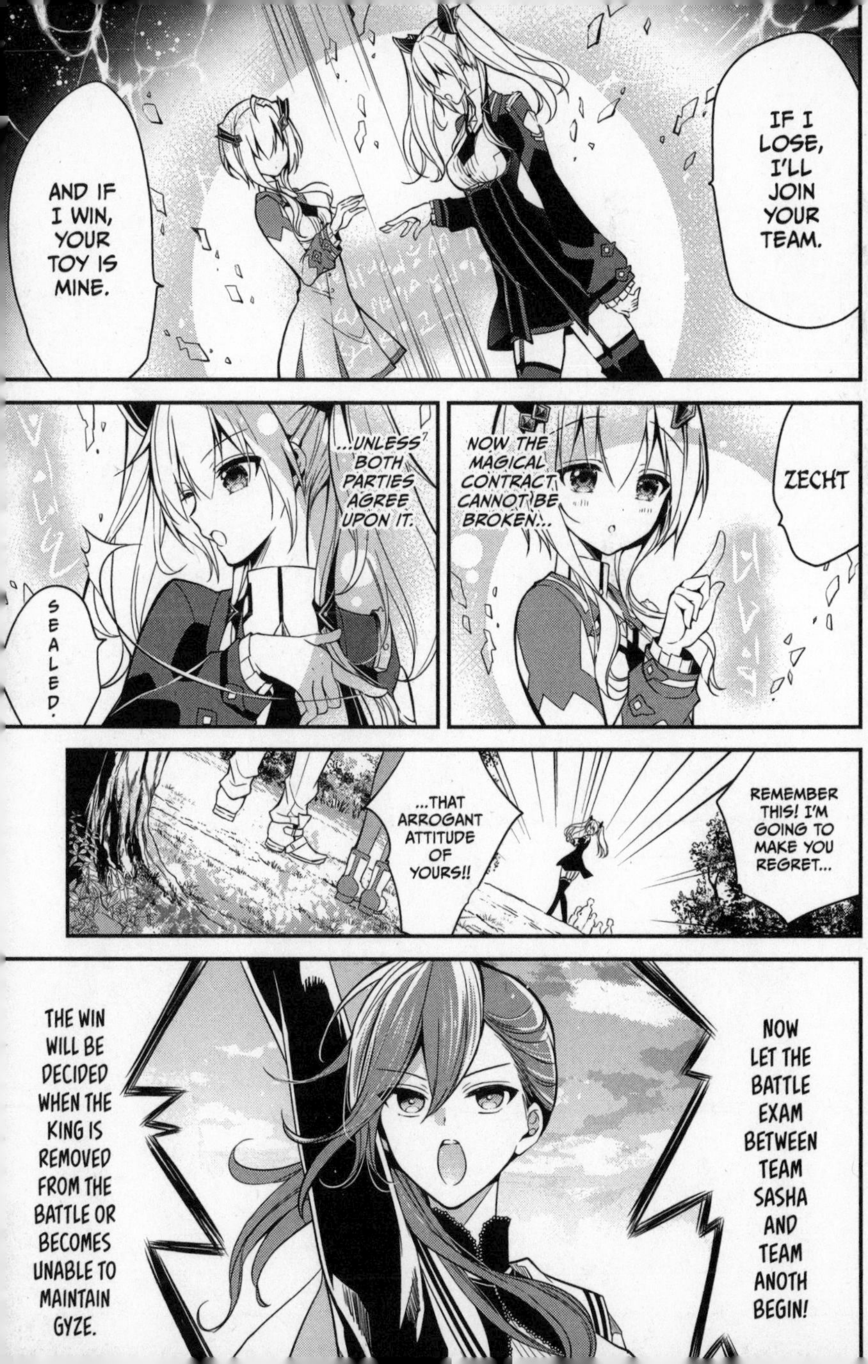
IF I LOSE, I'LL JOIN YOUR TEAM.
AND IF I WIN, YOUR TOY IS MINE.
ZECHT
NOW THE MAGICAL CONTRACT CANNOT BE BROKEN...
...UNLESS BOTH PARTIES AGREE UPON IT.
SEALED.
REMEMBER THIS! I'M GOING TO MAKE YOU REGRET...
...THAT ARROGANT ATTITUDE OF YOURS!!
NOW LET THE BATTLE EXAM BETWEEN TEAM SASHA AND TEAM ANOTH BEGIN!
THE WIN WILL BE DECIDED WHEN THE KING IS REMOVED FROM THE BATTLE OR BECOMES UNABLE TO MAINTAIN GYZE.

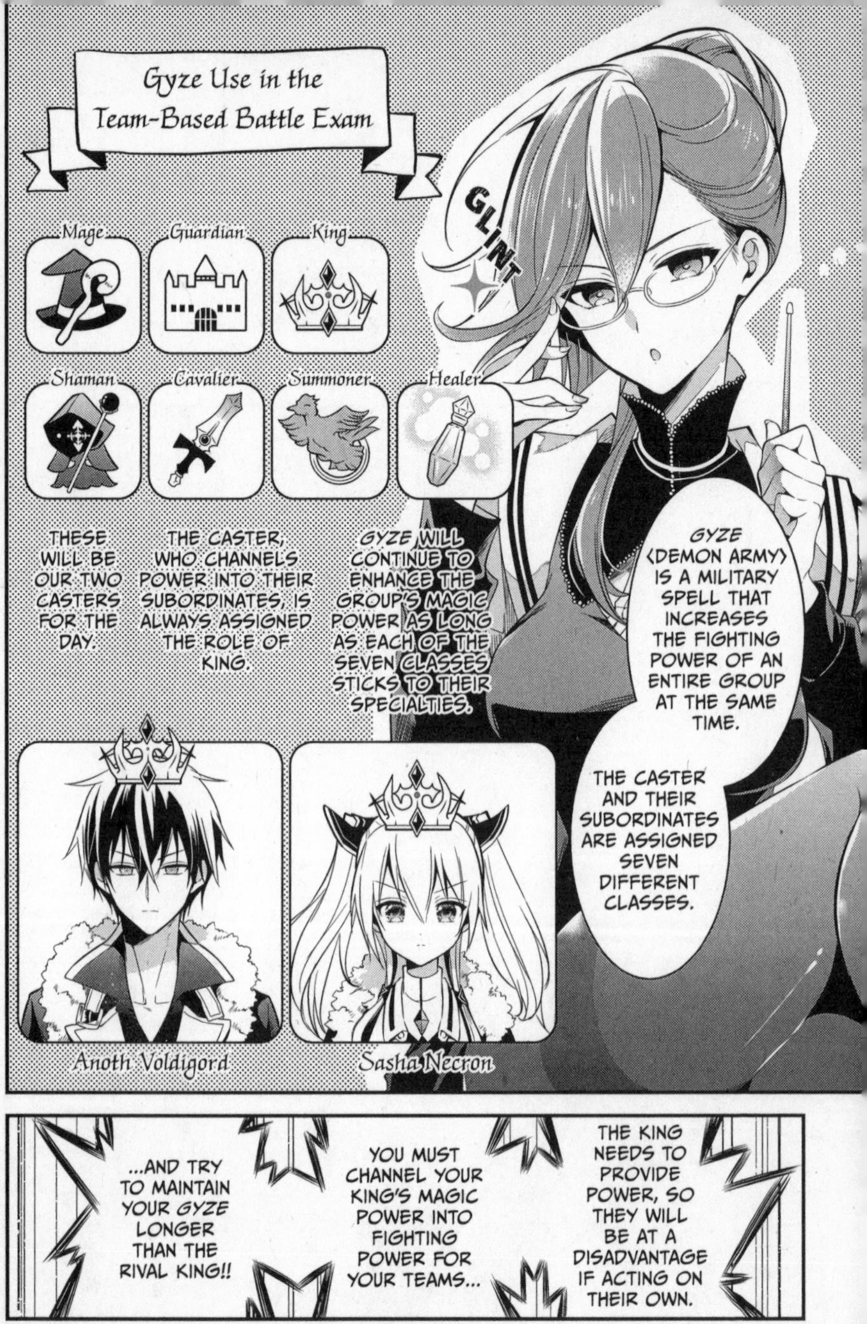
GYZE 〈DEMON ARMY〉 IS A MILITARY SPELL THAT INCREASES THE FIGHTING POWER OF AN ENTIRE GROUP AT THE SAME TIME.
THE CASTER AND THEIR SUBORDINATES ARE ASSIGNED SEVEN DIFFERENT CLASSES.
GLINT
Gyze Use in the Team-Based Battle Exam
King
Guardian
Mage
Healer
Summoner
Cavalier
Shaman
GYZE WILL CONTINUE TO ENHANCE THE GROUP'S MAGIC POWER AS LONG AS EACH OF THE SEVEN CLASSES STICKS TO THEIR SPECIALTIES.
THE CASTER, WHO CHANNELS POWER INTO THEIR SUBORDINATES, IS ALWAYS ASSIGNED THE ROLE OF KING.
THESE WILL BE OUR TWO CASTERS FOR THE DAY.
Sasha Necron
Anoth Voldigord
THE KING NEEDS TO PROVIDE POWER, SO THEY WILL BE AT A DISADVANTAGE IF ACTING ON THEIR OWN.
YOU MUST CHANNEL YOUR KING'S MAGIC POWER INTO FIGHTING POWER FOR YOUR TEAMS...
...AND TRY TO MAINTAIN YOUR GYZE LONGER THAN THE RIVAL KING!!

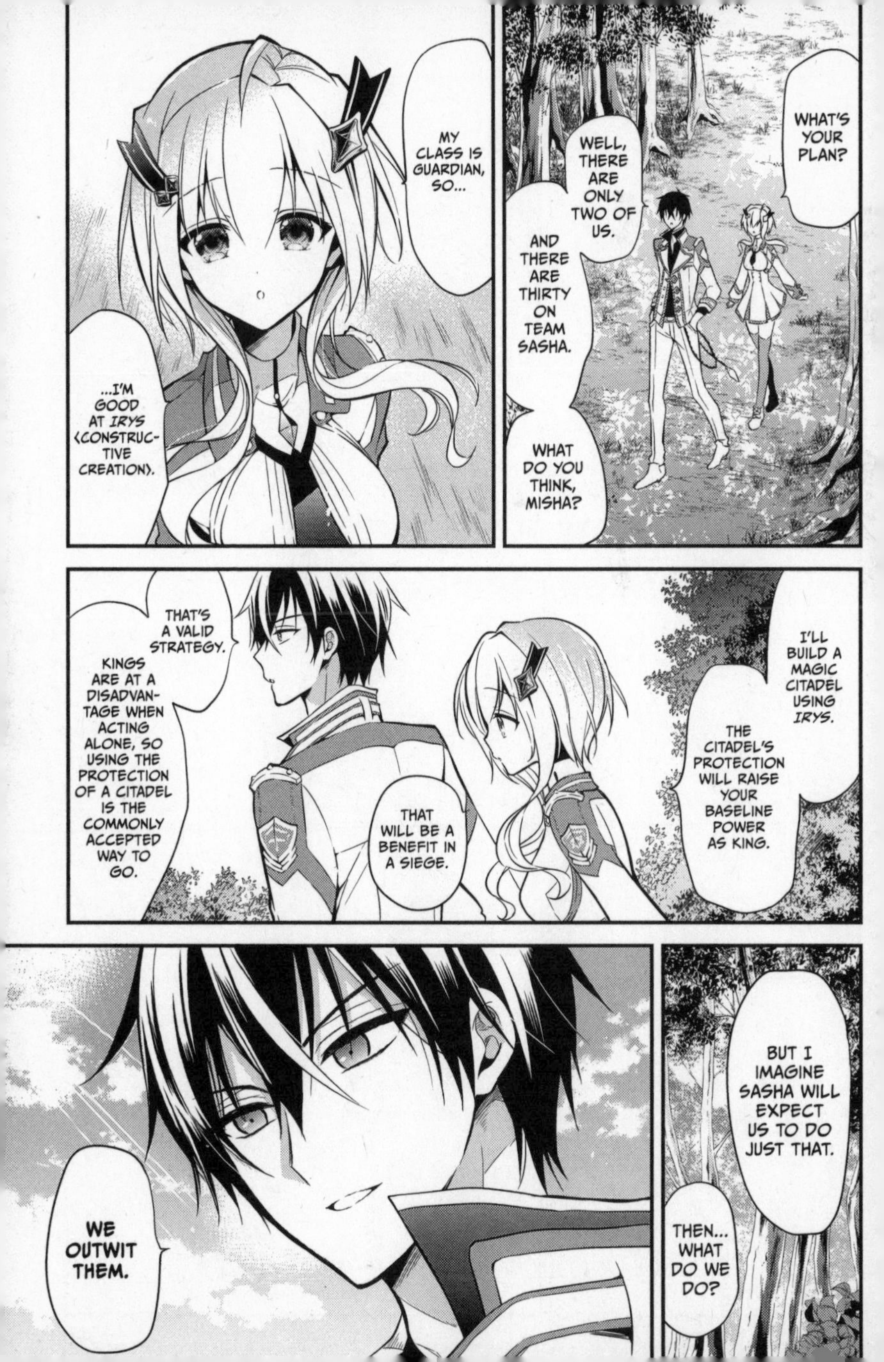
WHAT'S YOUR PLAN?
WELL, THERE ARE ONLY TWO OF US.
AND THERE ARE THIRTY ON TEAM SASHA.
WHAT DO YOU THINK, MISHA?
MY CLASS IS GUARDIAN, SO...
...I'M GOOD AT *IRYS* ‹CONSTRUCTIVE CREATION›.
I'LL BUILD A MAGIC CITADEL USING *IRYS*.
THE CITADEL'S PROTECTION WILL RAISE YOUR BASELINE POWER AS KING.
THAT WILL BE A BENEFIT IN A SIEGE.
THAT'S A VALID STRATEGY.
KINGS ARE AT A DISADVANTAGE WHEN ACTING ALONE, SO USING THE PROTECTION OF A CITADEL IS THE COMMONLY ACCEPTED WAY TO GO.
BUT I IMAGINE SASHA WILL EXPECT US TO DO JUST THAT.
THEN... WHAT DO WE DO?
WE OUTWIT THEM.

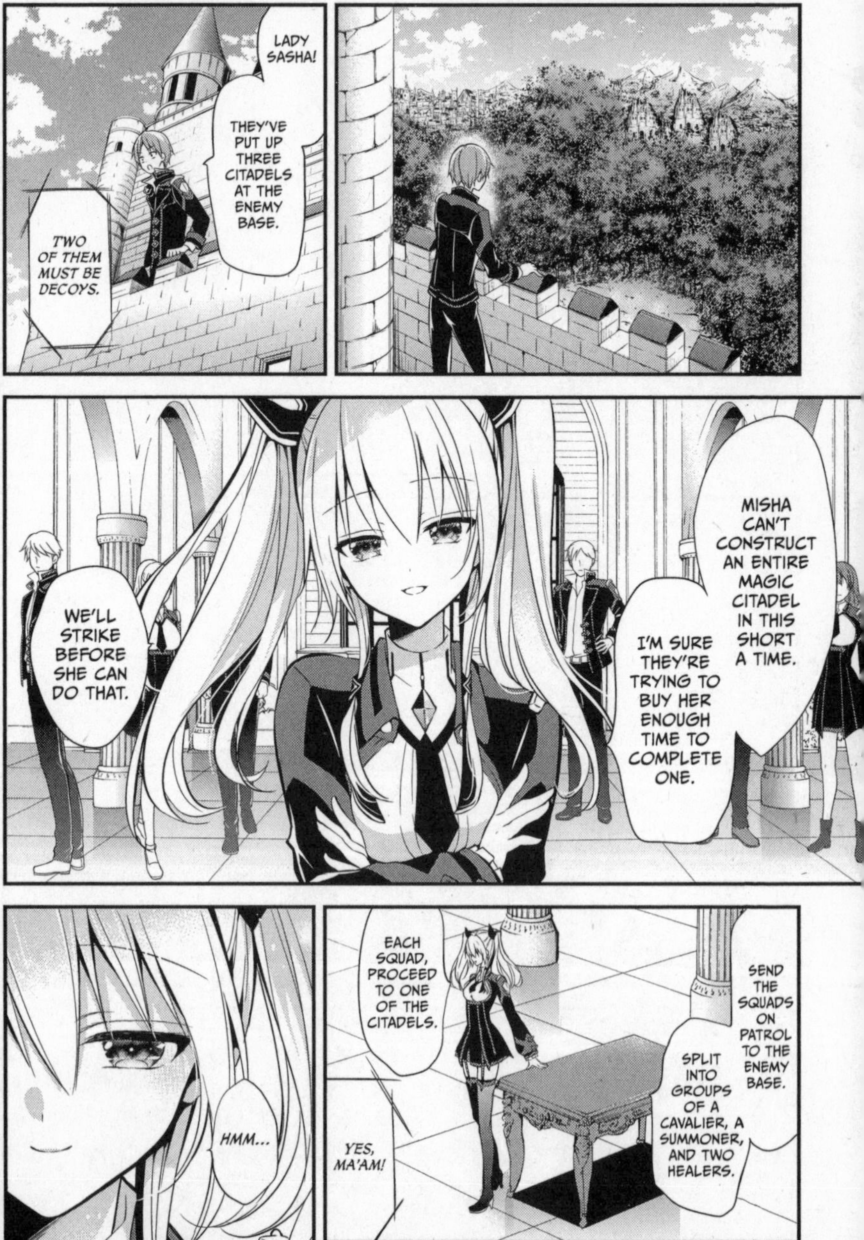
LADY SASHA!
THEY'VE PUT UP THREE CITADELS AT THE ENEMY BASE.
TWO OF THEM MUST BE DECOYS.
MISHA CAN'T CONSTRUCT AN ENTIRE MAGIC CITADEL IN THIS SHORT A TIME.
I'M SURE THEY'RE TRYING TO BUY HER ENOUGH TIME TO COMPLETE ONE.
WE'LL STRIKE BEFORE SHE CAN DO THAT.
SEND THE SQUADS ON PATROL TO THE ENEMY BASE.
SPLIT INTO GROUPS OF A CAVALIER, A SUMMONER, AND TWO HEALERS.
EACH SQUAD, PROCEED TO ONE OF THE CITADELS.
YES, MA'AM!
HMM...

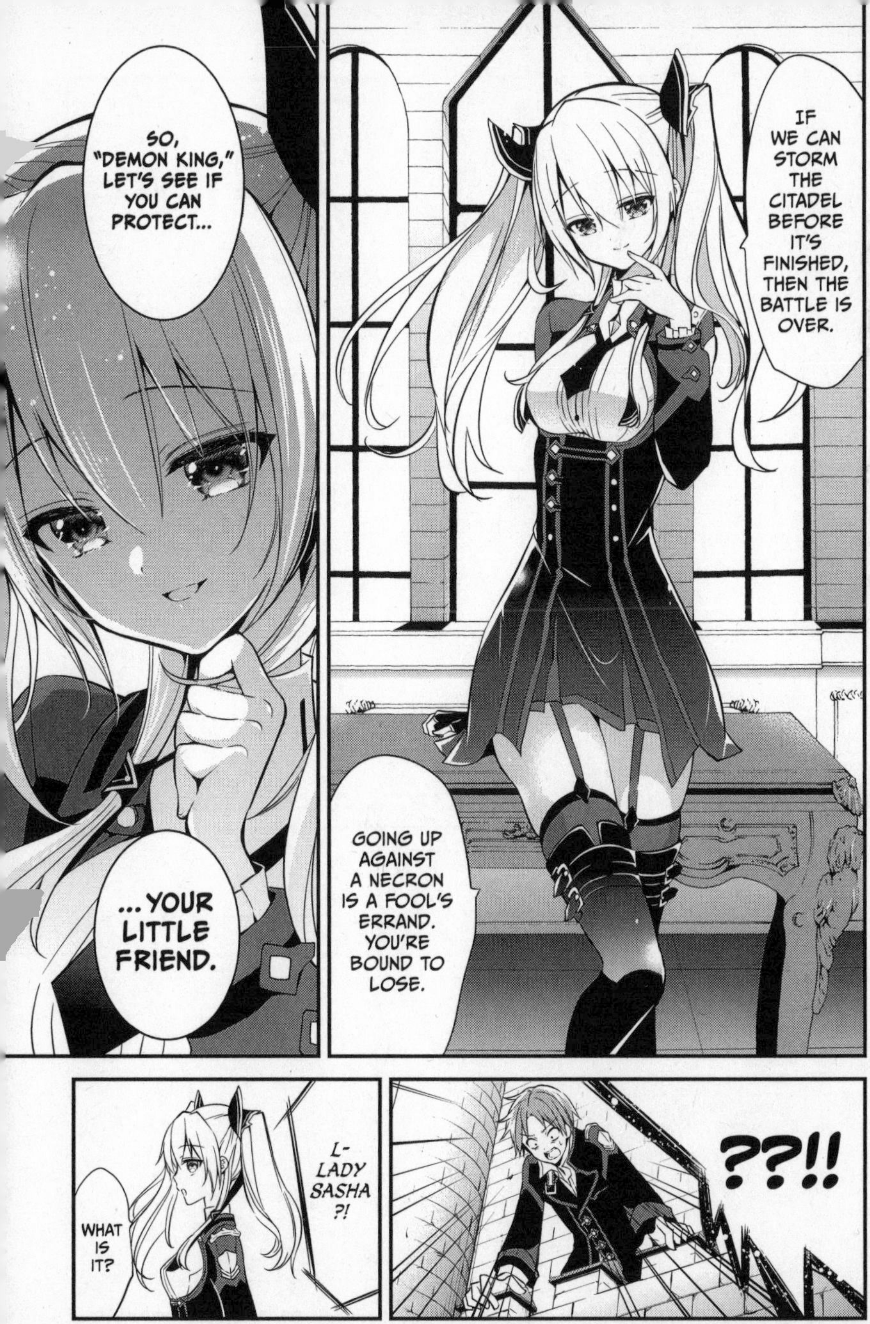
IF WE CAN STORM THE CITADEL BEFORE IT'S FINISHED, THEN THE BATTLE IS OVER.
GOING UP AGAINST A NECRON IS A FOOL'S ERRAND. YOU'RE BOUND TO LOSE.
SO, "DEMON KING," LET'S SEE IF YOU CAN PROTECT...
...YOUR LITTLE FRIEND.
??!!
L- LADY SASHA ?!
WHAT IS IT?

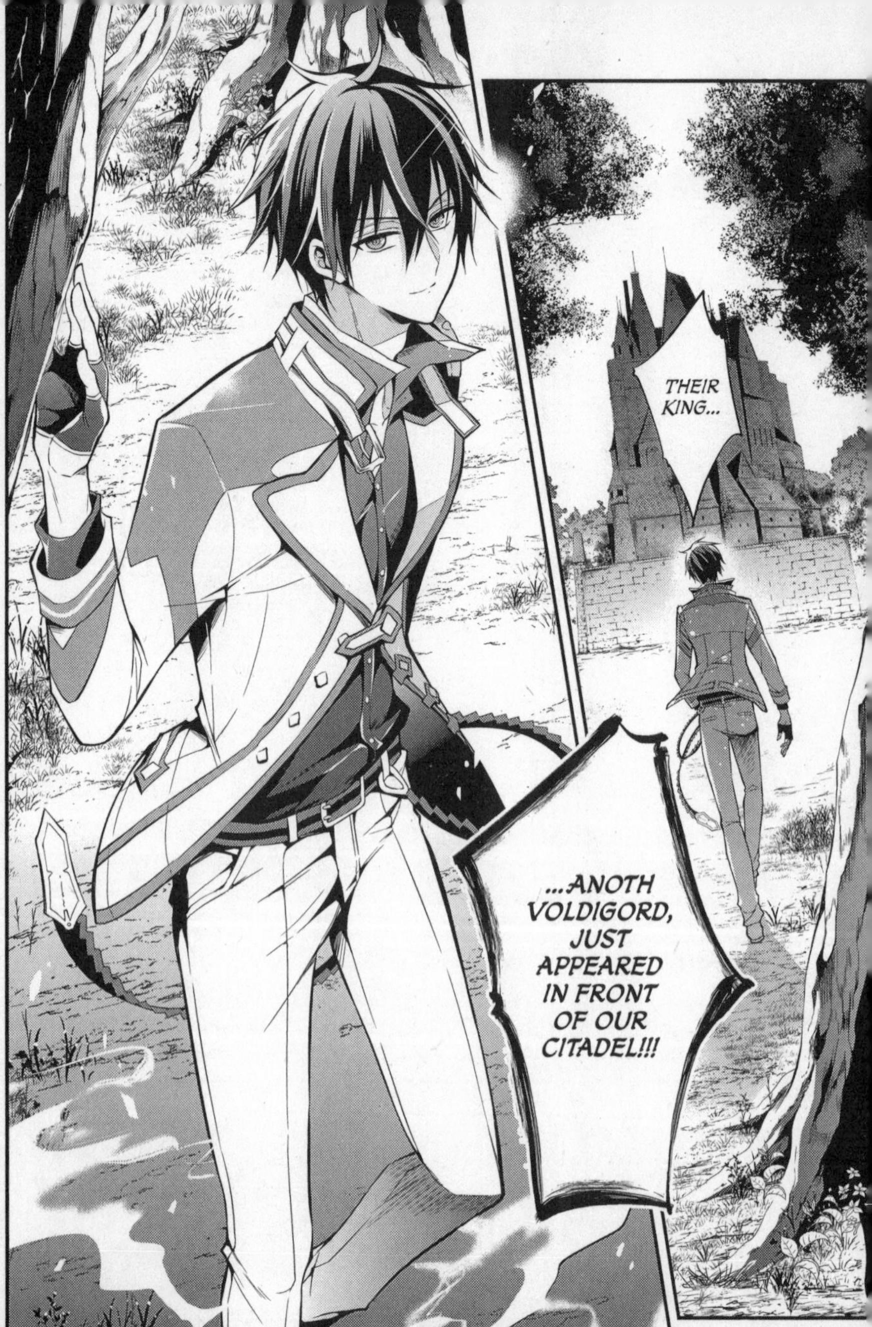
THEIR KING...
...ANOTH VOLDIGORD, JUST APPEARED IN FRONT OF OUR CITADEL!!!

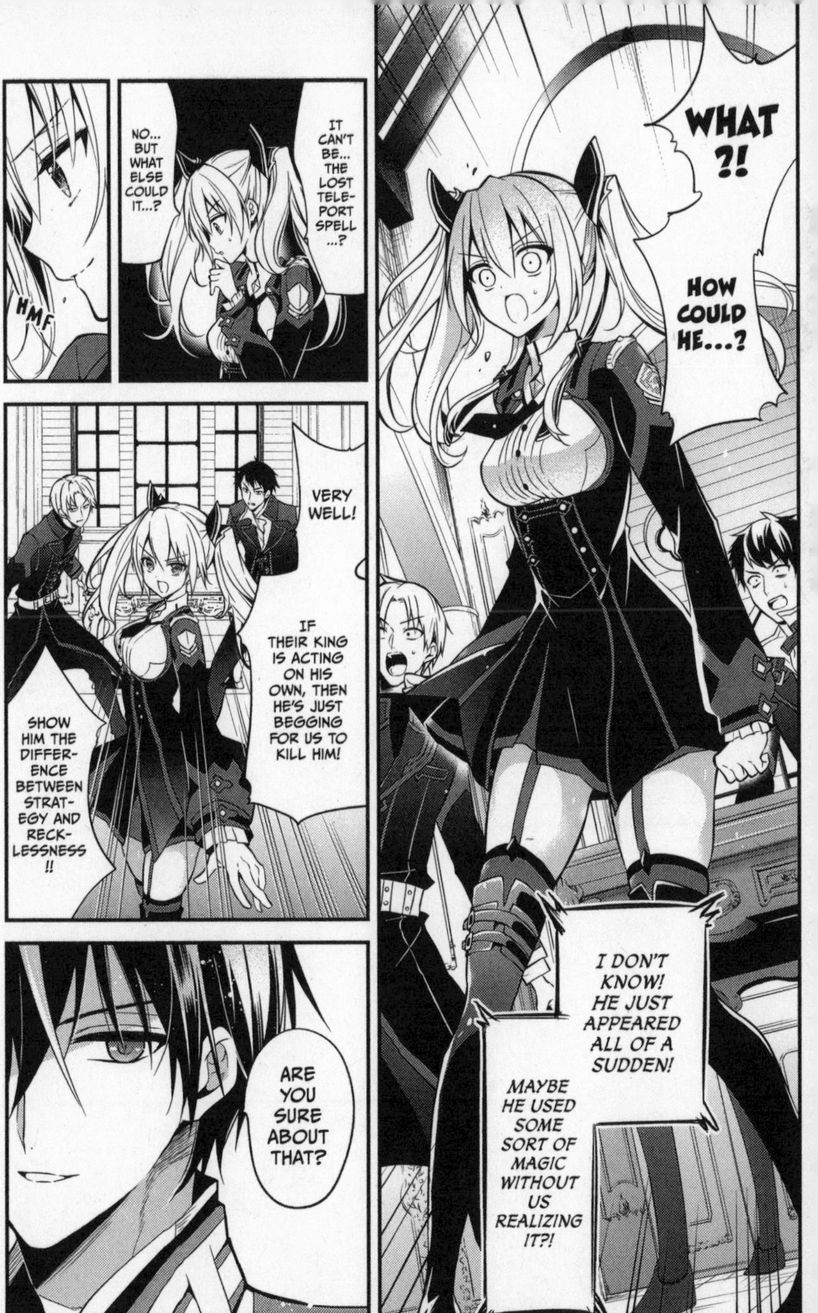
WHAT ?!
HOW COULD HE...?
I DON'T KNOW! HE JUST APPEARED ALL OF A SUDDEN!
MAYBE HE USED SOME SORT OF MAGIC WITHOUT US REALIZING IT?!
IT CAN'T BE... THE LOST TELEPORT SPELL ...?
NO... BUT WHAT ELSE COULD IT...?
HMF
VERY WELL!
IF THEIR KING IS ACTING ON HIS OWN, THEN HE'S JUST BEGGING FOR US TO KILL HIM!
SHOW HIM THE DIFFERENCE BETWEEN STRATEGY AND RECKLESSNESS !!
ARE YOU SURE ABOUT THAT?

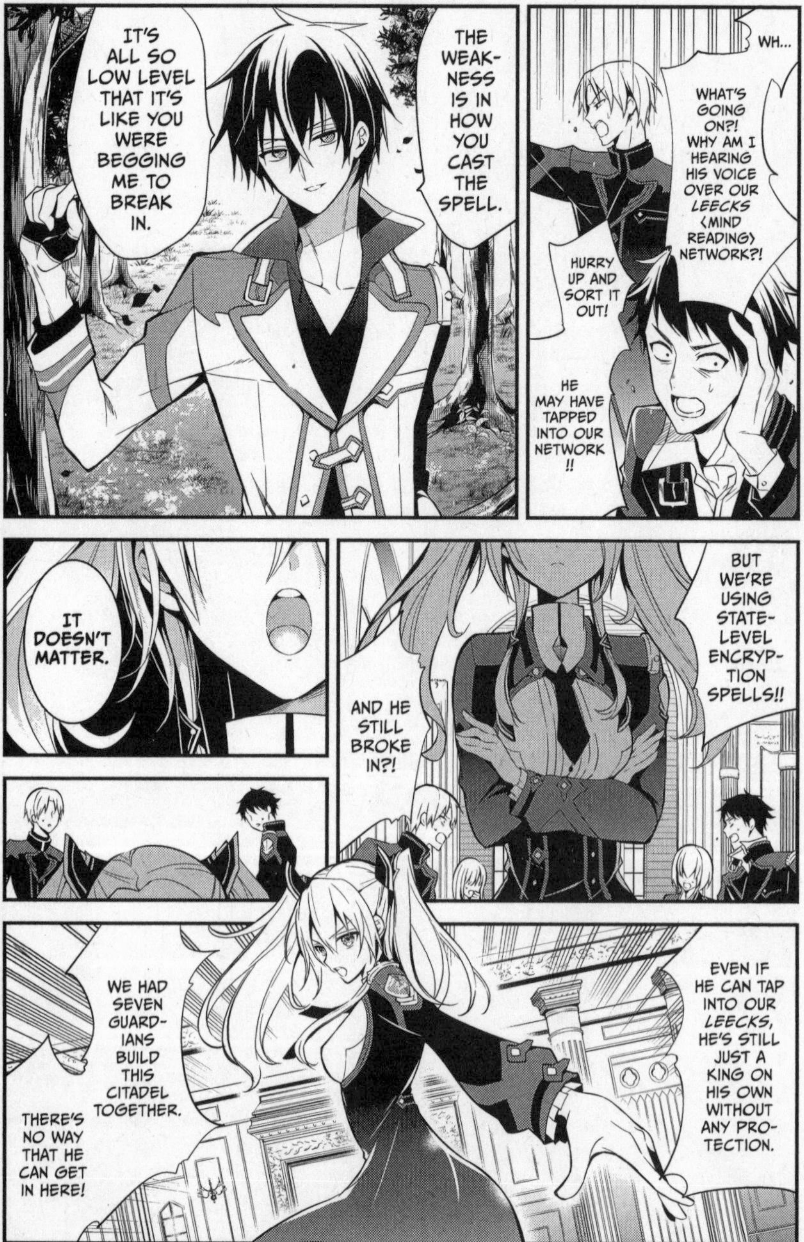
WH...
WHAT'S GOING ON?! WHY AM I HEARING HIS VOICE OVER OUR *LEECKS* ‹MIND READING› NETWORK?!
HURRY UP AND SORT IT OUT!
HE MAY HAVE TAPPED INTO OUR NETWORK !!
THE WEAKNESS IS IN HOW YOU CAST THE SPELL.
IT'S ALL SO LOW LEVEL THAT IT'S LIKE YOU WERE BEGGING ME TO BREAK IN.
BUT WE'RE USING STATE-LEVEL ENCRYPTION SPELLS!!
AND HE STILL BROKE IN?!
IT DOESN'T MATTER.
EVEN IF HE CAN TAP INTO OUR *LEECKS*, HE'S STILL JUST A KING ON HIS OWN WITHOUT ANY PROTECTION.
WE HAD SEVEN GUARDIANS BUILD THIS CITADEL TOGETHER.
THERE'S NO WAY THAT HE CAN GET IN HERE!

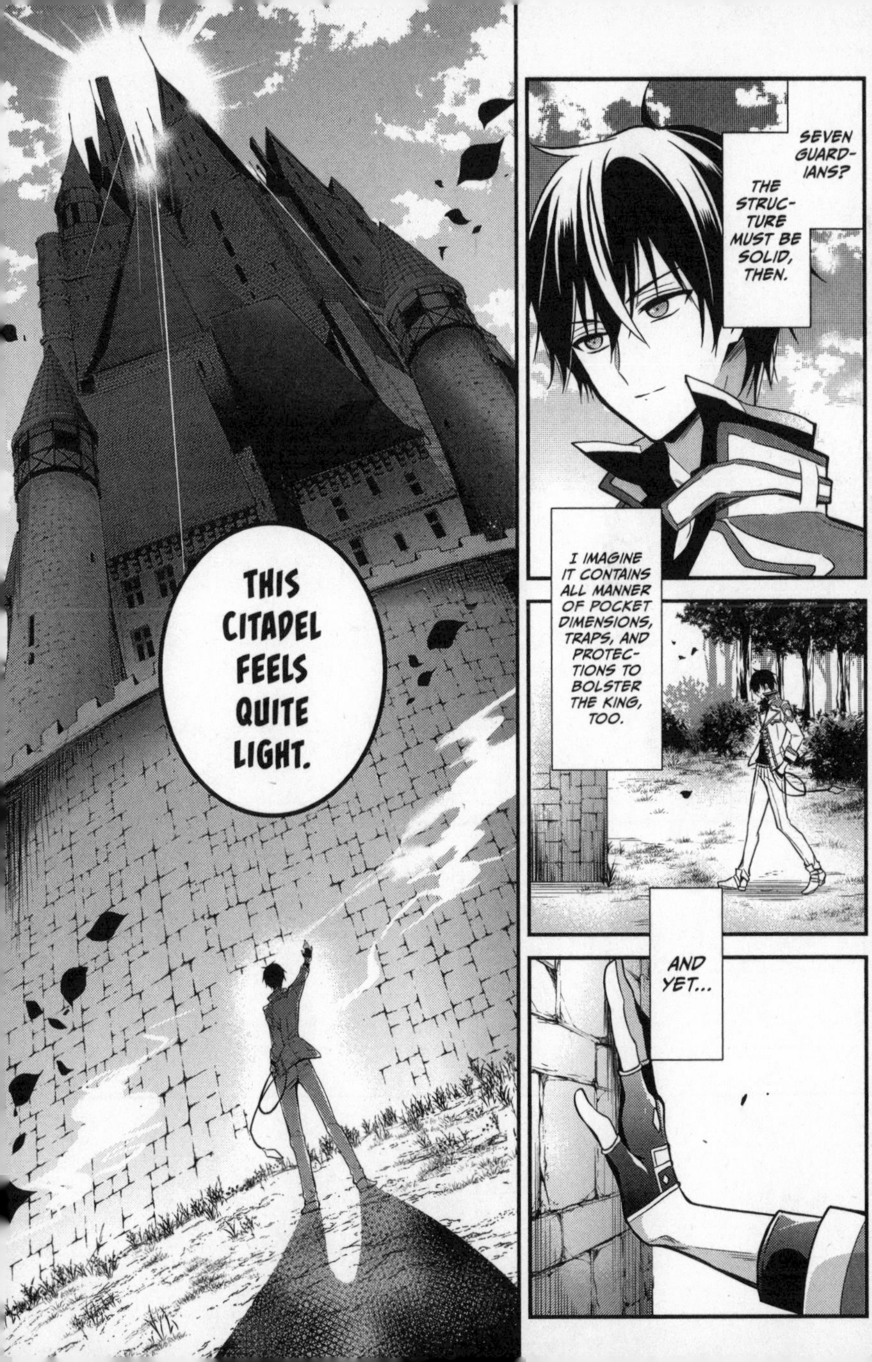
SEVEN GUARDIANS?
THE STRUCTURE MUST BE SOLID, THEN.
I IMAGINE IT CONTAINS ALL MANNER OF POCKET DIMENSIONS, TRAPS, AND PROTECTIONS TO BOLSTER THE KING, TOO.
AND YET...
THIS CITADEL FEELS QUITE LIGHT.

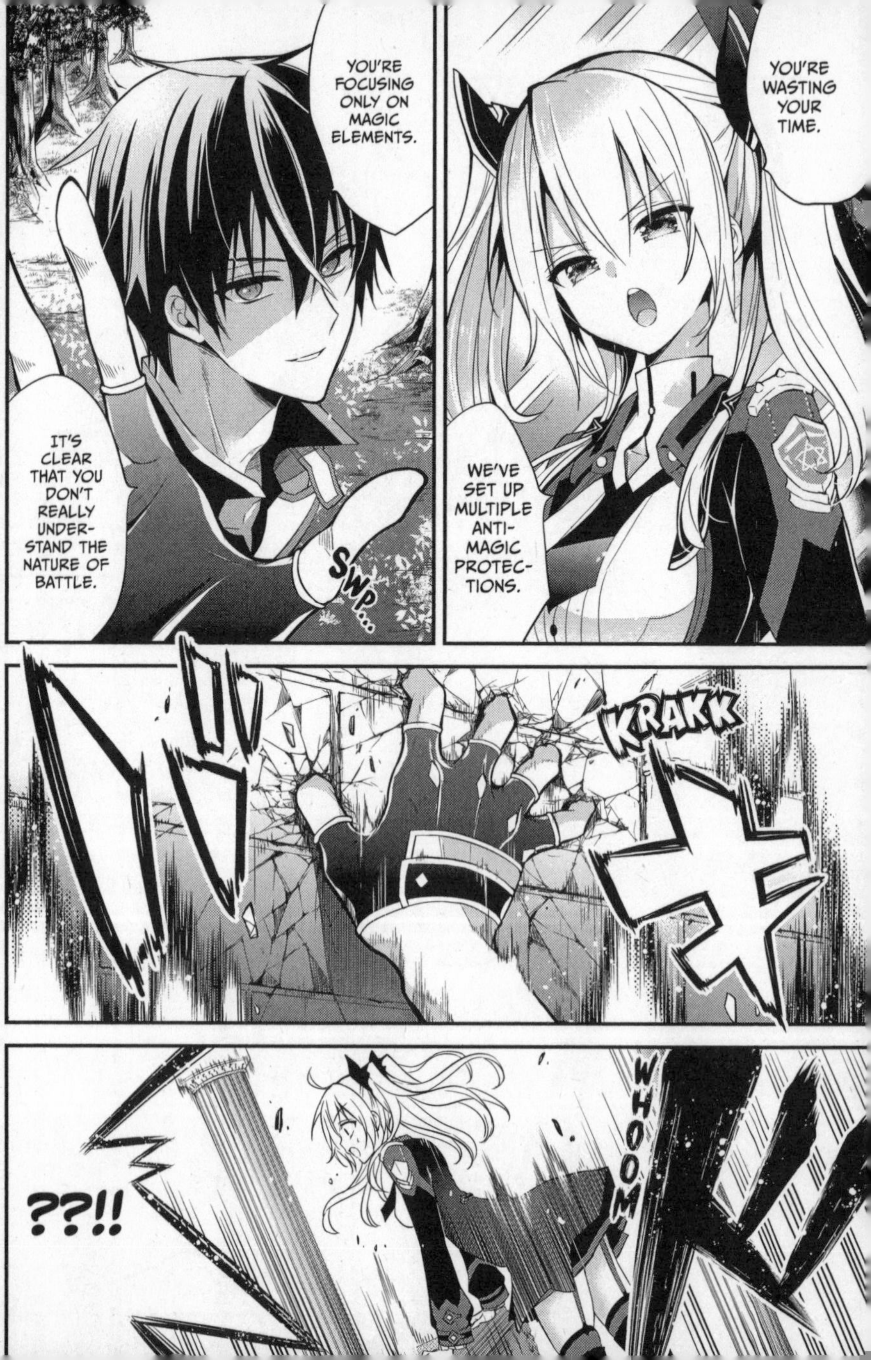
YOU'RE WASTING YOUR TIME.
WE'VE SET UP MULTIPLE ANTI-MAGIC PROTECTIONS.
YOU'RE FOCUSING ONLY ON MAGIC ELEMENTS.
IT'S CLEAR THAT YOU DON'T REALLY UNDER-STAND THE NATURE OF BATTLE.
SWP...
KRAKK
WHOOM
??!!

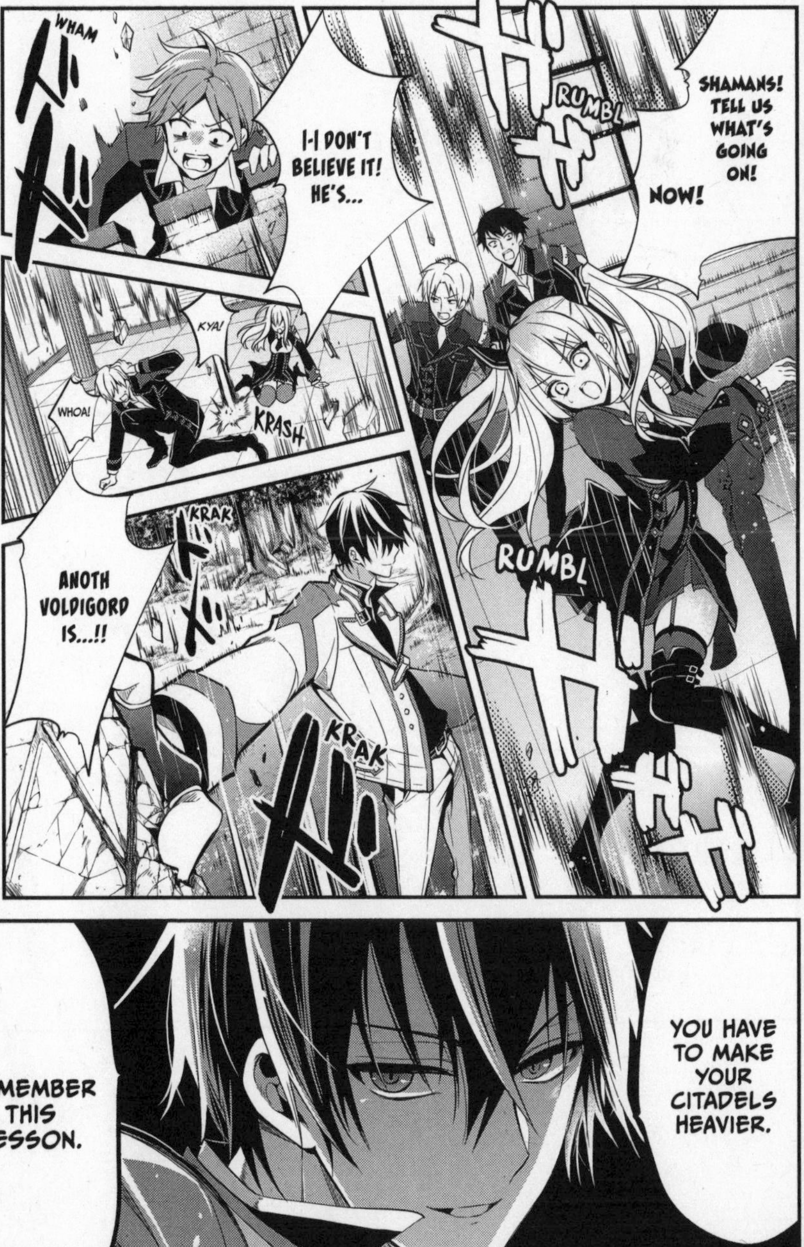

SHAMANS! TELL US WHAT'S GOING ON!
NOW!
RUMBL
RUMBL
WHAM
I-I DON'T BELIEVE IT! HE'S...
KYA!
WHOA!
KRASH
ANOTH VOLDIGORD IS...!!
KRAK
KRAK
YOU HAVE TO MAKE YOUR CITADELS HEAVIER.
REMEMBER THIS LESSON.

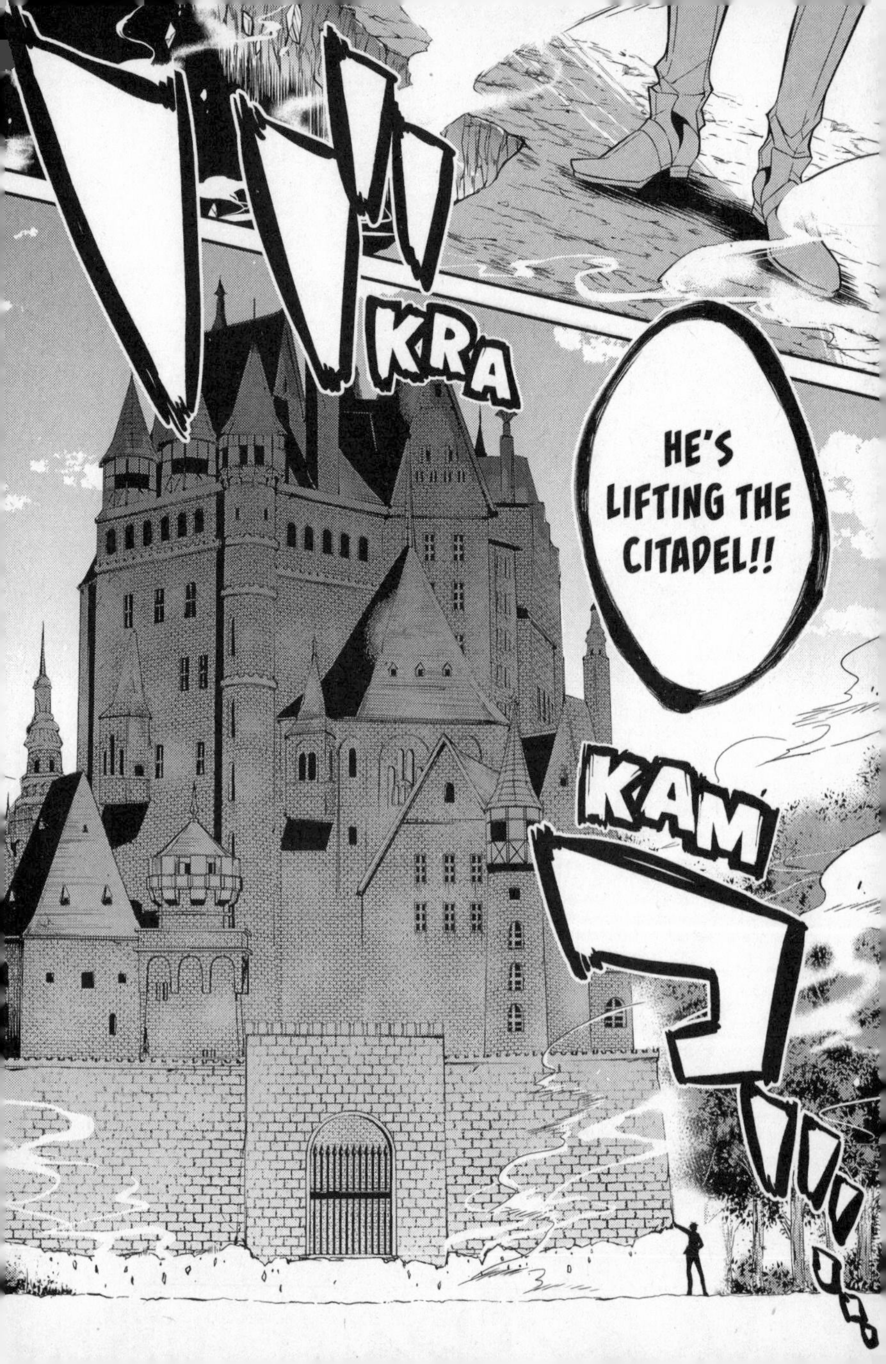
HE'S LIFTING THE CITADEL!!
KRA
KAM

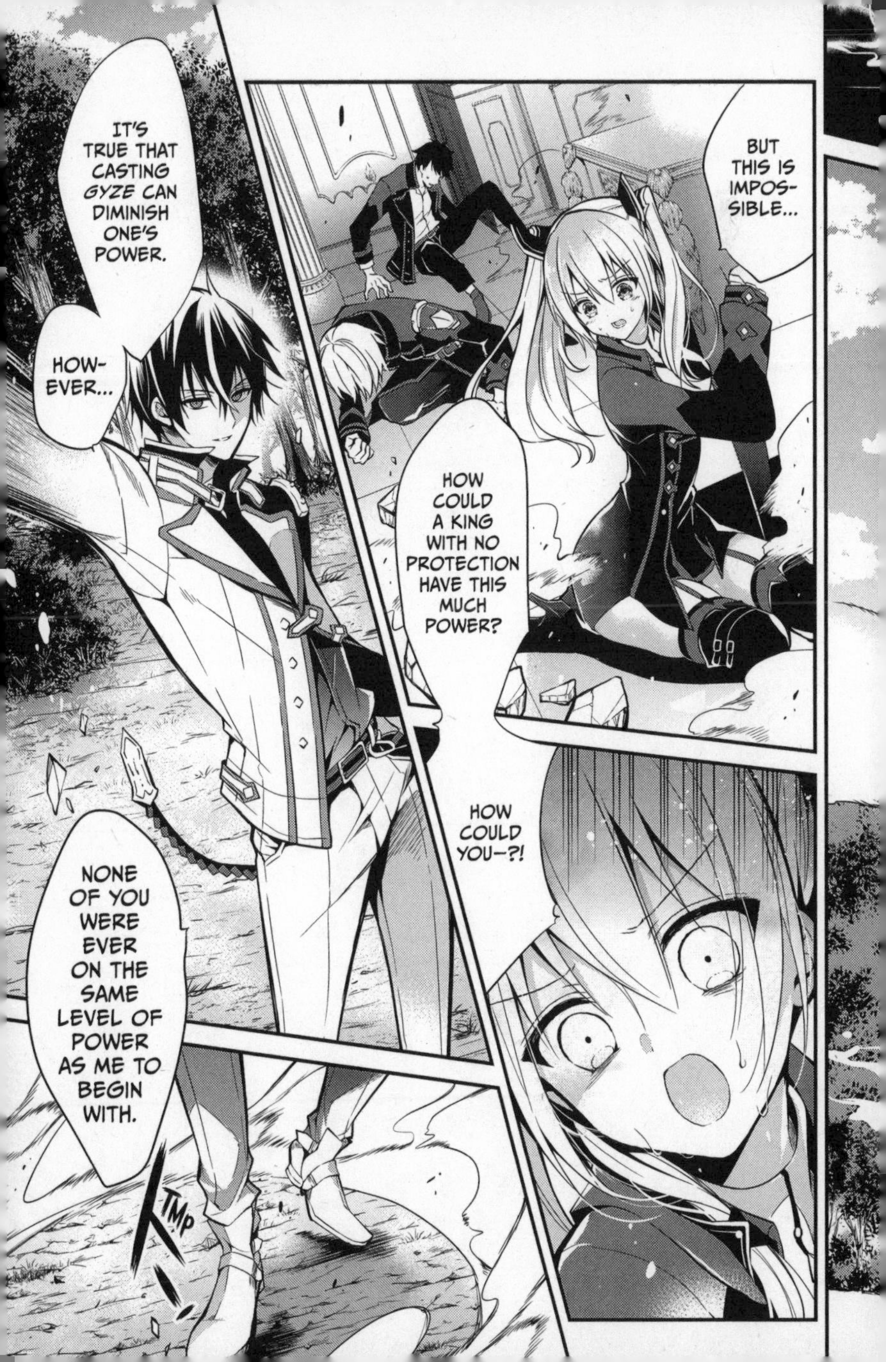
BUT THIS IS IMPOS-SIBLE...
HOW COULD A KING WITH NO PROTECTION HAVE THIS MUCH POWER?
HOW COULD YOU—?!
IT'S TRUE THAT CASTING GYZE CAN DIMINISH ONE'S POWER.
HOW-EVER...
NONE OF YOU WERE EVER ON THE SAME LEVEL OF POWER AS ME TO BEGIN WITH.
TMp

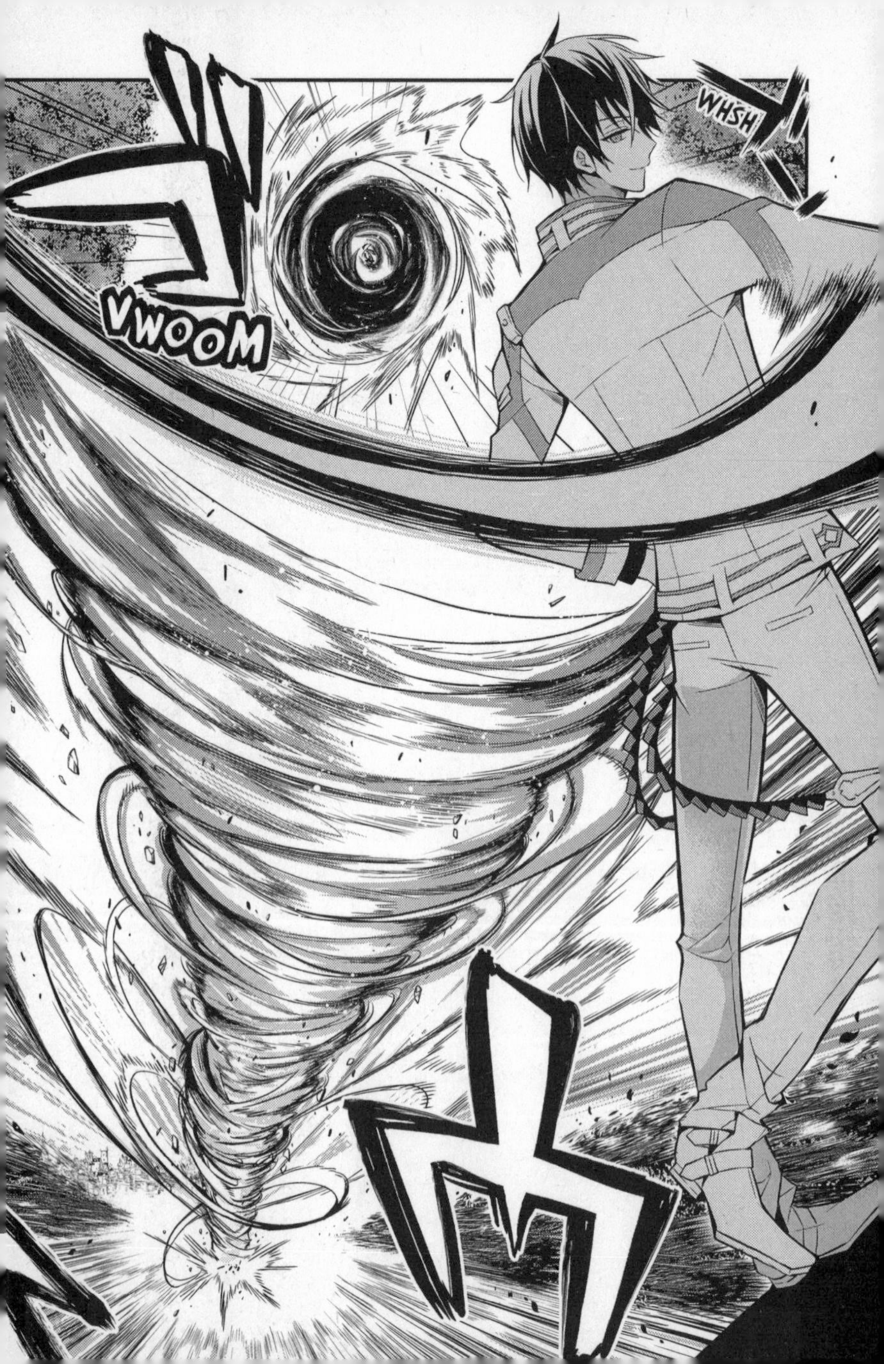
WHSH
VWOOM

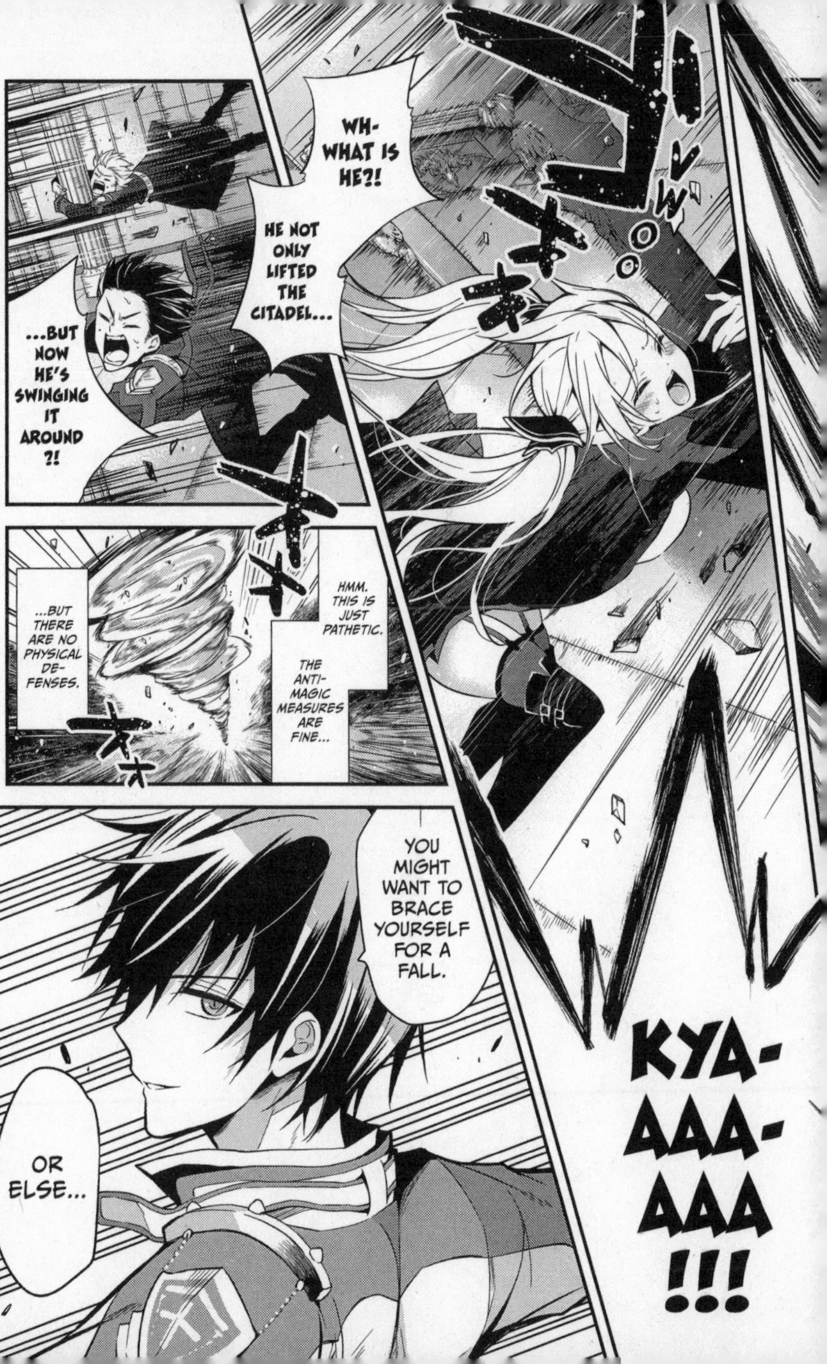
WH-WHAT IS HE?!
HE NOT ONLY LIFTED THE CITADEL...
...BUT NOW HE'S SWINGING IT AROUND?!
HMM. THIS IS JUST PATHETIC.
THE ANTI-MAGIC MEASURES ARE FINE...
...BUT THERE ARE NO PHYSICAL DE-FENSES.
YOU MIGHT WANT TO BRACE YOURSELF FOR A FALL.
OR ELSE...
KYA-AAA-AAA!!!

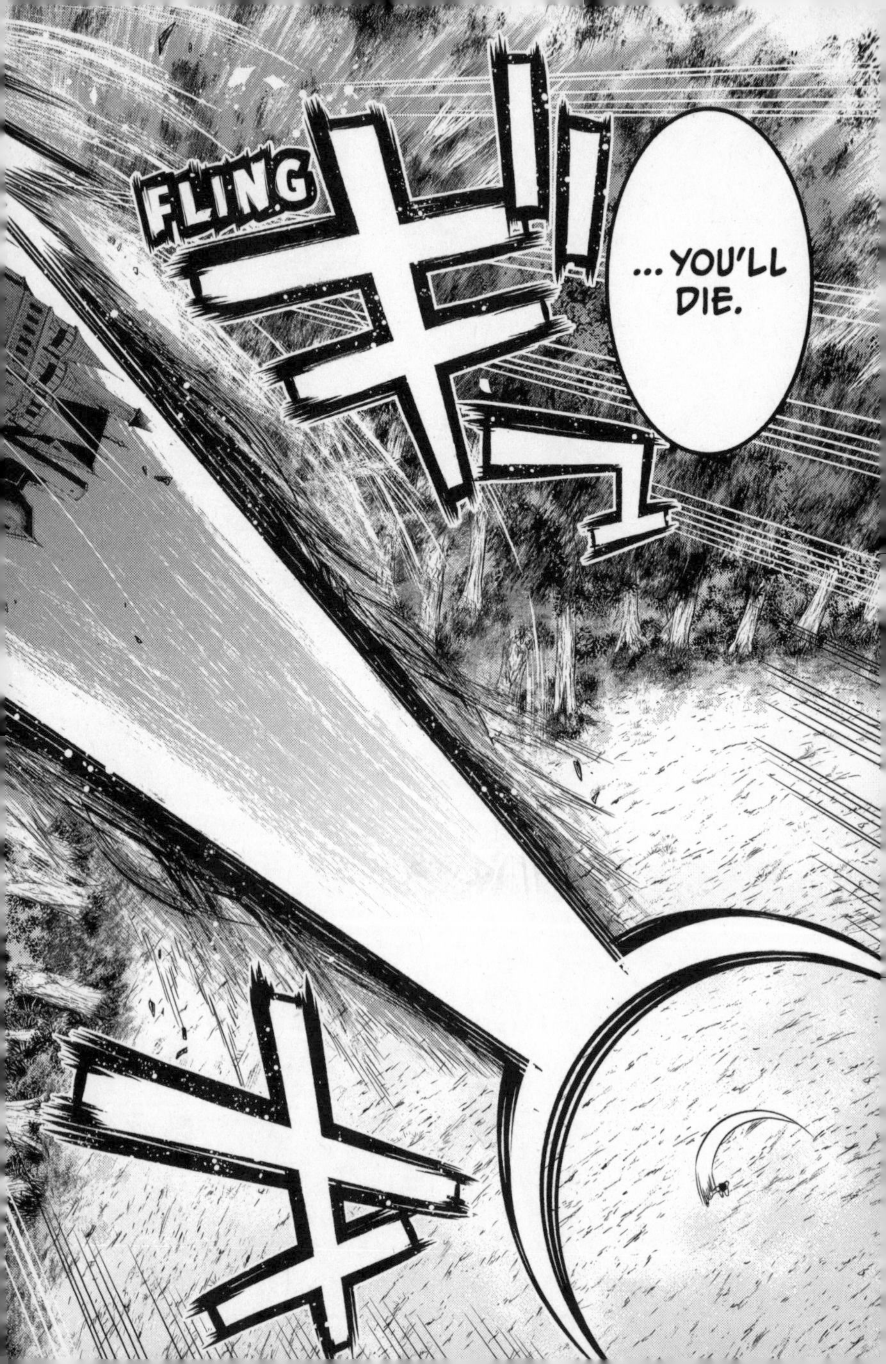
FLING
...YOU'LL DIE.

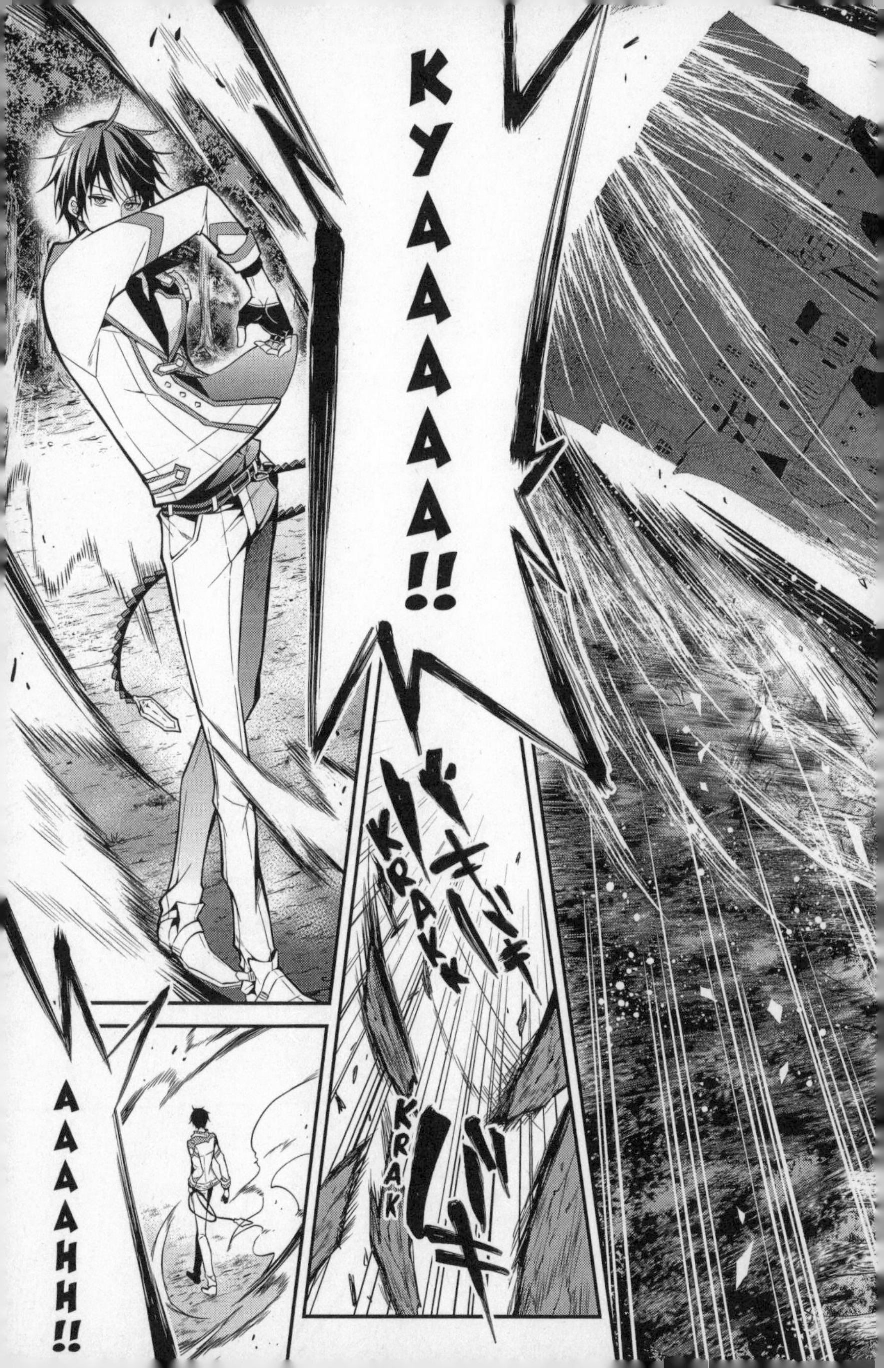
KYAAAAA!!
KRAKK
KRAK
AAAAAHH!!

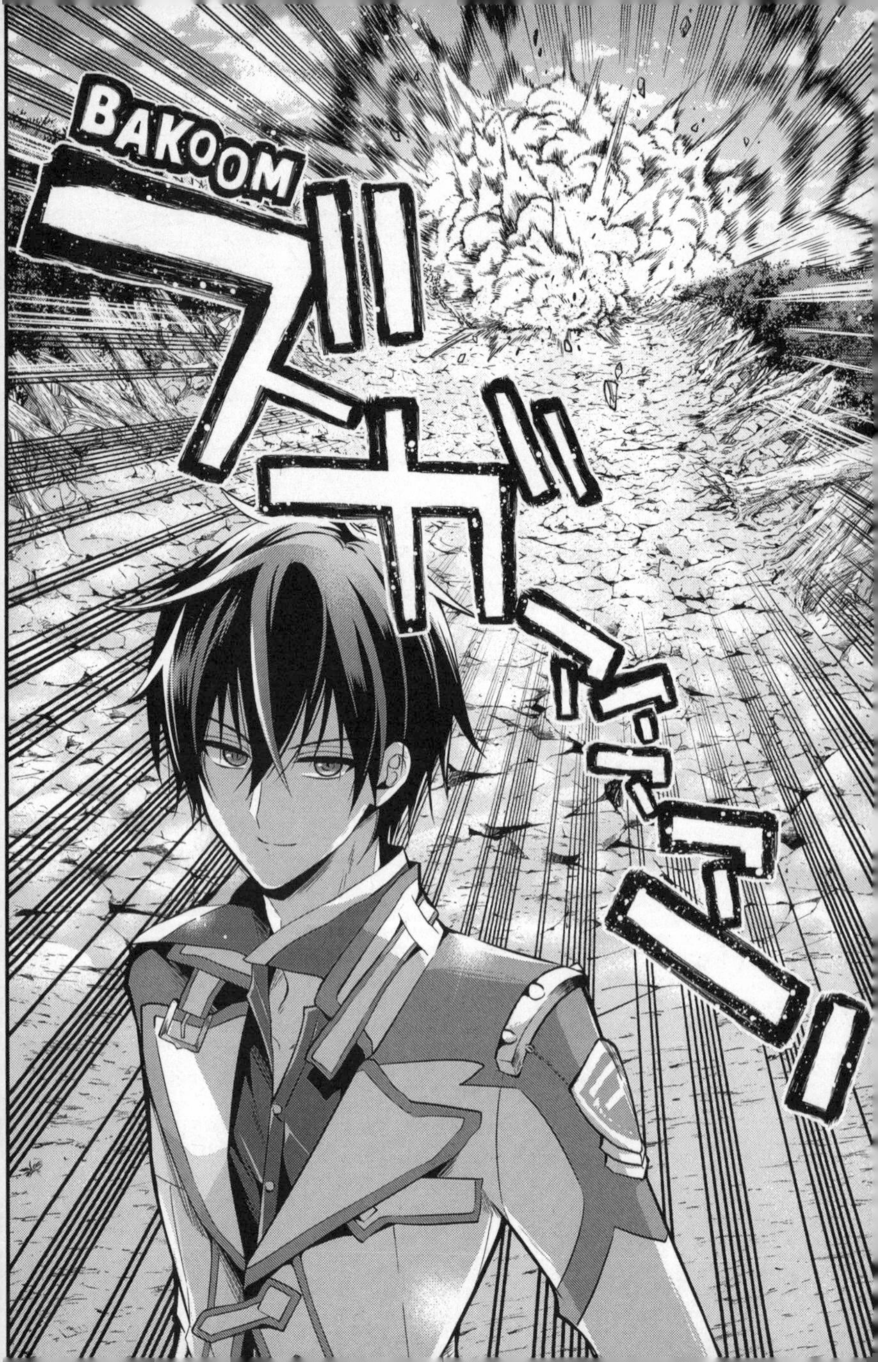
BAKOOM

The Misfit of Demon King Academy

HISTORY'S STRONGEST DEMON KING REINCARNATES AND GOES TO SCHOOL WITH HIS DESCENDANTS

The Misfit of
Demon King Academy

HISTORY'S STRONGEST DEMON KING REINCARNATES
AND GOES TO SCHOOL WITH HIS DESCENDANTS

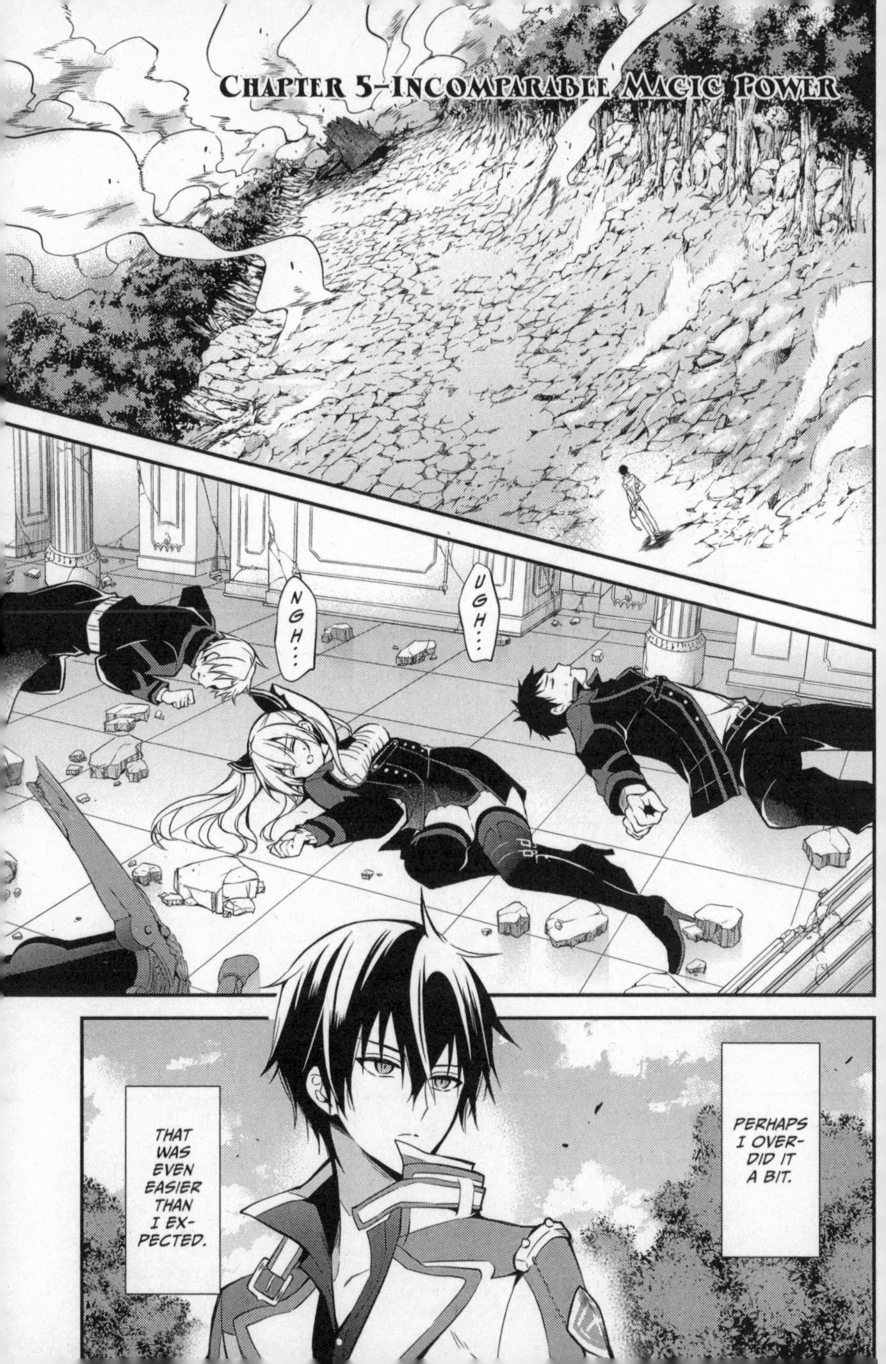
Chapter 5–Incomparable Magic Power
UGH...
NGH...
PERHAPS I OVER-DID IT A BIT.
THAT WAS EVEN EASIER THAN I EX-PECTED.

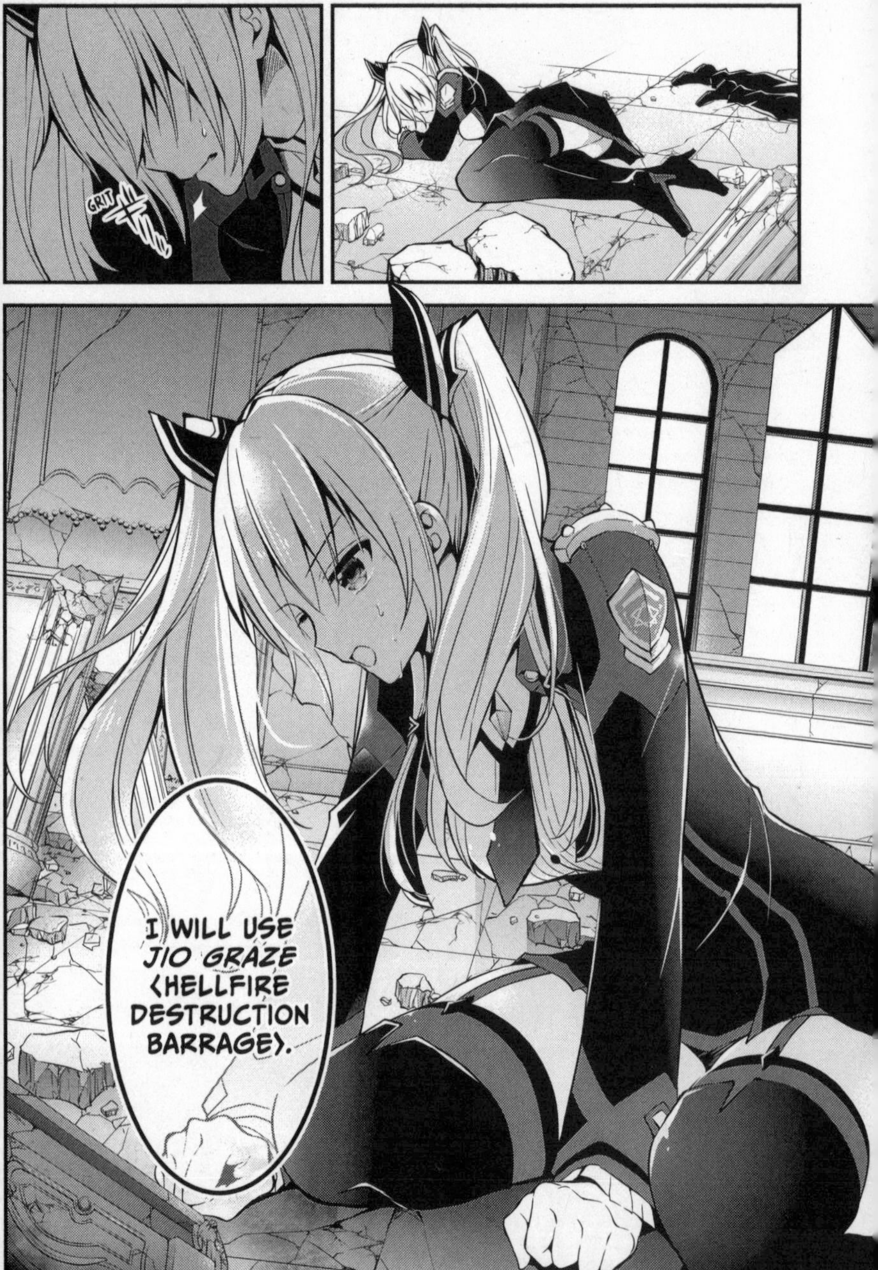
GRIT
I WILL USE JIO GRAZE <HELLFIRE DESTRUCTION BARRAGE>.

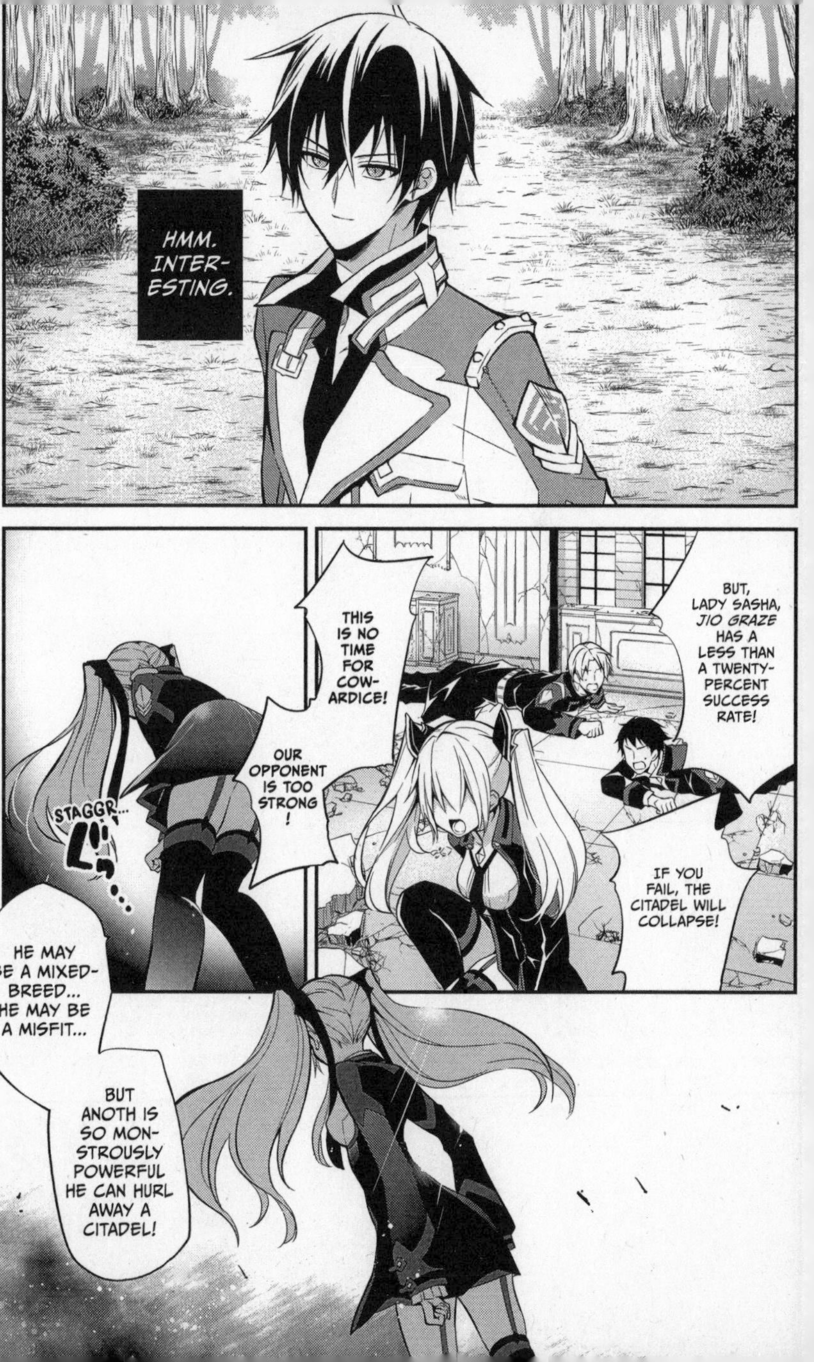
HMM. INTER-ESTING.
BUT, LADY SASHA, JIO GRAZE HAS A LESS THAN A TWENTY-PERCENT SUCCESS RATE!
THIS IS NO TIME FOR COW-ARDICE!
OUR OPPONENT IS TOO STRONG!
IF YOU FAIL, THE CITADEL WILL COLLAPSE!
STAGGR...
HE MAY BE A MIXED-BREED... HE MAY BE A MISFIT...
BUT ANOTH IS SO MON-STROUSLY POWERFUL HE CAN HURL AWAY A CITADEL!

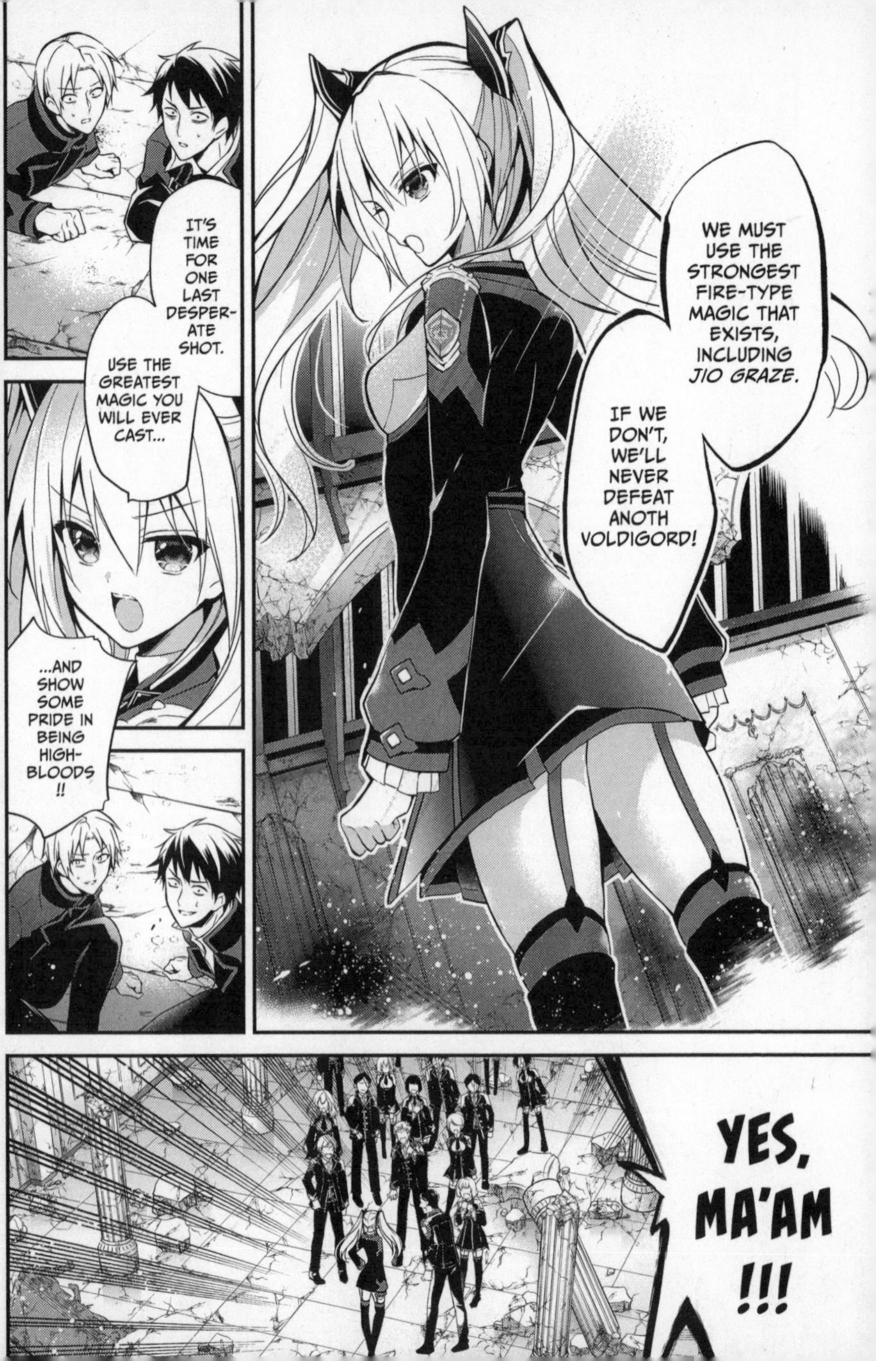
WE MUST USE THE STRONGEST FIRE-TYPE MAGIC THAT EXISTS, INCLUDING JIO GRAZE.
IF WE DON'T, WE'LL NEVER DEFEAT ANOTH VOLDIGORD!
IT'S TIME FOR ONE LAST DESPERATE SHOT.
USE THE GREATEST MAGIC YOU WILL EVER CAST...
...AND SHOW SOME PRIDE IN BEING HIGH-BLOODS!!
YES, MA'AM!!!

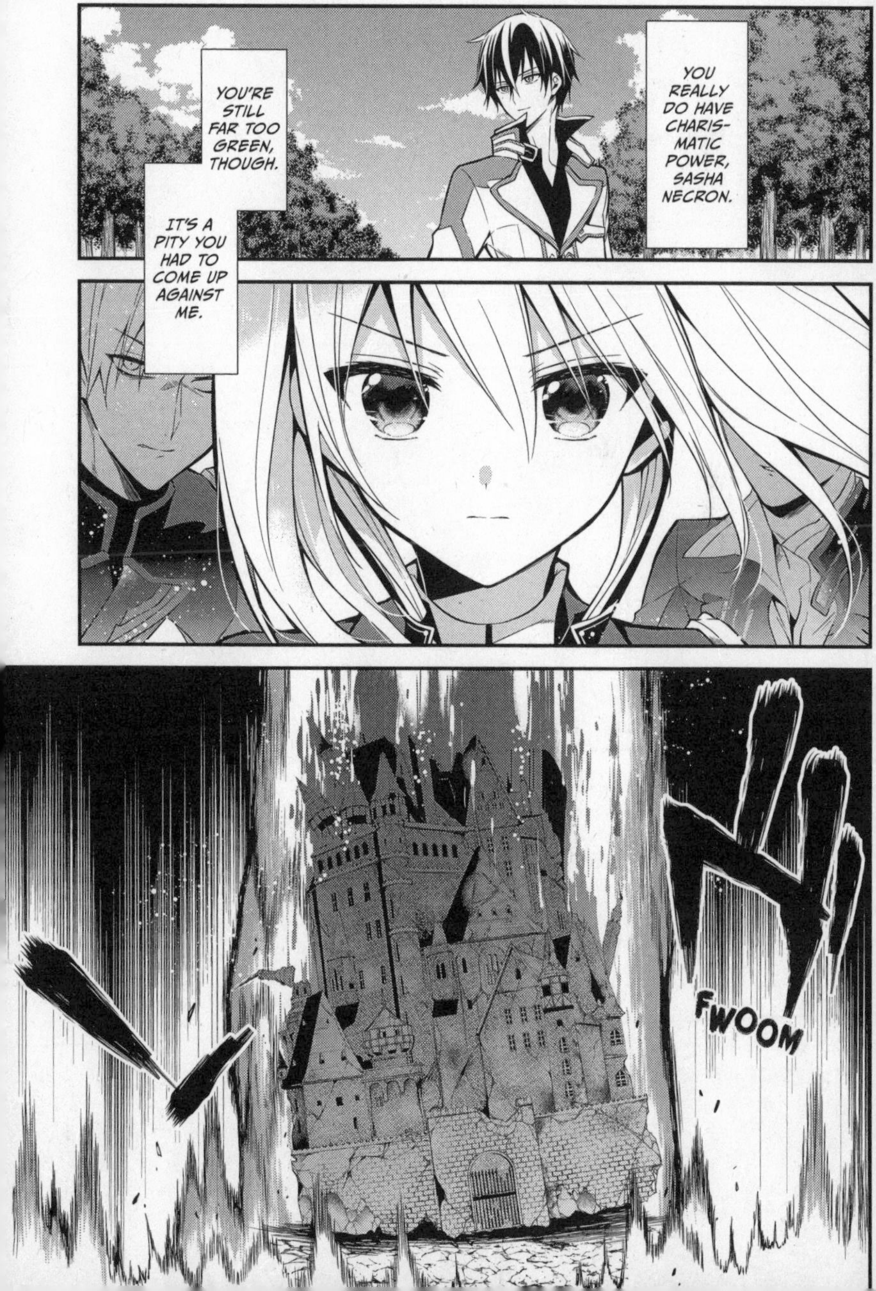
YOU REALLY DO HAVE CHARIS-MATIC POWER, SASHA NECRON.
YOU'RE STILL FAR TOO GREEN, THOUGH.
IT'S A PITY YOU HAD TO COME UP AGAINST ME.
FWOOM

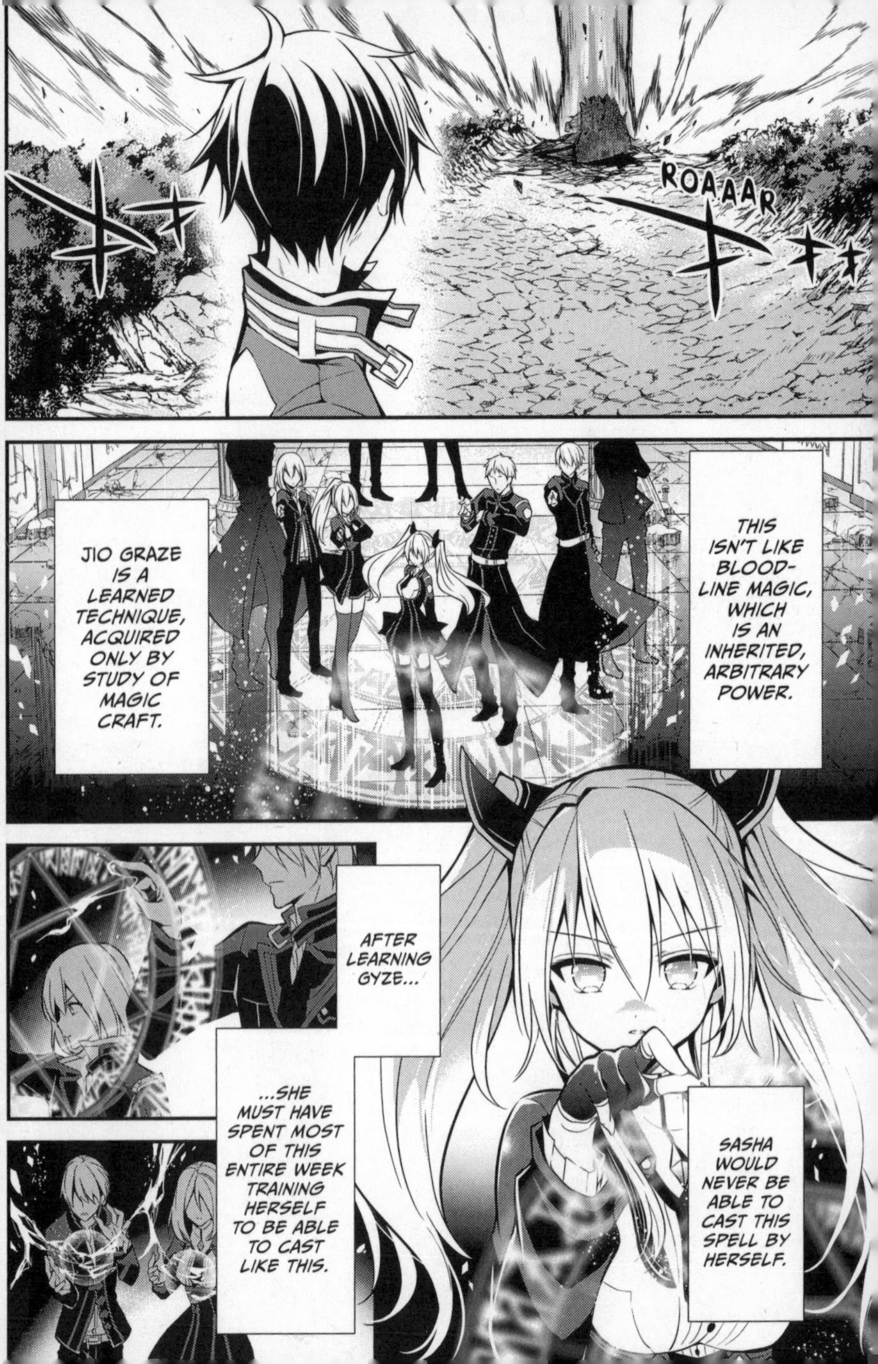
ROAAAR
THIS ISN'T LIKE BLOOD-LINE MAGIC, WHICH IS AN INHERITED, ARBITRARY POWER.
JIO GRAZE IS A LEARNED TECHNIQUE, ACQUIRED ONLY BY STUDY OF MAGIC CRAFT.
SASHA WOULD NEVER BE ABLE TO CAST THIS SPELL BY HERSELF.
AFTER LEARNING GYZE...
...SHE MUST HAVE SPENT MOST OF THIS ENTIRE WEEK TRAINING HERSELF TO BE ABLE TO CAST LIKE THIS.

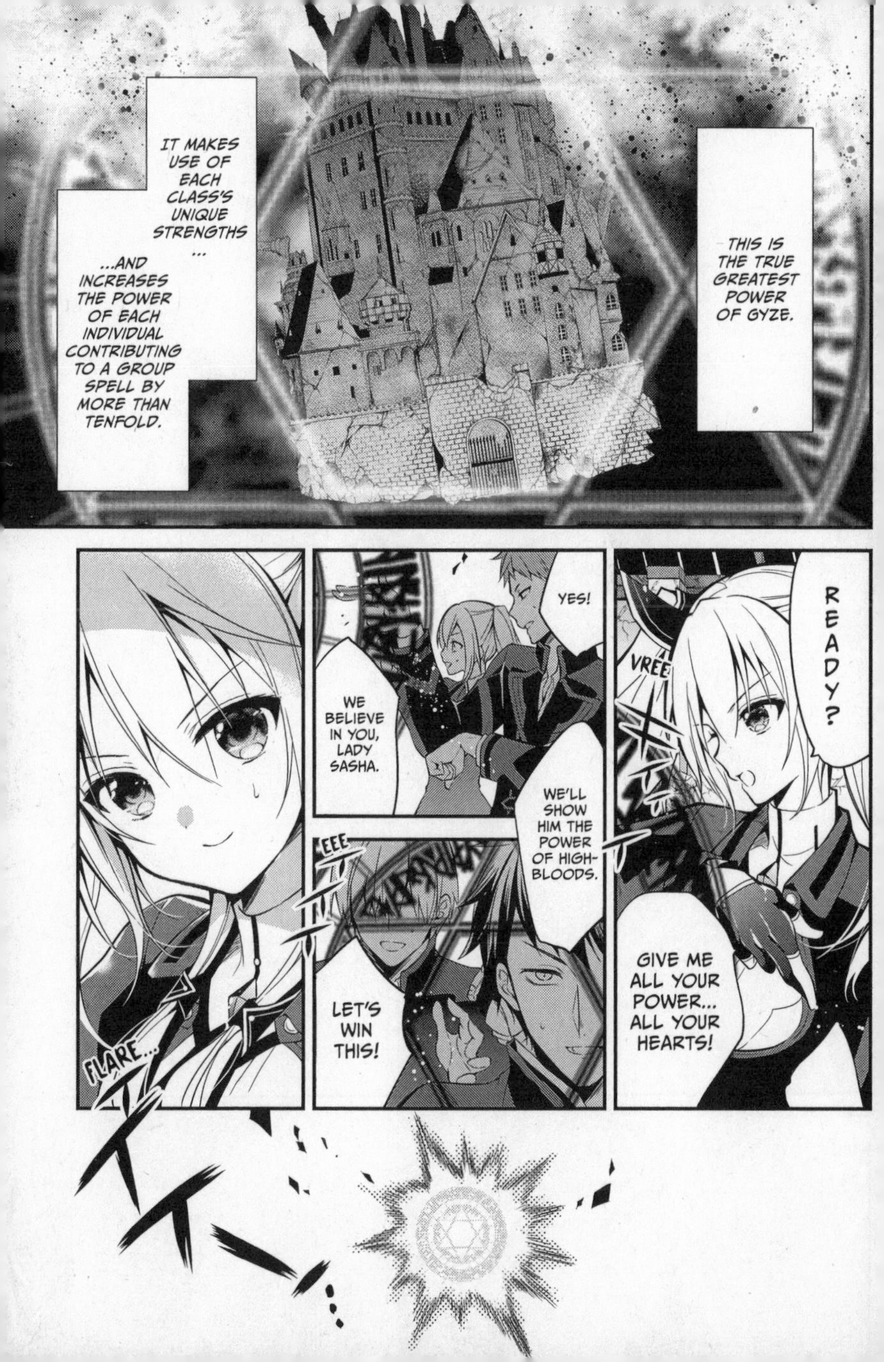
THIS IS THE TRUE GREATEST POWER OF GYZE.
IT MAKES USE OF EACH CLASS'S UNIQUE STRENGTHS...
...AND INCREASES THE POWER OF EACH INDIVIDUAL CONTRIBUTING TO A GROUP SPELL BY MORE THAN TENFOLD.
READY?
VREE
GIVE ME ALL YOUR POWER... ALL YOUR HEARTS!
YES!
WE BELIEVE IN YOU, LADY SASHA.
WE'LL SHOW HIM THE POWER OF HIGH-BLOODS.
EEE
LET'S WIN THIS!
FLARE...

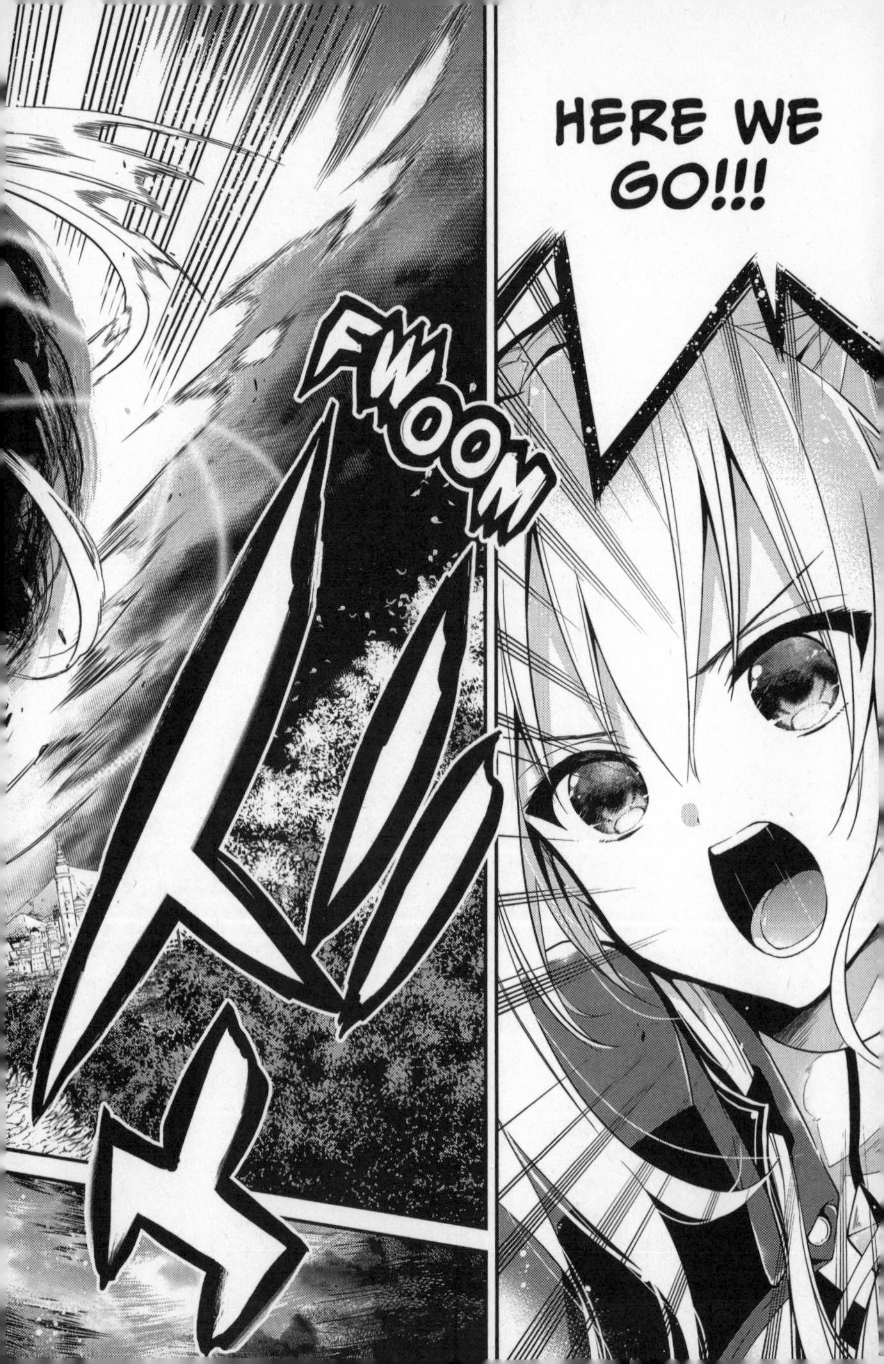
HERE WE GO!!!
FWOOM

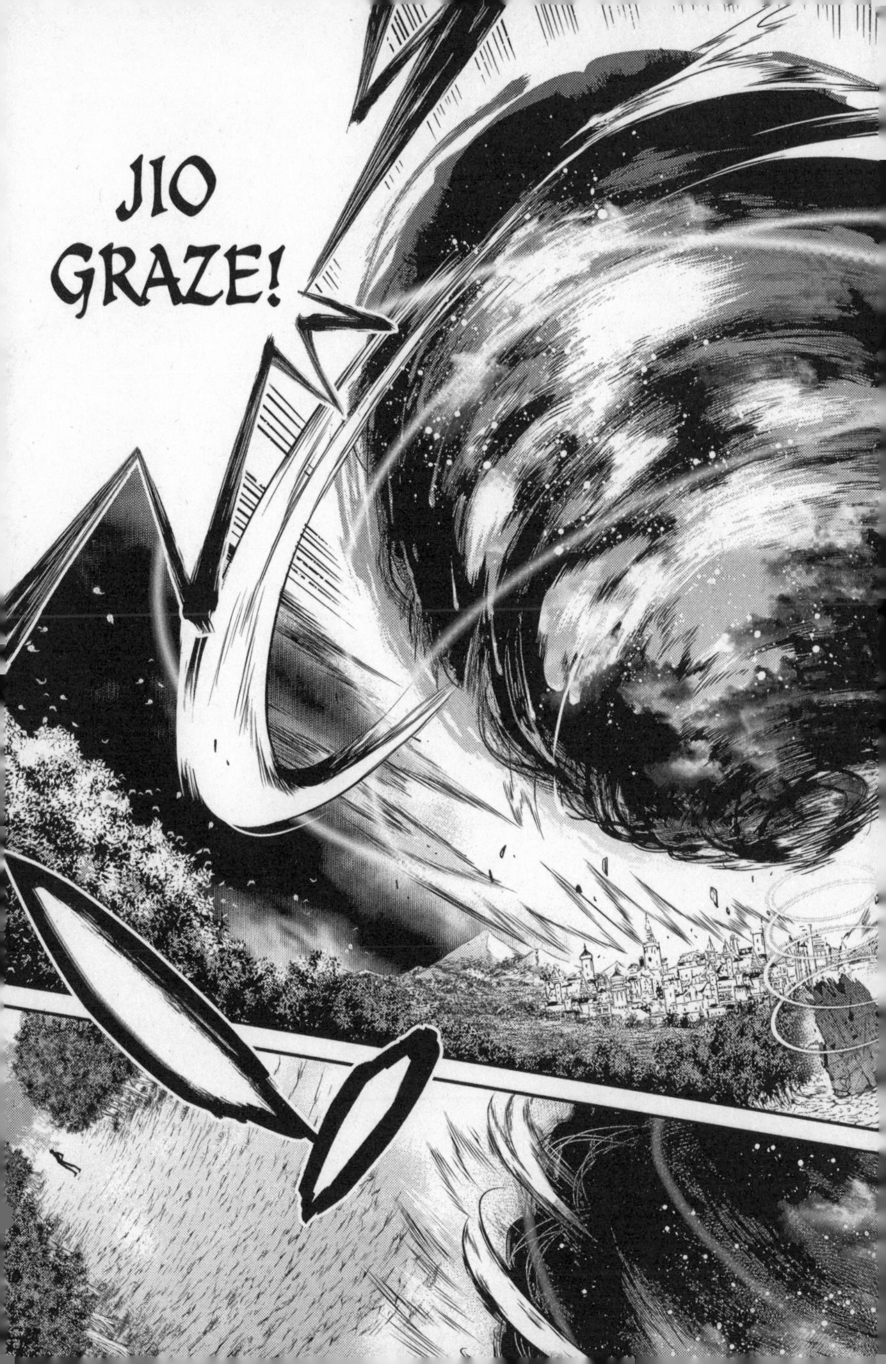
JIO GRAZE!

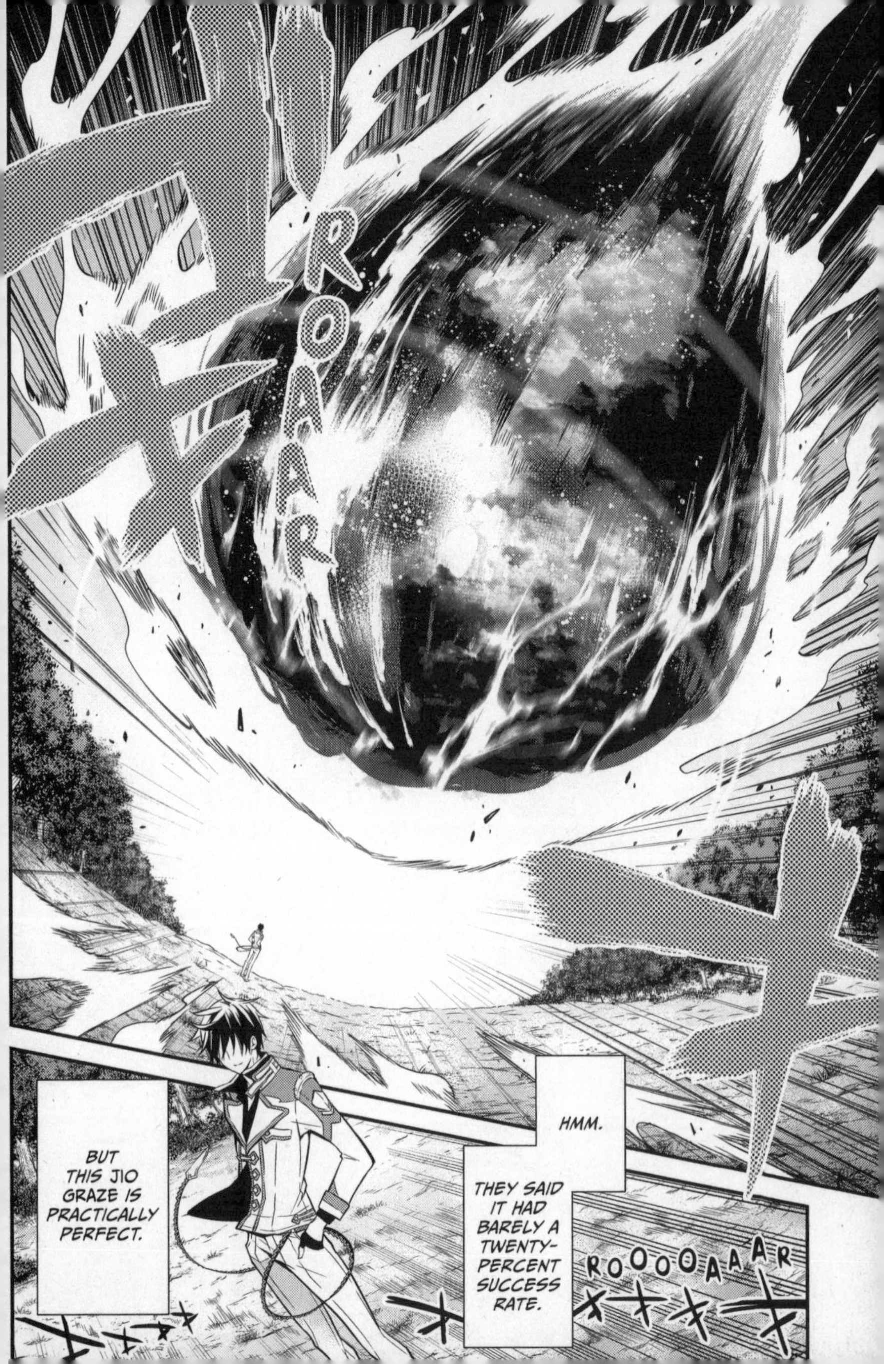
ROAAR
HMM.
THEY SAID IT HAD BARELY A TWENTY-PERCENT SUCCESS RATE.
ROOOOAAAR
BUT THIS JIO GRAZE IS PRACTICALLY PERFECT.

WELL DONE.

YOU DESERVE A REWARD FOR THAT.

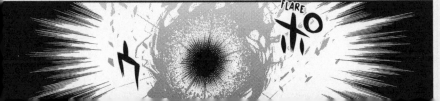

FLARE

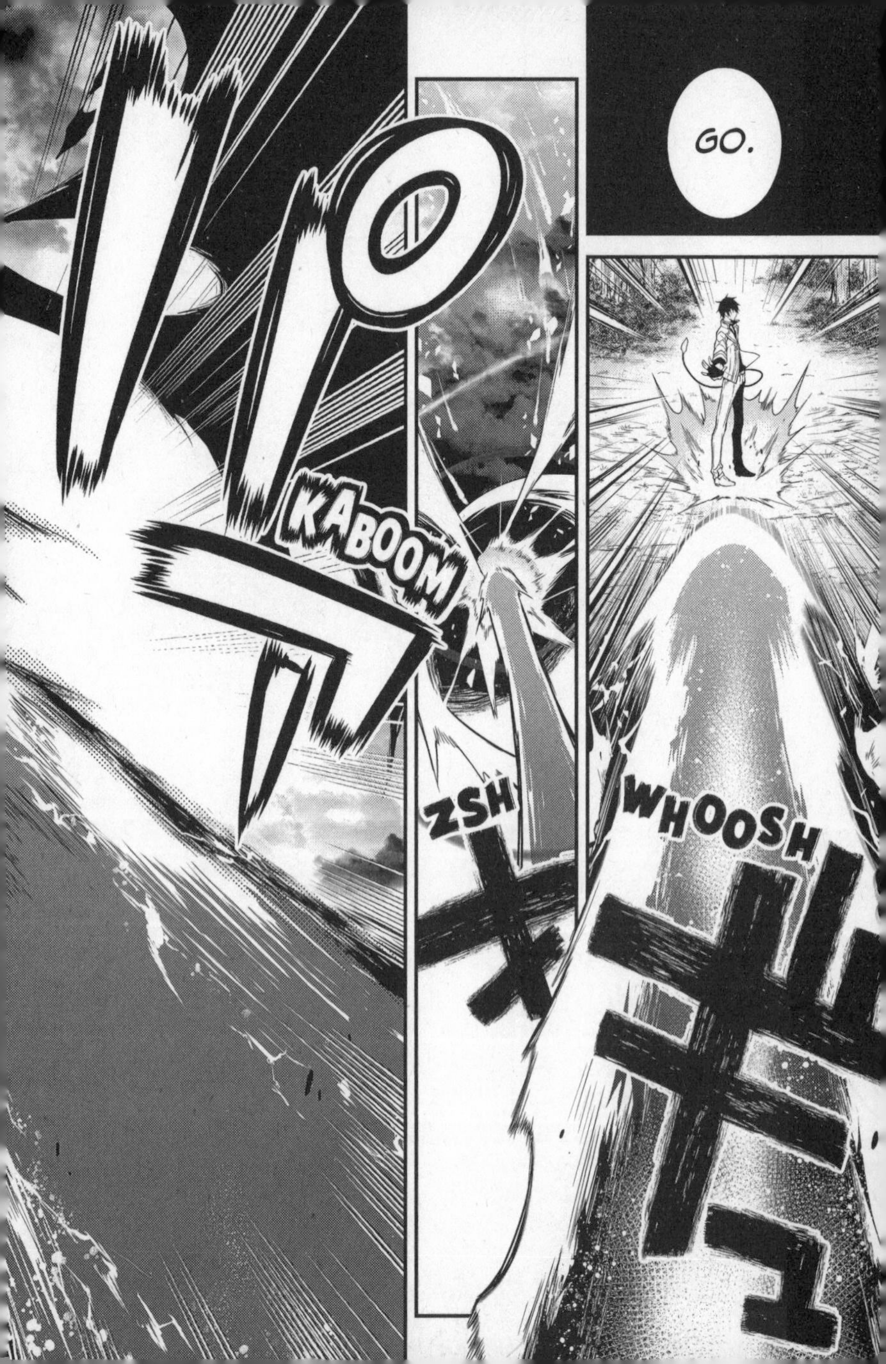
GO.
WHOOSH
ZSH
KABOOM

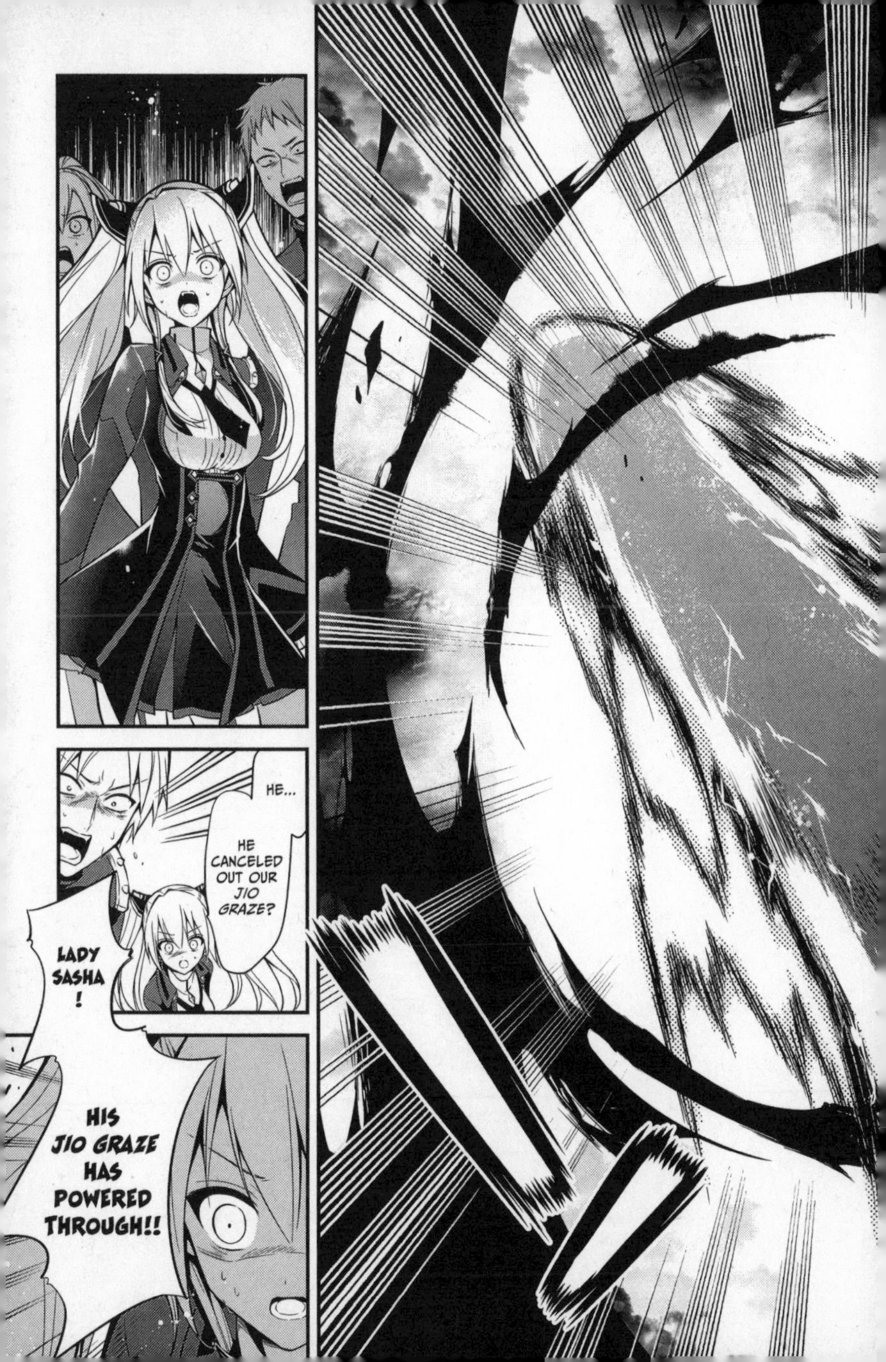
HE...
HE CANCELED OUT OUR JIO GRAZE?
LADY SASHA!
HIS JIO GRAZE HAS POWERED THROUGH!!

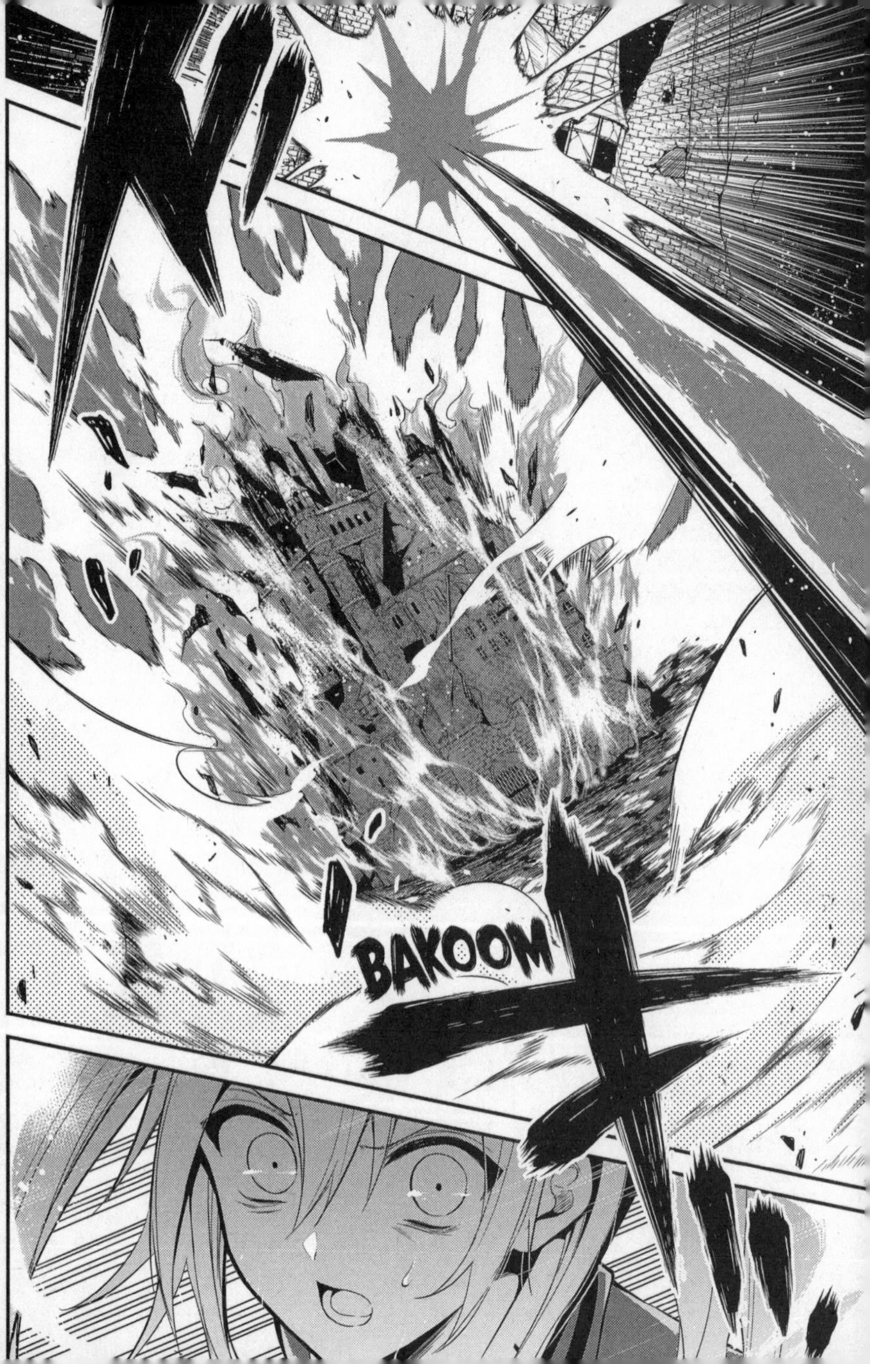
BAKOOM

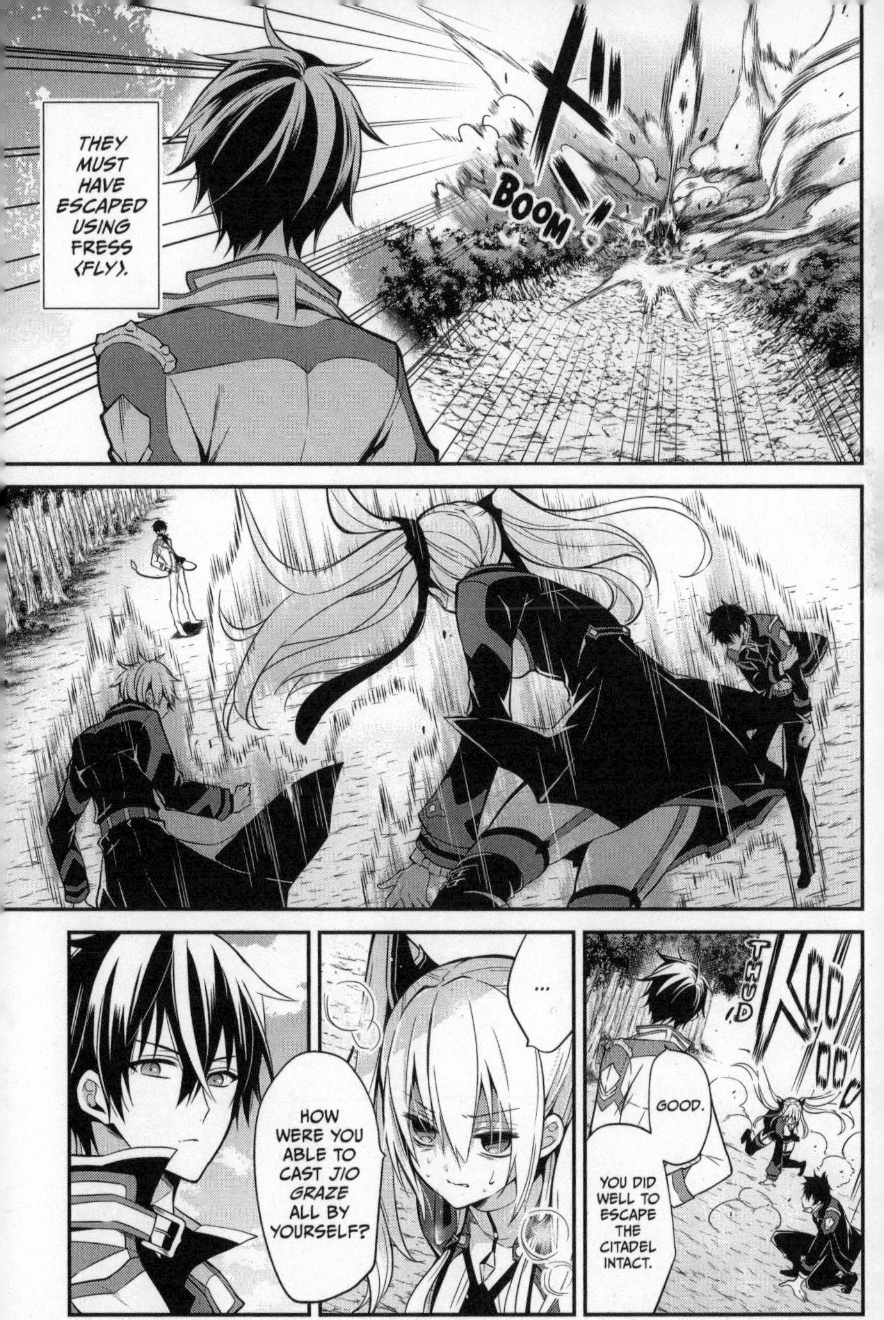
BOOM
THEY MUST HAVE ESCAPED USING FRESS ‹FLY›.
THUD
GOOD.
YOU DID WELL TO ESCAPE THE CITADEL INTACT.
...
HOW WERE YOU ABLE TO CAST JIO GRAZE ALL BY YOURSELF?

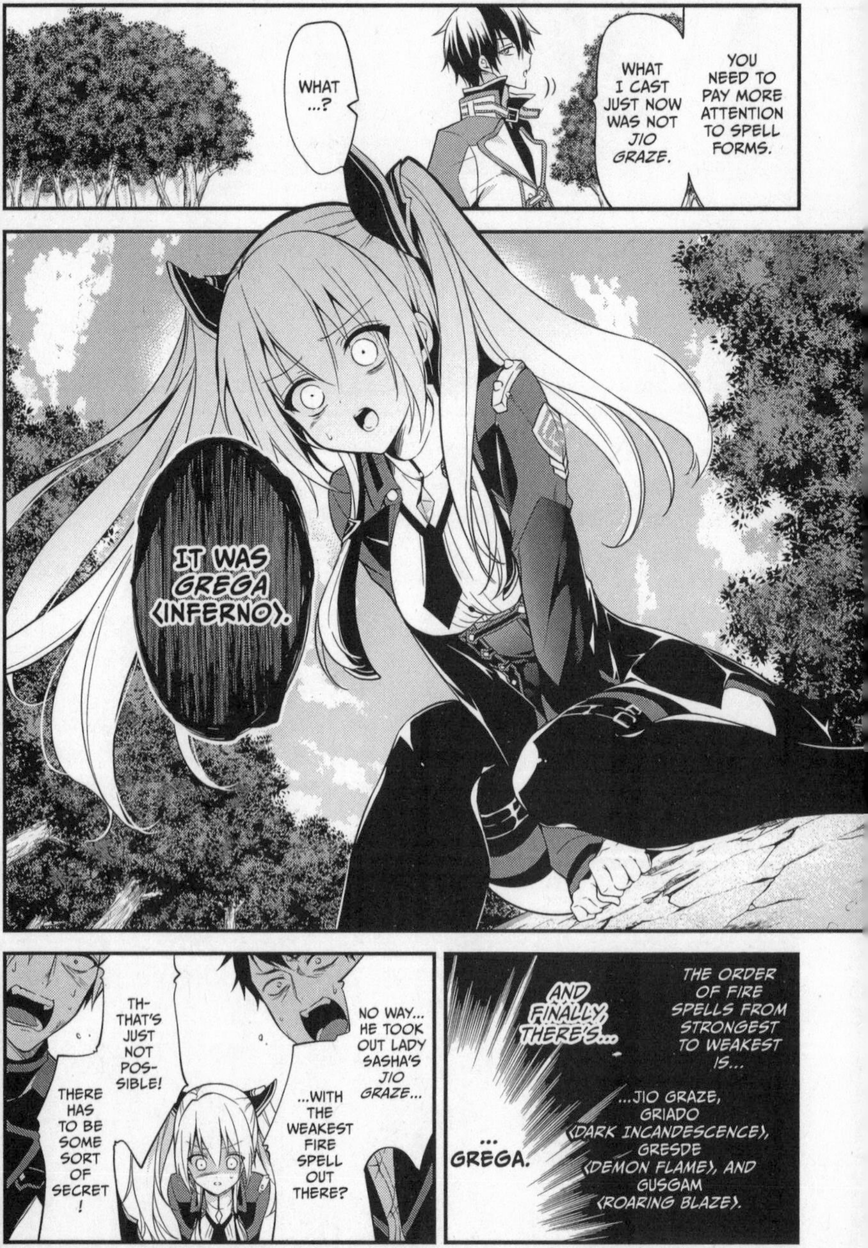
YOU NEED TO PAY MORE ATTENTION TO SPELL FORMS.
WHAT I CAST JUST NOW WAS NOT JIO GRAZE.
WHAT ...?
IT WAS GREGA 〈INFERNO〉.
THE ORDER OF FIRE SPELLS FROM STRONGEST TO WEAKEST IS...
...JIO GRAZE, GRIADO 〈DARK INCANDESCENCE〉, GRESDE 〈DEMON FLAME〉, AND GUSGAM 〈ROARING BLAZE〉.
AND FINALLY, THERE'S...
... GREGA.
NO WAY... HE TOOK OUT LADY SASHA'S JIO GRAZE...
...WITH THE WEAKEST FIRE SPELL OUT THERE?
TH-THAT'S JUST NOT POS-SIBLE!
THERE HAS TO BE SOME SORT OF SECRET!

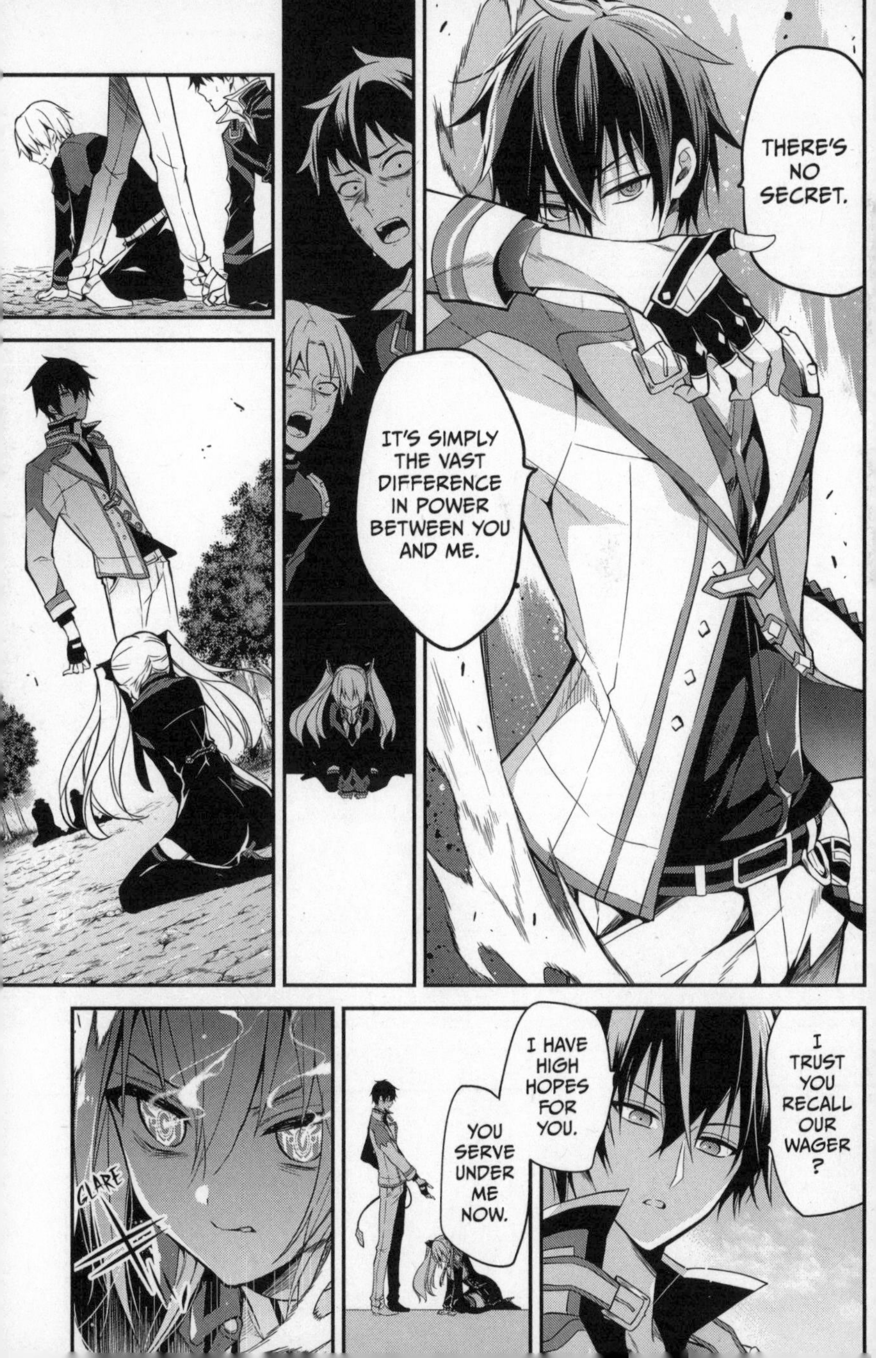
THERE'S NO SECRET.
IT'S SIMPLY THE VAST DIFFERENCE IN POWER BETWEEN YOU AND ME.
I TRUST YOU RECALL OUR WAGER?
I HAVE HIGH HOPES FOR YOU.
YOU SERVE UNDER ME NOW.
GLARE

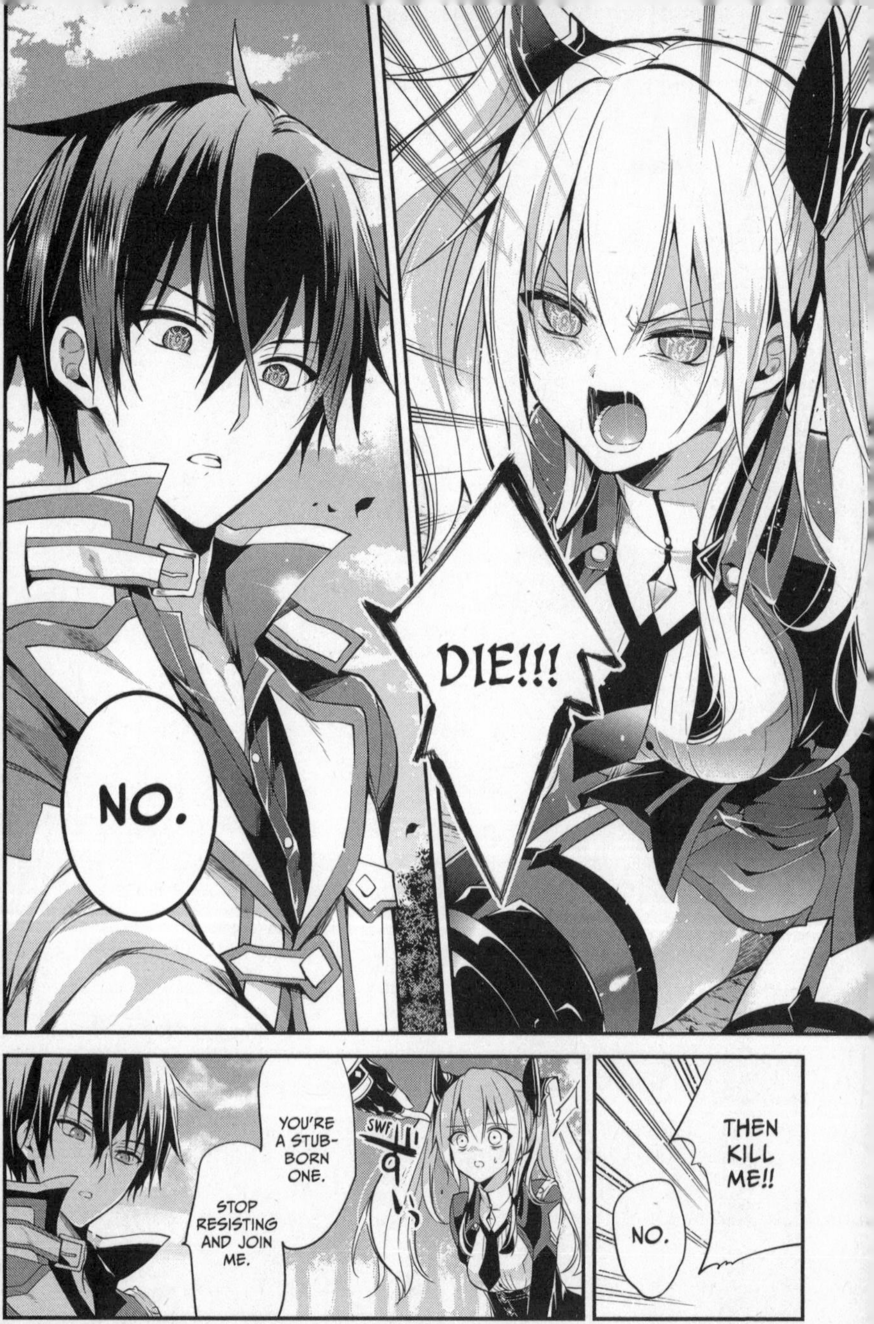
DIE!!!
NO.
THEN KILL ME!!
NO.
YOU'RE A STUB-BORN ONE.
STOP RESISTING AND JOIN ME.
SWF

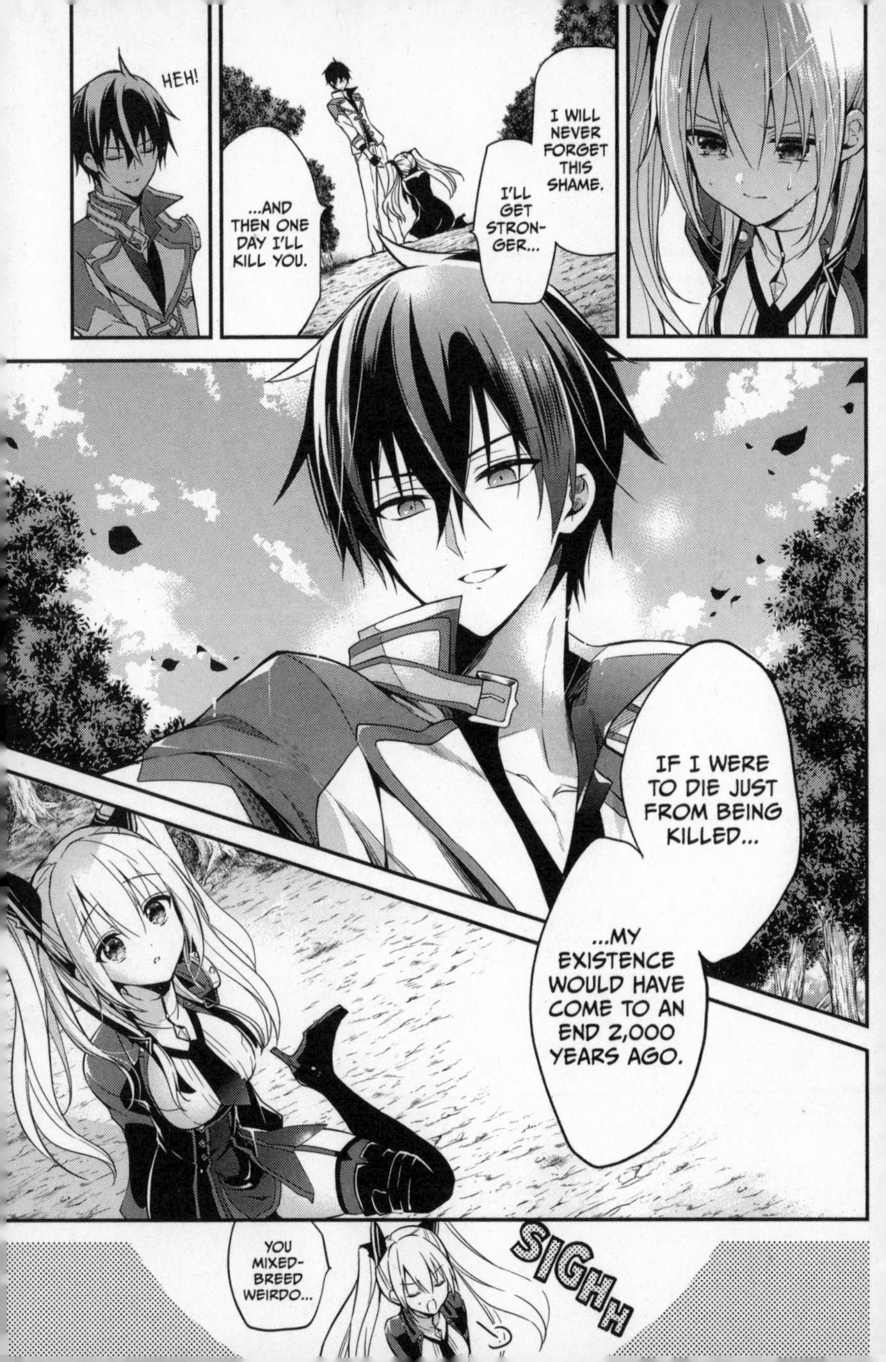
I WILL NEVER FORGET THIS SHAME.
I'LL GET STRONGER...
...AND THEN ONE DAY I'LL KILL YOU.
HEH!
IF I WERE TO DIE JUST FROM BEING KILLED...
...MY EXISTENCE WOULD HAVE COME TO AN END 2,000 YEARS AGO.
SIGHH
YOU MIXED-BREED WEIRDO...

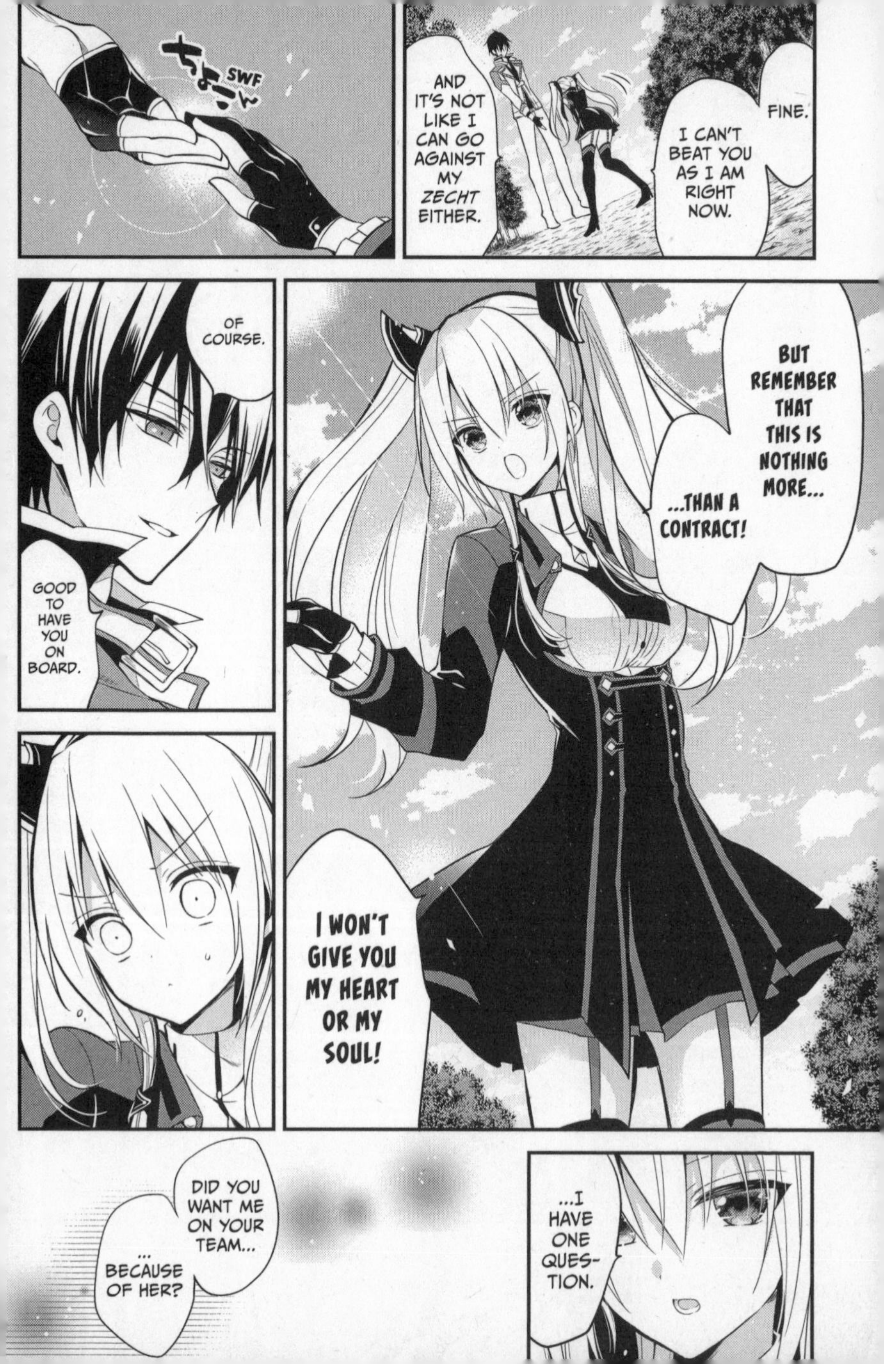
FINE.
I CAN'T BEAT YOU AS I AM RIGHT NOW.
AND IT'S NOT LIKE I CAN GO AGAINST MY *ZECHT* EITHER.
ちょこん
SWF
BUT REMEMBER THAT THIS IS NOTHING MORE...
...THAN A CONTRACT!
I WON'T GIVE YOU MY HEART OR MY SOUL!
OF COURSE.
GOOD TO HAVE YOU ON BOARD.
...I HAVE ONE QUES-TION.
DID YOU WANT ME ON YOUR TEAM...
...BECAUSE OF HER?

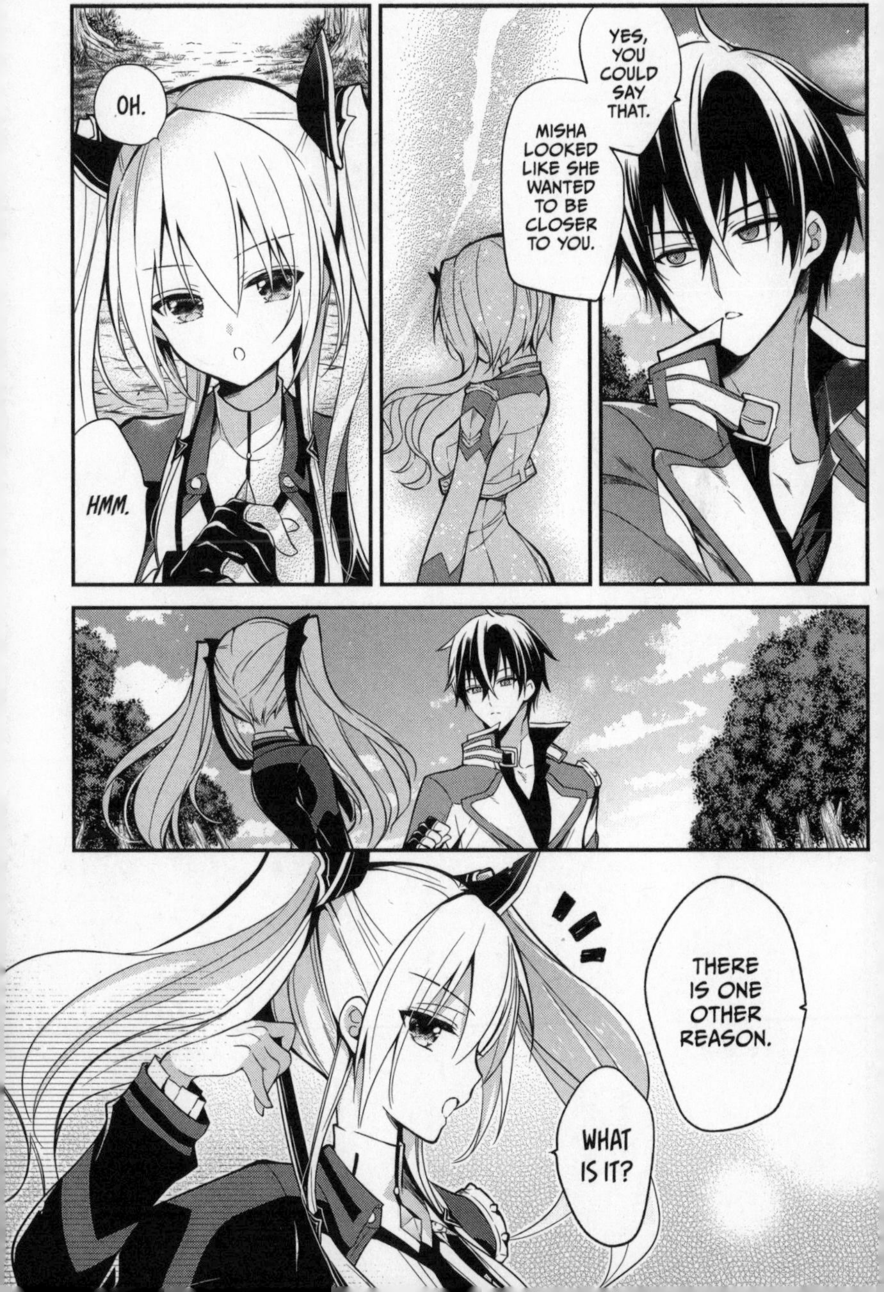
YES, YOU COULD SAY THAT.
MISHA LOOKED LIKE SHE WANTED TO BE CLOSER TO YOU.
OH.
HMM.
THERE IS ONE OTHER REASON.
WHAT IS IT?

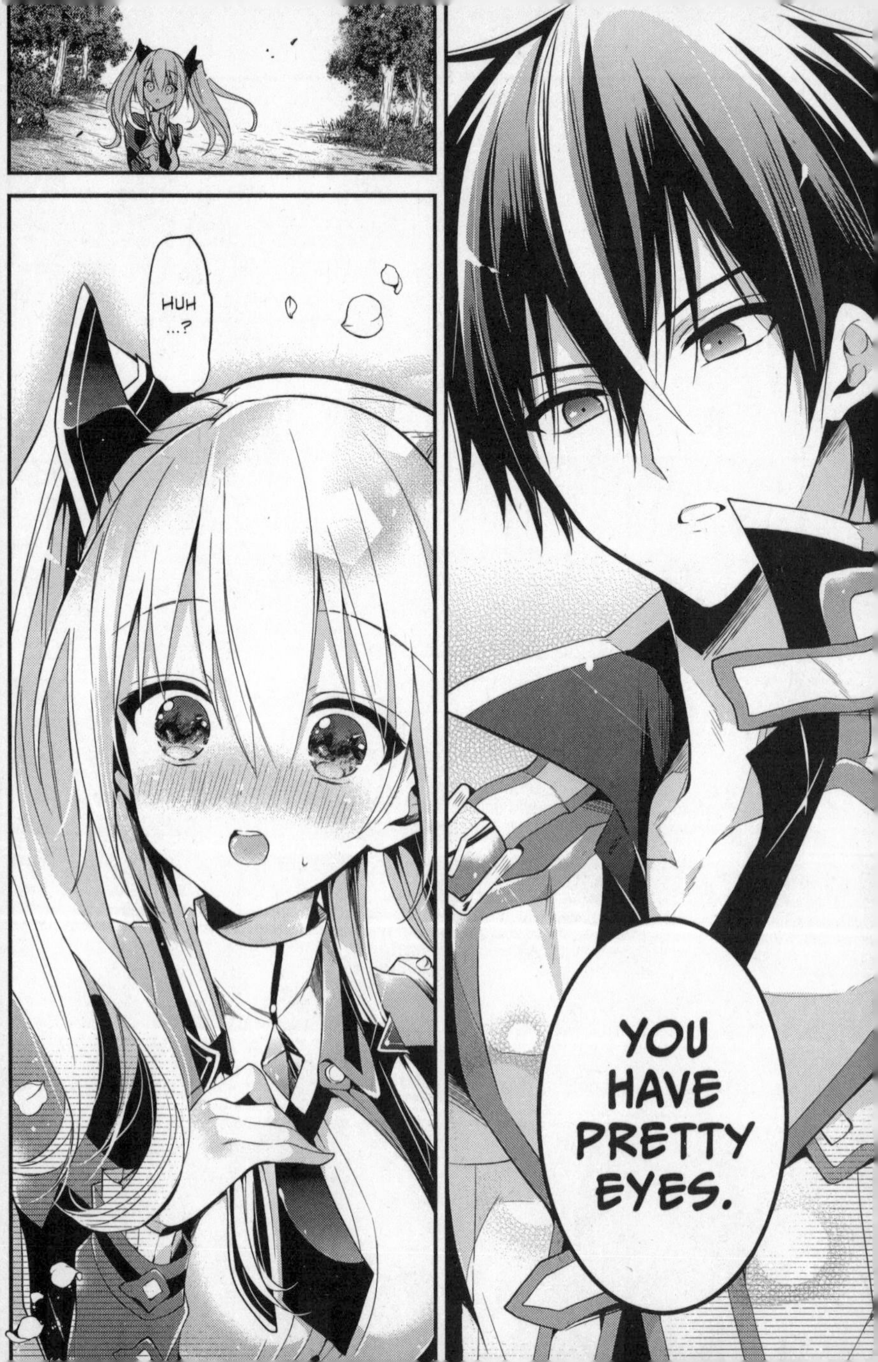
YOU HAVE PRETTY EYES.
HUH …?

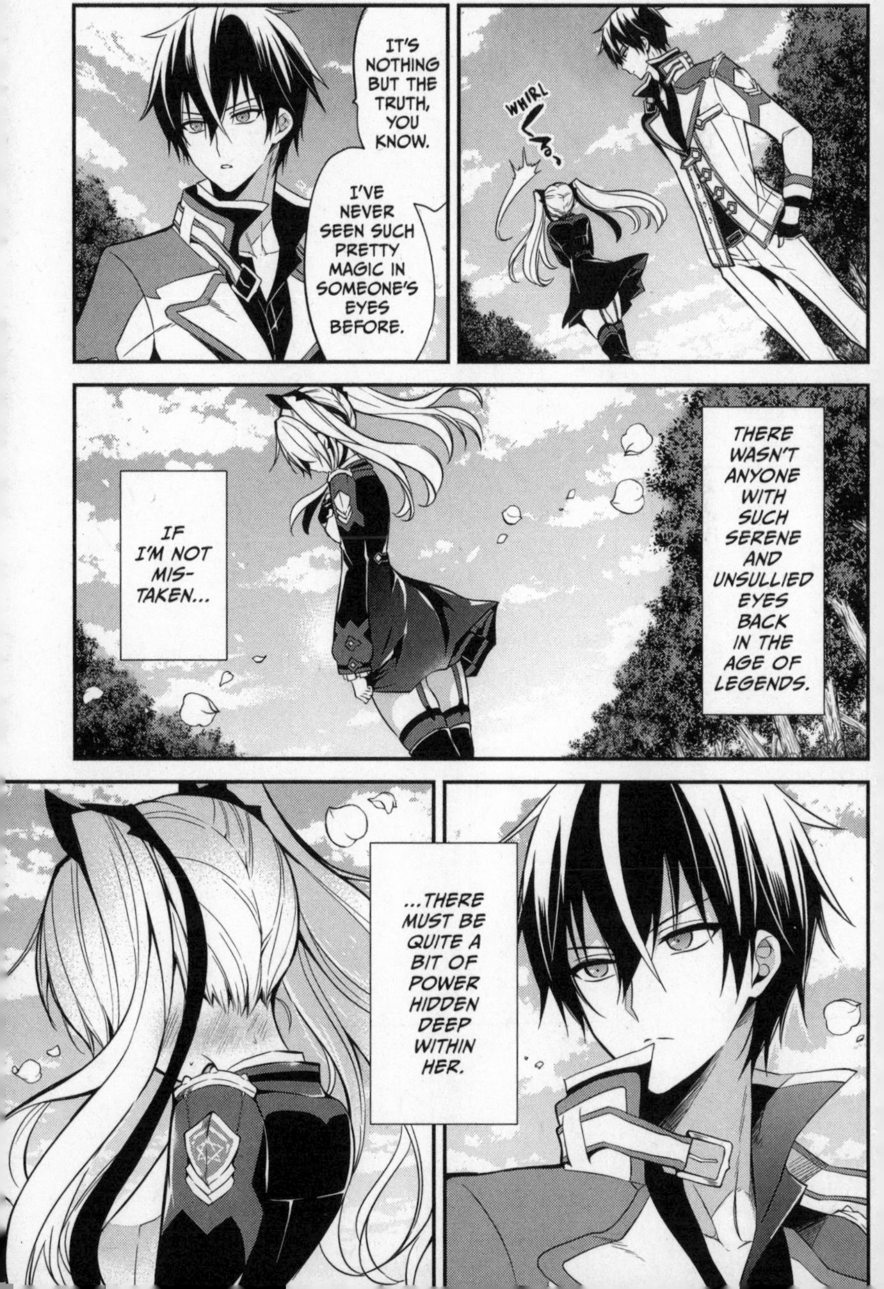
WHIRL
IT'S NOTHING BUT THE TRUTH, YOU KNOW.
I'VE NEVER SEEN SUCH PRETTY MAGIC IN SOMEONE'S EYES BEFORE.
THERE WASN'T ANYONE WITH SUCH SERENE AND UNSULLIED EYES BACK IN THE AGE OF LEGENDS.
IF I'M NOT MIS-TAKEN...
...THERE MUST BE QUITE A BIT OF POWER HIDDEN DEEP WITHIN HER.

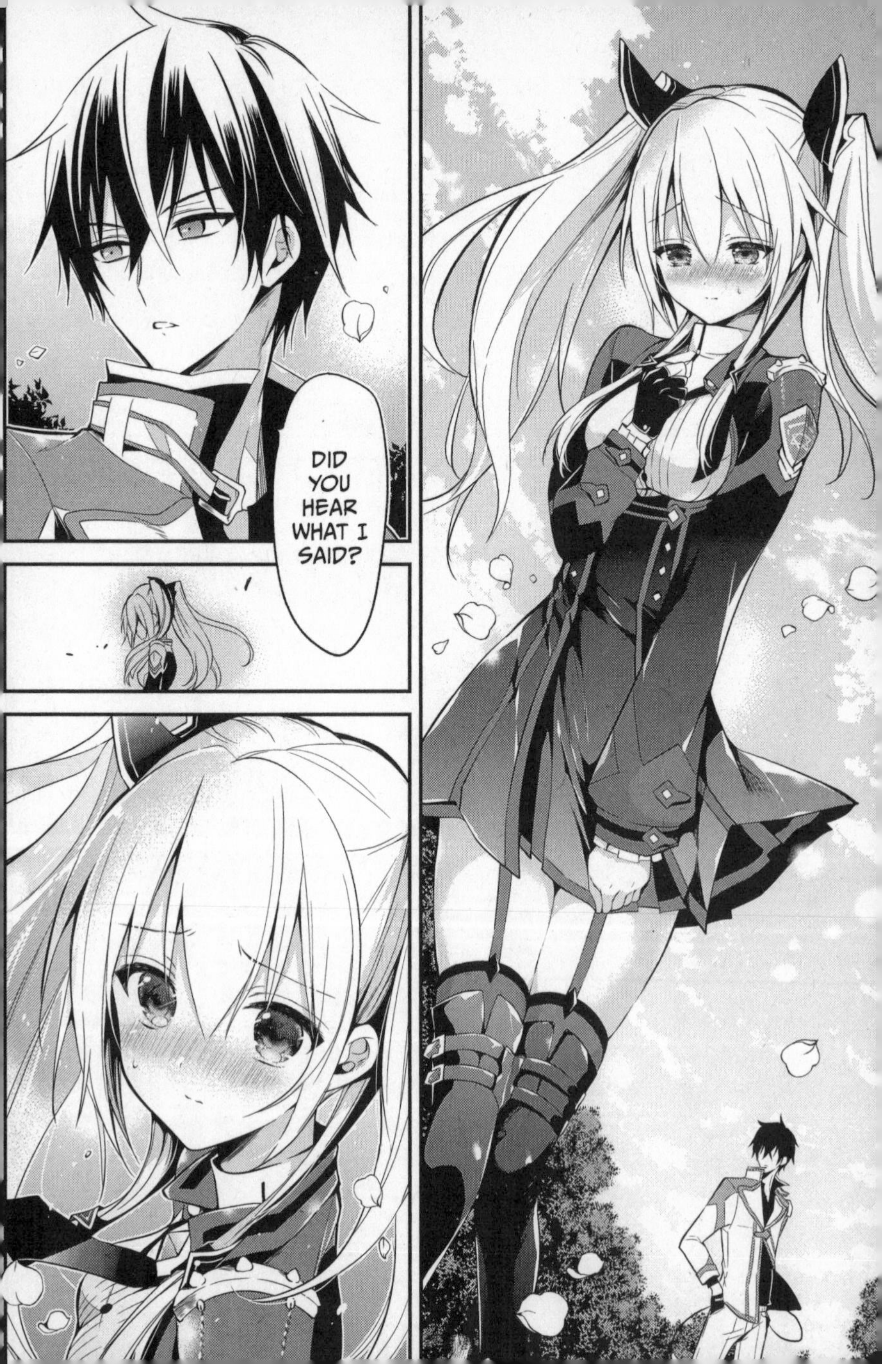
DID YOU HEAR WHAT I SAID?

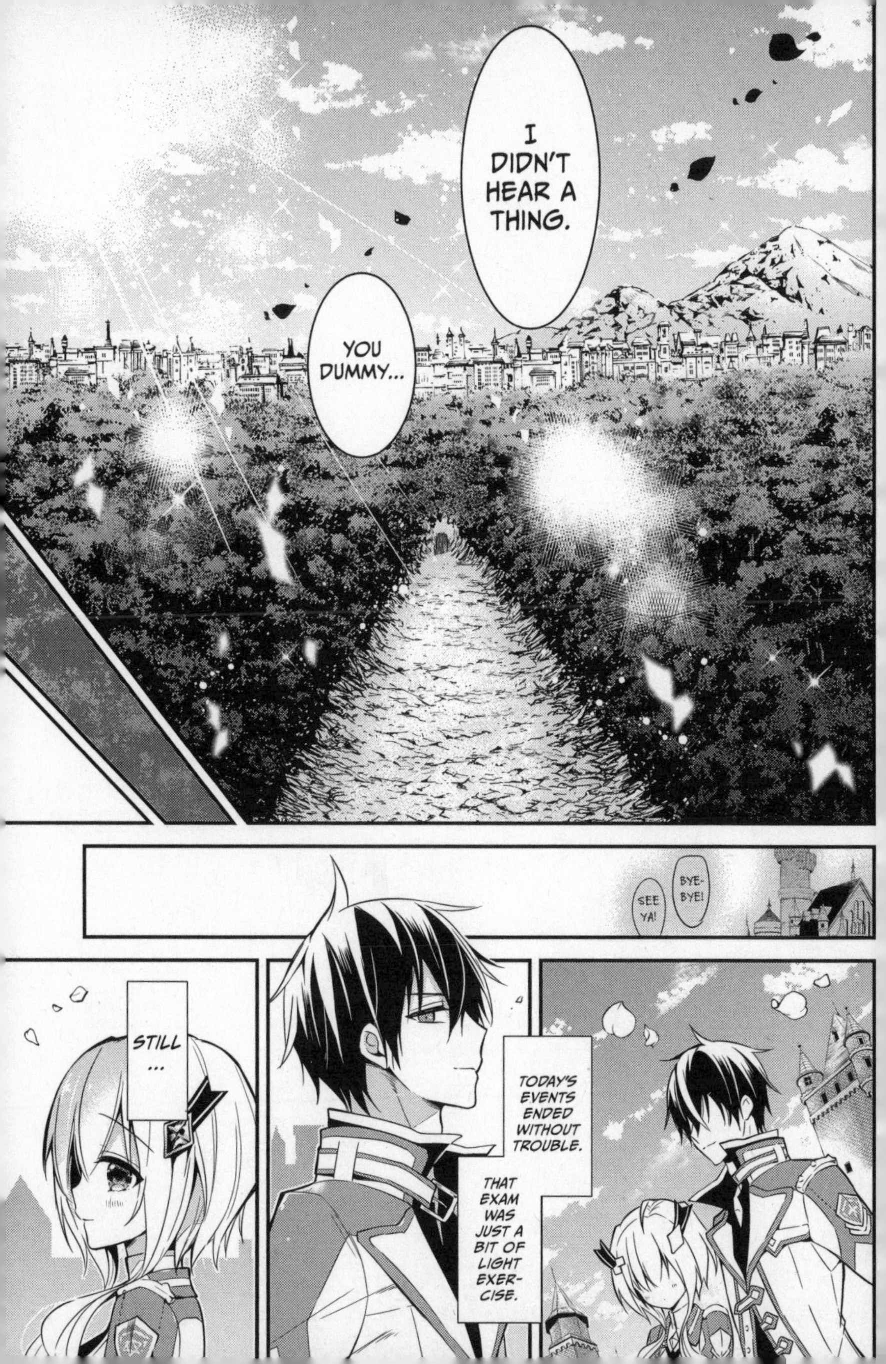
I DIDN'T HEAR A THING.
YOU DUMMY...
BYE-BYE!
SEE YA!
TODAY'S EVENTS ENDED WITHOUT TROUBLE.
THAT EXAM WAS JUST A BIT OF LIGHT EXER-CISE.
STILL ...

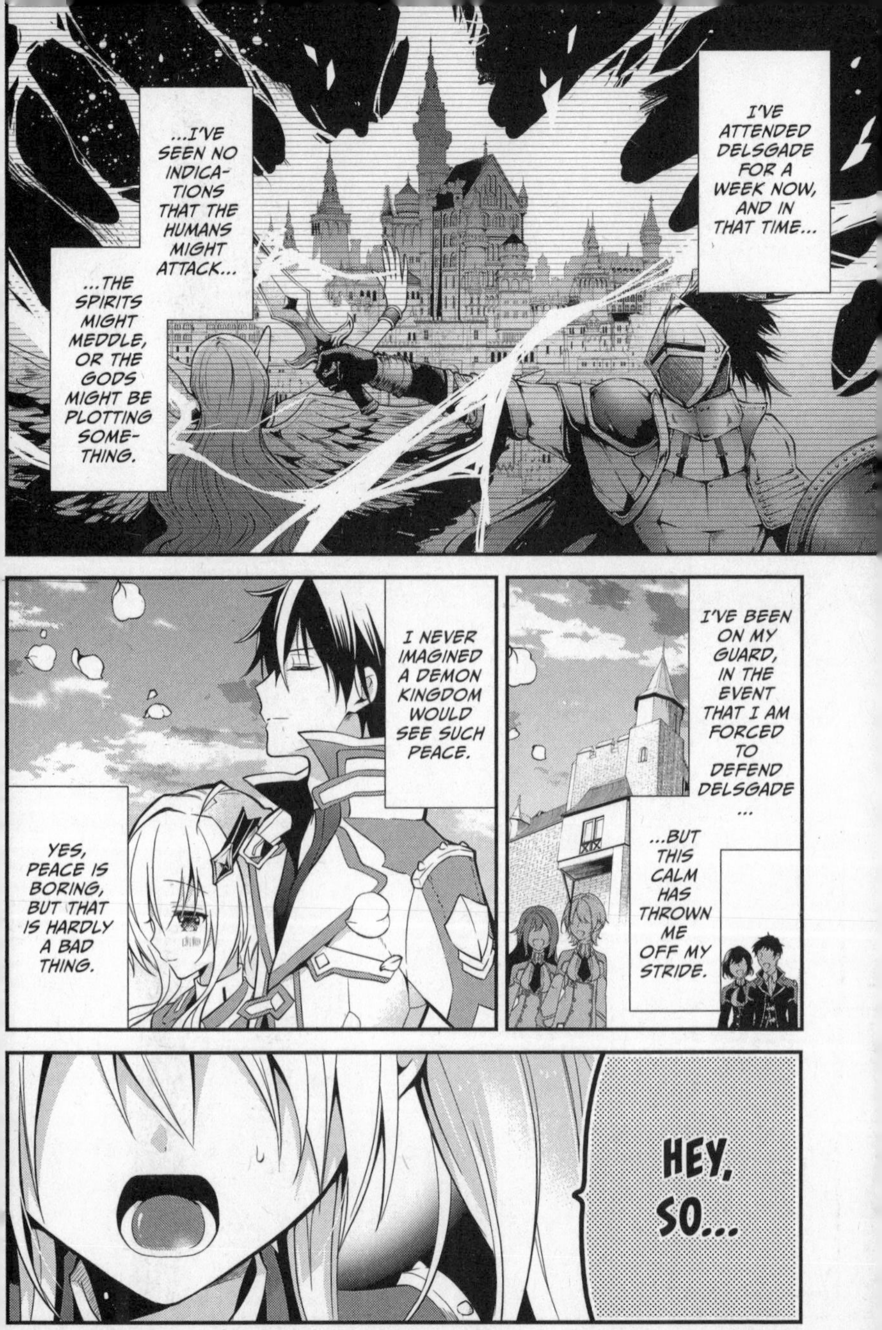
I'VE ATTENDED DELSGADE FOR A WEEK NOW, AND IN THAT TIME...
...I'VE SEEN NO INDICATIONS THAT THE HUMANS MIGHT ATTACK...
...THE SPIRITS MIGHT MEDDLE, OR THE GODS MIGHT BE PLOTTING SOMETHING.
I'VE BEEN ON MY GUARD, IN THE EVENT THAT I AM FORCED TO DEFEND DELSGADE...
...BUT THIS CALM HAS THROWN ME OFF MY STRIDE.
I NEVER IMAGINED A DEMON KINGDOM WOULD SEE SUCH PEACE.
YES, PEACE IS BORING, BUT THAT IS HARDLY A BAD THING.
HEY, SO...

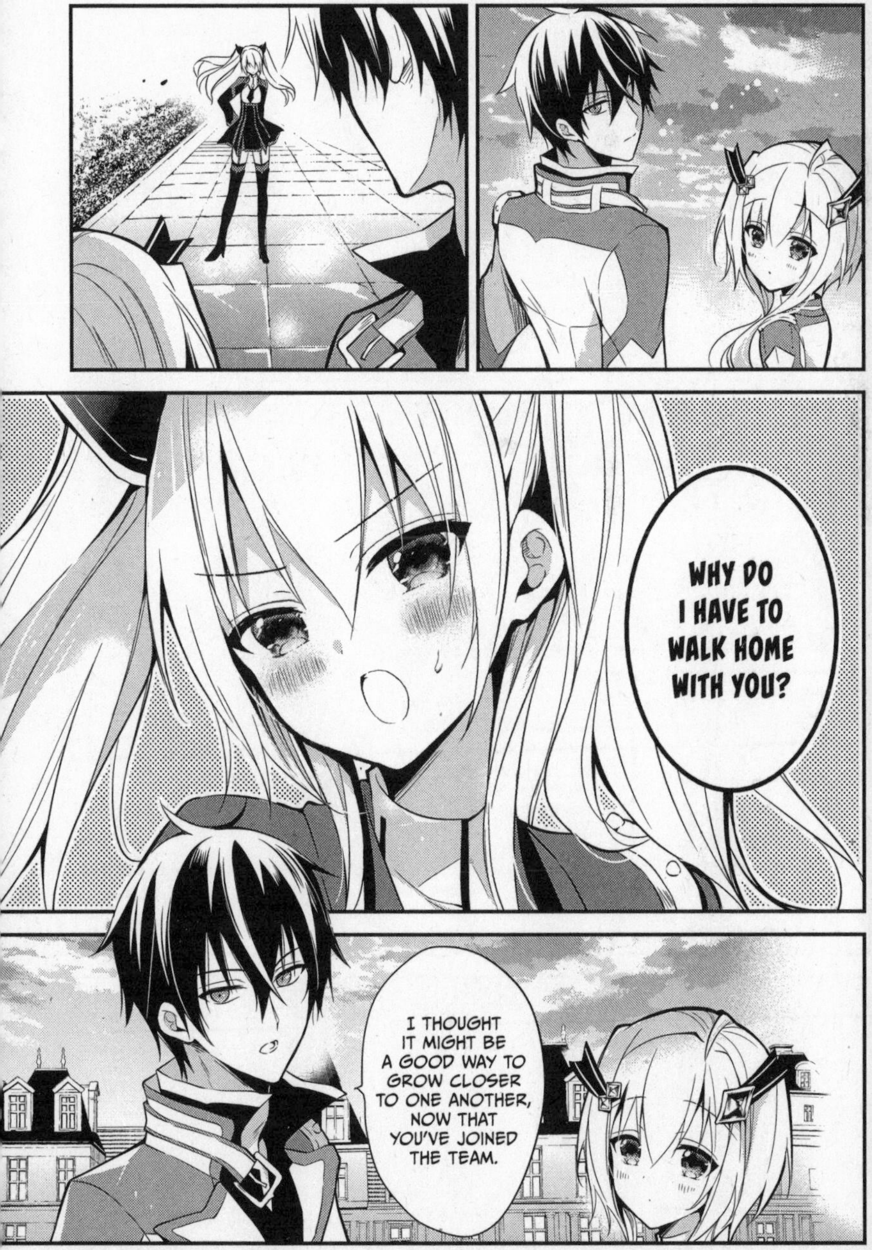
WHY DO I HAVE TO WALK HOME WITH YOU?
I THOUGHT IT MIGHT BE A GOOD WAY TO GROW CLOSER TO ONE ANOTHER, NOW THAT YOU'VE JOINED THE TEAM.

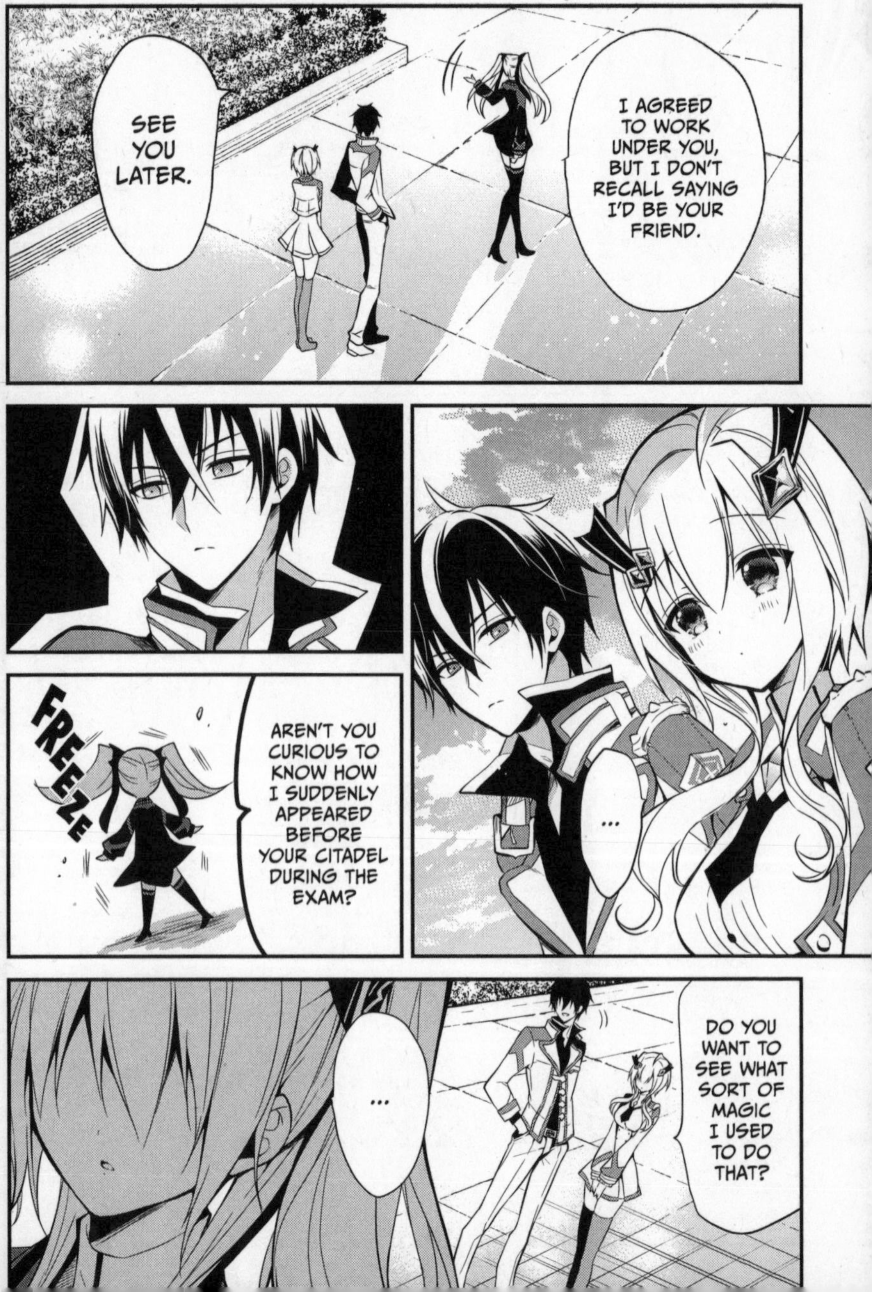
I AGREED TO WORK UNDER YOU, BUT I DON'T RECALL SAYING I'D BE YOUR FRIEND.
SEE YOU LATER.
...
AREN'T YOU CURIOUS TO KNOW HOW I SUDDENLY APPEARED BEFORE YOUR CITADEL DURING THE EXAM?
FREEZE
DO YOU WANT TO SEE WHAT SORT OF MAGIC I USED TO DO THAT?
...

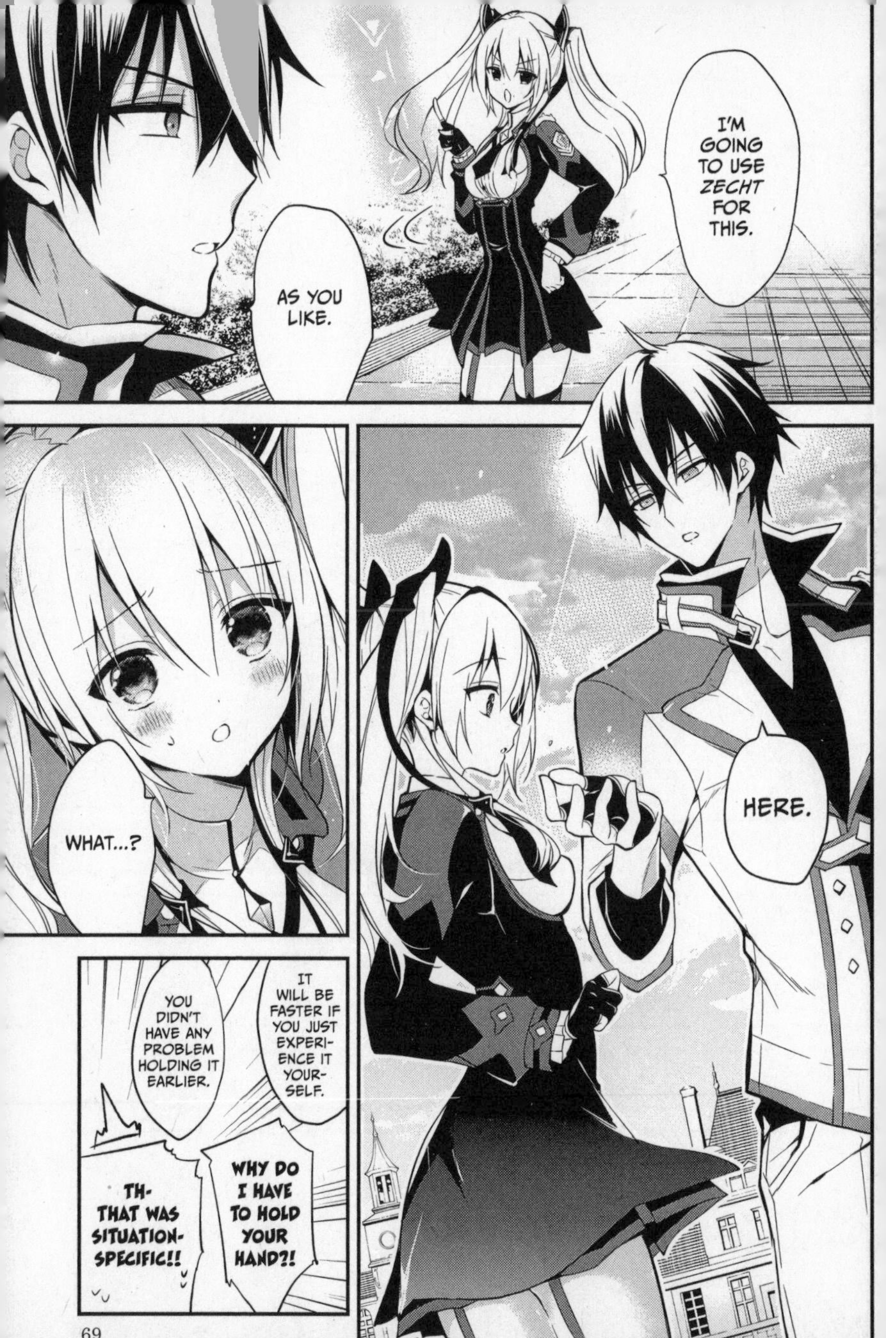
I'M GOING TO USE ZECHT FOR THIS.
AS YOU LIKE.
HERE.
WHAT...?
IT WILL BE FASTER IF YOU JUST EXPERIENCE IT YOURSELF.
YOU DIDN'T HAVE ANY PROBLEM HOLDING IT EARLIER.
WHY DO I HAVE TO HOLD YOUR HAND?!
TH- THAT WAS SITUATION-SPECIFIC!!

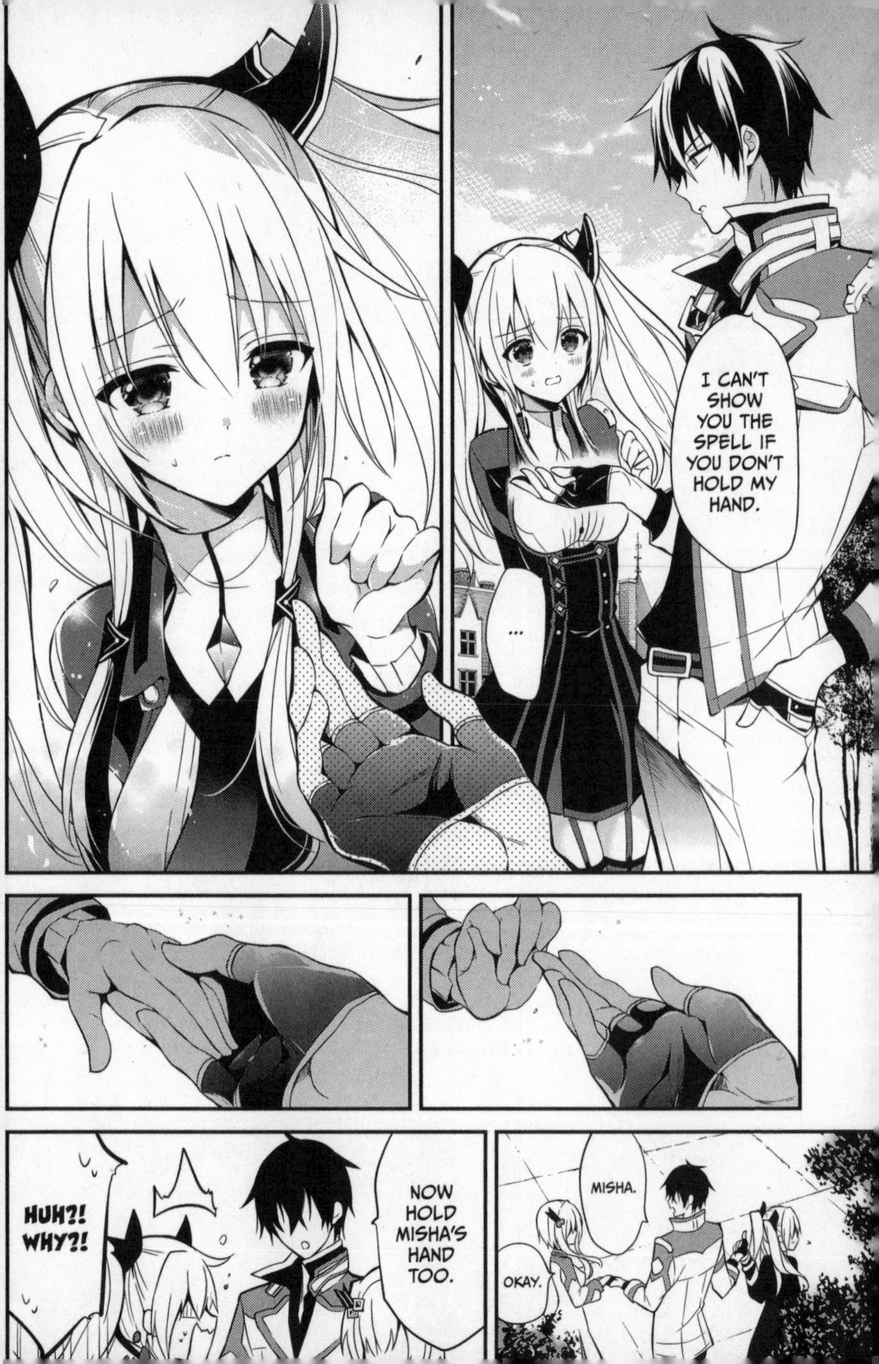
I CAN'T SHOW YOU THE SPELL IF YOU DON'T HOLD MY HAND.
...
MISHA.
OKAY.
NOW HOLD MISHA'S HAND TOO.
HUH?! WHY?!

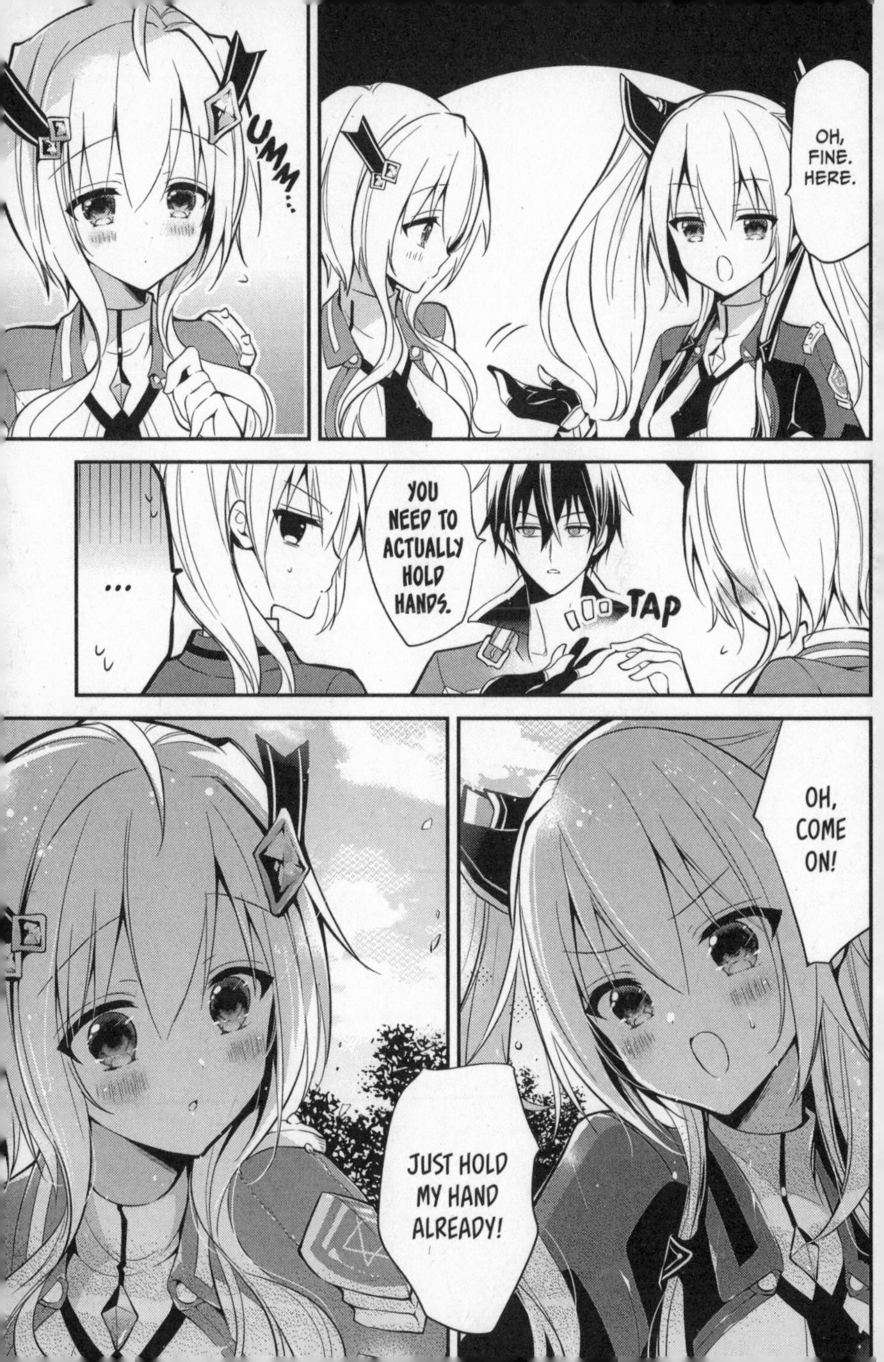
OH, FINE. HERE.
UMM...
TAP
YOU NEED TO ACTUALLY HOLD HANDS.
...
OH, COME ON!
JUST HOLD MY HAND ALREADY!

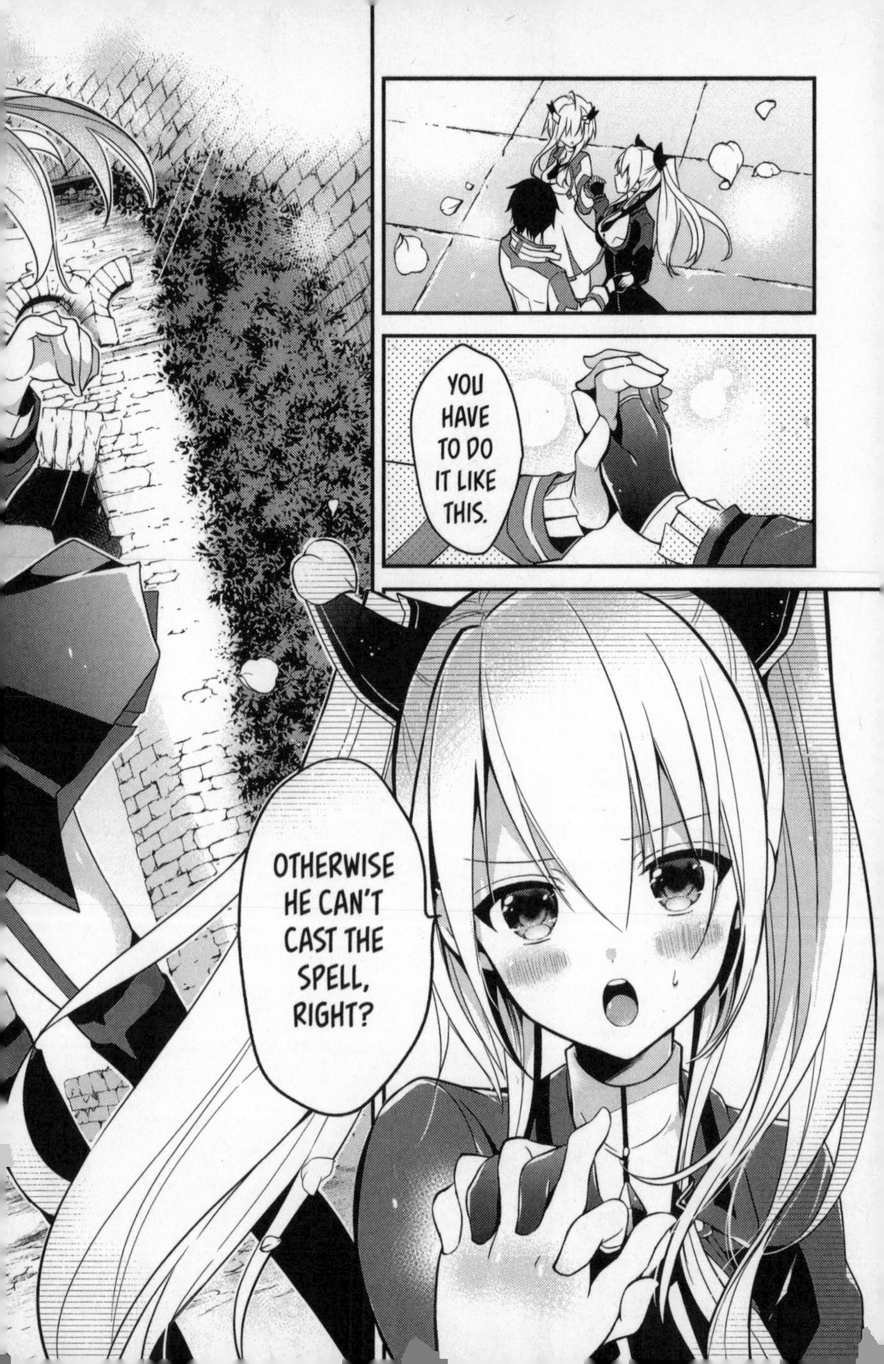
YOU HAVE TO DO IT LIKE THIS.
OTHERWISE HE CAN'T CAST THE SPELL, RIGHT?

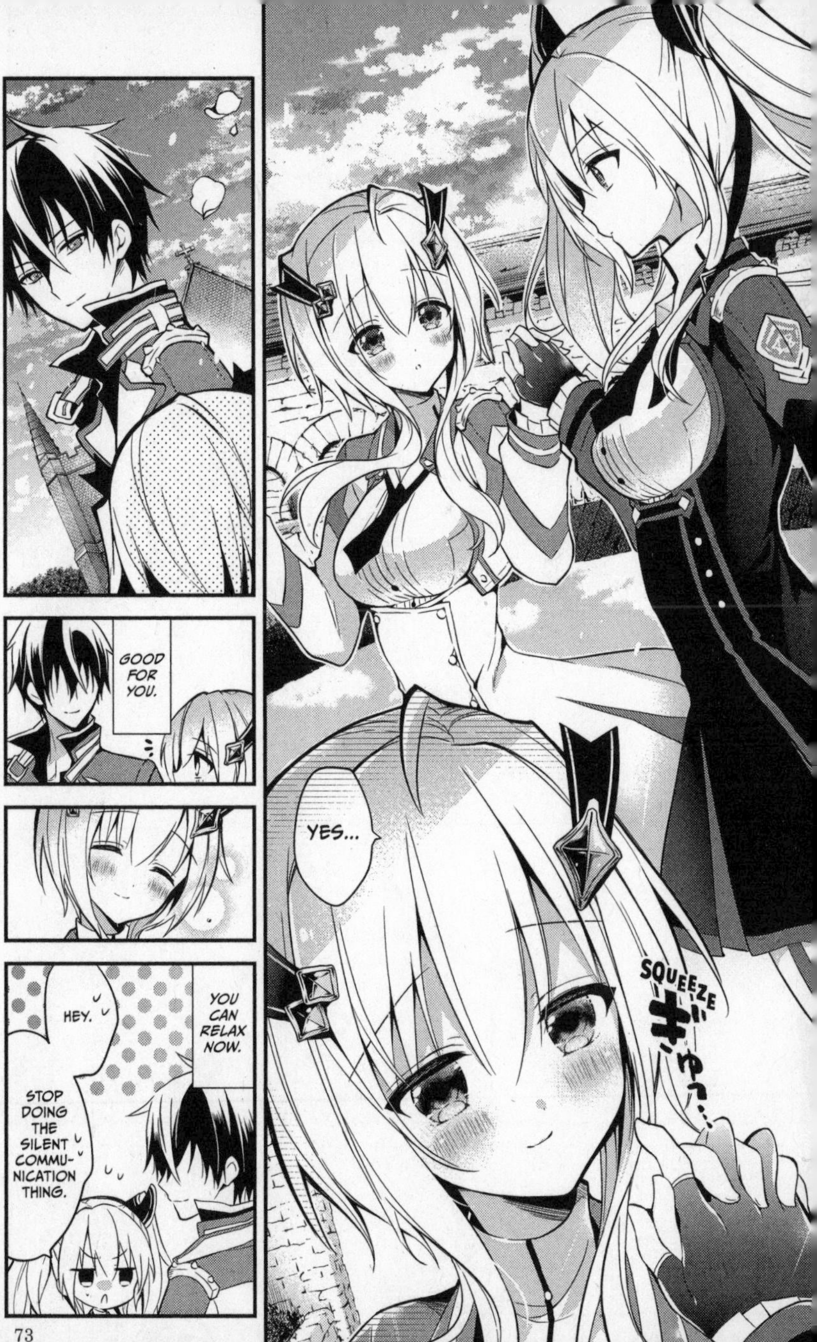
YES...
SQUEEZE
ぎゅっ…
GOOD FOR YOU.
YOU CAN RELAX NOW.
HEY.
STOP DOING THE SILENT COMMUNICATION THING.

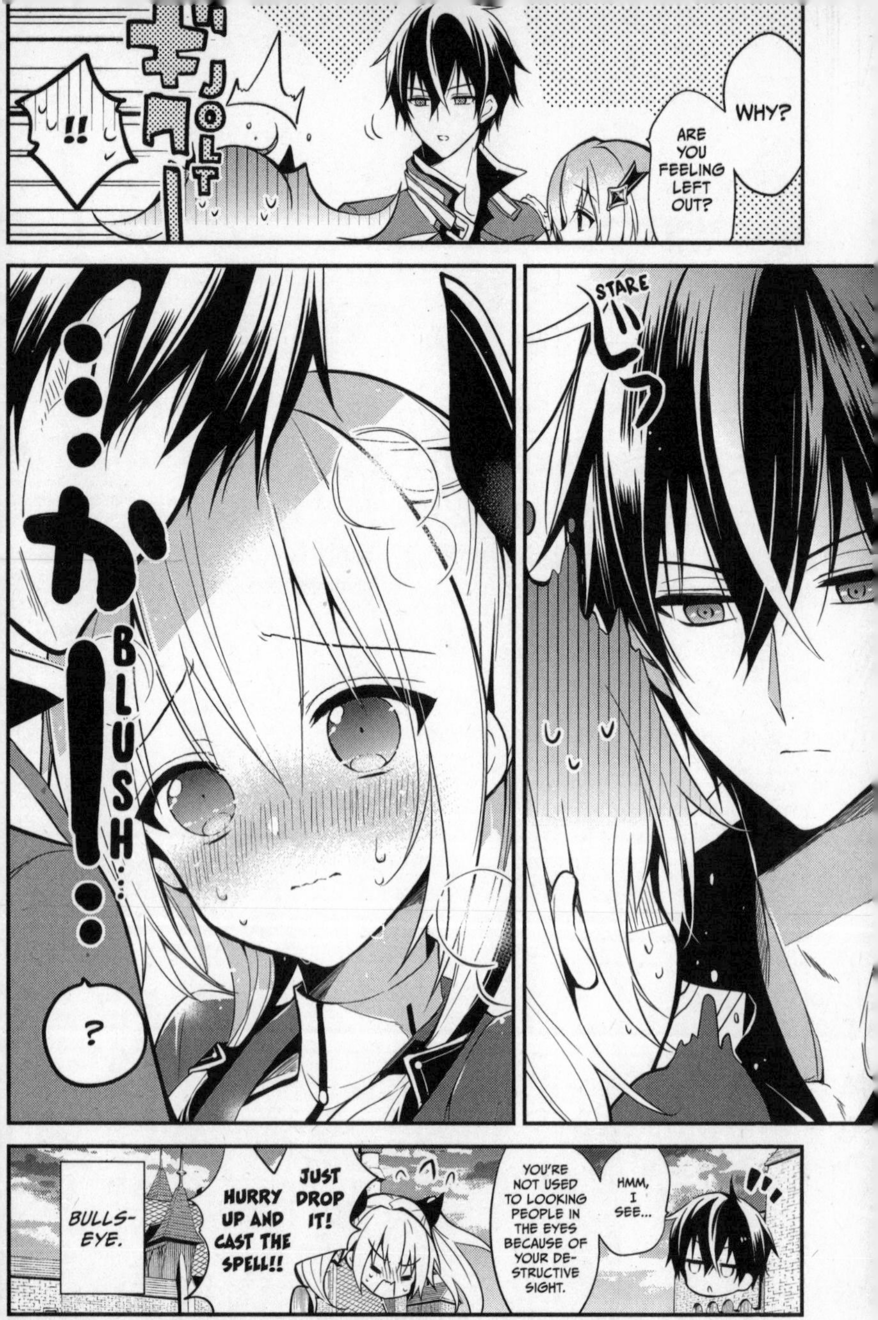
WHY?
ARE YOU FEELING LEFT OUT?
JOLT
!!
STARE
BLUSH...
?
HMM, I SEE...
YOU'RE NOT USED TO LOOKING PEOPLE IN THE EYES BECAUSE OF YOUR DESTRUCTIVE SIGHT.
JUST DROP IT!
HURRY UP AND CAST THE SPELL!!
BULLS-EYE.

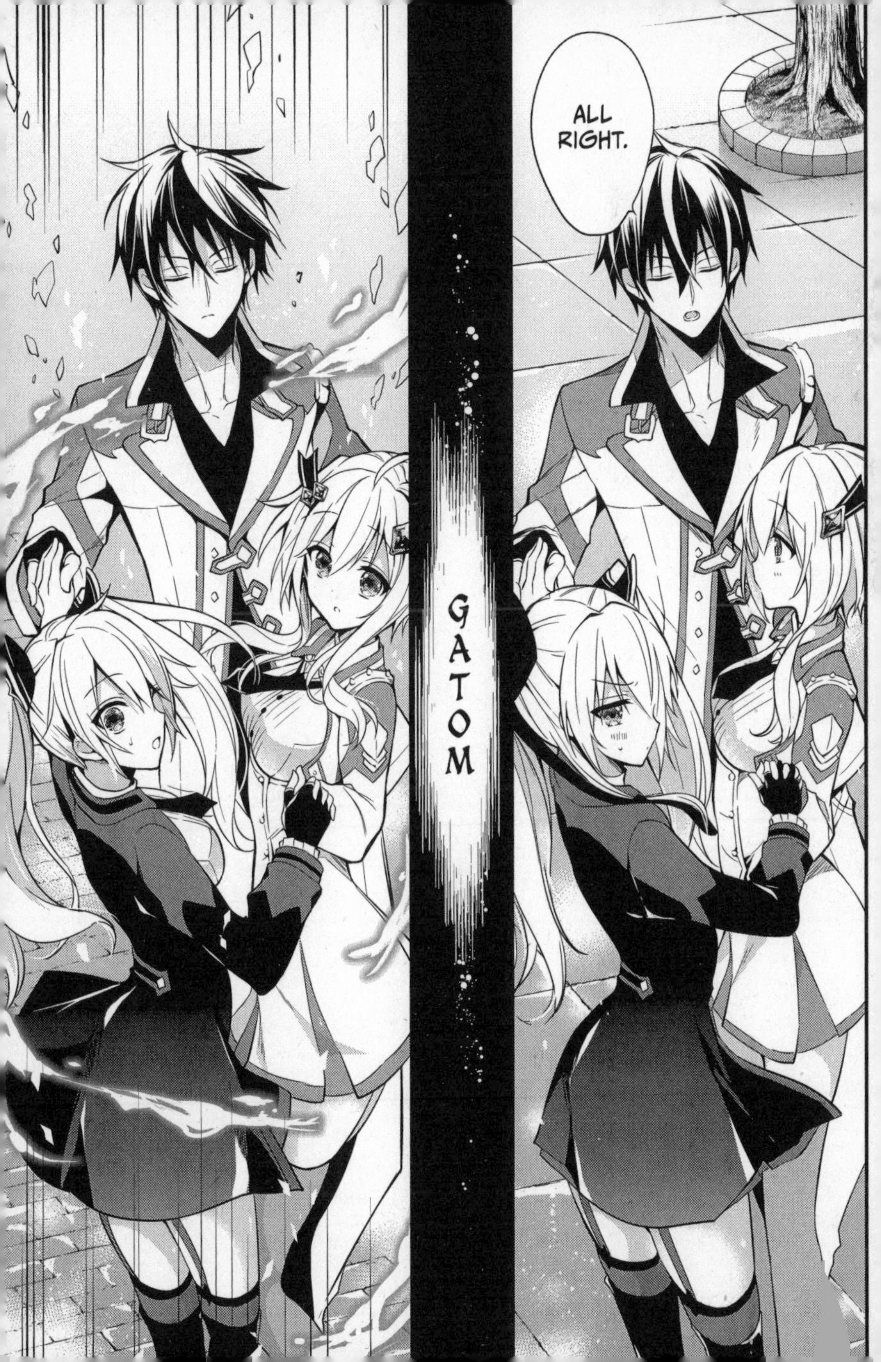
ALL RIGHT.
GATOM

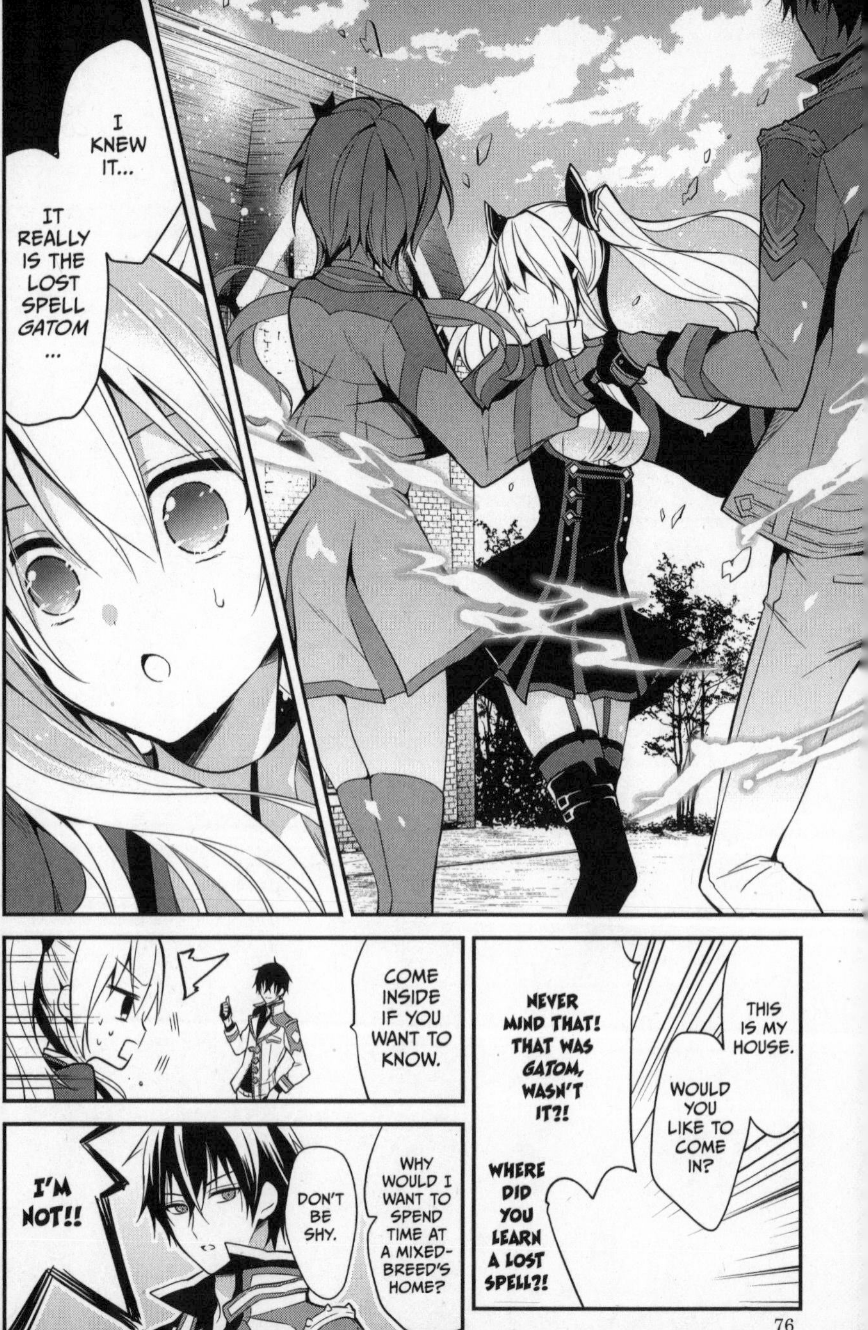
I KNEW IT...
IT REALLY IS THE LOST SPELL GATOM ...
THIS IS MY HOUSE.
WOULD YOU LIKE TO COME IN?
NEVER MIND THAT! THAT WAS GATOM, WASN'T IT?!
WHERE DID YOU LEARN A LOST SPELL?!
COME INSIDE IF YOU WANT TO KNOW.
WHY WOULD I WANT TO SPEND TIME AT A MIXED-BREED'S HOME?
DON'T BE SHY.
I'M NOT!!

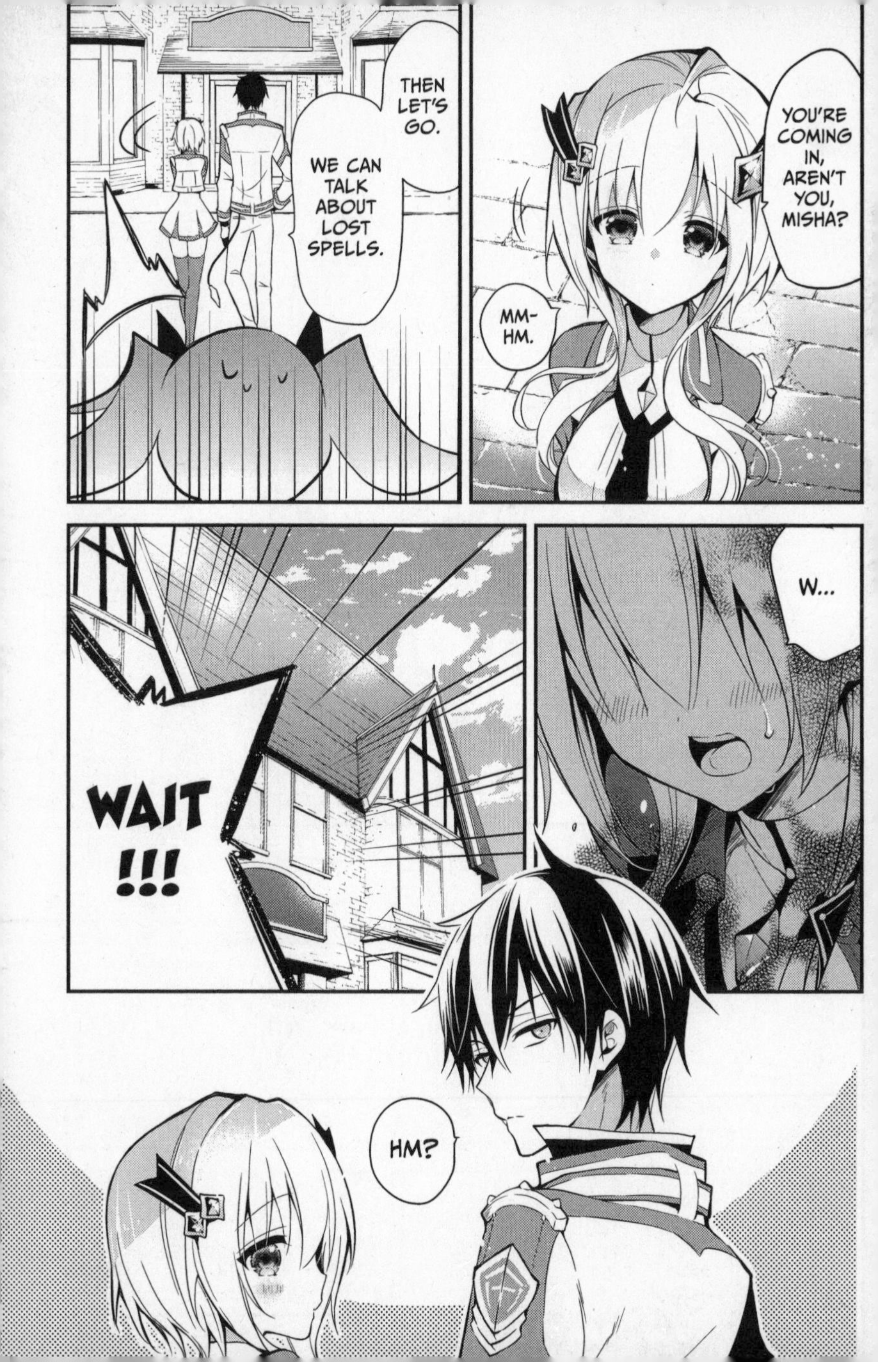
YOU'RE COMING IN, AREN'T YOU, MISHA?
MM-HM.
THEN LET'S GO.
WE CAN TALK ABOUT LOST SPELLS.
W...
WAIT !!!
HM?

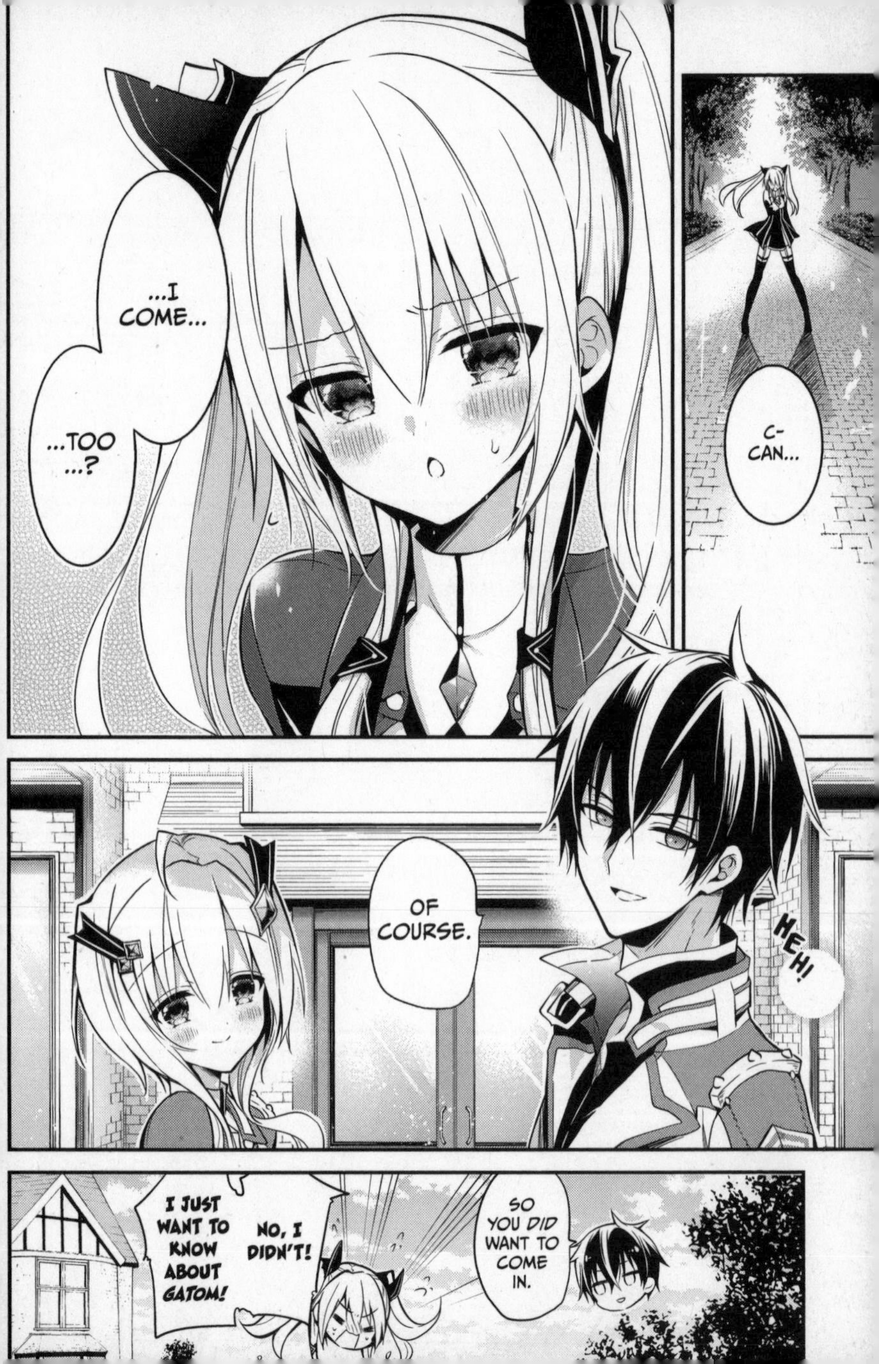
C-CAN...
...I COME...
...TOO ...?
HEH!
OF COURSE.
SO YOU DID WANT TO COME IN.
NO, I DIDN'T!
I JUST WANT TO KNOW ABOUT GATOM!

The Misfit of Demon King Academy

HISTORY'S STRONGEST DEMON KING REINCARNATES
AND GOES TO SCHOOL WITH HIS DESCENDANTS

The Misfit of Demon King Academy

HISTORY'S STRONGEST DEMON KING REINCARNATES AND GOES TO SCHOOL WITH HIS DESCENDANTS

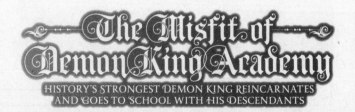

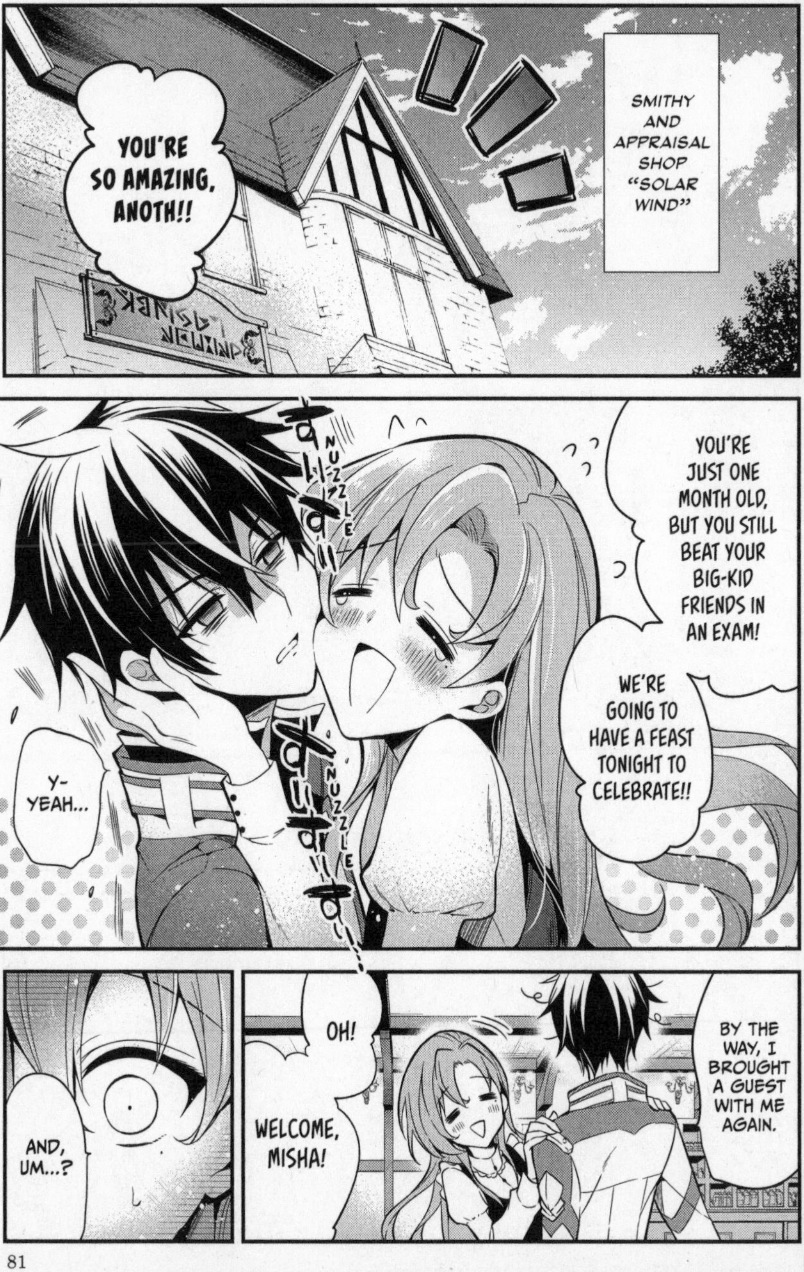
SMITHY AND APPRAISAL SHOP "SOLAR WIND"
YOU'RE SO AMAZING, ANOTH!!
YOU'RE JUST ONE MONTH OLD, BUT YOU STILL BEAT YOUR BIG-KID FRIENDS IN AN EXAM!
WE'RE GOING TO HAVE A FEAST TONIGHT TO CELEBRATE!!
NUZZLE
NUZZLE
Y-YEAH...
BY THE WAY, I BROUGHT A GUEST WITH ME AGAIN.
OH!
WELCOME, MISHA!
AND, UM...?

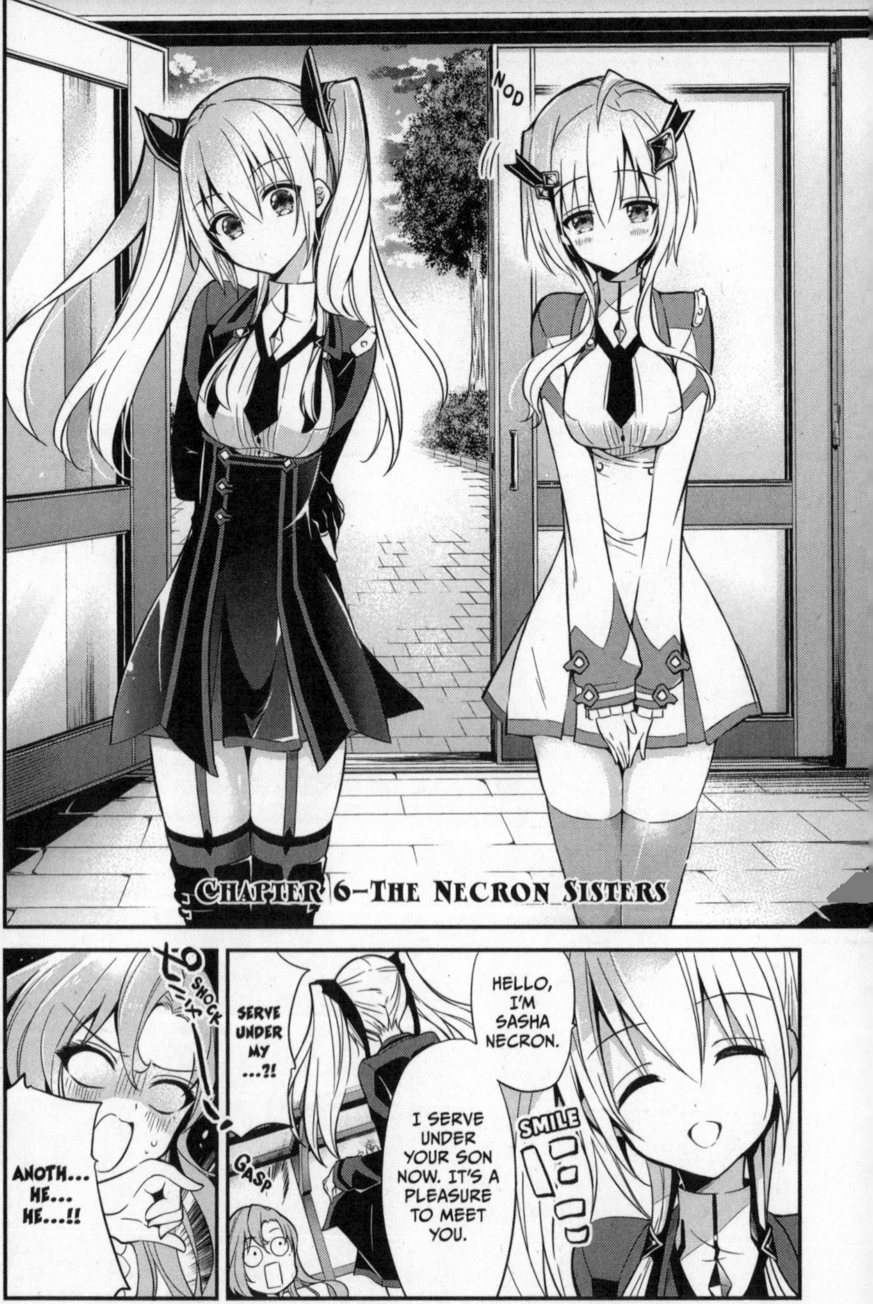
NOD
Chapter 6–The Necron Sisters
HELLO, I'M SASHA NECRON.
SMILE
I SERVE UNDER YOUR SON NOW. IT'S A PLEASURE TO MEET YOU.
SERVE UNDER MY ...?!
GASP
SHOCK
ANOTH... HE... HE...!!

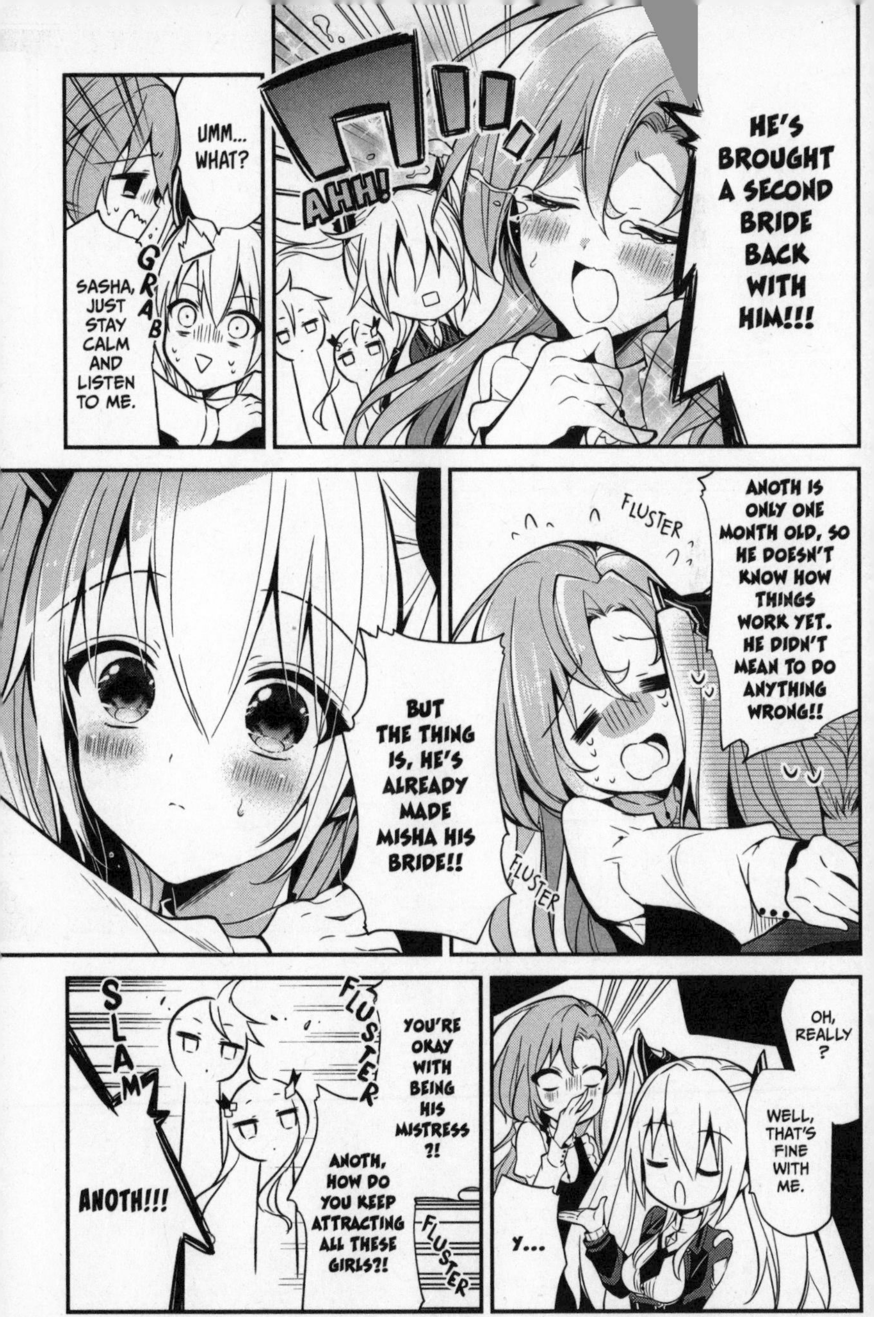
AHH!
HE'S BROUGHT A SECOND BRIDE BACK WITH HIM!!!
UMM... WHAT?
GRAB
SASHA, JUST STAY CALM AND LISTEN TO ME.
FLUSTER
ANOTH IS ONLY ONE MONTH OLD, SO HE DOESN'T KNOW HOW THINGS WORK YET. HE DIDN'T MEAN TO DO ANYTHING WRONG!!
FLUSTER
...
BUT THE THING IS, HE'S ALREADY MADE MISHA HIS BRIDE!!
OH, REALLY?
WELL, THAT'S FINE WITH ME.
Y...
FLUSTER
YOU'RE OKAY WITH BEING HIS MISTRESS?!
SLAM
ANOTH, HOW DO YOU KEEP ATTRACTING ALL THESE GIRLS?!
FLUSTER
ANOTH!!!

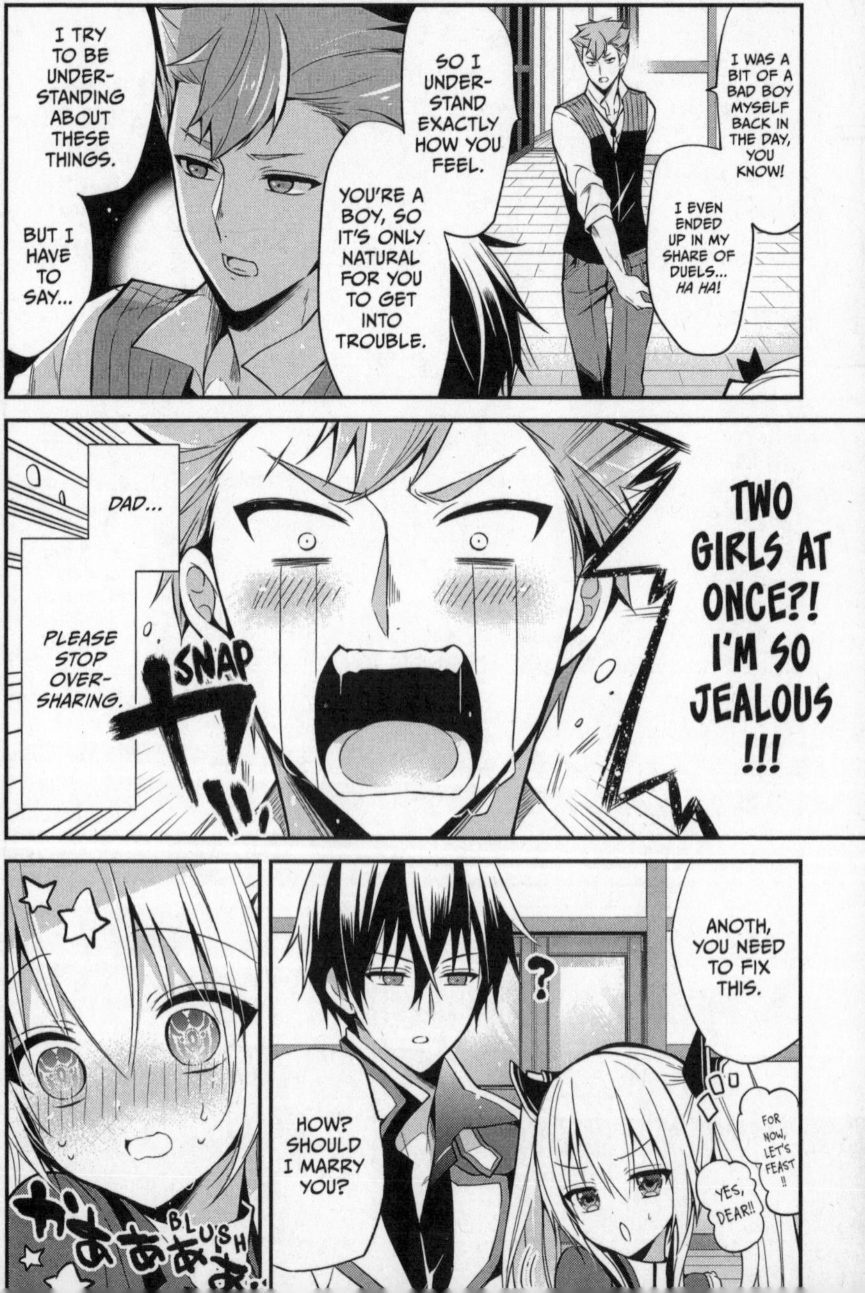
I WAS A BIT OF A BAD BOY MYSELF BACK IN THE DAY, YOU KNOW!
I EVEN ENDED UP IN MY SHARE OF DUELS... HA HA!
SO I UNDER-STAND EXACTLY HOW YOU FEEL.
YOU'RE A BOY, SO IT'S ONLY NATURAL FOR YOU TO GET INTO TROUBLE.
I TRY TO BE UNDER-STANDING ABOUT THESE THINGS.
BUT I HAVE TO SAY...
TWO GIRLS AT ONCE?! I'M SO JEALOUS!!!
SNAP
DAD...
PLEASE STOP OVER-SHARING.
ANOTH, YOU NEED TO FIX THIS.
HOW? SHOULD I MARRY YOU?
FOR NOW, LET'S FEAST!!
YES, DEAR!!
BLUSH

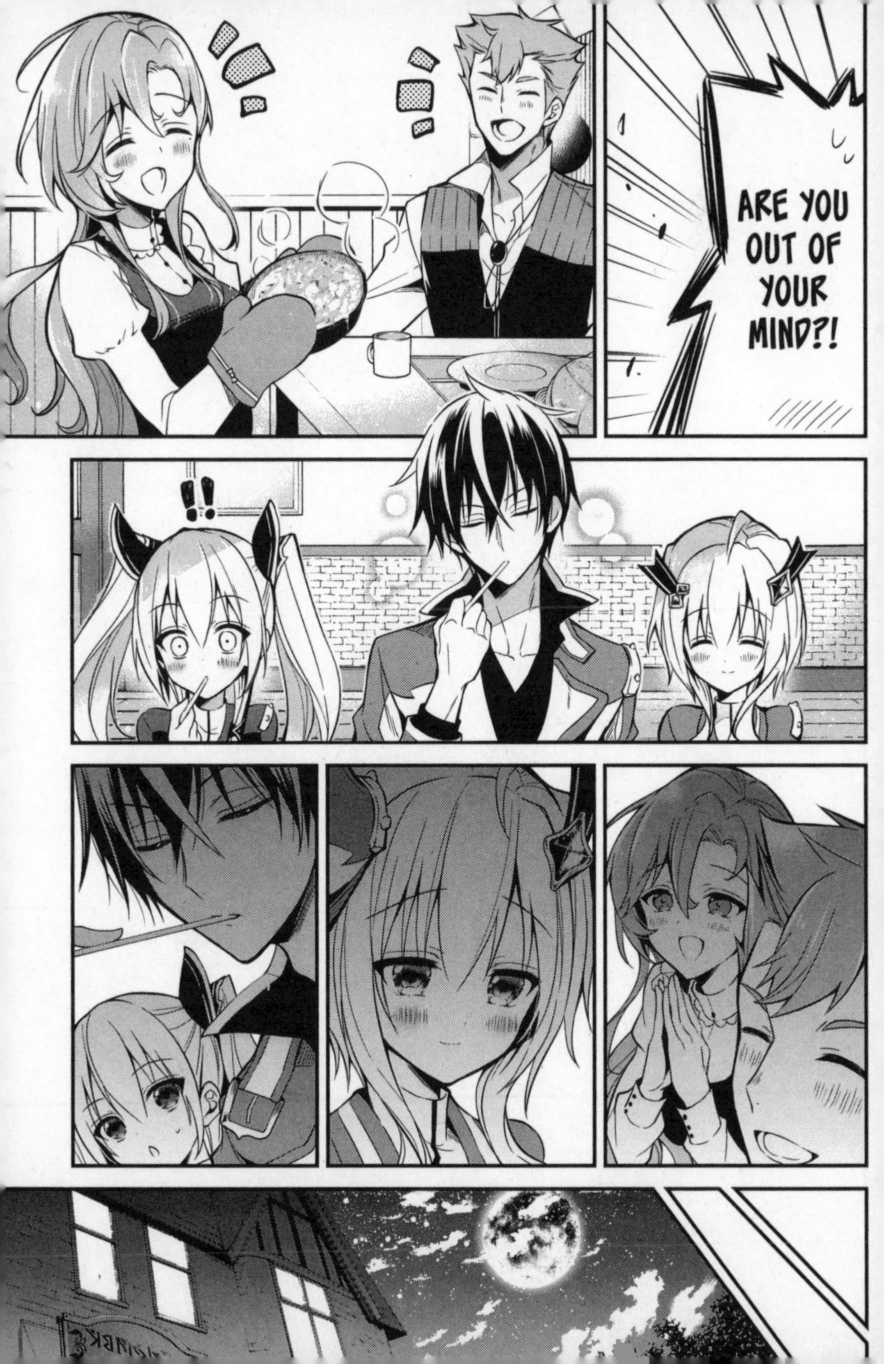
ARE YOU OUT OF YOUR MIND?!

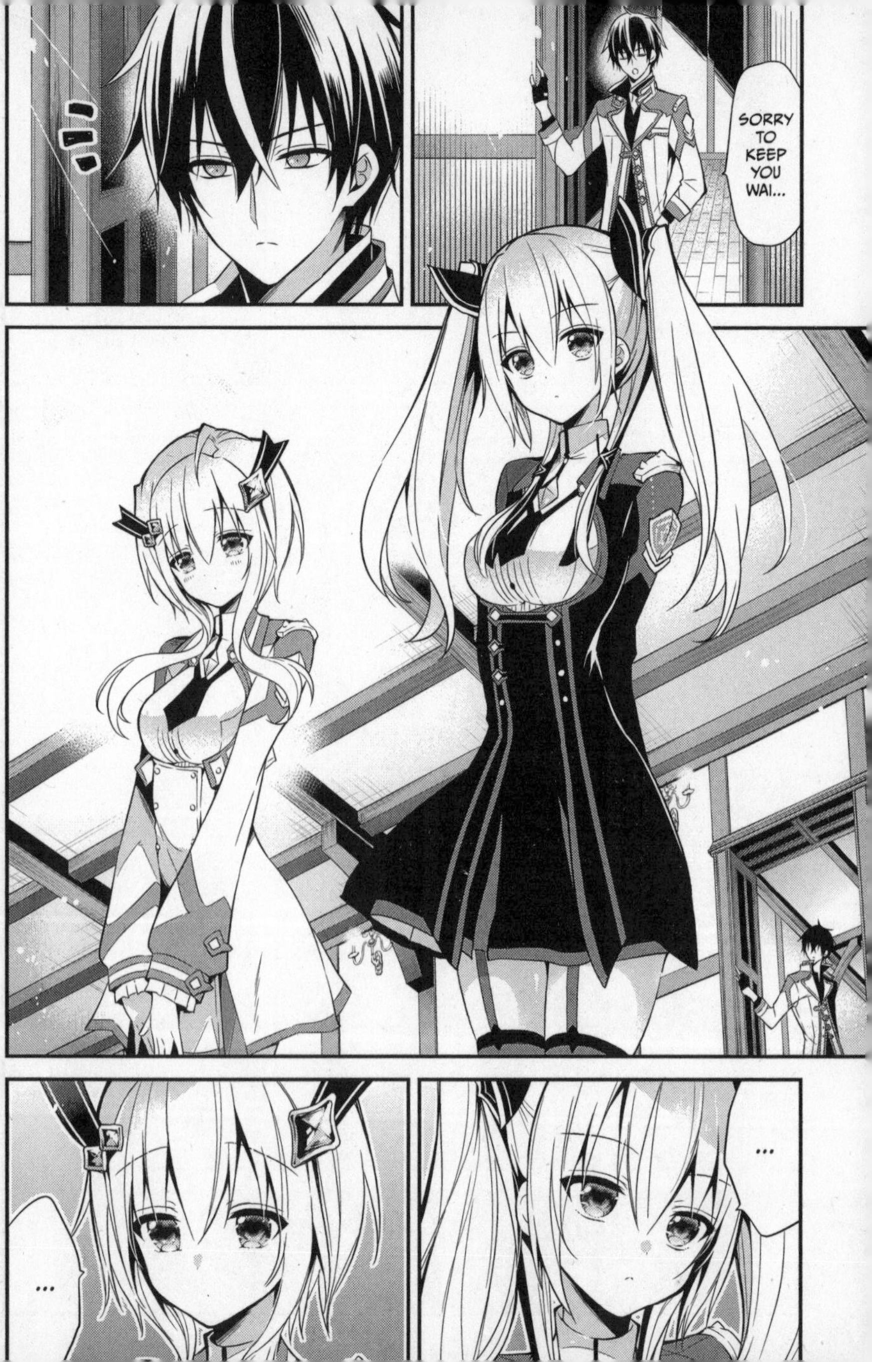
SORRY TO KEEP YOU WAI...
...
...

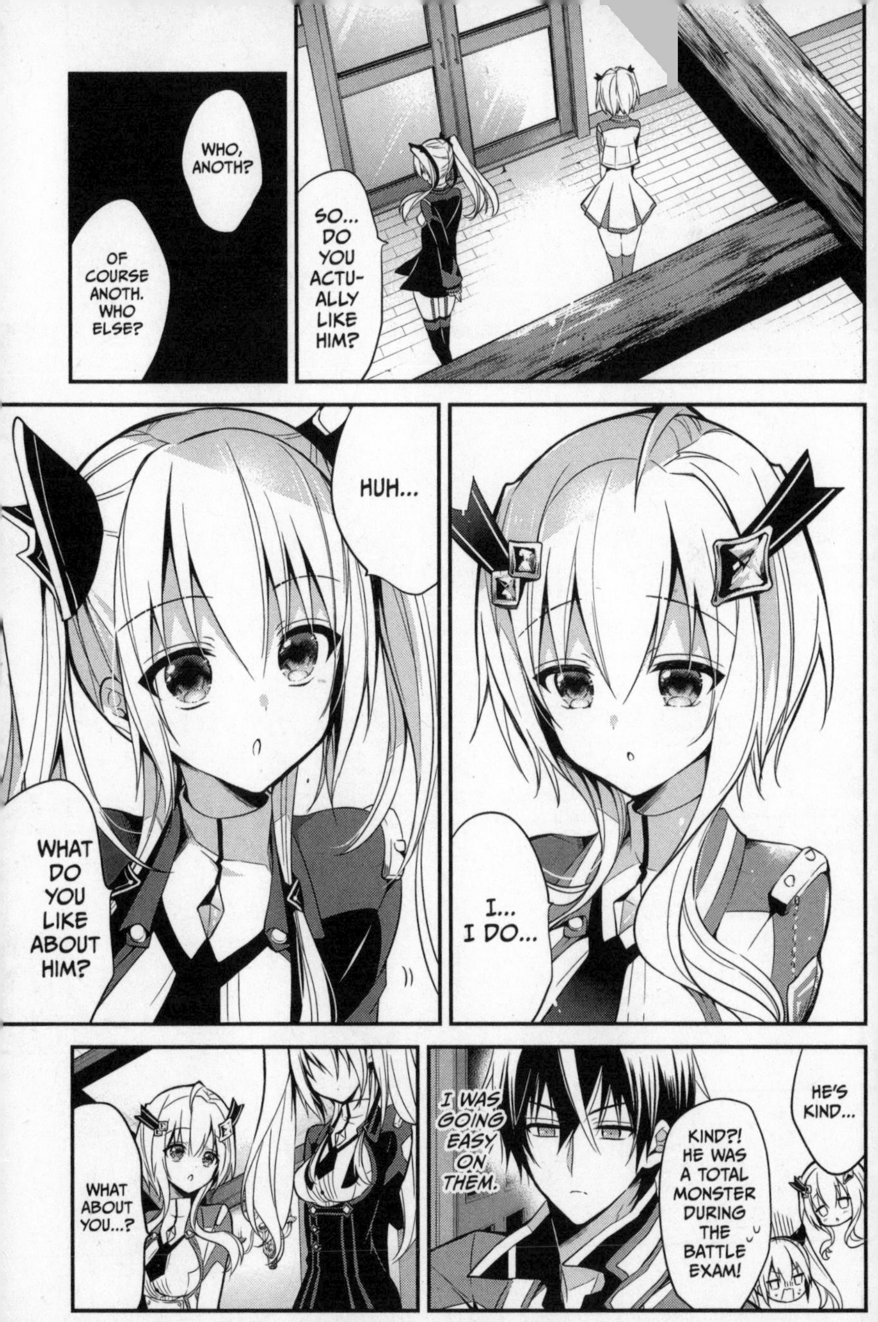
SO... DO YOU ACTU-ALLY LIKE HIM?
WHO, ANOTH?
OF COURSE ANOTH. WHO ELSE?
I... I DO...
HUH...
WHAT DO YOU LIKE ABOUT HIM?
HE'S KIND...
KIND?! HE WAS A TOTAL MONSTER DURING THE BATTLE EXAM!
I WAS GOING EASY ON THEM.
WHAT ABOUT YOU...?

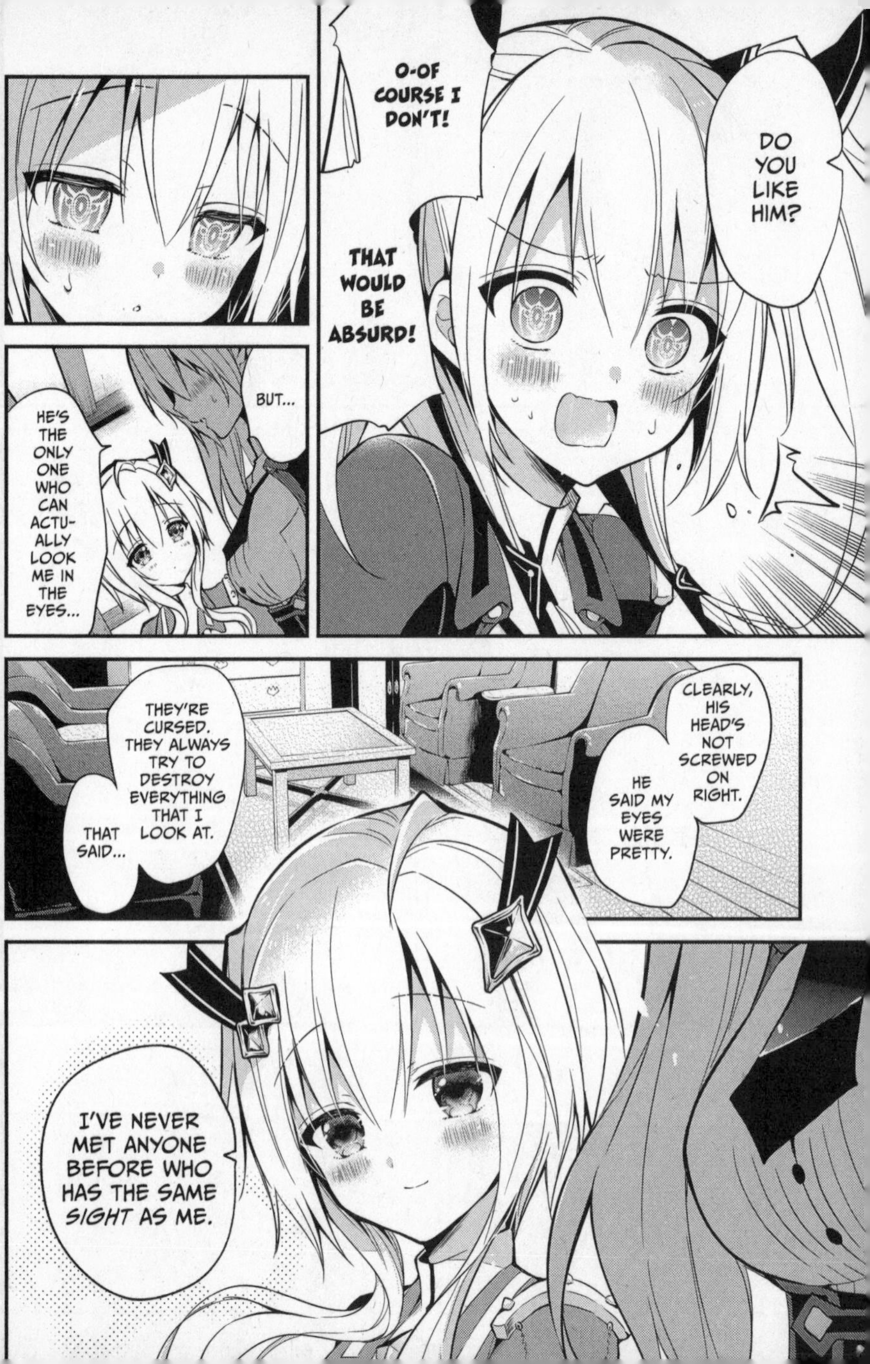
DO YOU LIKE HIM?
O-OF COURSE I DON'T!
THAT WOULD BE ABSURD!
BUT...
HE'S THE ONLY ONE WHO CAN ACTU-ALLY LOOK ME IN THE EYES...
CLEARLY, HIS HEAD'S NOT SCREWED ON RIGHT.
HE SAID MY EYES WERE PRETTY.
THEY'RE CURSED. THEY ALWAYS TRY TO DESTROY EVERYTHING THAT I LOOK AT.
THAT SAID...
I'VE NEVER MET ANYONE BEFORE WHO HAS THE SAME *SIGHT* AS ME.

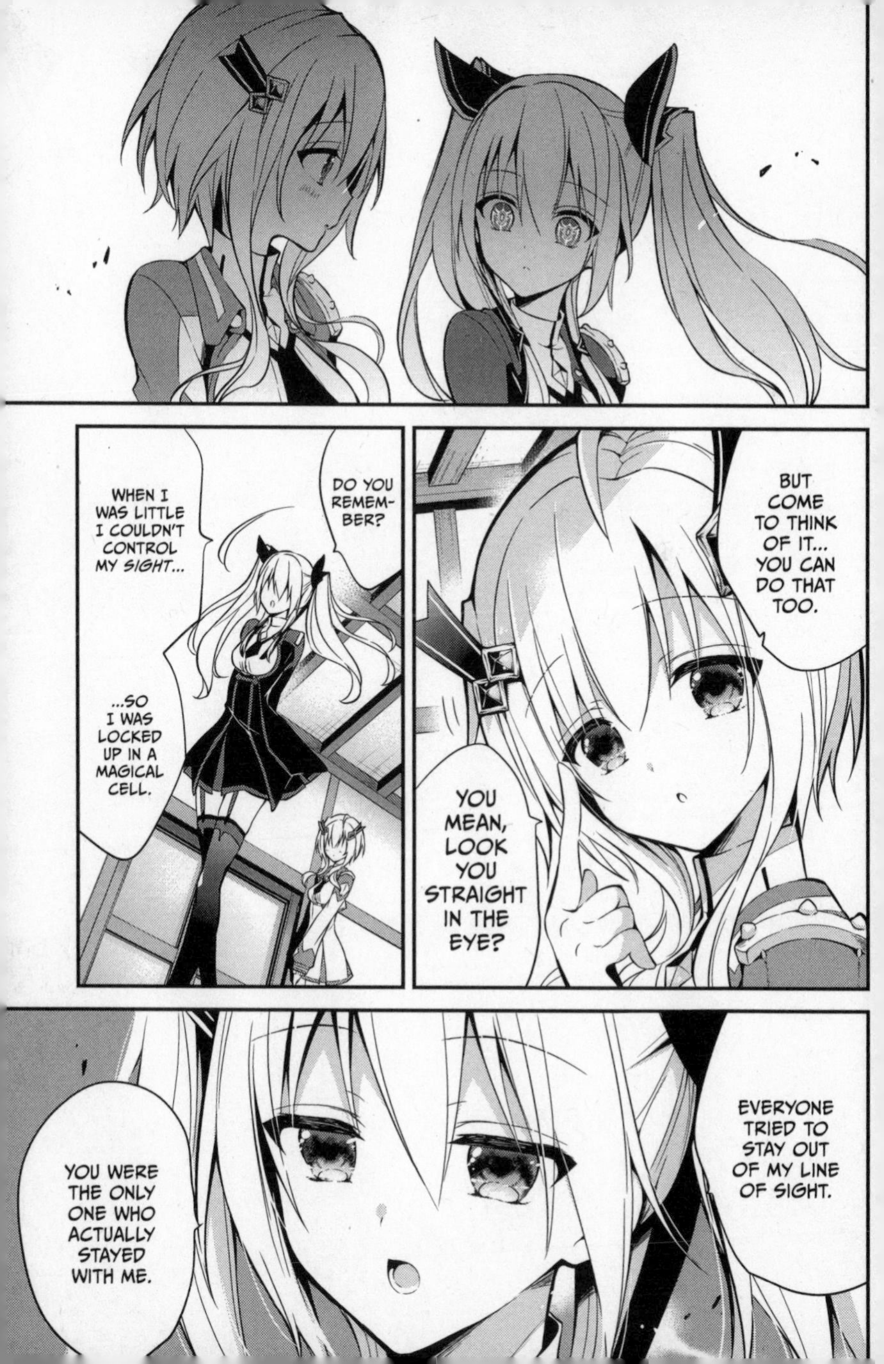
BUT COME TO THINK OF IT... YOU CAN DO THAT TOO.
YOU MEAN, LOOK YOU STRAIGHT IN THE EYE?
DO YOU REMEMBER?
WHEN I WAS LITTLE I COULDN'T CONTROL MY *SIGHT*...
...SO I WAS LOCKED UP IN A MAGICAL CELL.
EVERYONE TRIED TO STAY OUT OF MY LINE OF SIGHT.
YOU WERE THE ONLY ONE WHO ACTUALLY STAYED WITH ME.

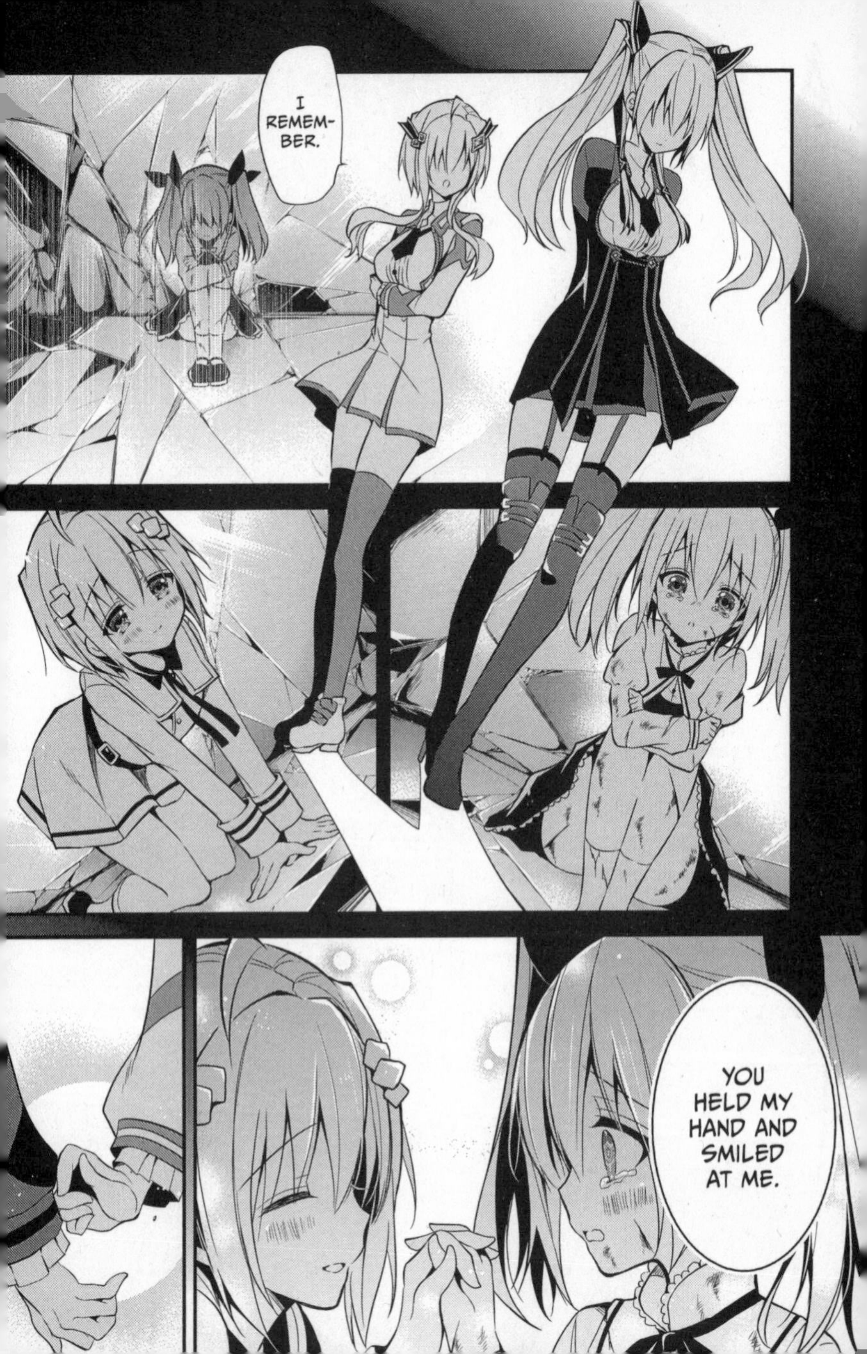
I REMEMBER.
YOU HELD MY HAND AND SMILED AT ME.

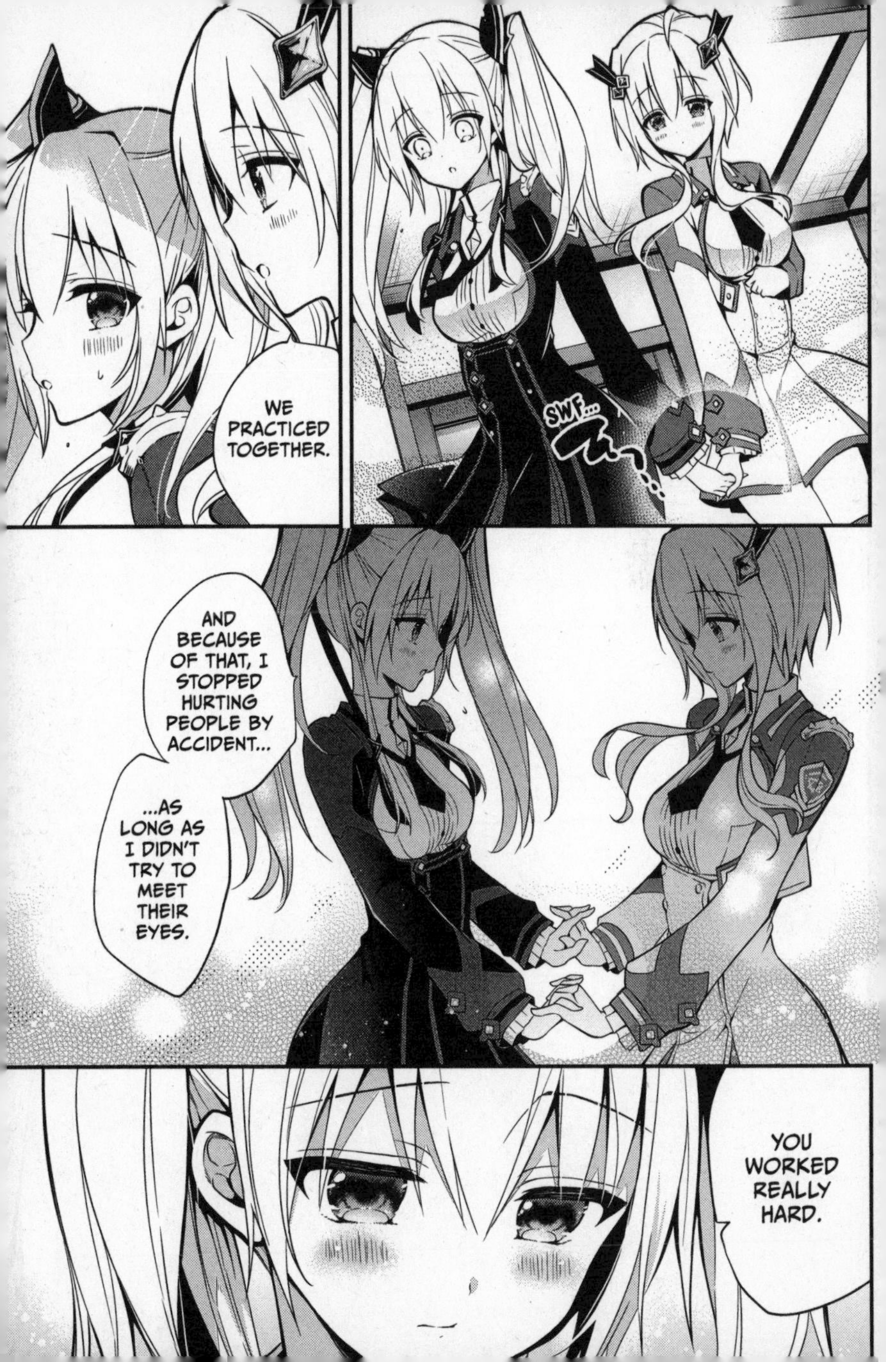
SWF...
WE PRACTICED TOGETHER.
AND BECAUSE OF THAT, I STOPPED HURTING PEOPLE BY ACCIDENT...
...AS LONG AS I DIDN'T TRY TO MEET THEIR EYES.
YOU WORKED REALLY HARD.

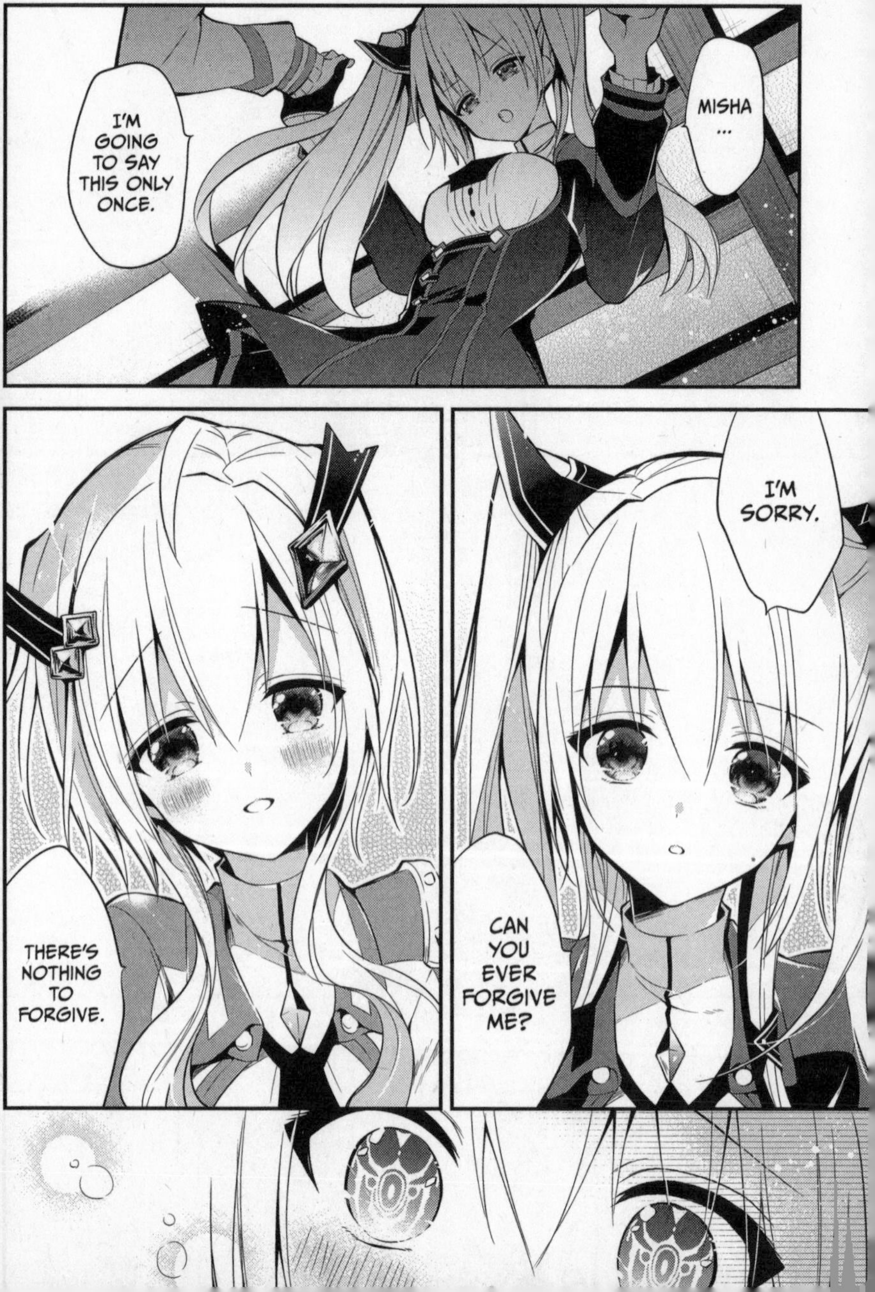
MISHA ...
I'M GOING TO SAY THIS ONLY ONCE.
I'M SORRY.
CAN YOU EVER FORGIVE ME?
THERE'S NOTHING TO FORGIVE.

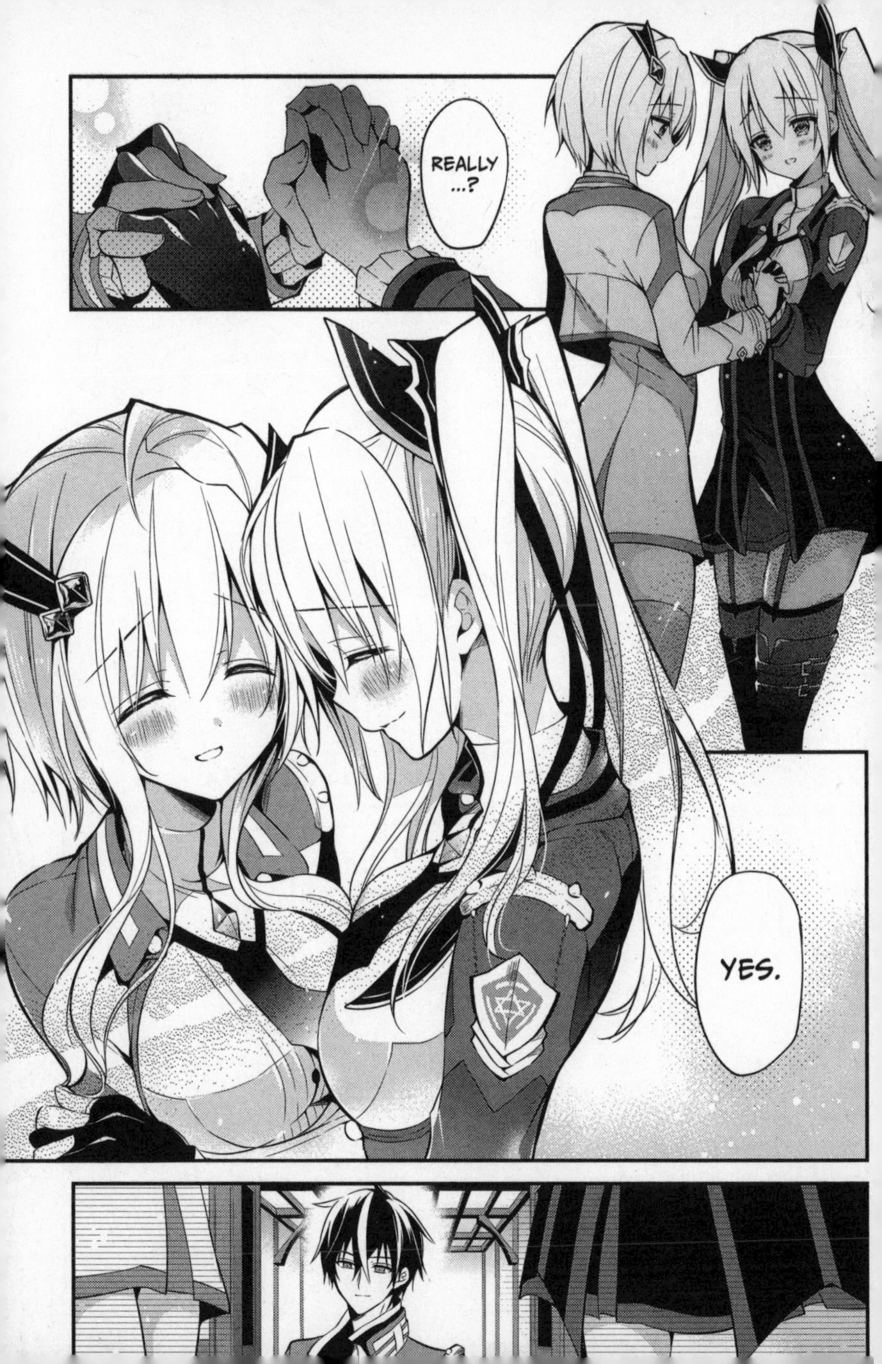
REALLY
...?
YES.

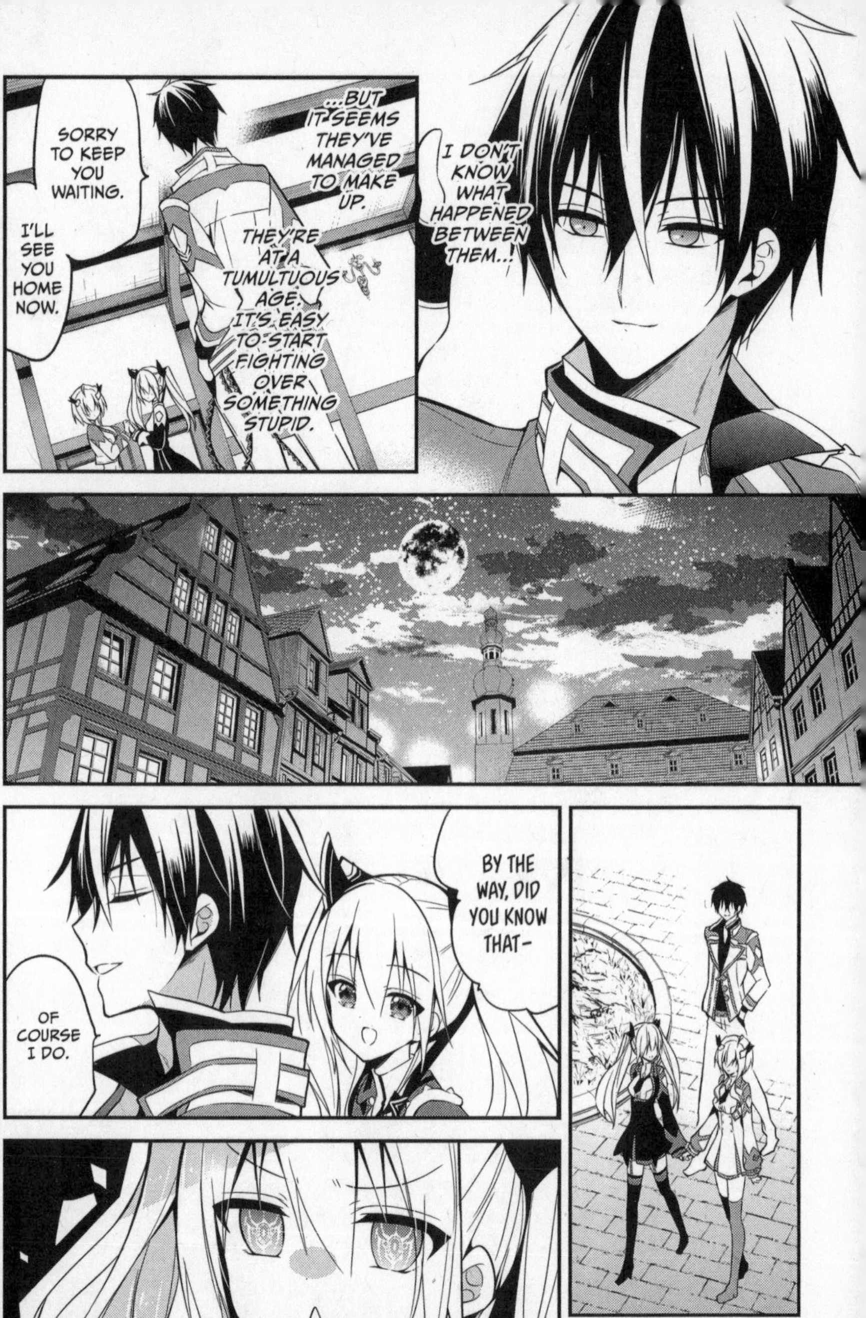
I DON'T KNOW WHAT HAPPENED BETWEEN THEM..!
...BUT IT SEEMS THEY'VE MANAGED TO MAKE UP.
THEY'RE AT A TUMULTUOUS AGE. IT'S EASY TO START FIGHTING OVER SOMETHING STUPID.
SORRY TO KEEP YOU WAITING.
I'LL SEE YOU HOME NOW.
BY THE WAY, DID YOU KNOW THAT-
OF COURSE I DO.

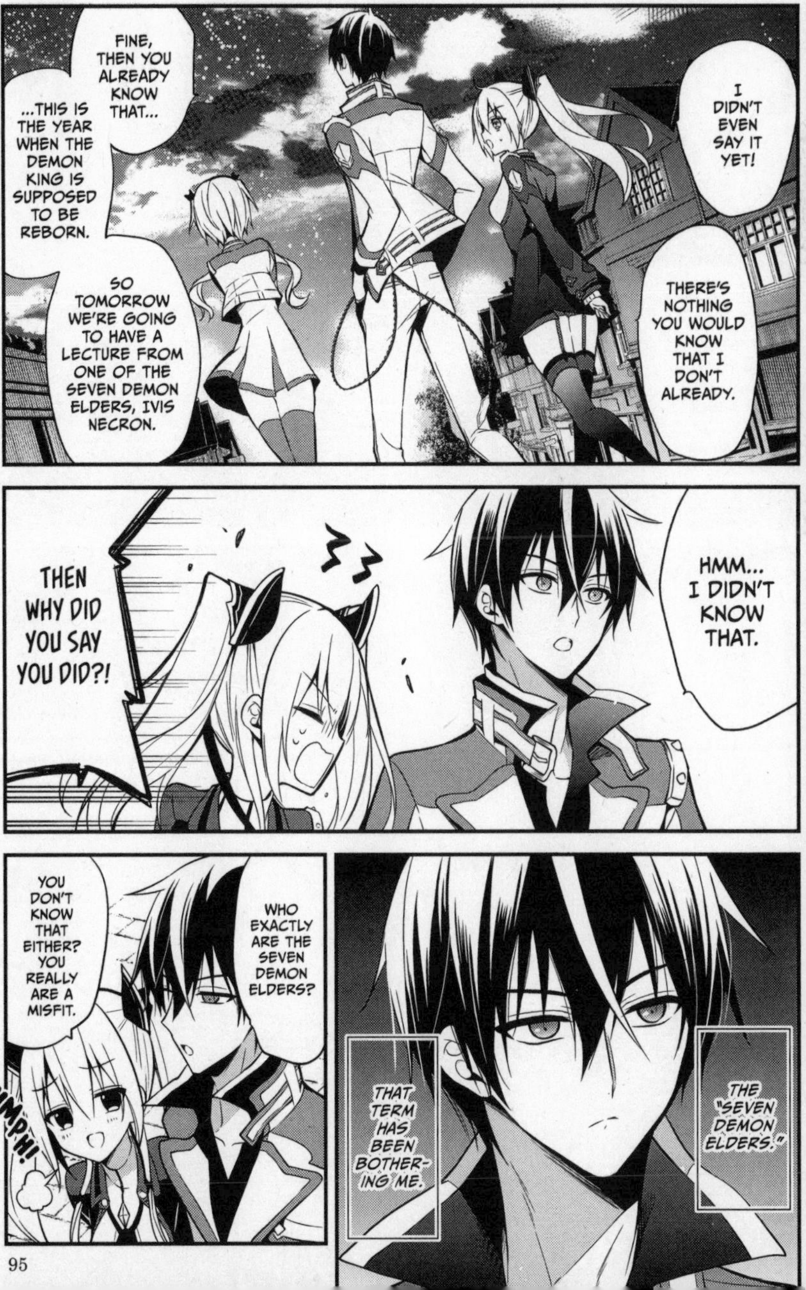

I DIDN'T EVEN SAY IT YET!
THERE'S NOTHING YOU WOULD KNOW THAT I DON'T ALREADY.
FINE, THEN YOU ALREADY KNOW THAT...
...THIS IS THE YEAR WHEN THE DEMON KING IS SUPPOSED TO BE REBORN.
SO TOMORROW WE'RE GOING TO HAVE A LECTURE FROM ONE OF THE SEVEN DEMON ELDERS, IVIS NECRON.
HMM... I DIDN'T KNOW THAT.
THEN WHY DID YOU SAY YOU DID?!
THE "SEVEN DEMON ELDERS."
THAT TERM HAS BEEN BOTHERING ME.
WHO EXACTLY ARE THE SEVEN DEMON ELDERS?
YOU DON'T KNOW THAT EITHER? YOU REALLY ARE A MISFIT.
HMPH!

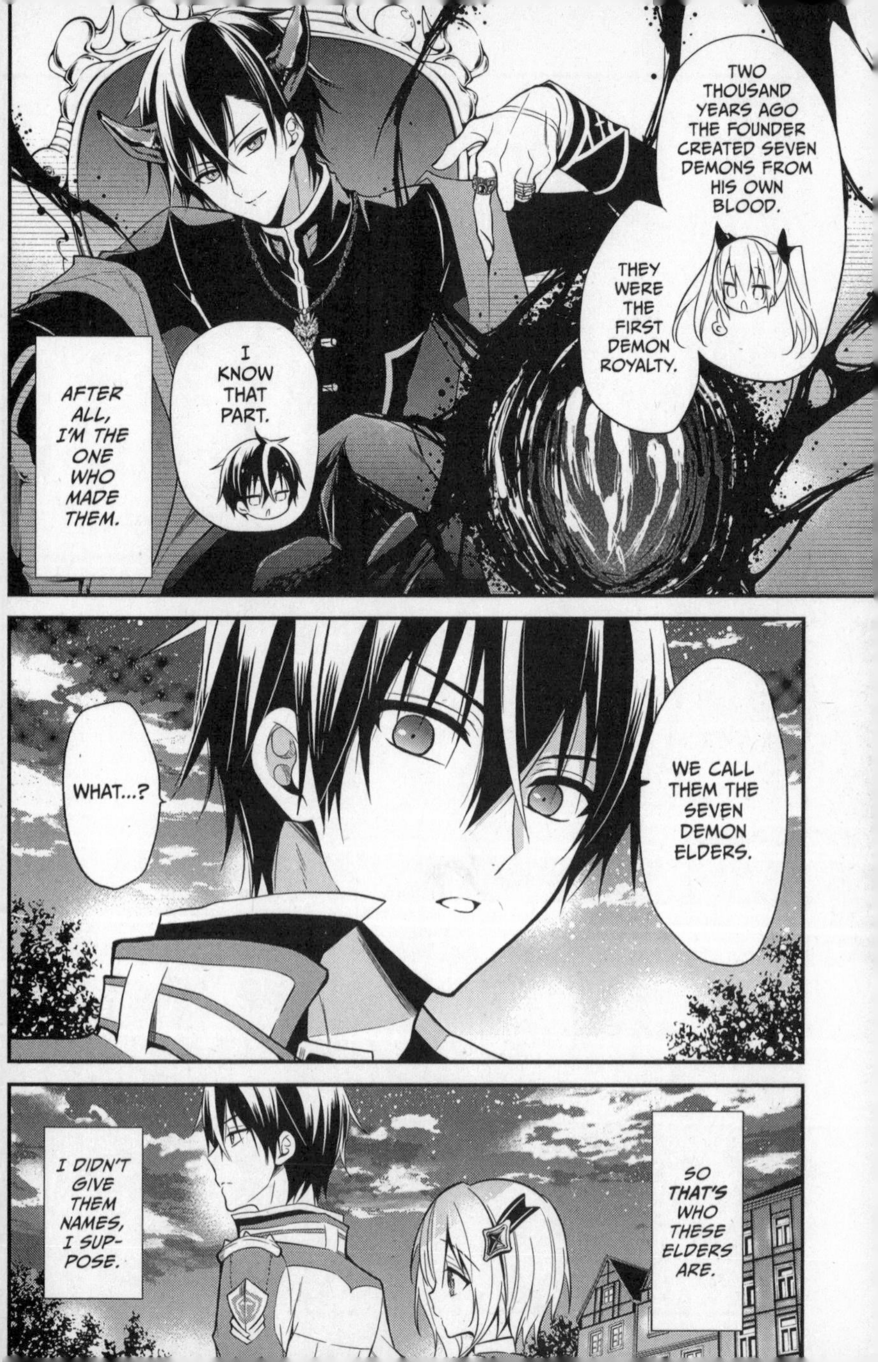
TWO THOUSAND YEARS AGO THE FOUNDER CREATED SEVEN DEMONS FROM HIS OWN BLOOD.
THEY WERE THE FIRST DEMON ROYALTY.
I KNOW THAT PART.
AFTER ALL, I'M THE ONE WHO MADE THEM.
WE CALL THEM THE SEVEN DEMON ELDERS.
WHAT...?
SO THAT'S WHO THESE ELDERS ARE.
I DIDN'T GIVE THEM NAMES, I SUPPOSE.

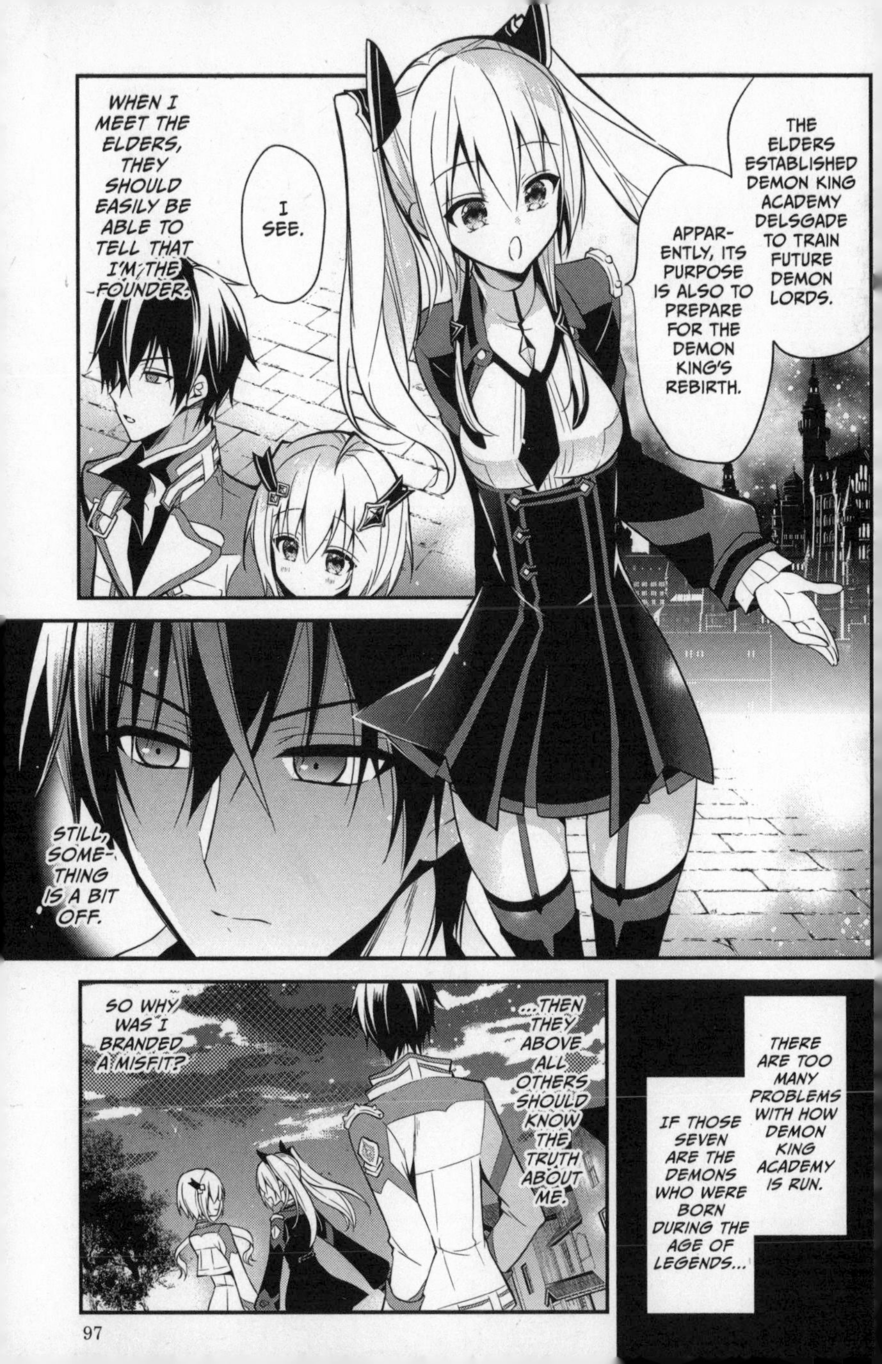
THE ELDERS ESTABLISHED DEMON KING ACADEMY DELSGADE TO TRAIN FUTURE DEMON LORDS.
APPARENTLY, ITS PURPOSE IS ALSO TO PREPARE FOR THE DEMON KING'S REBIRTH.
I SEE.
WHEN I MEET THE ELDERS, THEY SHOULD EASILY BE ABLE TO TELL THAT I'M THE FOUNDER.
STILL, SOMETHING IS A BIT OFF.
THERE ARE TOO MANY PROBLEMS WITH HOW DEMON KING ACADEMY IS RUN.
IF THOSE SEVEN ARE THE DEMONS WHO WERE BORN DURING THE AGE OF LEGENDS...
...THEN THEY ABOVE ALL OTHERS SHOULD KNOW THE TRUTH ABOUT ME.
SO WHY WAS I BRANDED A MISFIT?

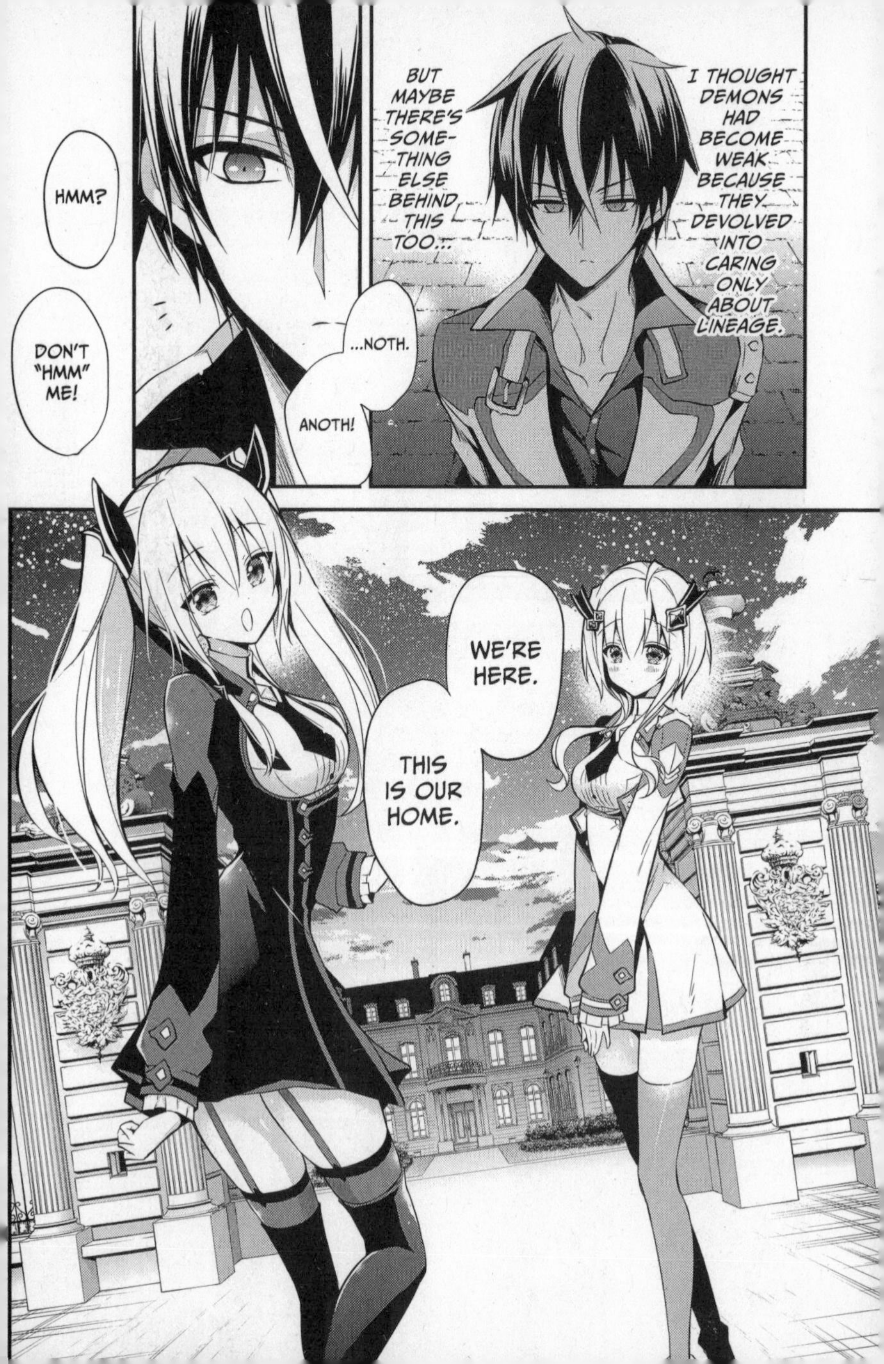
I THOUGHT DEMONS HAD BECOME WEAK BECAUSE THEY DEVOLVED INTO CARING ONLY ABOUT LINEAGE.
BUT MAYBE THERE'S SOME-THING ELSE BEHIND THIS TOO...
...NOTH.
ANOTH!
HMM?
DON'T "HMM" ME!
WE'RE HERE.
THIS IS OUR HOME.

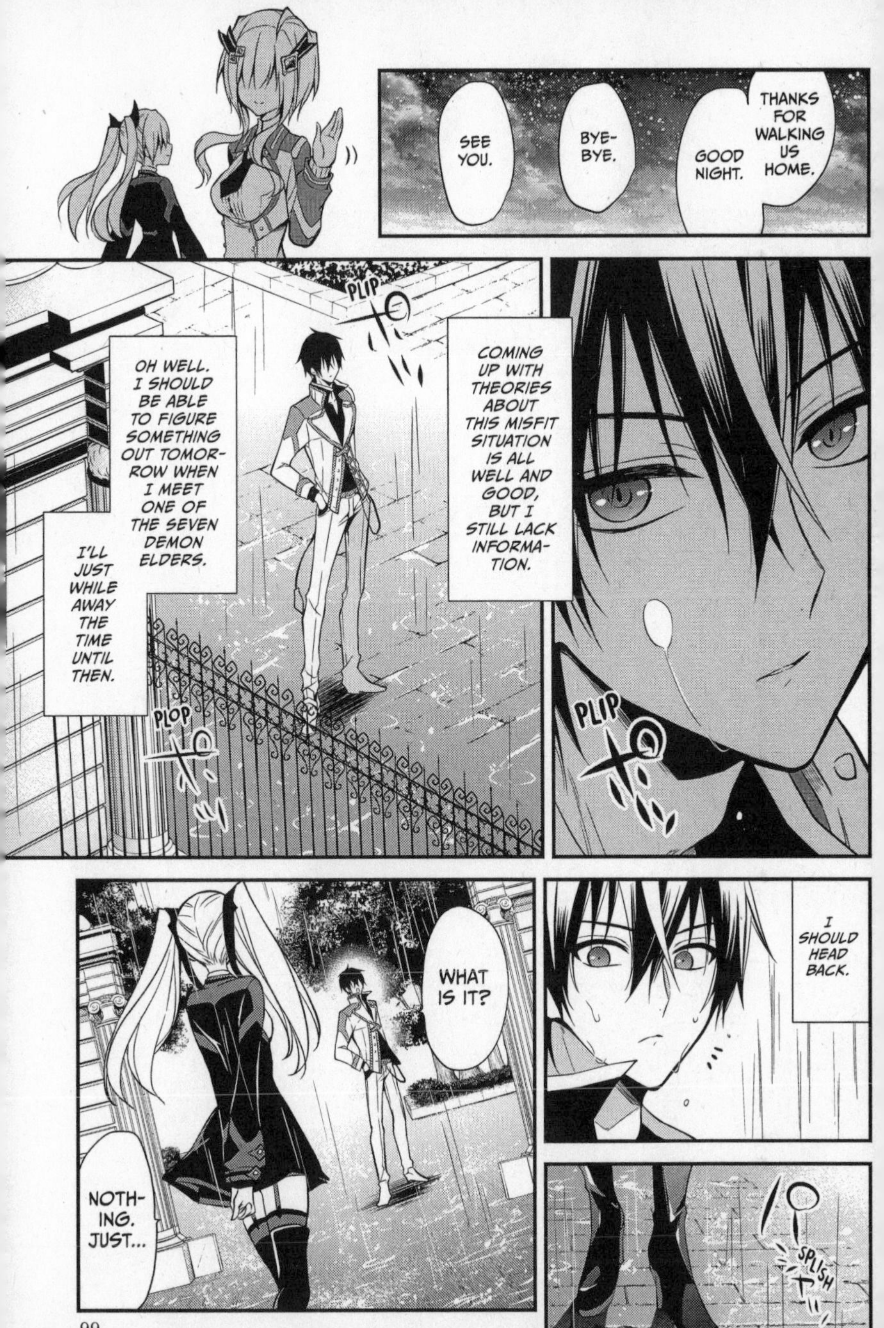
THANKS FOR WALKING US HOME.
GOOD NIGHT.
BYE-BYE.
SEE YOU.
PLIP
PLIP
COMING UP WITH THEORIES ABOUT THIS MISFIT SITUATION IS ALL WELL AND GOOD, BUT I STILL LACK INFORMATION.
OH WELL. I SHOULD BE ABLE TO FIGURE SOMETHING OUT TOMORROW WHEN I MEET ONE OF THE SEVEN DEMON ELDERS.
I'LL JUST WHILE AWAY THE TIME UNTIL THEN.
PLOP
I SHOULD HEAD BACK.
SPLISH
WHAT IS IT?
NOTH-ING. JUST...

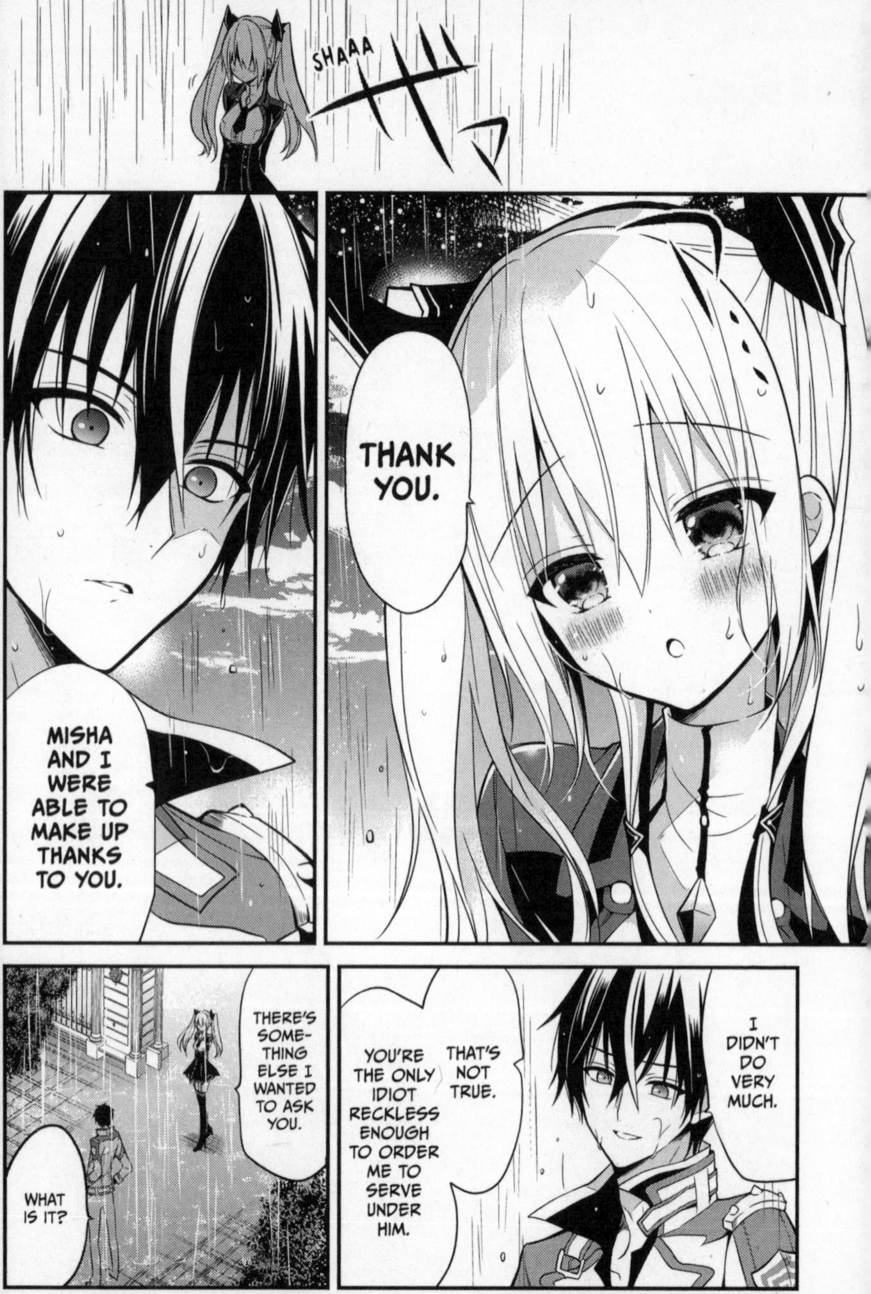
SHAAA
THANK YOU.
MISHA AND I WERE ABLE TO MAKE UP THANKS TO YOU.
I DIDN'T DO VERY MUCH.
THAT'S NOT TRUE.
YOU'RE THE ONLY IDIOT RECKLESS ENOUGH TO ORDER ME TO SERVE UNDER HIM.
THERE'S SOME-THING ELSE I WANTED TO ASK YOU.
WHAT IS IT?

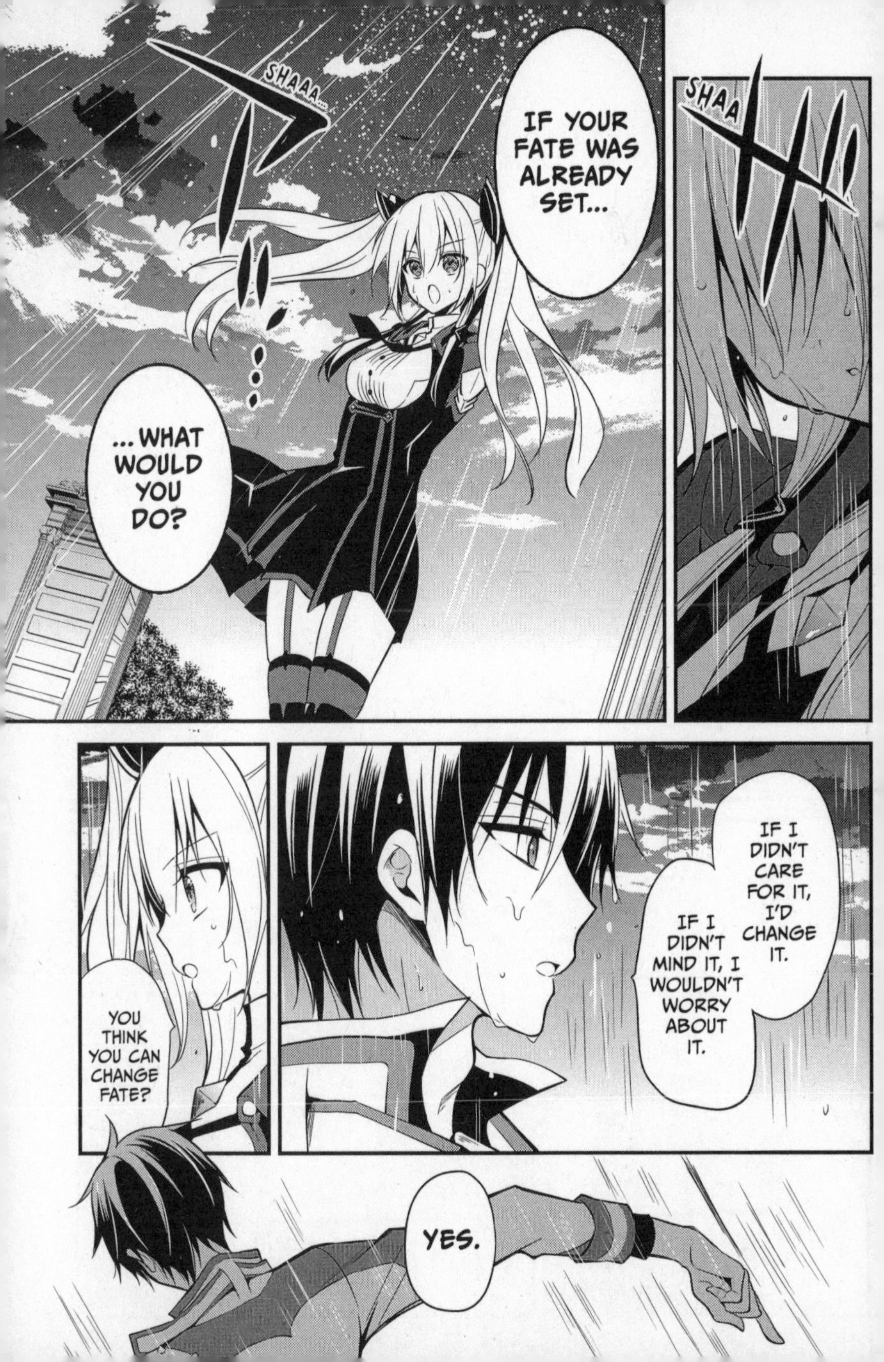
SHAA
IF YOUR FATE WAS ALREADY SET...
SHAAA...
...WHAT WOULD YOU DO?
IF I DIDN'T CARE FOR IT, I'D CHANGE IT.
IF I DIDN'T MIND IT, I WOULDN'T WORRY ABOUT IT.
YOU THINK YOU CAN CHANGE FATE?
YES.

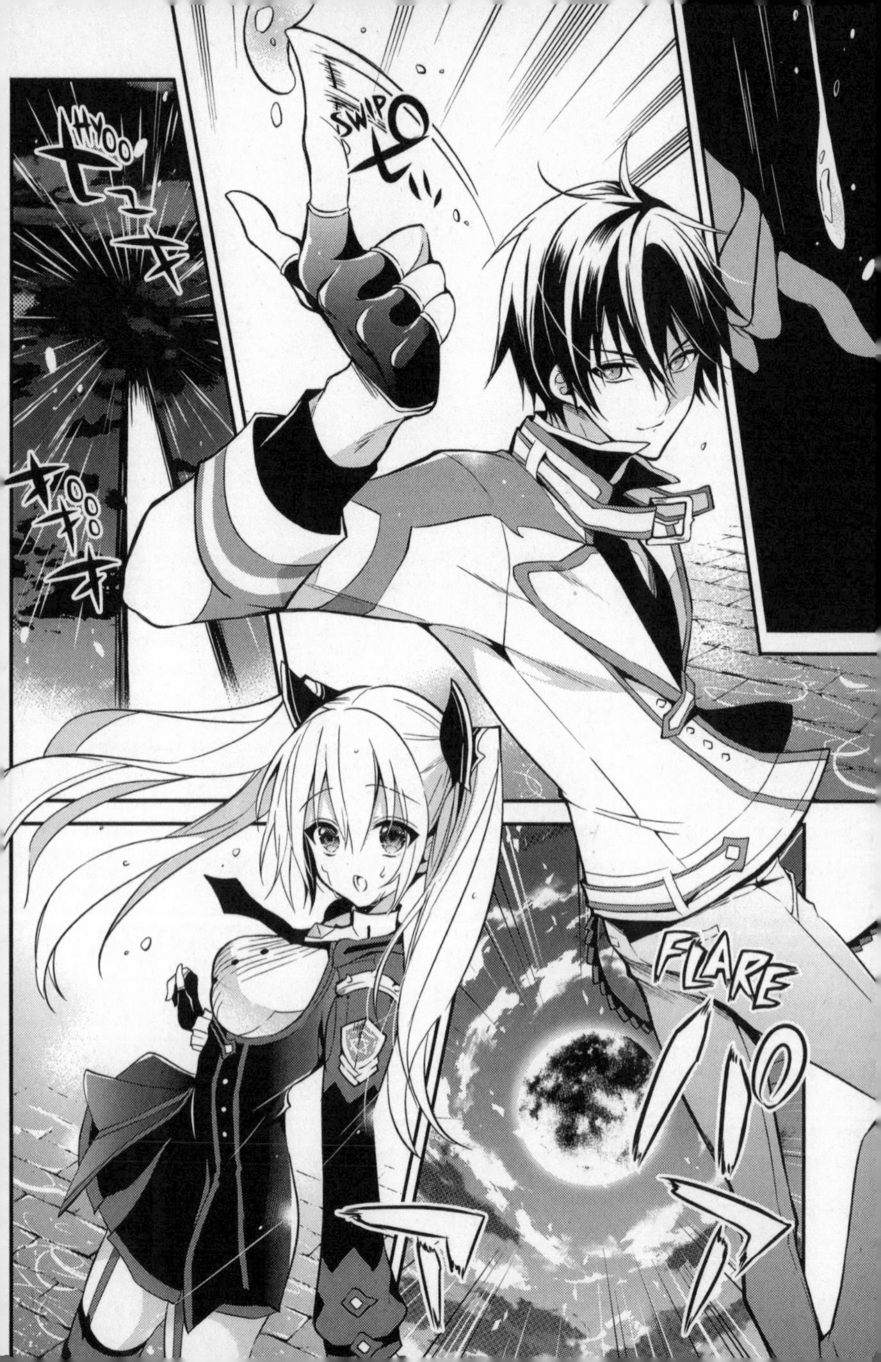
SWIP
HYOO
FLARE

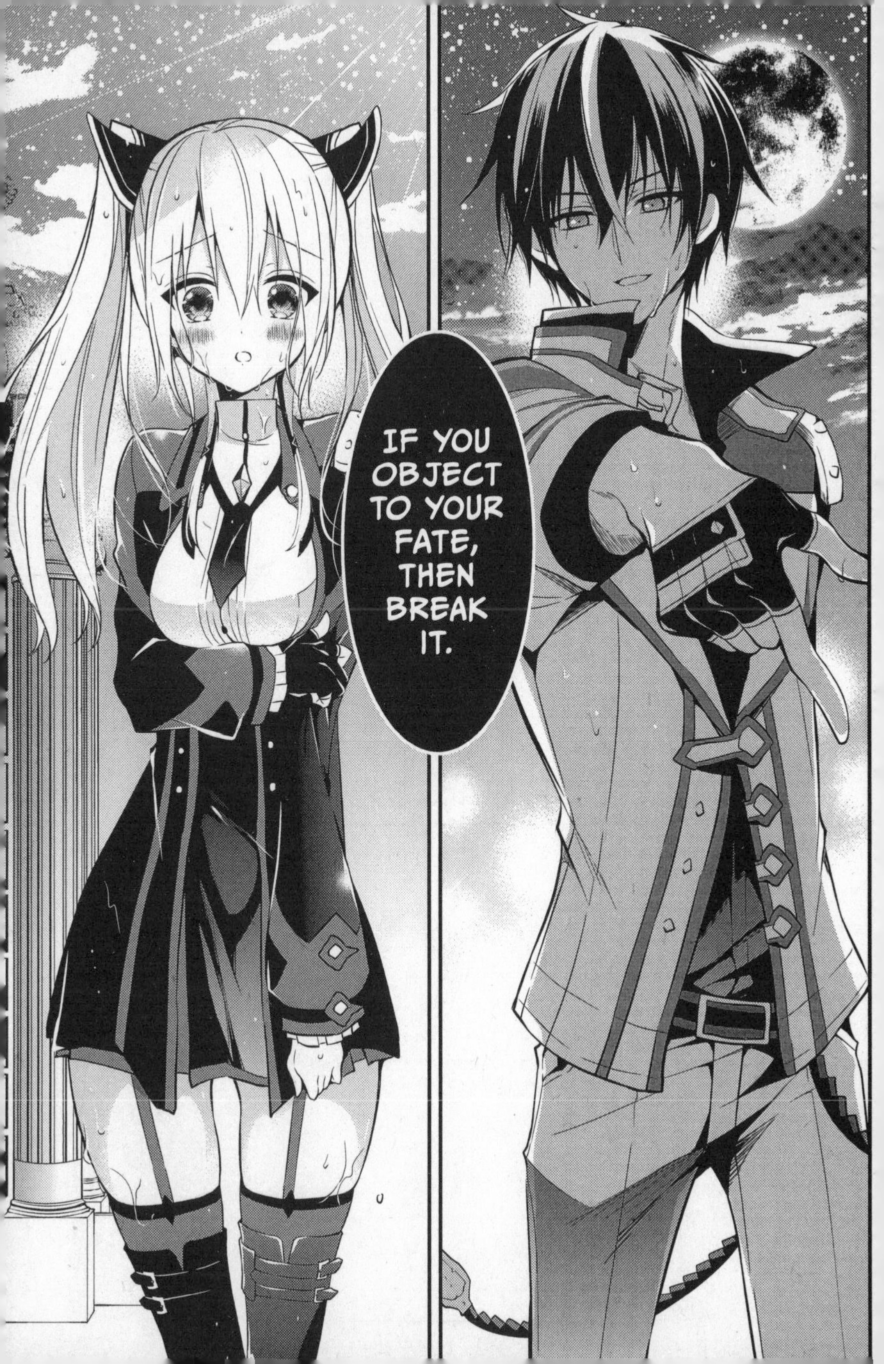
IF YOU OBJECT TO YOUR FATE, THEN BREAK IT.

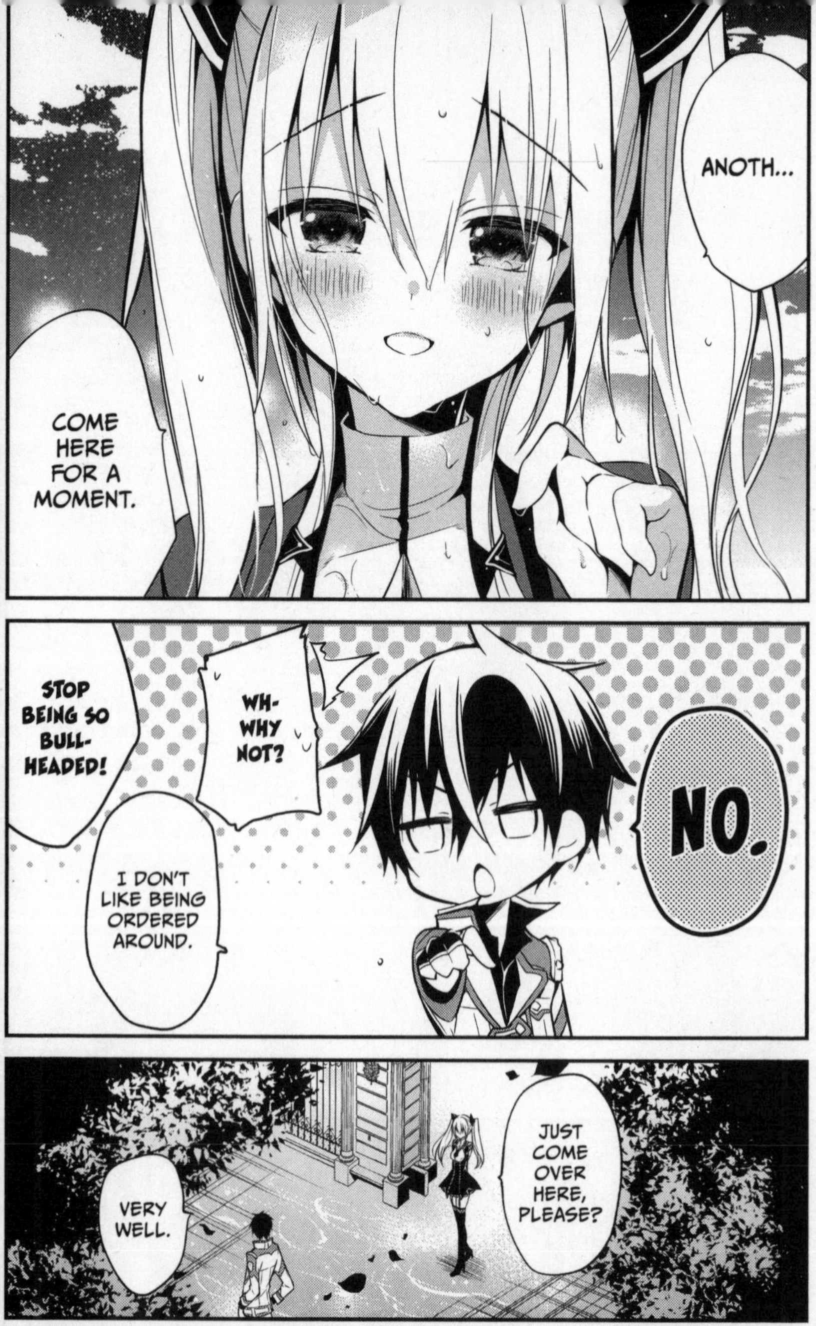
ANOTH...
COME HERE FOR A MOMENT.
NO.
WH- WHY NOT?
STOP BEING SO BULL-HEADED!
I DON'T LIKE BEING ORDERED AROUND.
JUST COME OVER HERE, PLEASE?
VERY WELL.

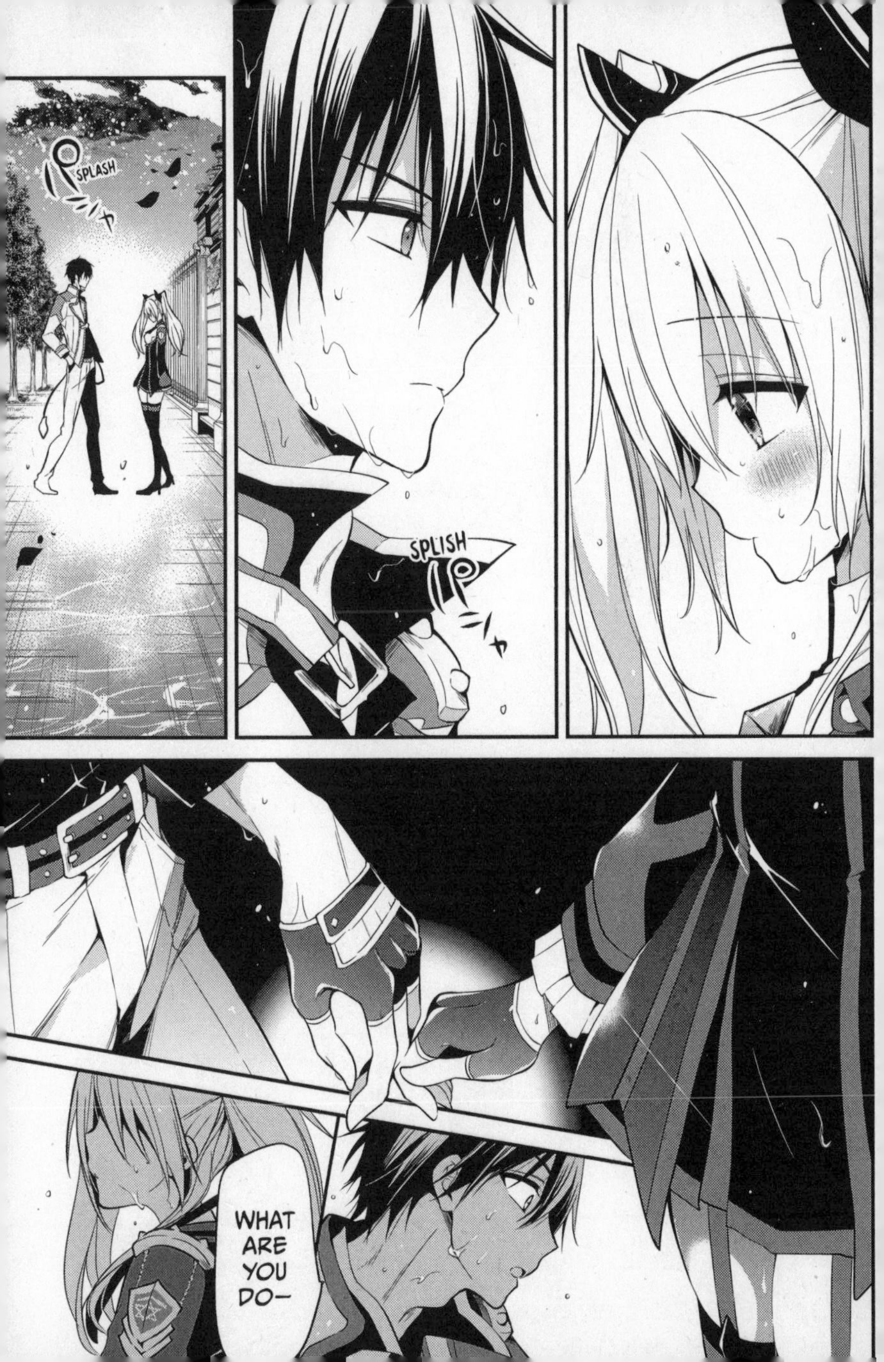
SPLISH
SPLASH
WHAT ARE YOU DO—

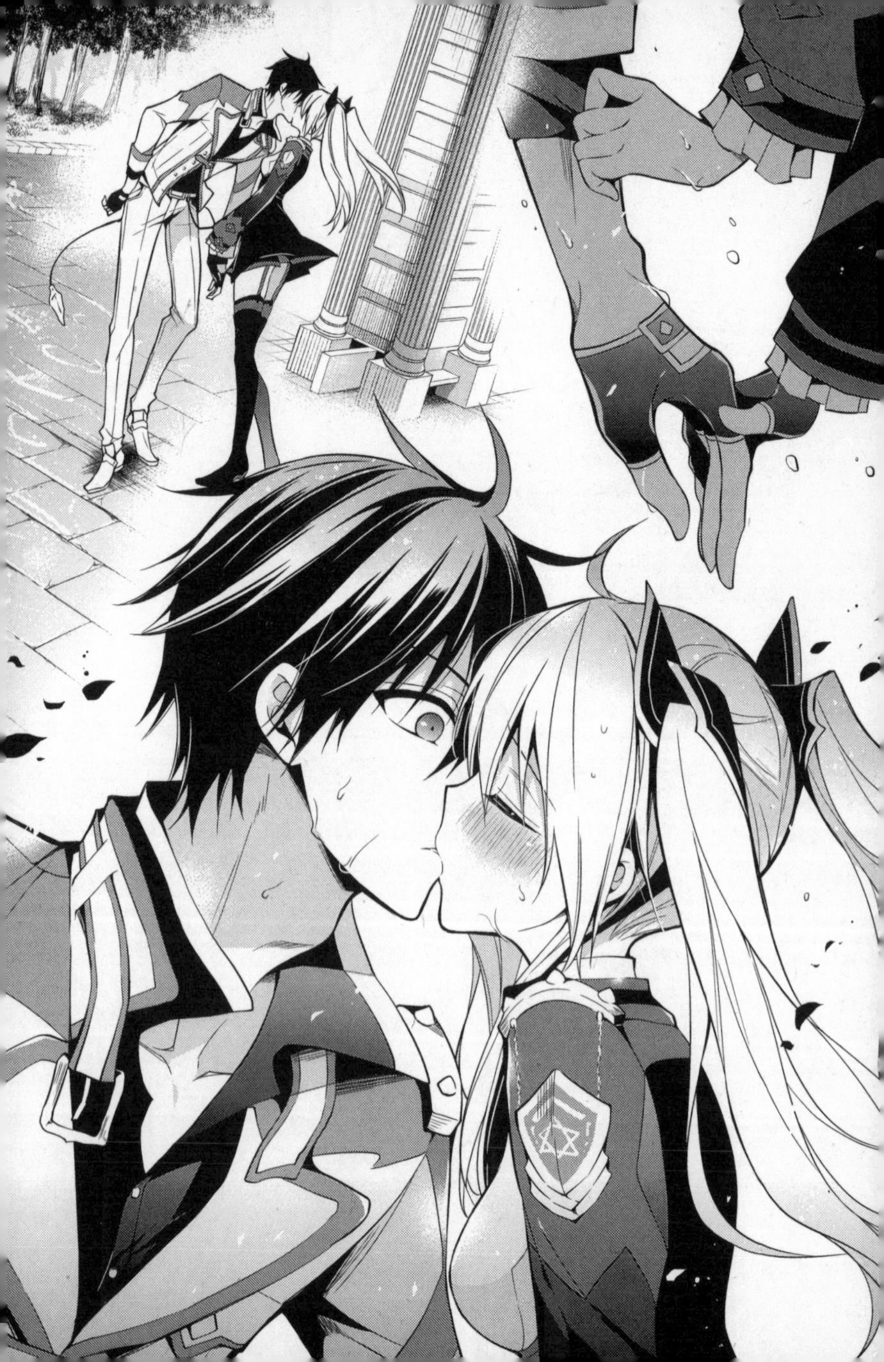

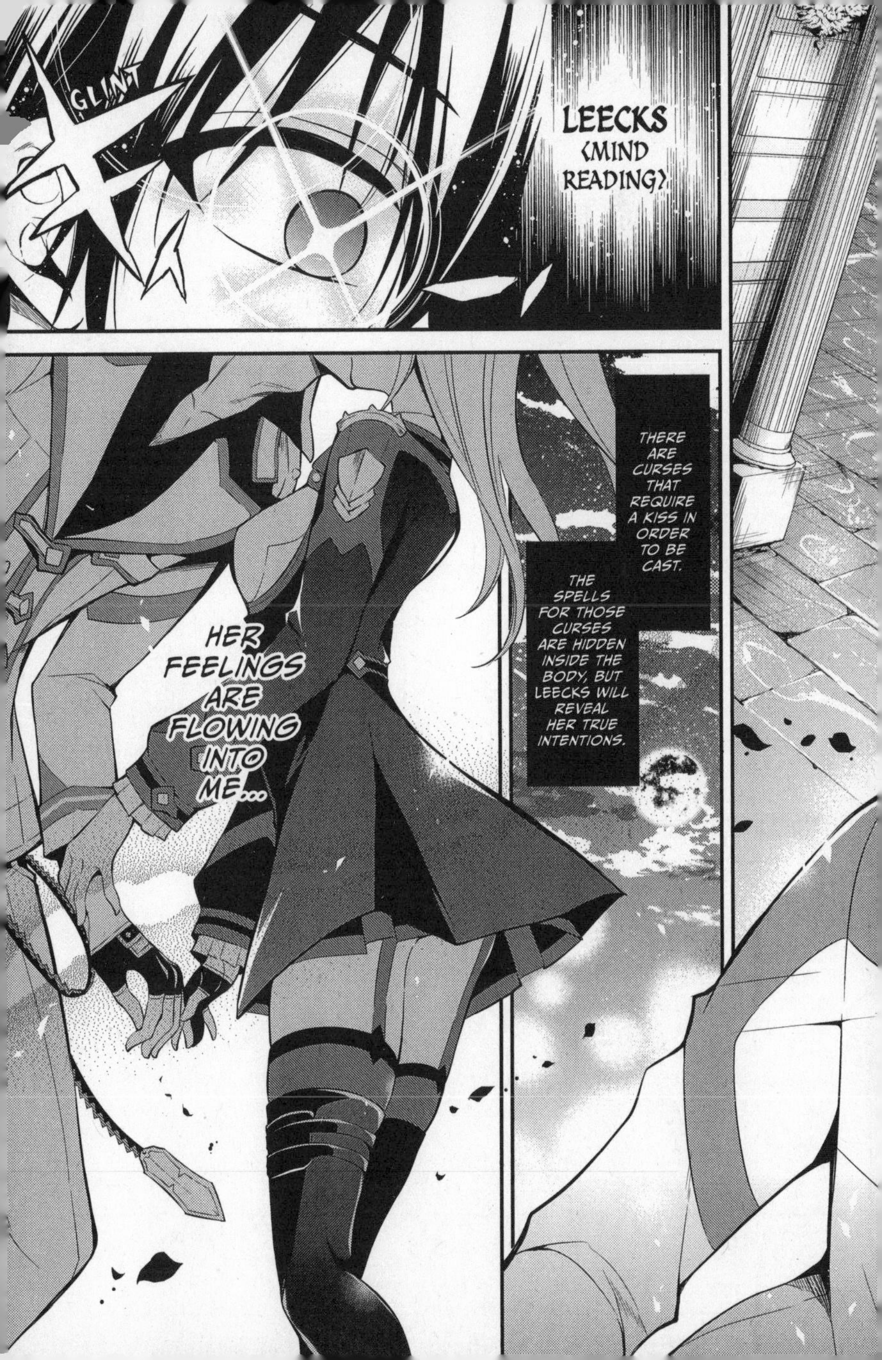
LEECKS <MIND READING>
GLINT
THERE ARE CURSES THAT REQUIRE A KISS IN ORDER TO BE CAST.
THE SPELLS FOR THOSE CURSES ARE HIDDEN INSIDE THE BODY, BUT LEECKS WILL REVEAL HER TRUE INTENTIONS.
HER FEELINGS ARE FLOWING INTO ME...

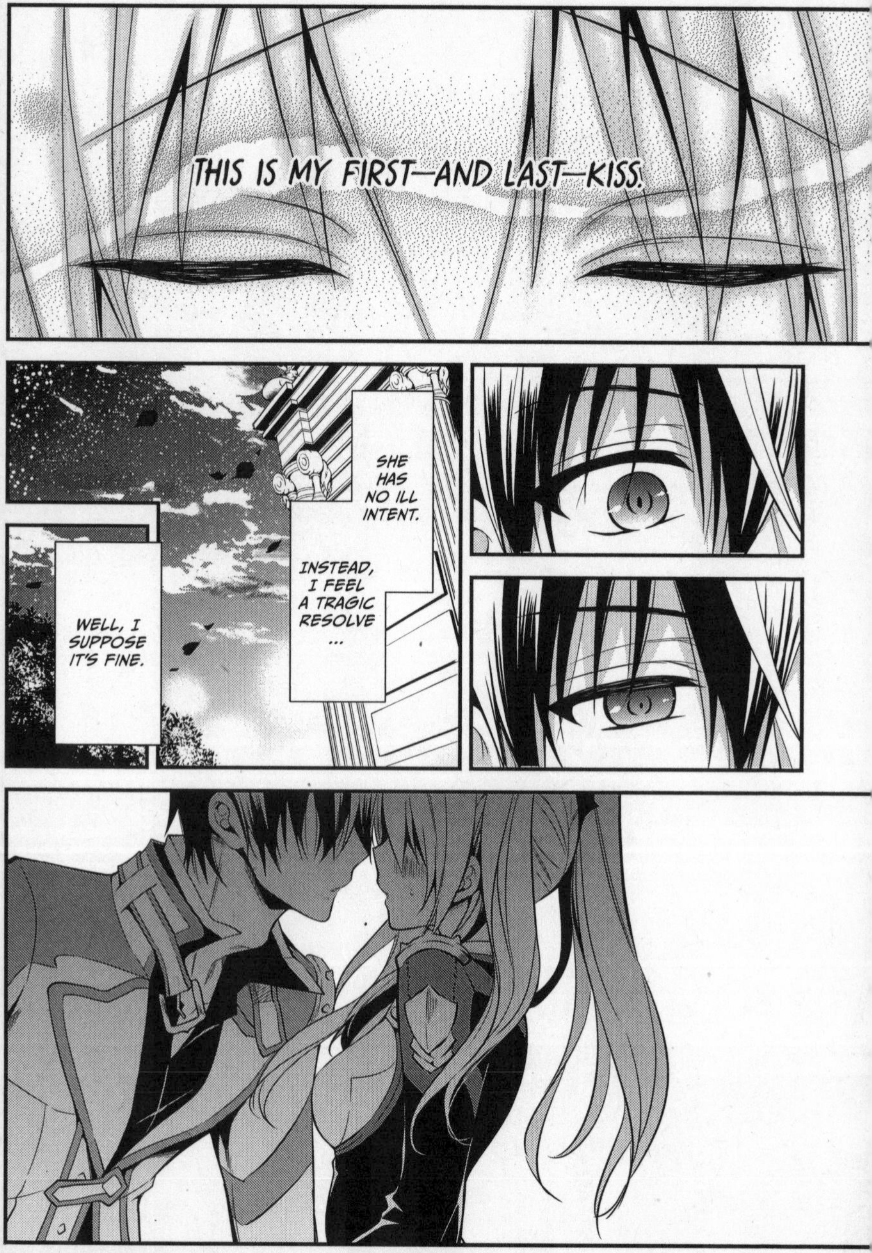
THIS IS MY FIRST—AND LAST—KISS.
SHE HAS NO ILL INTENT.
INSTEAD, I FEEL A TRAGIC RESOLVE ...
WELL, I SUPPOSE IT'S FINE.

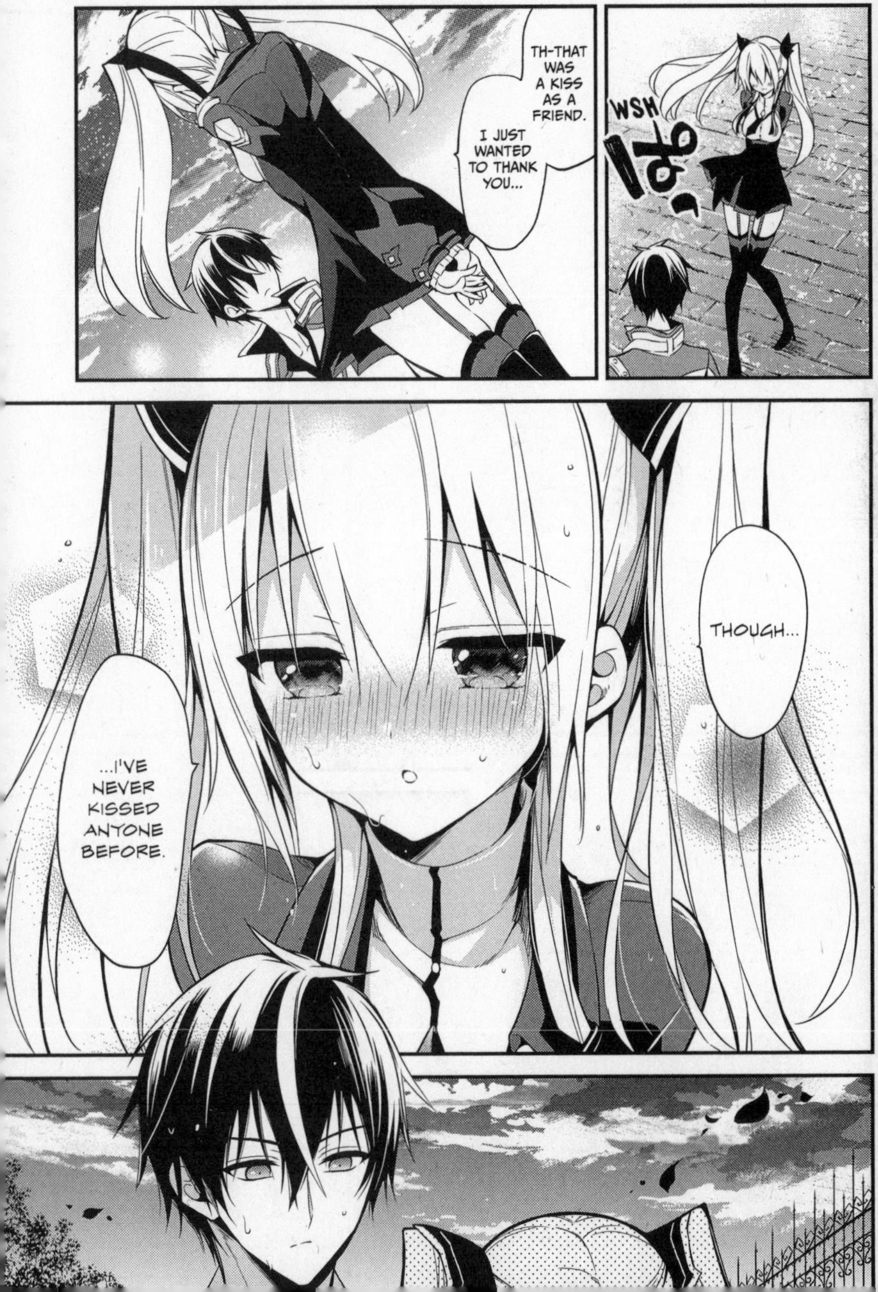
WSH
TH-THAT WAS A KISS AS A FRIEND.
I JUST WANTED TO THANK YOU...
THOUGH...
...I'VE NEVER KISSED ANYONE BEFORE.

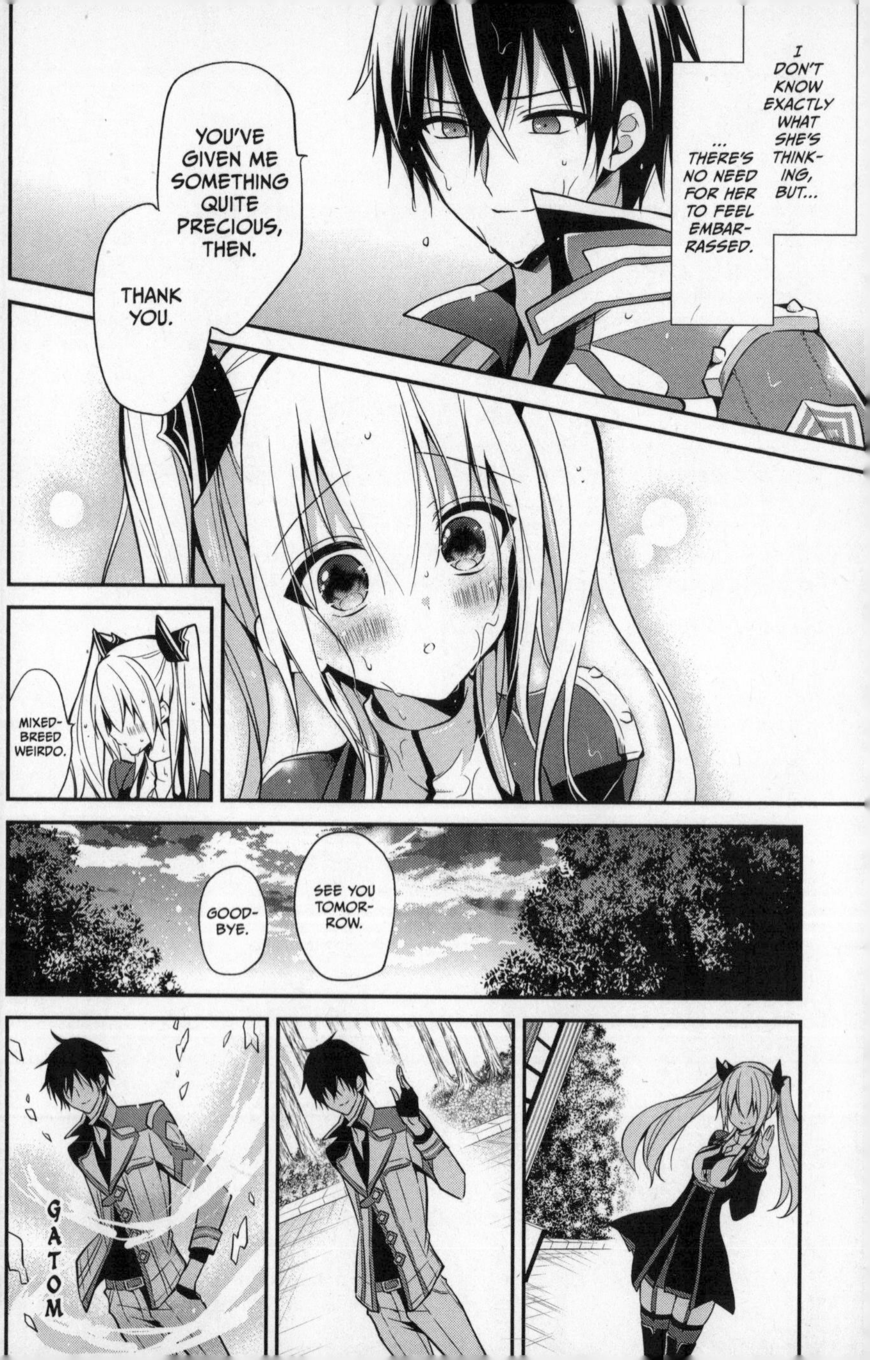
I DON'T KNOW EXACTLY WHAT SHE'S THINKING, BUT...
...THERE'S NO NEED FOR HER TO FEEL EMBARRASSED.
YOU'VE GIVEN ME SOMETHING QUITE PRECIOUS, THEN.
THANK YOU.
MIXED-BREED WEIRDO.
SEE YOU TOMORROW.
GOODBYE.
GATOM

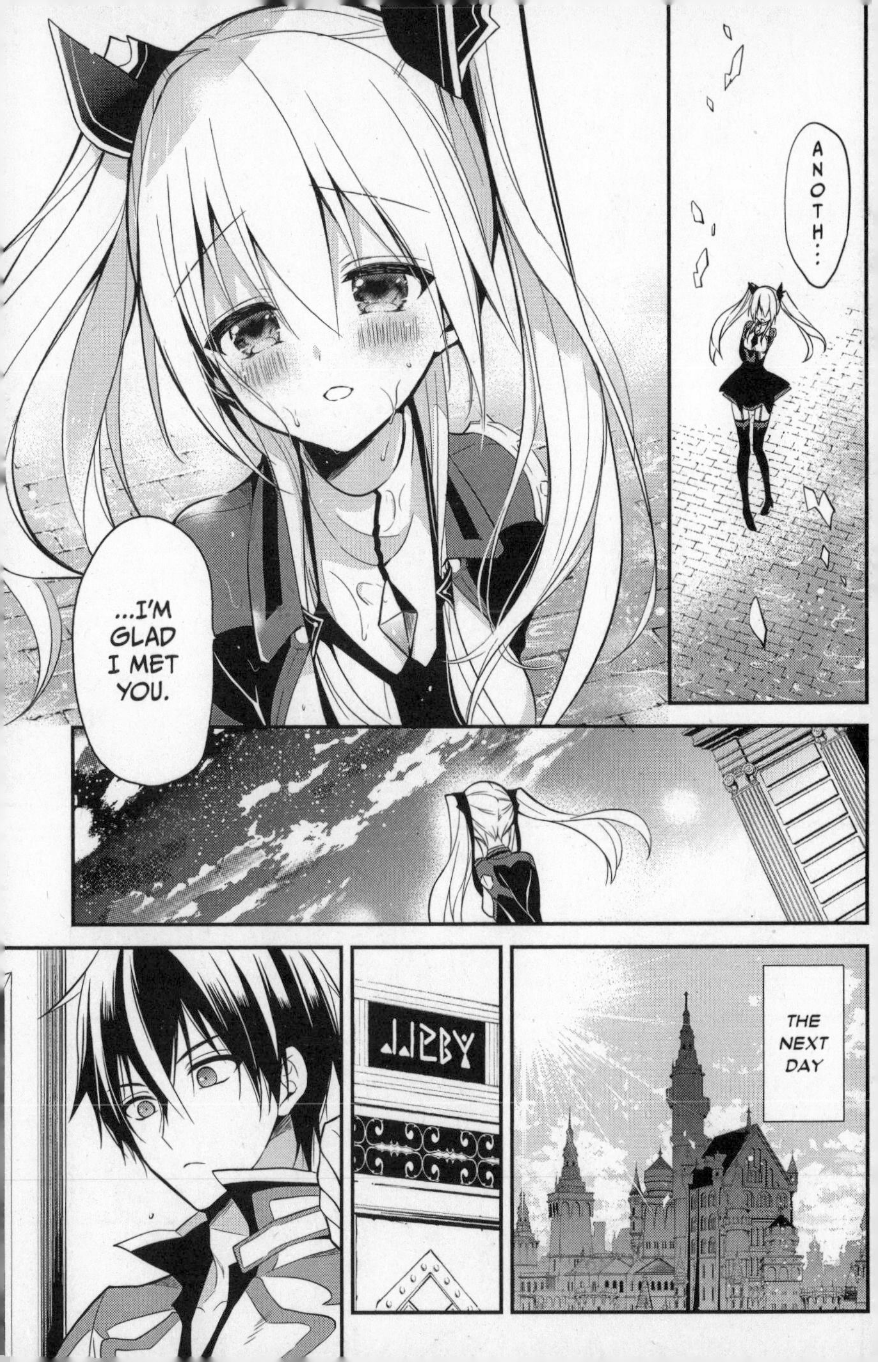
ANOTH...
...I'M GLAD I MET YOU.
THE NEXT DAY

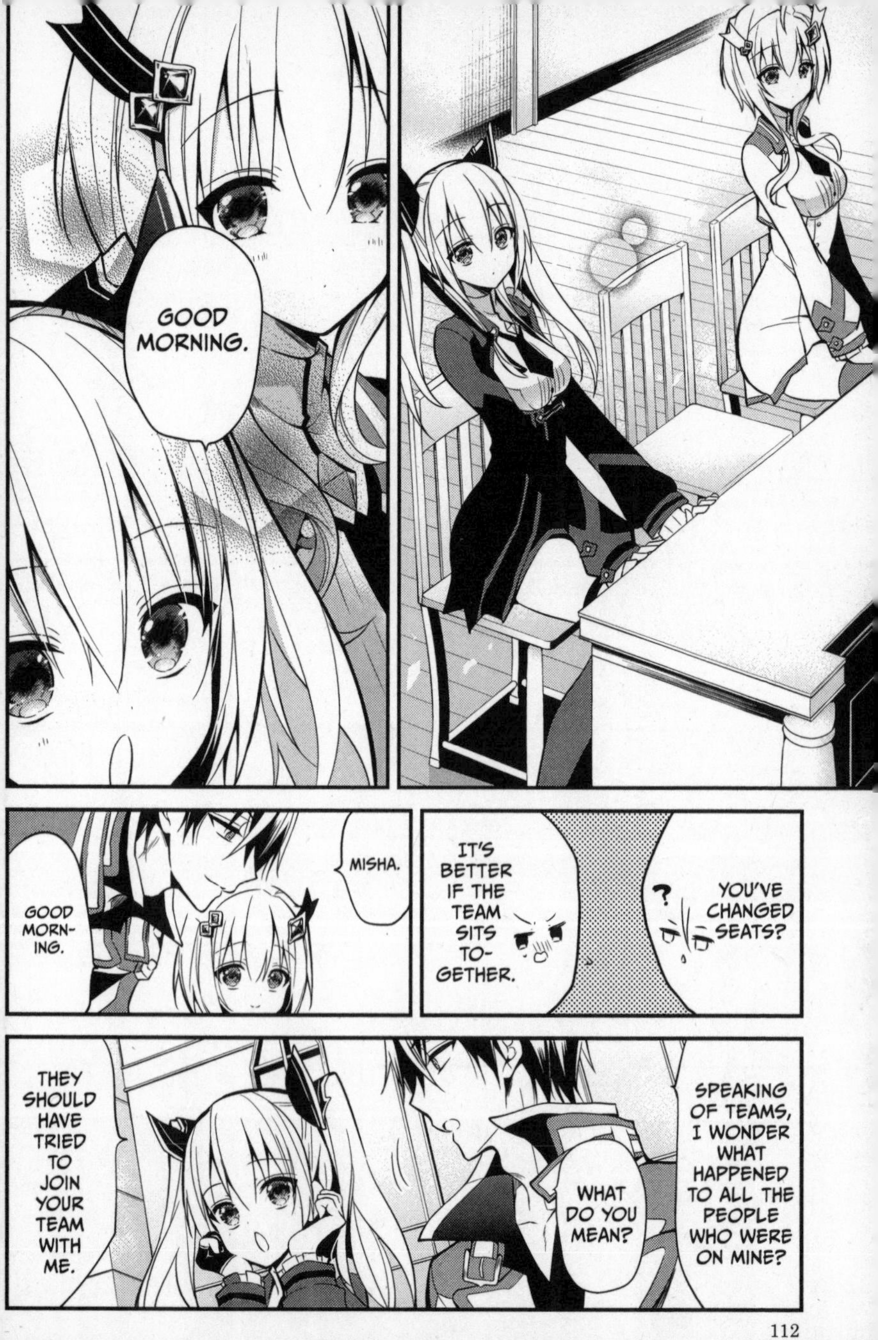
GOOD MORNING.
YOU'VE CHANGED SEATS?
IT'S BETTER IF THE TEAM SITS TOGETHER.
MISHA.
GOOD MORNING.
SPEAKING OF TEAMS, I WONDER WHAT HAPPENED TO ALL THE PEOPLE WHO WERE ON MINE?
WHAT DO YOU MEAN?
THEY SHOULD HAVE TRIED TO JOIN YOUR TEAM WITH ME.

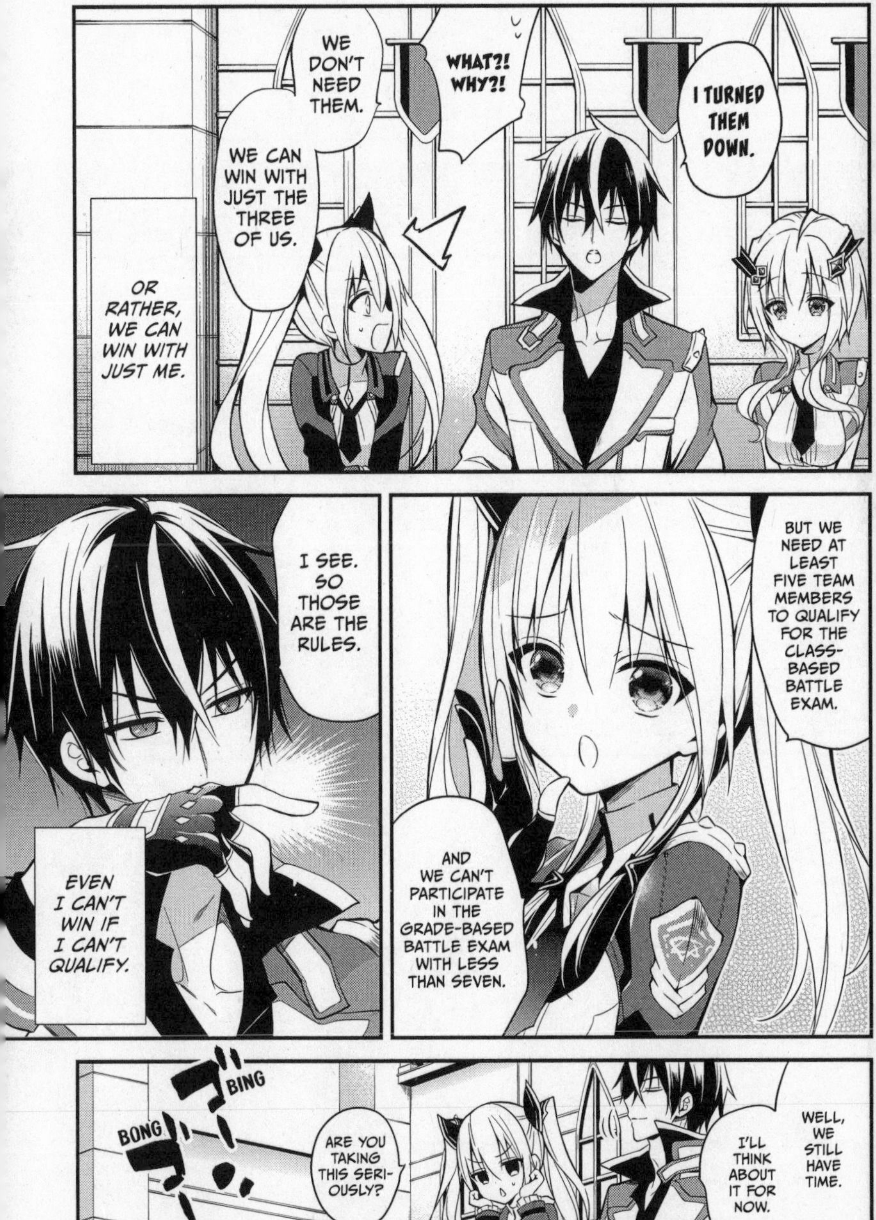
I TURNED THEM DOWN.
WHAT?! WHY?!
WE DON'T NEED THEM.
WE CAN WIN WITH JUST THE THREE OF US.
OR RATHER, WE CAN WIN WITH JUST ME.
BUT WE NEED AT LEAST FIVE TEAM MEMBERS TO QUALIFY FOR THE CLASS-BASED BATTLE EXAM.
AND WE CAN'T PARTICIPATE IN THE GRADE-BASED BATTLE EXAM WITH LESS THAN SEVEN.
I SEE. SO THOSE ARE THE RULES.
EVEN I CAN'T WIN IF I CAN'T QUALIFY.
WELL, WE STILL HAVE TIME.
I'LL THINK ABOUT IT FOR NOW.
ARE YOU TAKING THIS SERI-OUSLY?
BING
BONG

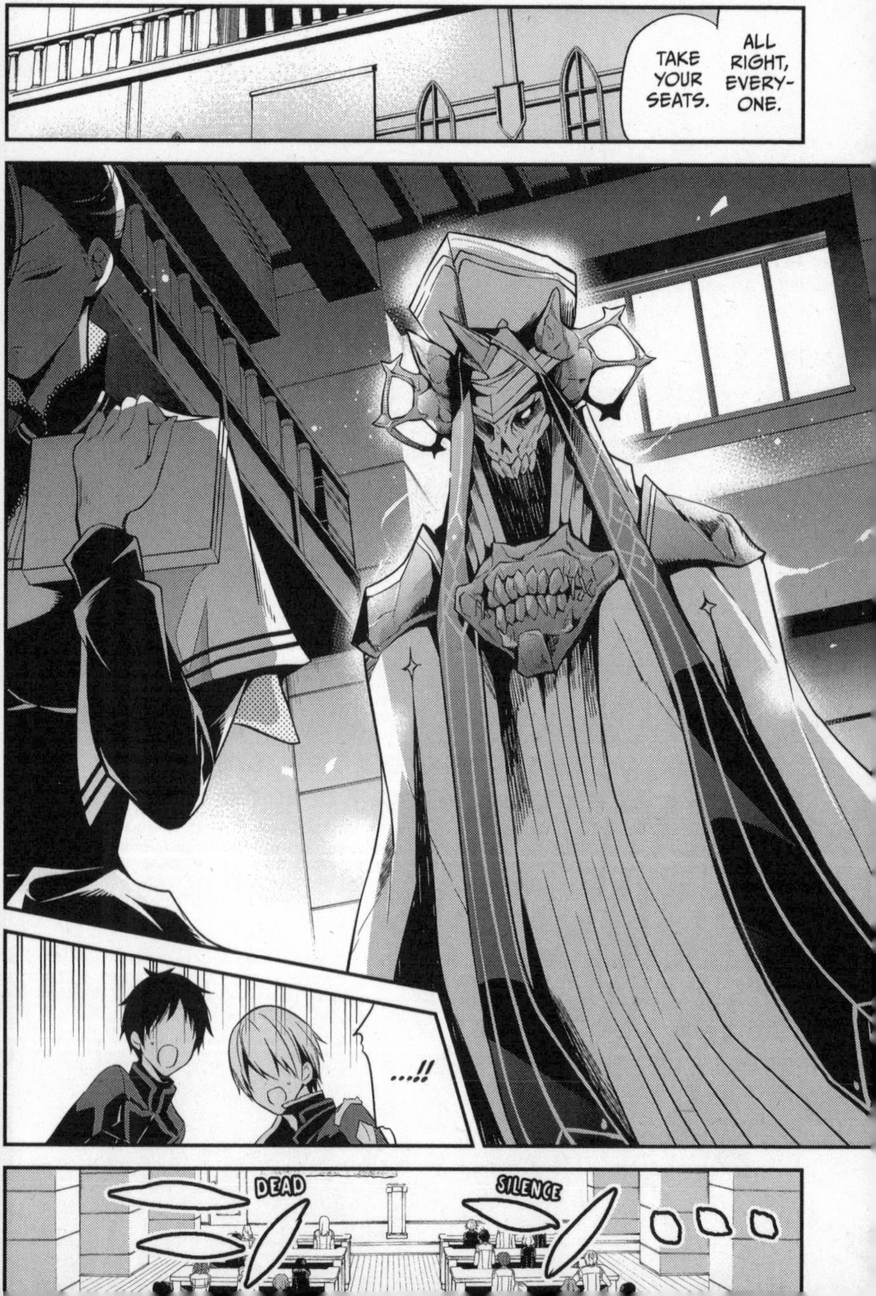
ALL RIGHT, EVERY-ONE.
TAKE YOUR SEATS.
...!!
DEAD
SILENCE

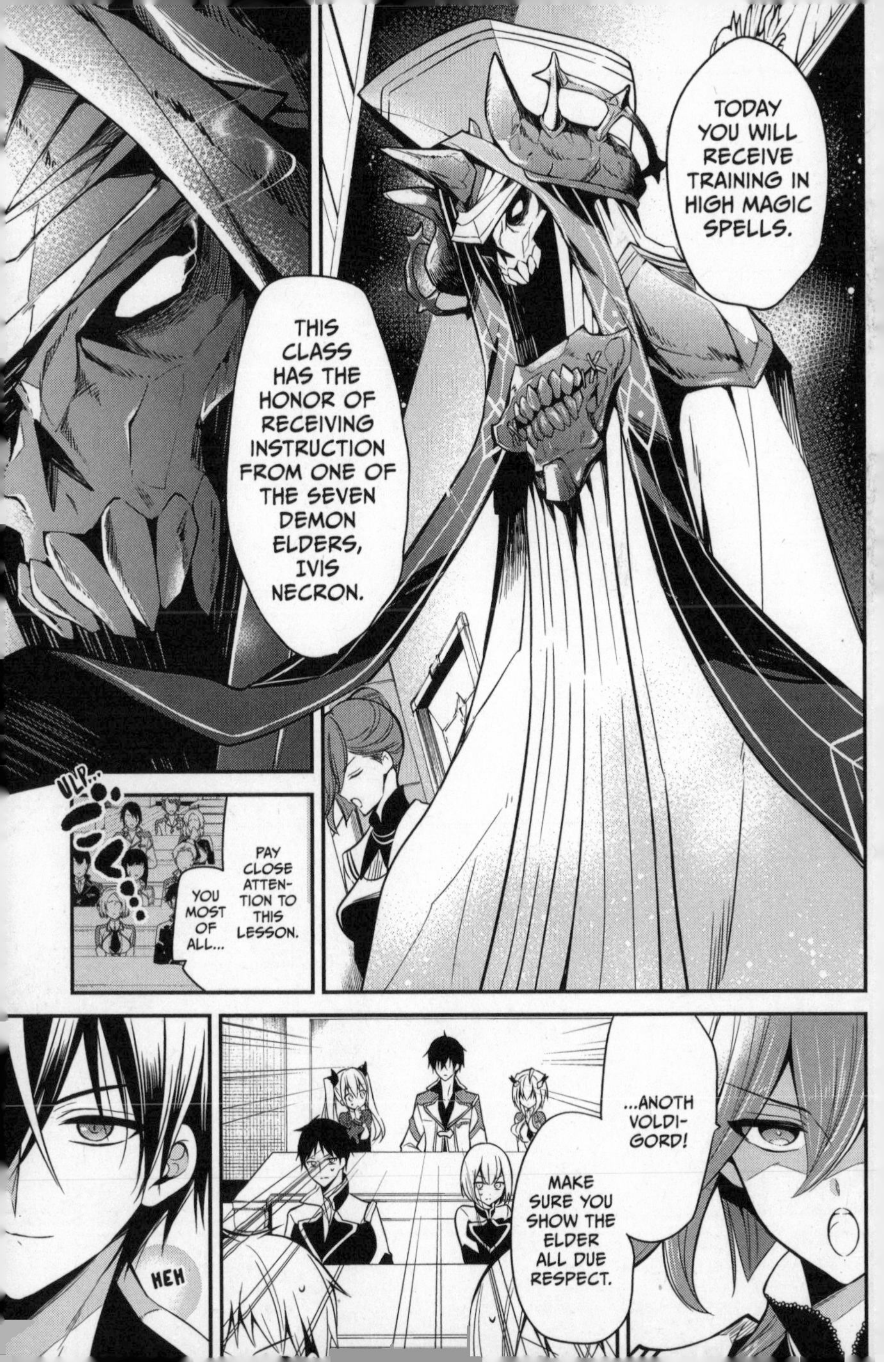
TODAY YOU WILL RECEIVE TRAINING IN HIGH MAGIC SPELLS.
THIS CLASS HAS THE HONOR OF RECEIVING INSTRUCTION FROM ONE OF THE SEVEN DEMON ELDERS, IVIS NECRON.
PAY CLOSE ATTEN-TION TO THIS LESSON.
YOU MOST OF ALL...
ULP...
...ANOTH VOLDI-GORD!
MAKE SURE YOU SHOW THE ELDER ALL DUE RESPECT.
HEH

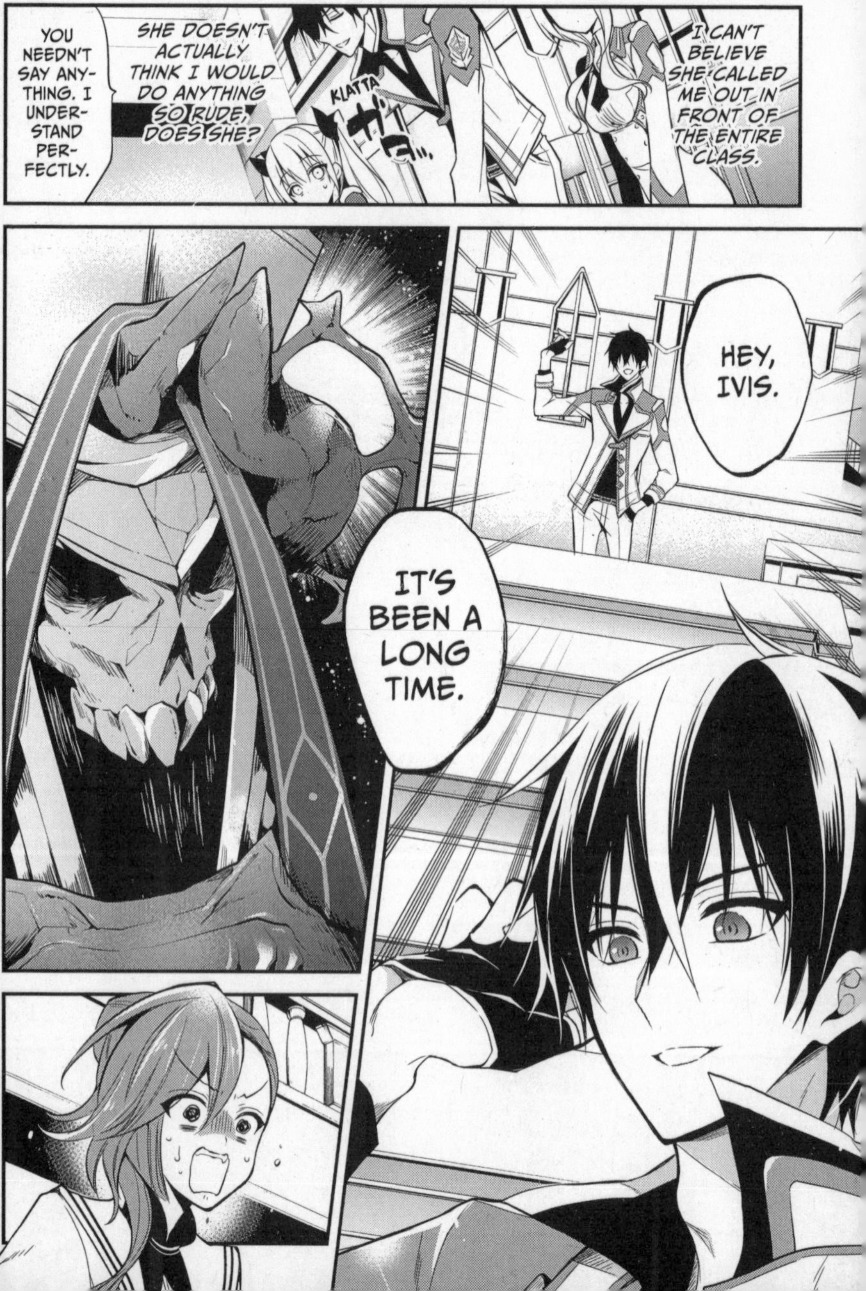
I CAN'T BELIEVE SHE CALLED ME OUT IN FRONT OF THE ENTIRE CLASS.
SHE DOESN'T ACTUALLY THINK I WOULD DO ANYTHING SO RUDE, DOES SHE?
KLATTA
YOU NEEDN'T SAY ANY-THING. I UNDER-STAND PER-FECTLY.
HEY, IVIS.
IT'S BEEN A LONG TIME.

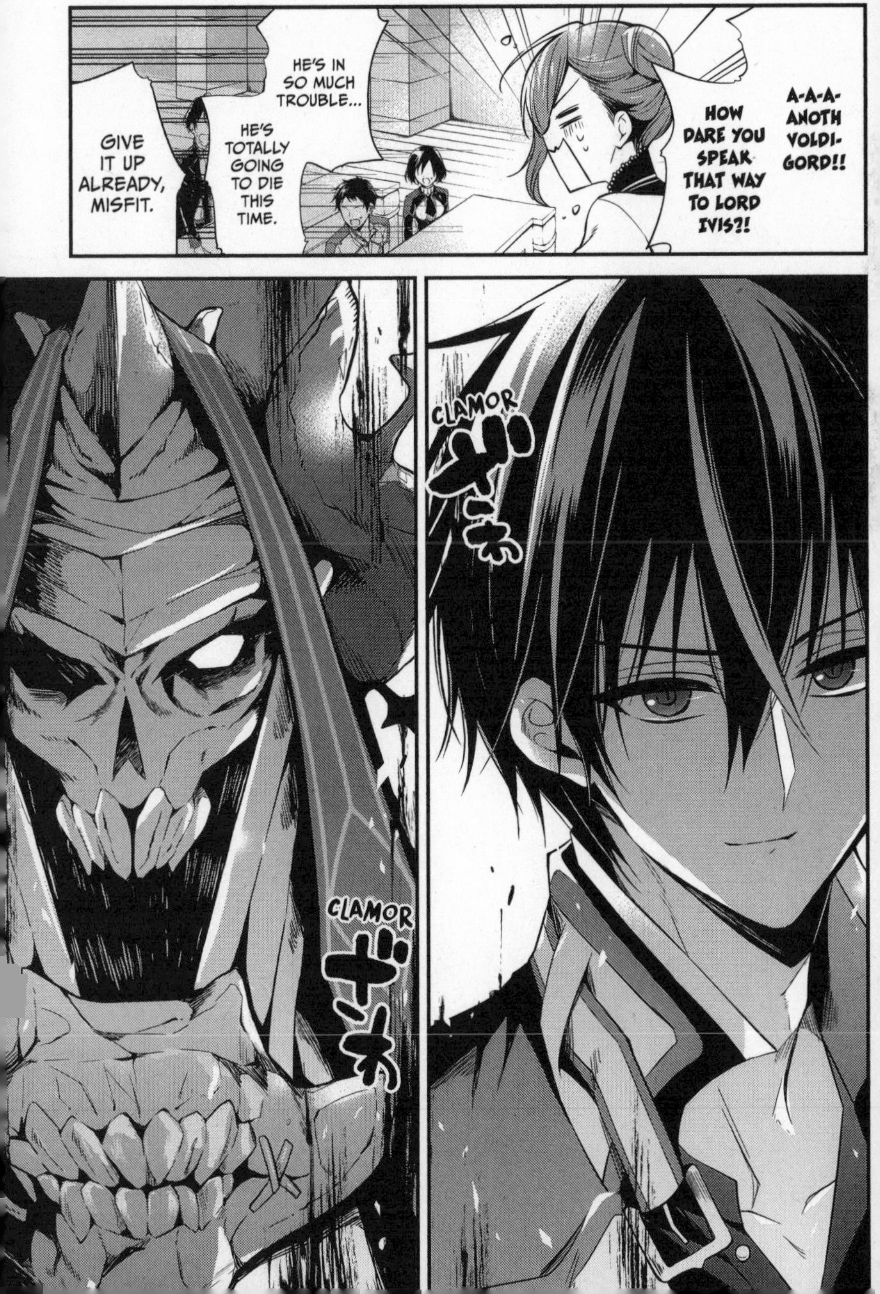
A-A-A-ANOTH VOLDIGORD!!
HOW DARE YOU SPEAK THAT WAY TO LORD IVIS?!
HE'S IN SO MUCH TROUBLE...
HE'S TOTALLY GOING TO DIE THIS TIME.
GIVE IT UP ALREADY, MISFIT.
CLAMOR
CLAMOR

The Misfit of Demon King Academy

HISTORY'S STRONGEST DEMON KING REINCARNATES
AND GOES TO SCHOOL WITH HIS DESCENDANTS

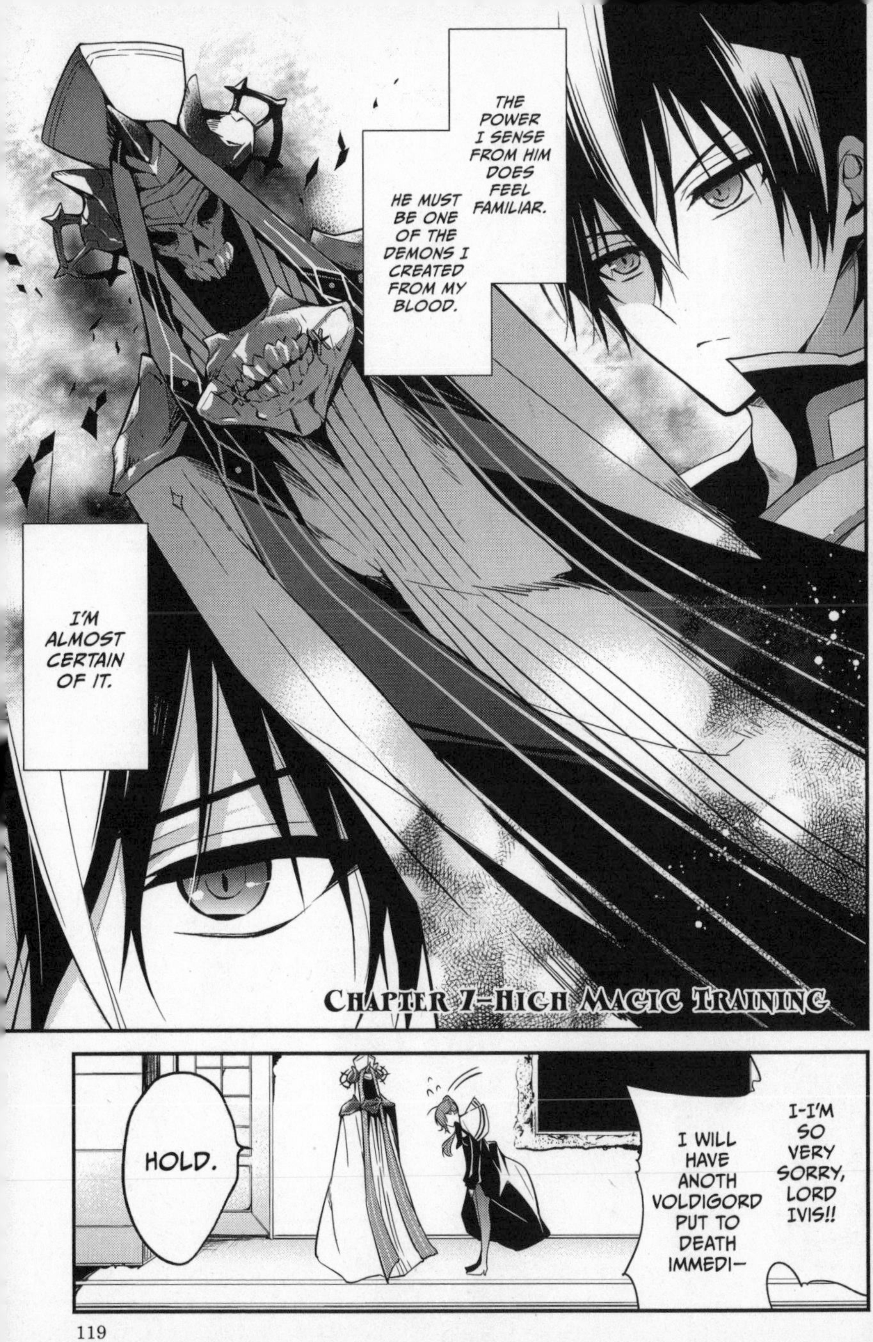
THE POWER I SENSE FROM HIM DOES FEEL FAMILIAR.
HE MUST BE ONE OF THE DEMONS I CREATED FROM MY BLOOD.
I'M ALMOST CERTAIN OF IT.
Chapter 7–High Magic Training
I-I'M SO VERY SORRY, LORD IVIS!!
I WILL HAVE ANOTH VOLDIGORD PUT TO DEATH IMMEDI—
HOLD.

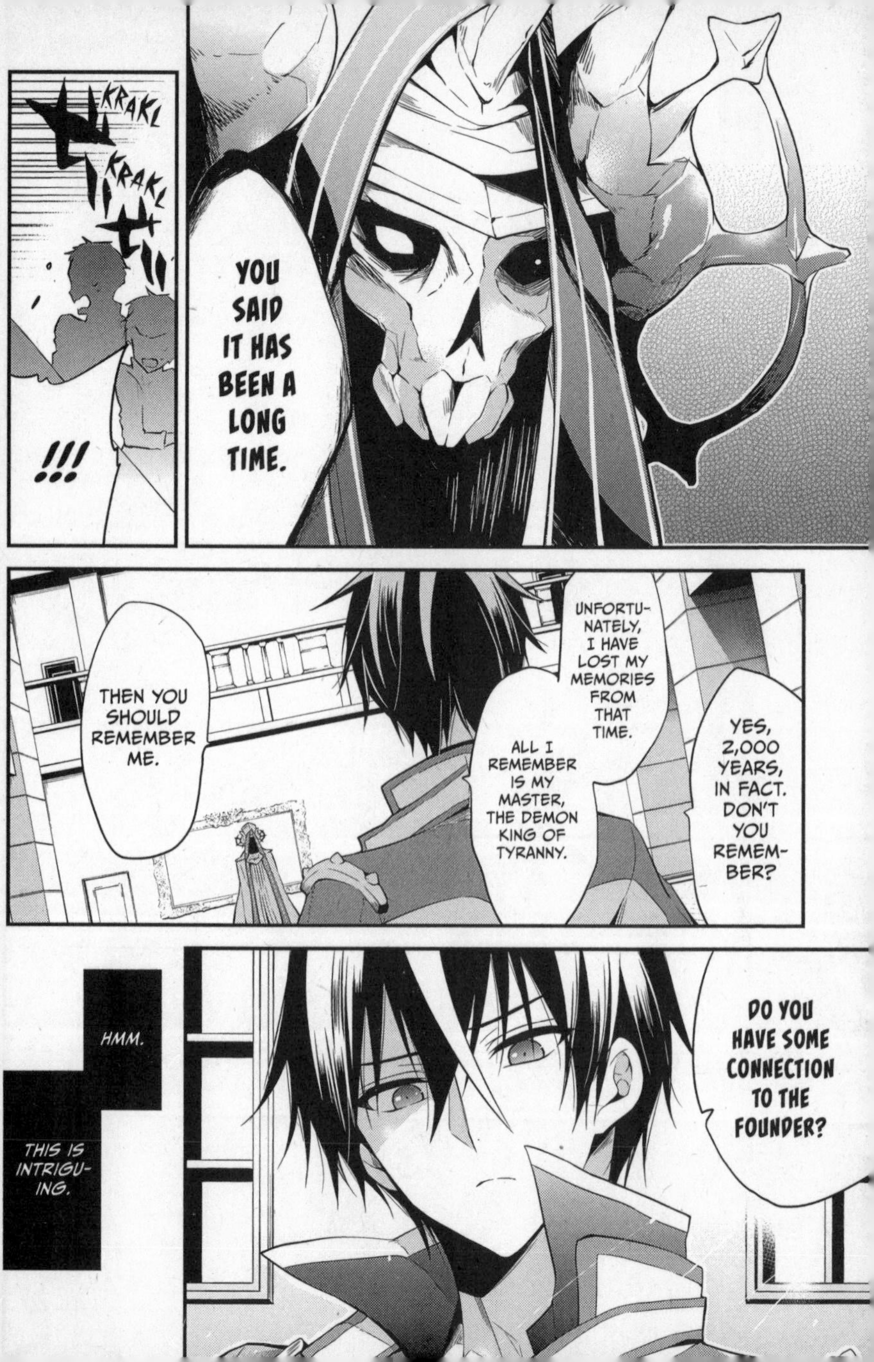
YOU SAID IT HAS BEEN A LONG TIME.
KRAKL
KRAKL
!!!
YES, 2,000 YEARS, IN FACT. DON'T YOU REMEMBER?
UNFORTUNATELY, I HAVE LOST MY MEMORIES FROM THAT TIME.
ALL I REMEMBER IS MY MASTER, THE DEMON KING OF TYRANNY.
THEN YOU SHOULD REMEMBER ME.
DO YOU HAVE SOME CONNECTION TO THE FOUNDER?
HMM.
THIS IS INTRIGUING.

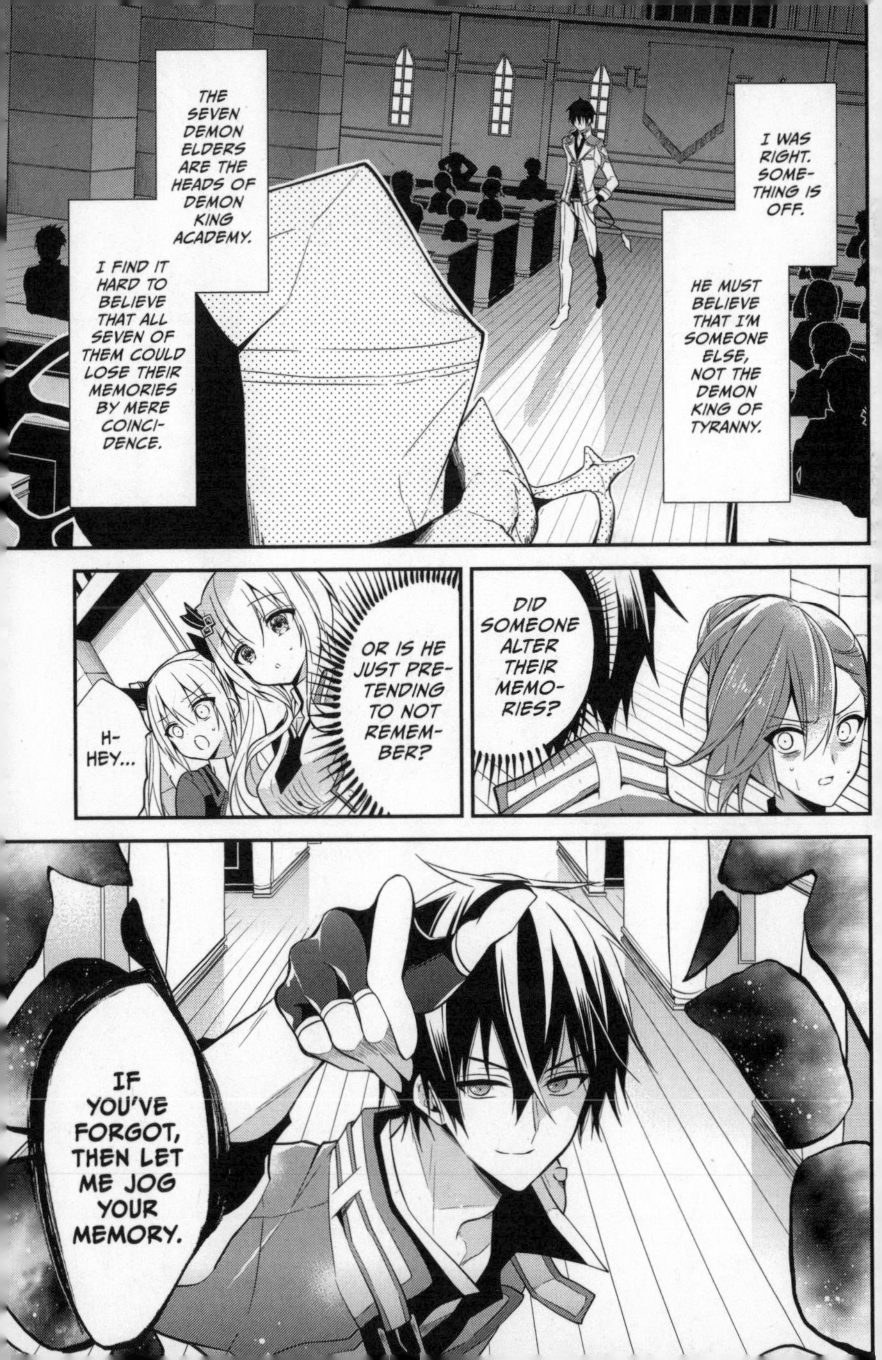
I WAS RIGHT. SOME-THING IS OFF.
HE MUST BELIEVE THAT I'M SOMEONE ELSE, NOT THE DEMON KING OF TYRANNY.
THE SEVEN DEMON ELDERS ARE THE HEADS OF DEMON KING ACADEMY.
I FIND IT HARD TO BELIEVE THAT ALL SEVEN OF THEM COULD LOSE THEIR MEMORIES BY MERE COINCI-DENCE.
DID SOMEONE ALTER THEIR MEMO-RIES?
OR IS HE JUST PRE-TENDING TO NOT REMEM-BER?
H-HEY...
IF YOU'VE FORGOT, THEN LET ME JOG YOUR MEMORY.

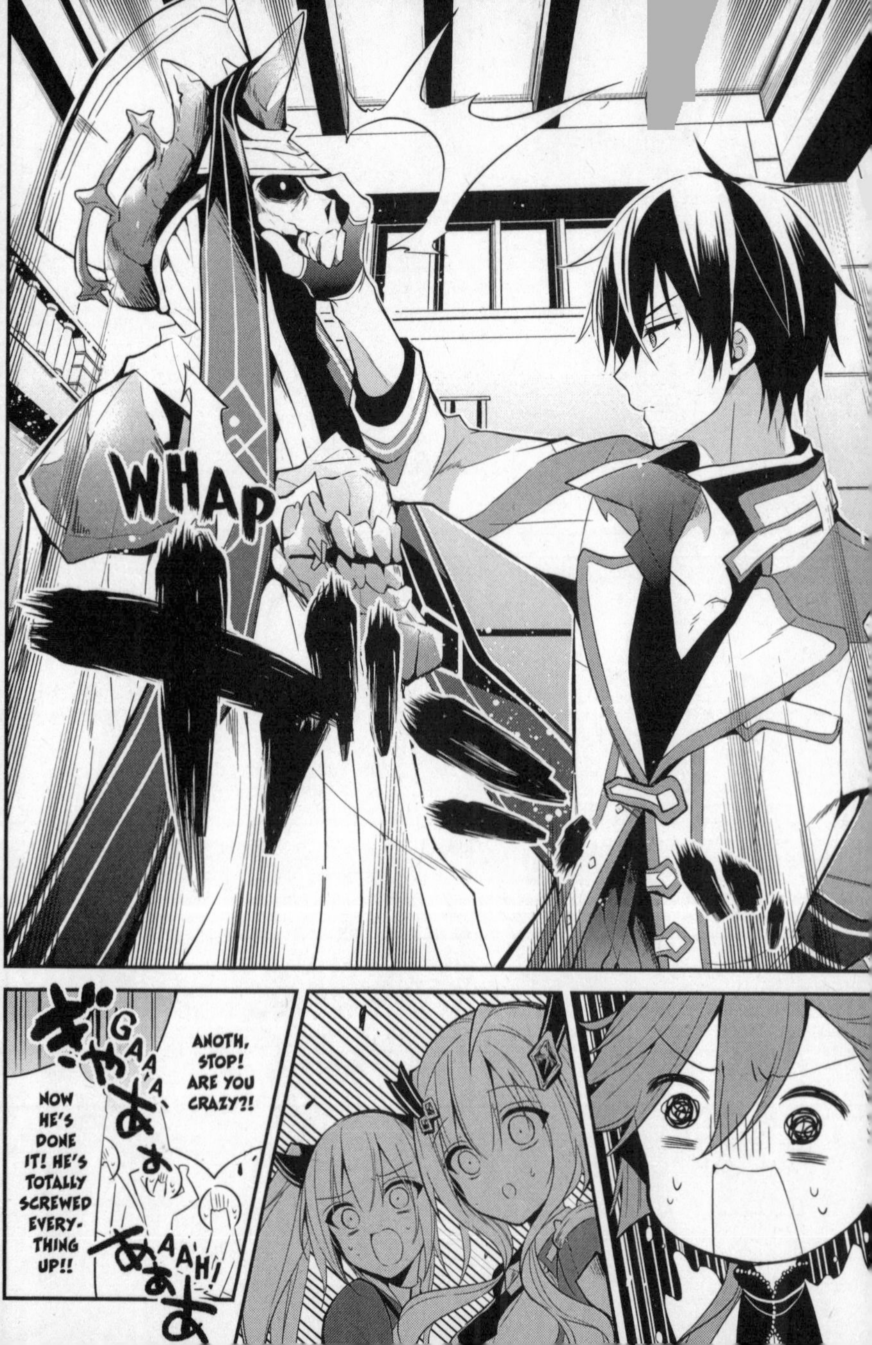
WHAP
ANOTH, STOP! ARE YOU CRAZY?!
GAAAA
NOW HE'S DONE IT! HE'S TOTALLY SCREWED EVERYTHING UP!!
AAH!

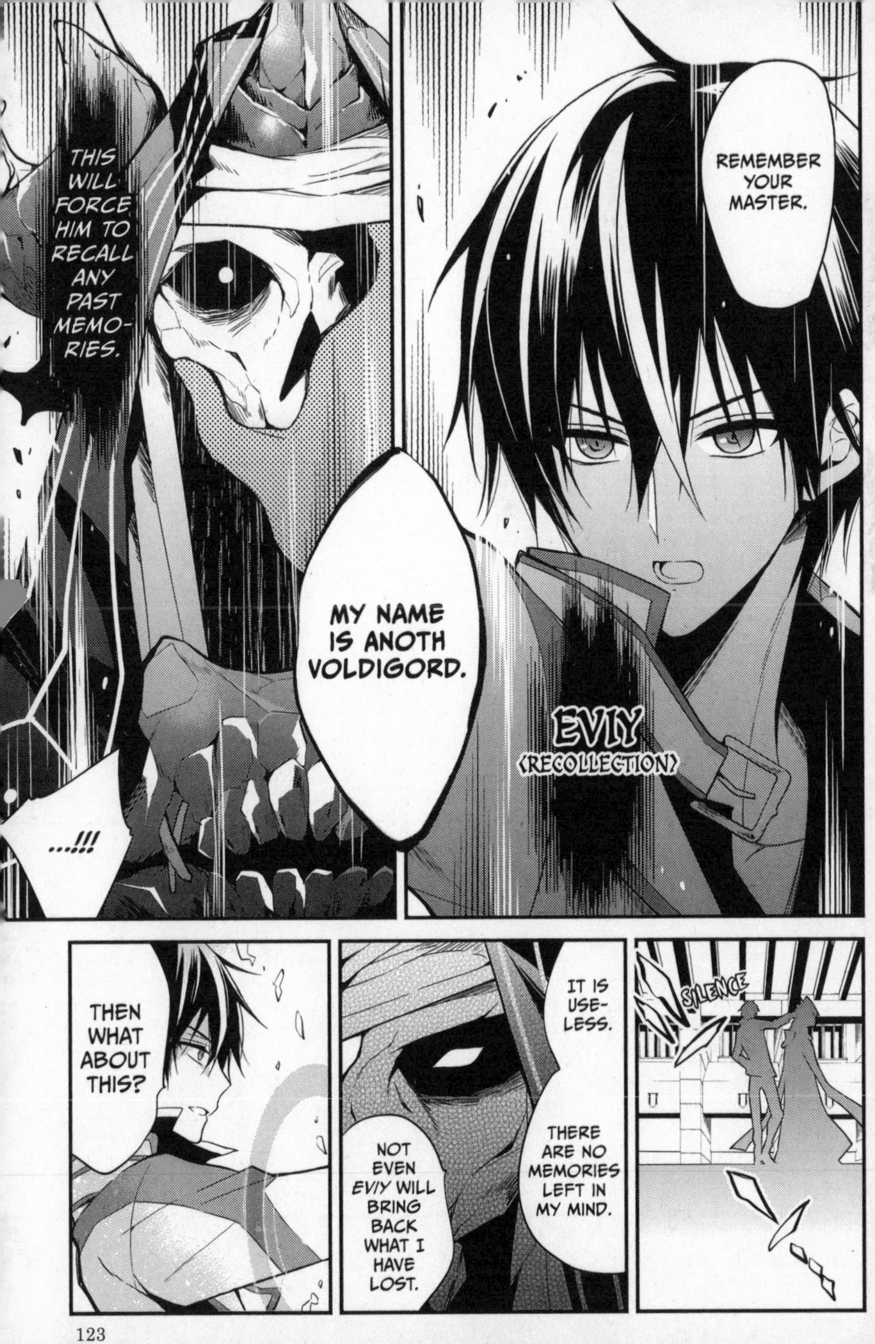
REMEMBER YOUR MASTER.
MY NAME IS ANOTH VOLDIGORD.
EVIY
〈RECOLLECTION〉
THIS WILL FORCE HIM TO RECALL ANY PAST MEMO-RIES.
...!!!
SILENCE
IT IS USE-LESS.
THERE ARE NO MEMORIES LEFT IN MY MIND.
NOT EVEN *EVIY* WILL BRING BACK WHAT I HAVE LOST.
THEN WHAT ABOUT THIS?

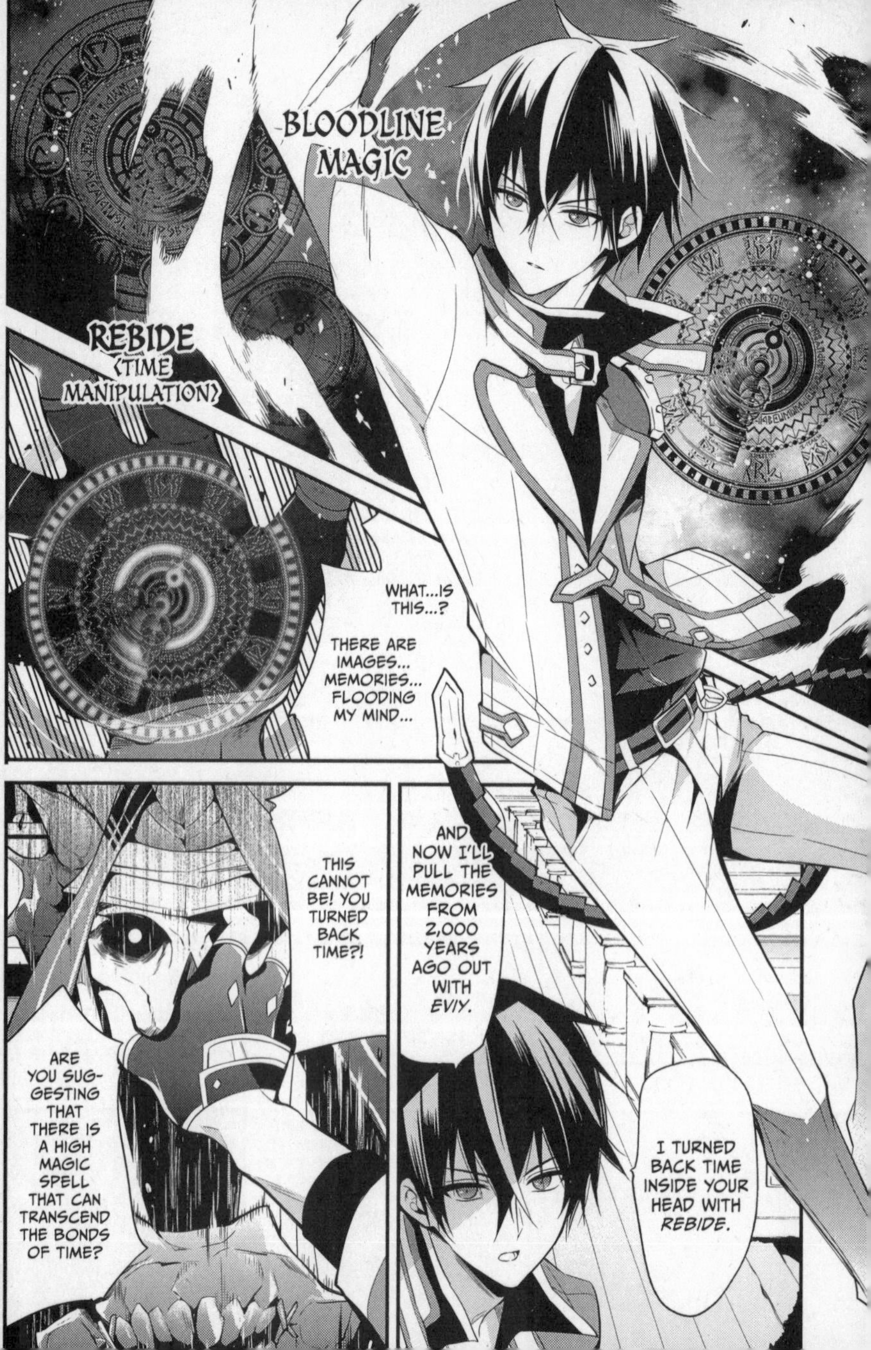
BLOODLINE MAGIC
REBIDE ‹TIME MANIPULATION›
WHAT...IS THIS...?
THERE ARE IMAGES... MEMORIES... FLOODING MY MIND...
AND NOW I'LL PULL THE MEMORIES FROM 2,000 YEARS AGO OUT WITH *EVIY*.
I TURNED BACK TIME INSIDE YOUR HEAD WITH *REBIDE*.
THIS CANNOT BE! YOU TURNED BACK TIME?!
ARE YOU SUG-GESTING THAT THERE IS A HIGH MAGIC SPELL THAT CAN TRANSCEND THE BONDS OF TIME?

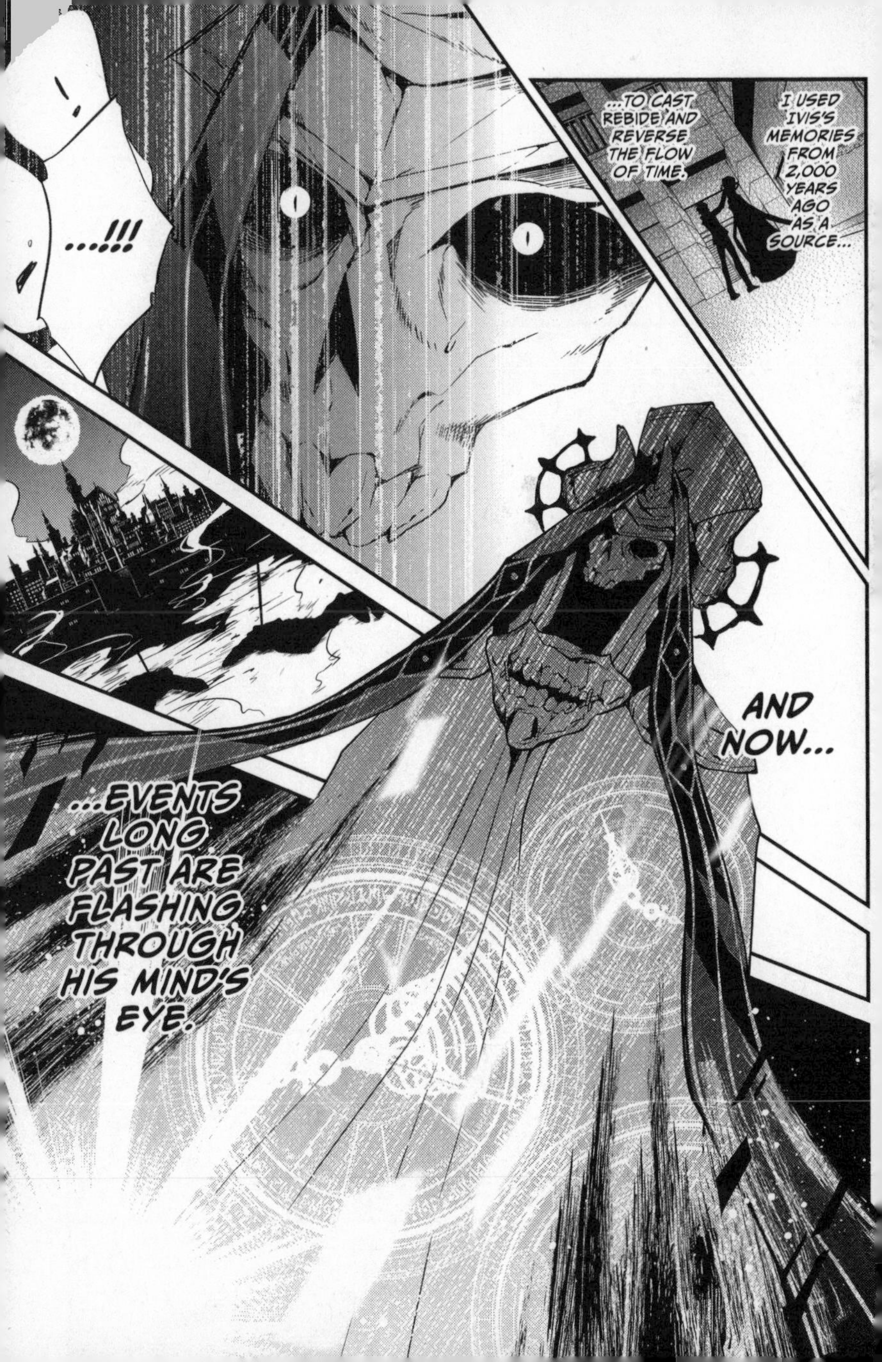
I USED IVIS'S MEMORIES FROM 2,000 YEARS AGO AS A SOURCE...
...TO CAST REBIDE AND REVERSE THE FLOW OF TIME.
...!!!
AND NOW...
...EVENTS LONG PAST ARE FLASHING THROUGH HIS MIND'S EYE.

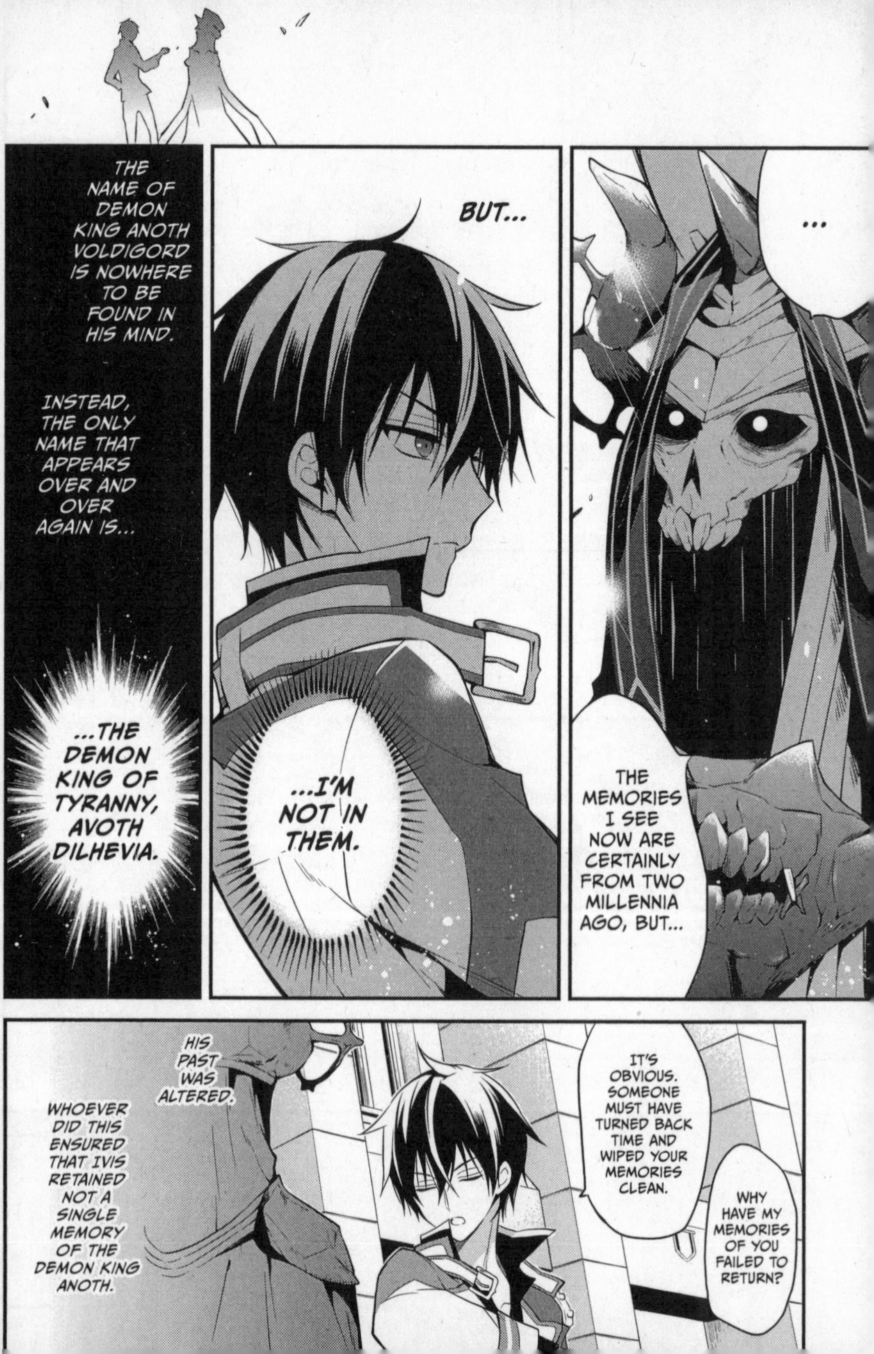
...
THE MEMORIES I SEE NOW ARE CERTAINLY FROM TWO MILLENNIA AGO, BUT...
BUT...
...I'M NOT IN THEM.
THE NAME OF DEMON KING ANOTH VOLDIGORD IS NOWHERE TO BE FOUND IN HIS MIND.
INSTEAD, THE ONLY NAME THAT APPEARS OVER AND OVER AGAIN IS...
...THE DEMON KING OF TYRANNY, AVOTH DILHEVIA.
WHY HAVE MY MEMORIES OF YOU FAILED TO RETURN?
IT'S OBVIOUS. SOMEONE MUST HAVE TURNED BACK TIME AND WIPED YOUR MEMORIES CLEAN.
HIS PAST WAS ALTERED.
WHOEVER DID THIS ENSURED THAT IVIS RETAINED NOT A SINGLE MEMORY OF THE DEMON KING ANOTH.

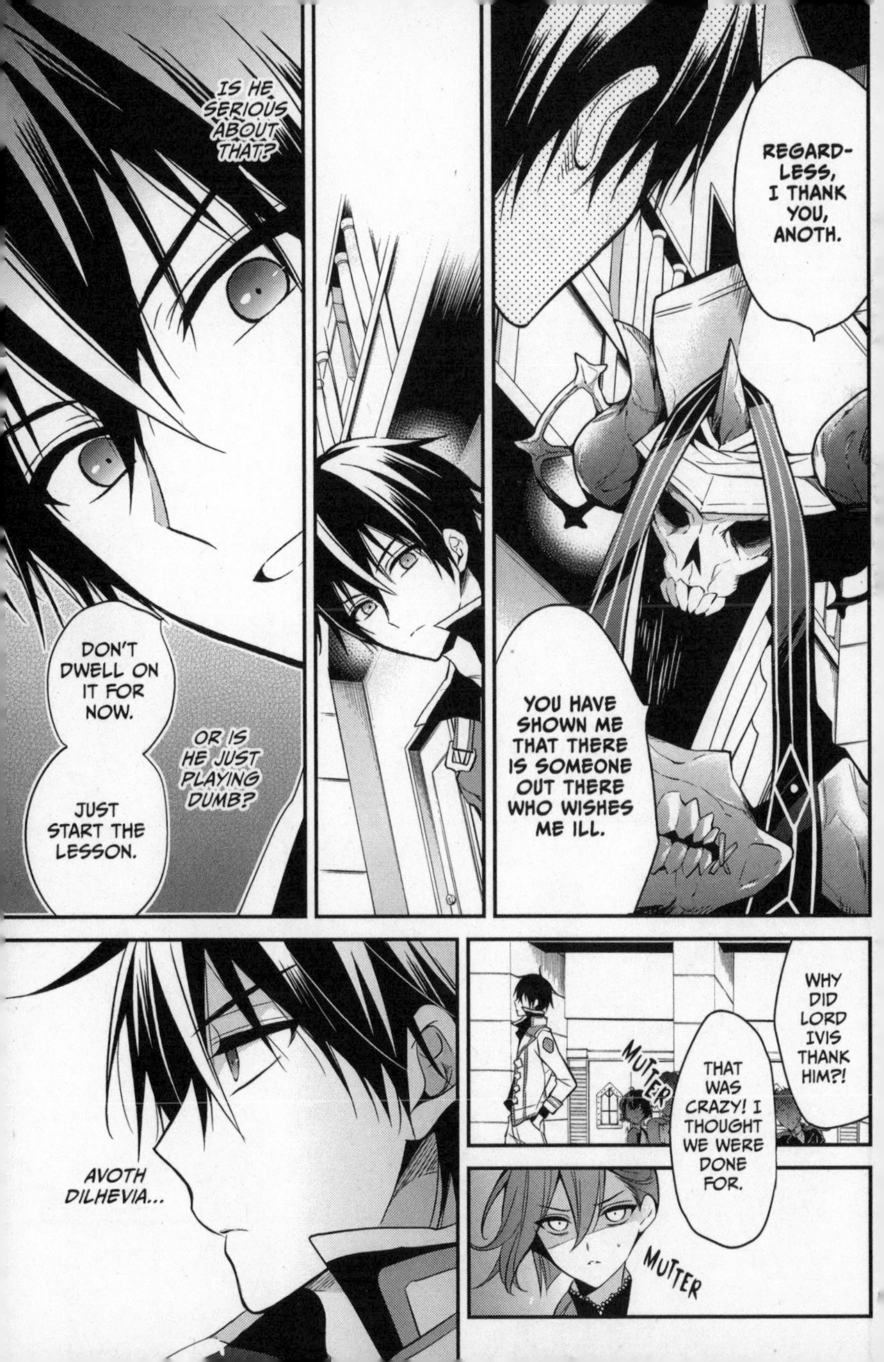
REGARD-LESS, I THANK YOU, ANOTH.
YOU HAVE SHOWN ME THAT THERE IS SOMEONE OUT THERE WHO WISHES ME ILL.
IS HE SERIOUS ABOUT THAT?
DON'T DWELL ON IT FOR NOW.
OR IS HE JUST PLAYING DUMB?
JUST START THE LESSON.
WHY DID LORD IVIS THANK HIM?!
MUTTER
THAT WAS CRAZY! I THOUGHT WE WERE DONE FOR.
MUTTER
AVOTH DILHEVIA...

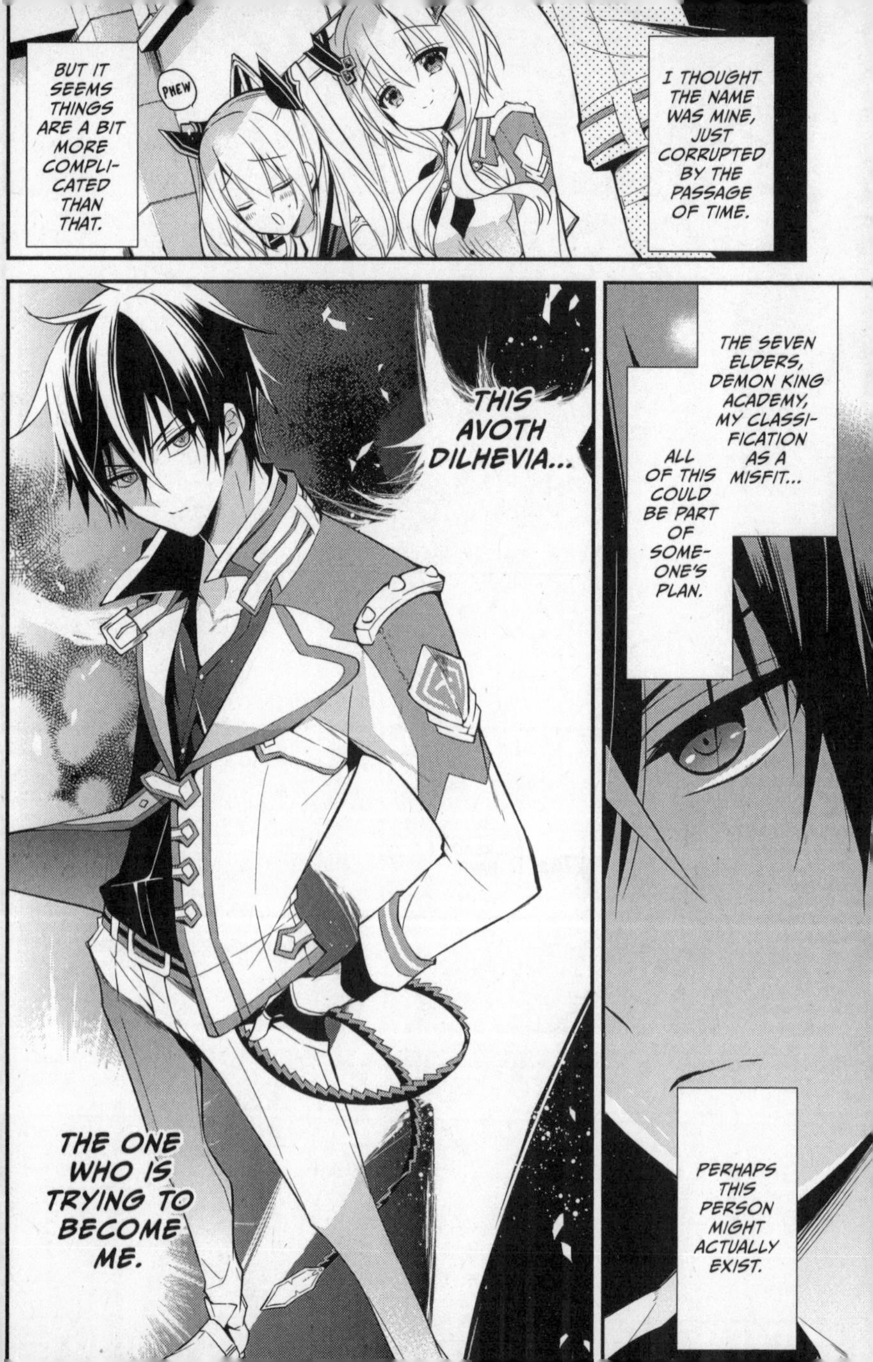
I THOUGHT THE NAME WAS MINE, JUST CORRUPTED BY THE PASSAGE OF TIME.
PHEW
BUT IT SEEMS THINGS ARE A BIT MORE COMPLICATED THAN THAT.
THE SEVEN ELDERS, DEMON KING ACADEMY, MY CLASSIFICATION AS A MISFIT...
ALL OF THIS COULD BE PART OF SOMEONE'S PLAN.
PERHAPS THIS PERSON MIGHT ACTUALLY EXIST.
THIS AVOTH DILHEVIA...
THE ONE WHO IS TRYING TO BECOME ME.

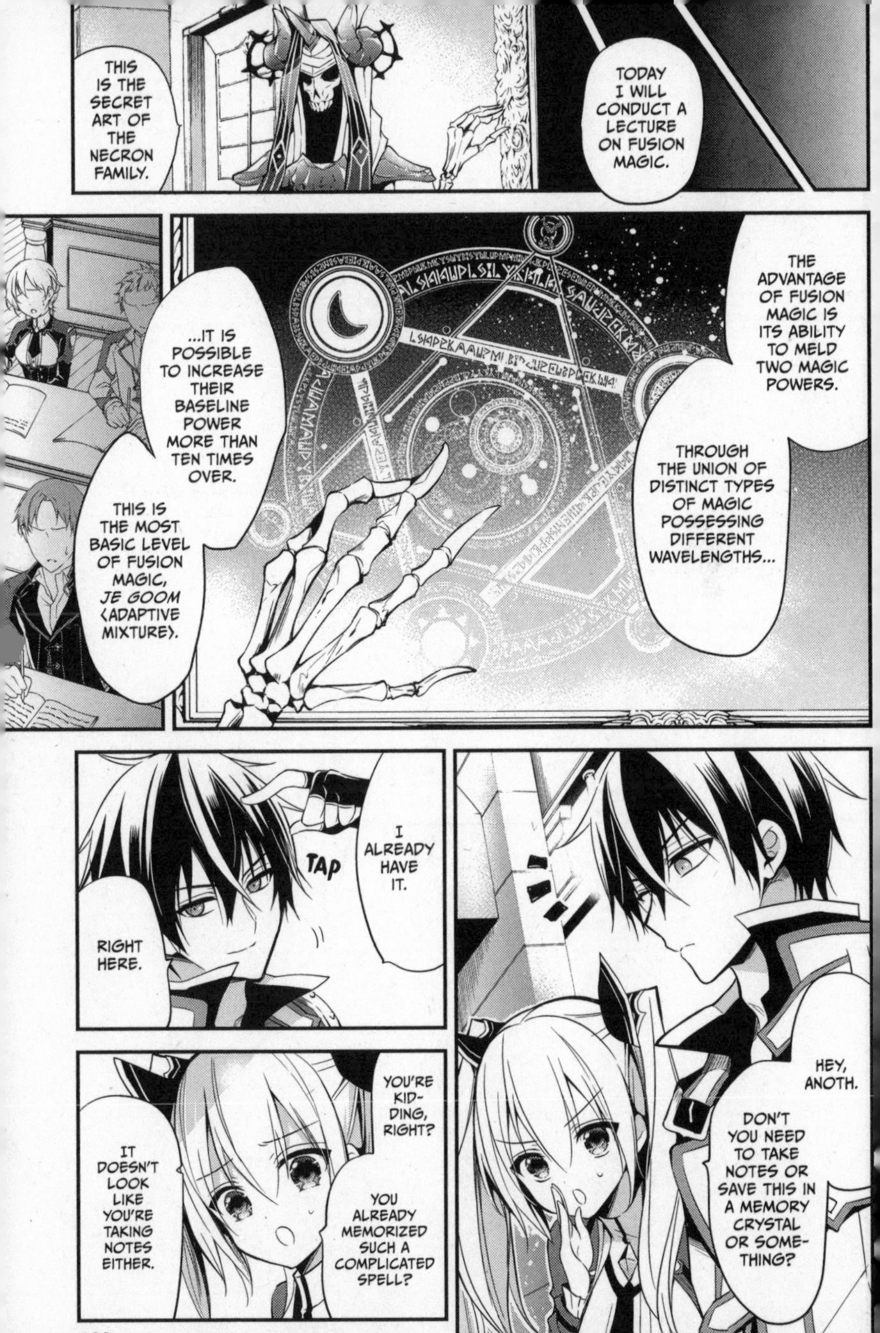
TODAY I WILL CONDUCT A LECTURE ON FUSION MAGIC.
THIS IS THE SECRET ART OF THE NECRON FAMILY.
THE ADVANTAGE OF FUSION MAGIC IS ITS ABILITY TO MELD TWO MAGIC POWERS.
THROUGH THE UNION OF DISTINCT TYPES OF MAGIC POSSESSING DIFFERENT WAVELENGTHS...
...IT IS POSSIBLE TO INCREASE THEIR BASELINE POWER MORE THAN TEN TIMES OVER.
THIS IS THE MOST BASIC LEVEL OF FUSION MAGIC, JE GOOM <ADAPTIVE MIXTURE>.
HEY, ANOTH.
DON'T YOU NEED TO TAKE NOTES OR SAVE THIS IN A MEMORY CRYSTAL OR SOME-THING?
I ALREADY HAVE IT.
TAP
RIGHT HERE.
YOU'RE KID-DING, RIGHT?
YOU ALREADY MEMORIZED SUCH A COMPLICATED SPELL?
IT DOESN'T LOOK LIKE YOU'RE TAKING NOTES EITHER.

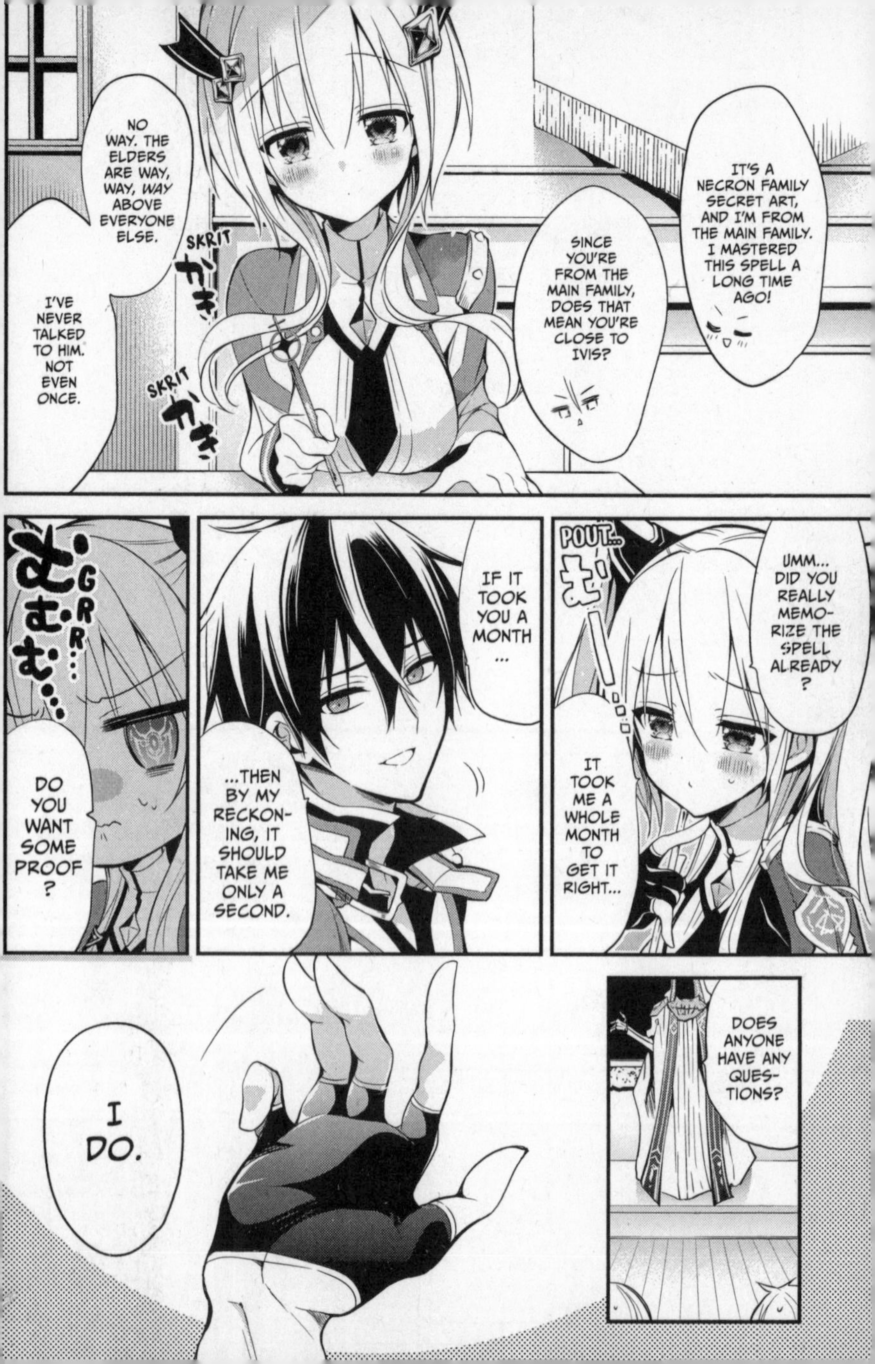
IT'S A NECRON FAMILY SECRET ART, AND I'M FROM THE MAIN FAMILY. I MASTERED THIS SPELL A LONG TIME AGO!
SINCE YOU'RE FROM THE MAIN FAMILY, DOES THAT MEAN YOU'RE CLOSE TO IVIS?
SKRIT かき
NO WAY. THE ELDERS ARE WAY, WAY, WAY ABOVE EVERYONE ELSE.
SKRIT かき
I'VE NEVER TALKED TO HIM. NOT EVEN ONCE.
UMM... DID YOU REALLY MEMO-RIZE THE SPELL ALREADY?
POUT... む
IT TOOK ME A WHOLE MONTH TO GET IT RIGHT...
IF IT TOOK YOU A MONTH...
...THEN BY MY RECKON-ING, IT SHOULD TAKE ME ONLY A SECOND.
GRR... むむむ...
DO YOU WANT SOME PROOF?
DOES ANYONE HAVE ANY QUES-TIONS?
I DO.

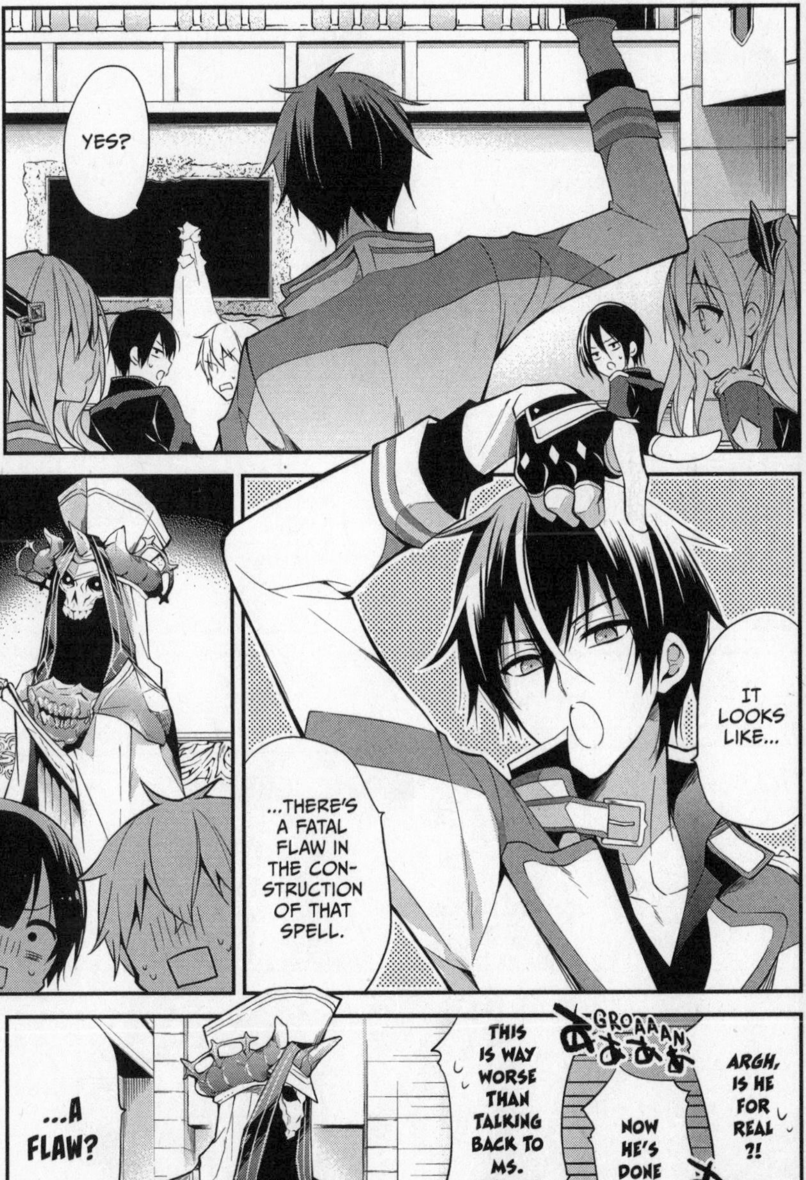
YES?
IT LOOKS LIKE...
...THERE'S A FATAL FLAW IN THE CON-STRUCTION OF THAT SPELL.
ARGH, IS HE FOR REAL?!
あああ
GROAAAN
あああ
NOW HE'S DONE IT!
THIS IS WAY WORSE THAN TALKING BACK TO MS. EMILIA!
...A FLAW?

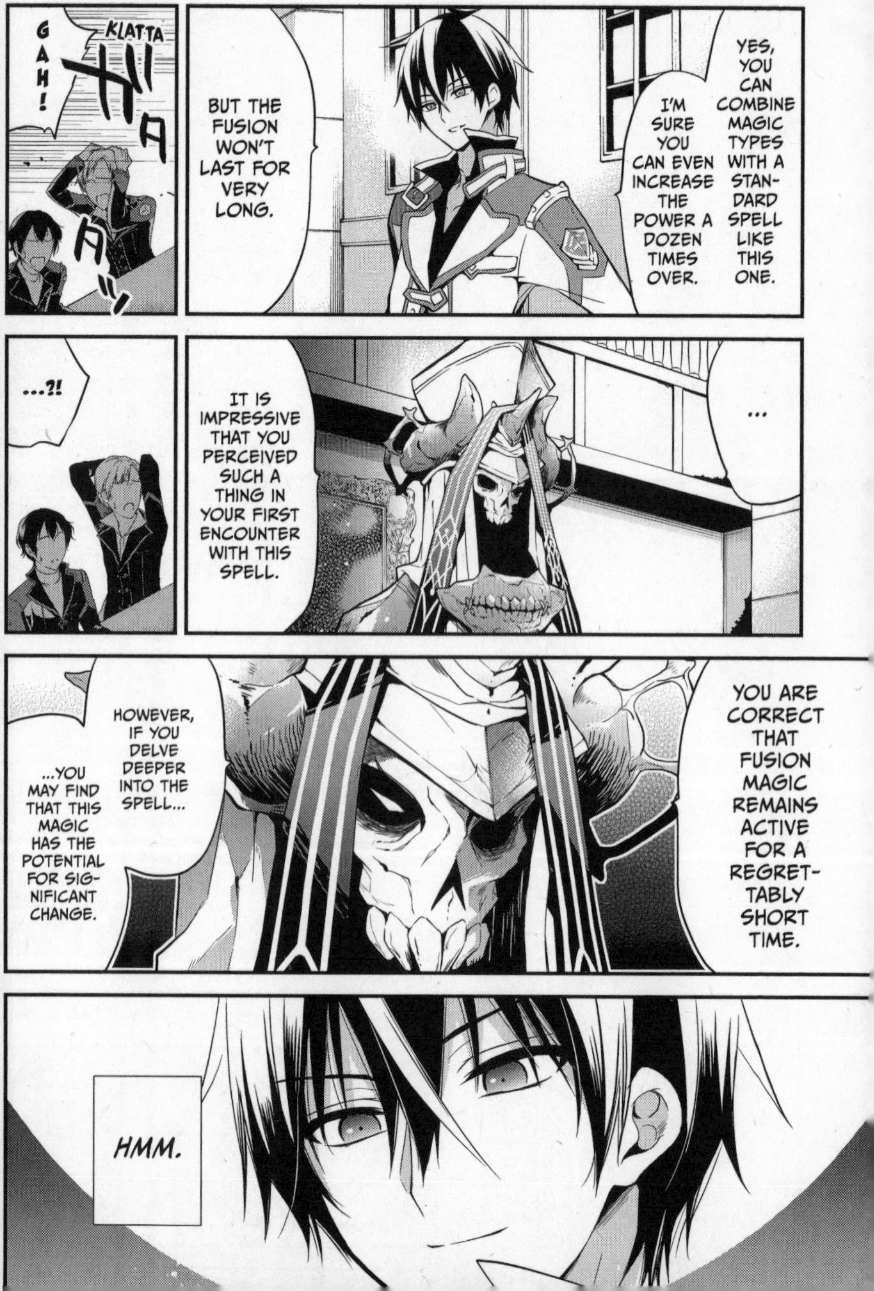
YES, YOU CAN COMBINE MAGIC TYPES WITH A STANDARD SPELL LIKE THIS ONE.
I'M SURE YOU CAN EVEN INCREASE THE POWER A DOZEN TIMES OVER.
BUT THE FUSION WON'T LAST FOR VERY LONG.
GAH!
KLATTA
...
IT IS IMPRESSIVE THAT YOU PERCEIVED SUCH A THING IN YOUR FIRST ENCOUNTER WITH THIS SPELL.
...?!
YOU ARE CORRECT THAT FUSION MAGIC REMAINS ACTIVE FOR A REGRETTABLY SHORT TIME.
HOWEVER, IF YOU DELVE DEEPER INTO THE SPELL...
...YOU MAY FIND THAT THIS MAGIC HAS THE POTENTIAL FOR SIGNIFICANT CHANGE.
HMM.

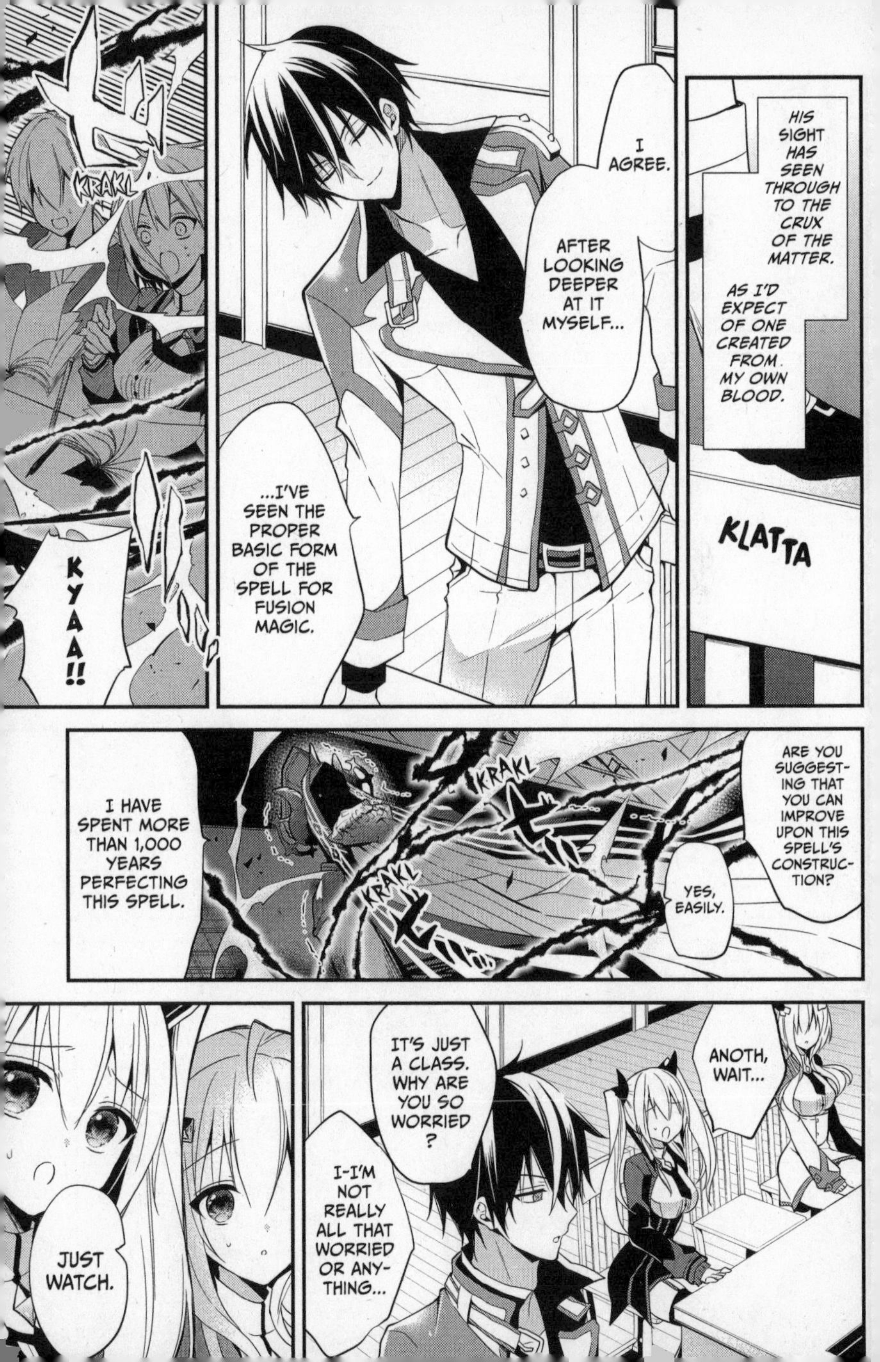
HIS SIGHT HAS SEEN THROUGH TO THE CRUX OF THE MATTER.
AS I'D EXPECT OF ONE CREATED FROM MY OWN BLOOD.
KLATTA
I AGREE.
AFTER LOOKING DEEPER AT IT MYSELF...
...I'VE SEEN THE PROPER BASIC FORM OF THE SPELL FOR FUSION MAGIC.
KRAKL
KYAA!!
ARE YOU SUGGESTING THAT YOU CAN IMPROVE UPON THIS SPELL'S CONSTRUCTION?
YES, EASILY.
KRAKL
KRAKL
I HAVE SPENT MORE THAN 1,000 YEARS PERFECTING THIS SPELL.
ANOTH, WAIT...
IT'S JUST A CLASS. WHY ARE YOU SO WORRIED?
I-I'M NOT REALLY ALL THAT WORRIED OR ANYTHING...
JUST WATCH.

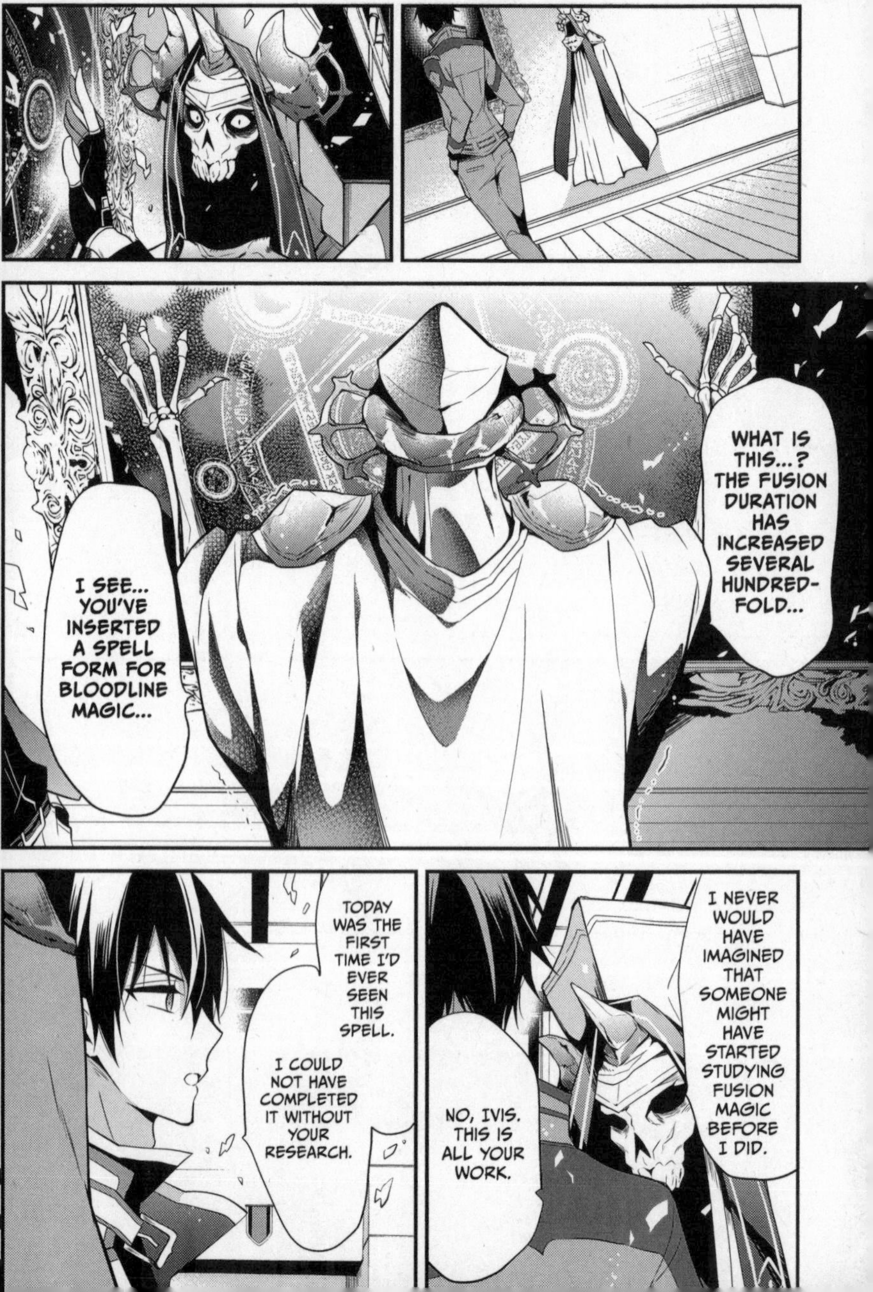
WHAT IS THIS...? THE FUSION DURATION HAS INCREASED SEVERAL HUNDRED-FOLD...
I SEE... YOU'VE INSERTED A SPELL FORM FOR BLOODLINE MAGIC...
I NEVER WOULD HAVE IMAGINED THAT SOMEONE MIGHT HAVE STARTED STUDYING FUSION MAGIC BEFORE I DID.
NO, IVIS. THIS IS ALL YOUR WORK.
TODAY WAS THE FIRST TIME I'D EVER SEEN THIS SPELL.
I COULD NOT HAVE COMPLETED IT WITHOUT YOUR RESEARCH.

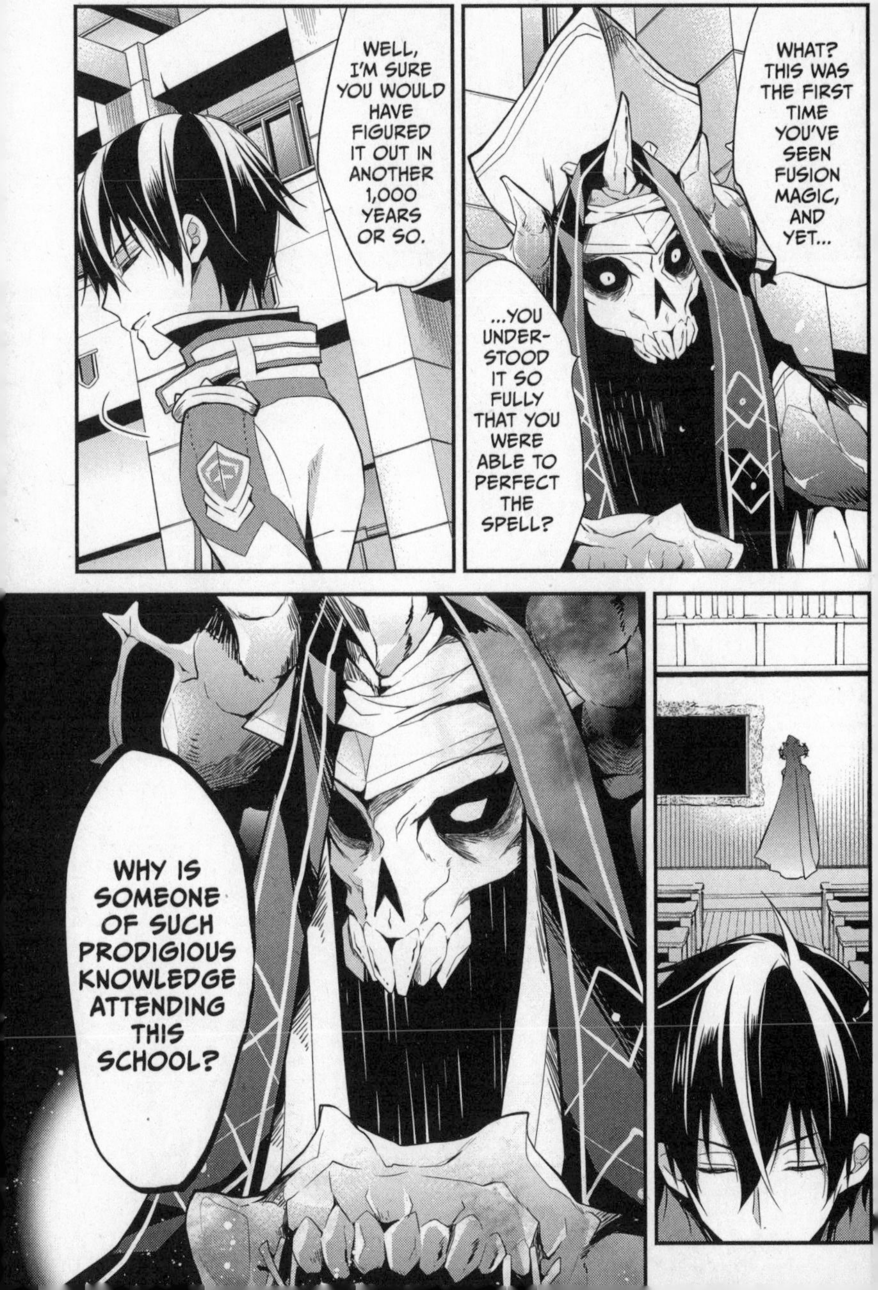
WHAT? THIS WAS THE FIRST TIME YOU'VE SEEN FUSION MAGIC, AND YET...
...YOU UNDERSTOOD IT SO FULLY THAT YOU WERE ABLE TO PERFECT THE SPELL?
WELL, I'M SURE YOU WOULD HAVE FIGURED IT OUT IN ANOTHER 1,000 YEARS OR SO.
WHY IS SOMEONE OF SUCH PRODIGIOUS KNOWLEDGE ATTENDING THIS SCHOOL?

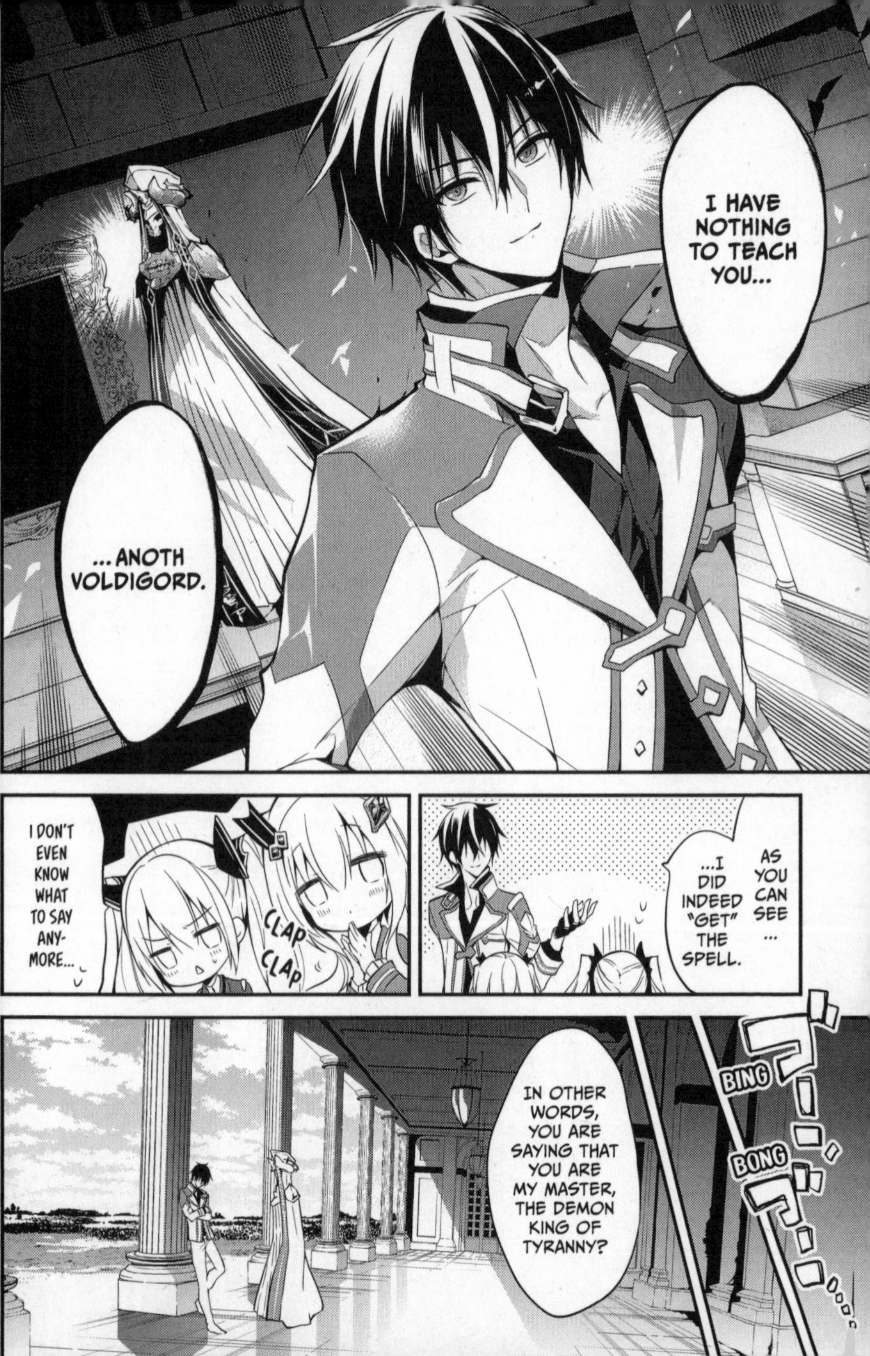

I HAVE NOTHING TO TEACH YOU...
...ANOTH VOLDIGORD.
AS YOU CAN SEE...
...I DID INDEED "GET" THE SPELL.
I DON'T EVEN KNOW WHAT TO SAY ANY-MORE...
CLAP CLAP
BING
BONG
IN OTHER WORDS, YOU ARE SAYING THAT YOU ARE MY MASTER, THE DEMON KING OF TYRANNY?

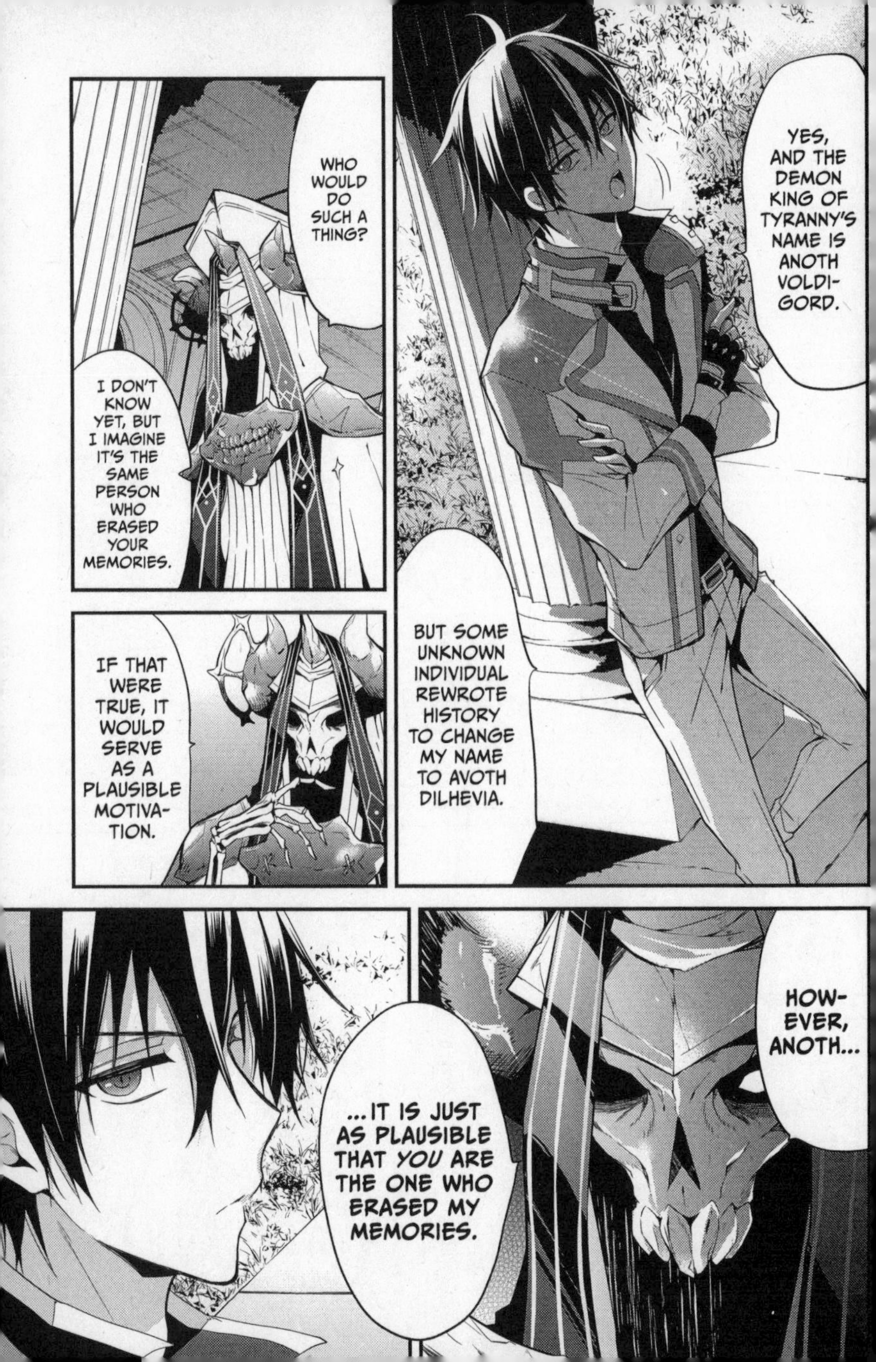
YES, AND THE DEMON KING OF TYRANNY'S NAME IS ANOTH VOLDIGORD.
BUT SOME UNKNOWN INDIVIDUAL REWROTE HISTORY TO CHANGE MY NAME TO AVOTH DILHEVIA.
WHO WOULD DO SUCH A THING?
I DON'T KNOW YET, BUT I IMAGINE IT'S THE SAME PERSON WHO ERASED YOUR MEMORIES.
IF THAT WERE TRUE, IT WOULD SERVE AS A PLAUSIBLE MOTIVATION.
HOWEVER, ANOTH...
...IT IS JUST AS PLAUSIBLE THAT *YOU* ARE THE ONE WHO ERASED MY MEMORIES.

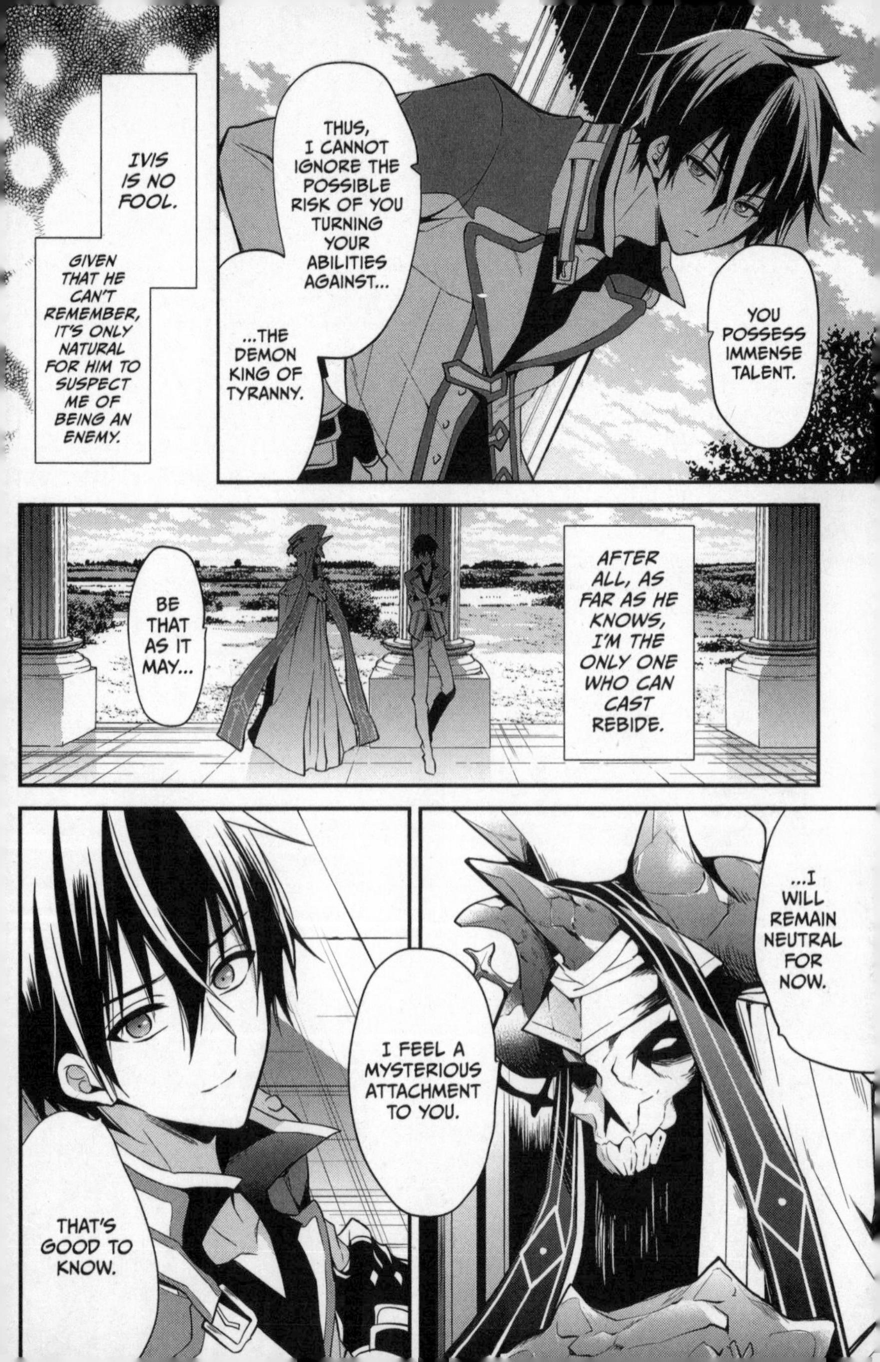
YOU POSSESS IMMENSE TALENT.
THUS, I CANNOT IGNORE THE POSSIBLE RISK OF YOU TURNING YOUR ABILITIES AGAINST...
...THE DEMON KING OF TYRANNY.
IVIS IS NO FOOL.
GIVEN THAT HE CAN'T REMEMBER, IT'S ONLY NATURAL FOR HIM TO SUSPECT ME OF BEING AN ENEMY.
AFTER ALL, AS FAR AS HE KNOWS, I'M THE ONLY ONE WHO CAN CAST REBIDE.
BE THAT AS IT MAY...
...I WILL REMAIN NEUTRAL FOR NOW.
I FEEL A MYSTERIOUS ATTACHMENT TO YOU.
THAT'S GOOD TO KNOW.

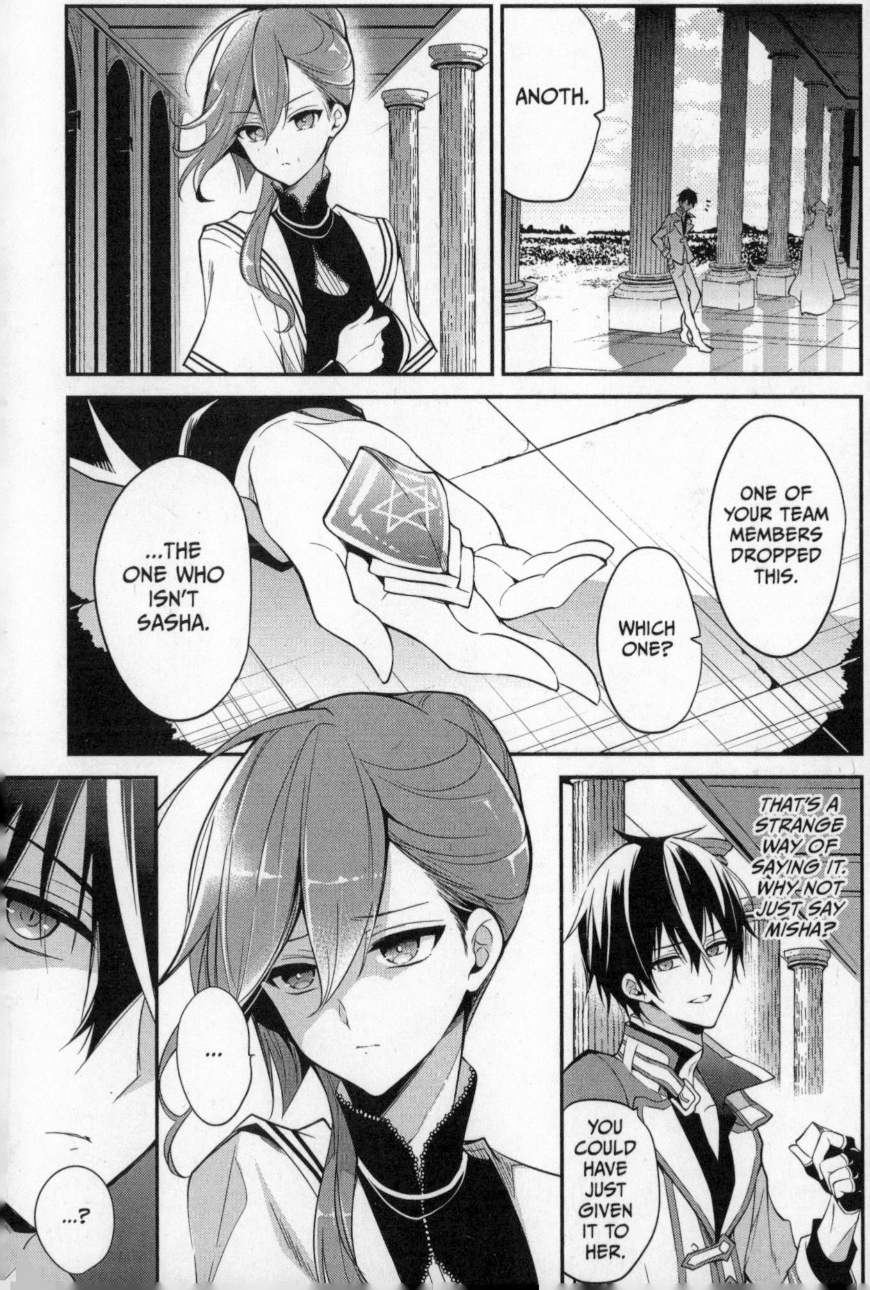
ANOTH.
ONE OF YOUR TEAM MEMBERS DROPPED THIS.
WHICH ONE?
...THE ONE WHO ISN'T SASHA.
THAT'S A STRANGE WAY OF SAYING IT. WHY NOT JUST SAY MISHA?
YOU COULD HAVE JUST GIVEN IT TO HER.
...
...?

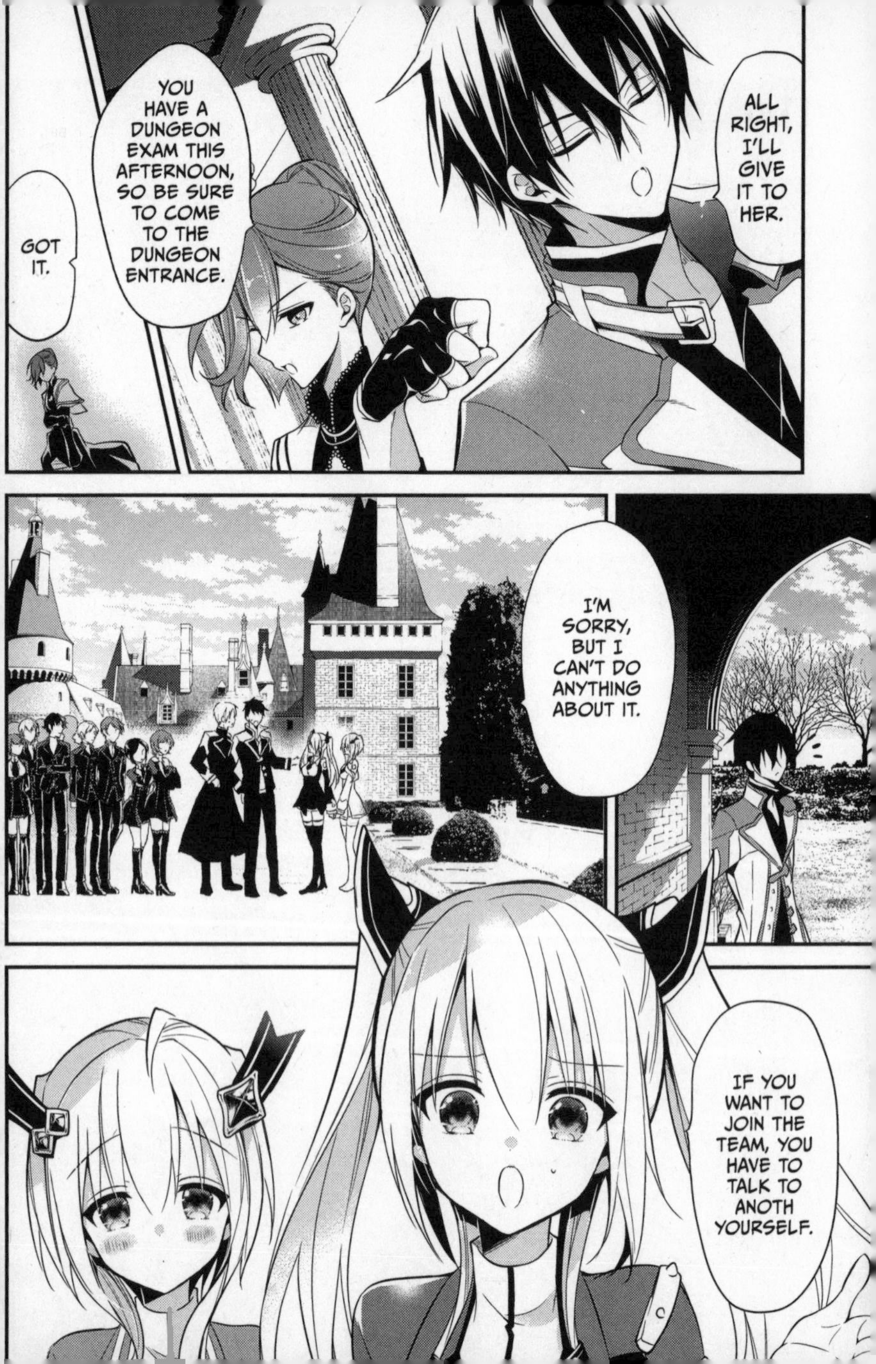
ALL RIGHT, I'LL GIVE IT TO HER.
YOU HAVE A DUNGEON EXAM THIS AFTERNOON, SO BE SURE TO COME TO THE DUNGEON ENTRANCE.
GOT IT.
I'M SORRY, BUT I CAN'T DO ANYTHING ABOUT IT.
IF YOU WANT TO JOIN THE TEAM, YOU HAVE TO TALK TO ANOTH YOURSELF.

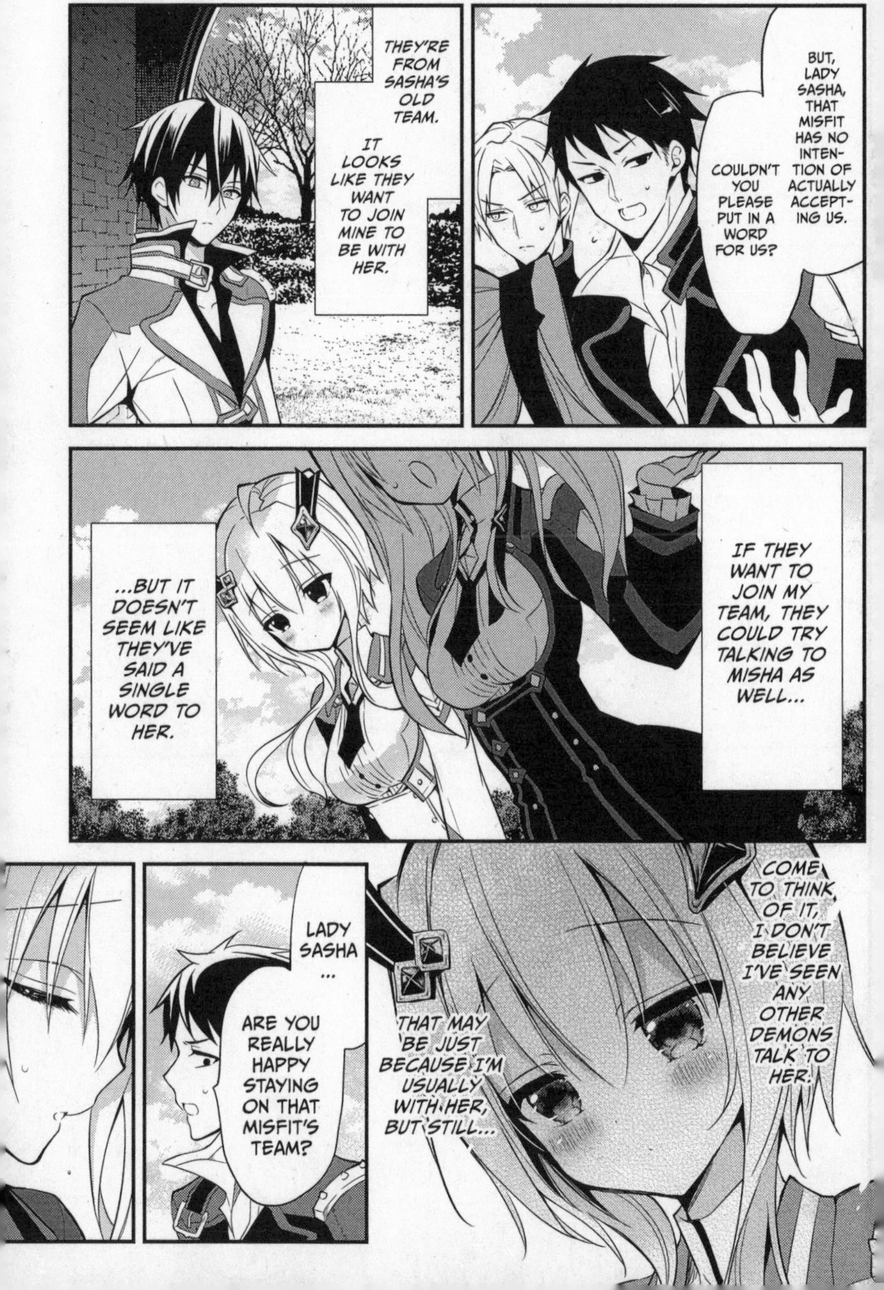
BUT, LADY SASHA, THAT MISFIT HAS NO INTENTION OF ACTUALLY ACCEPTING US.
COULDN'T YOU PLEASE PUT IN A WORD FOR US?
THEY'RE FROM SASHA'S OLD TEAM.
IT LOOKS LIKE THEY WANT TO JOIN MINE TO BE WITH HER.
IF THEY WANT TO JOIN MY TEAM, THEY COULD TRY TALKING TO MISHA AS WELL...
...BUT IT DOESN'T SEEM LIKE THEY'VE SAID A SINGLE WORD TO HER.
COME TO THINK OF IT, I DON'T BELIEVE I'VE SEEN ANY OTHER DEMONS TALK TO HER.
THAT MAY BE JUST BECAUSE I'M USUALLY WITH HER, BUT STILL...
LADY SASHA ...
ARE YOU REALLY HAPPY STAYING ON THAT MISFIT'S TEAM?

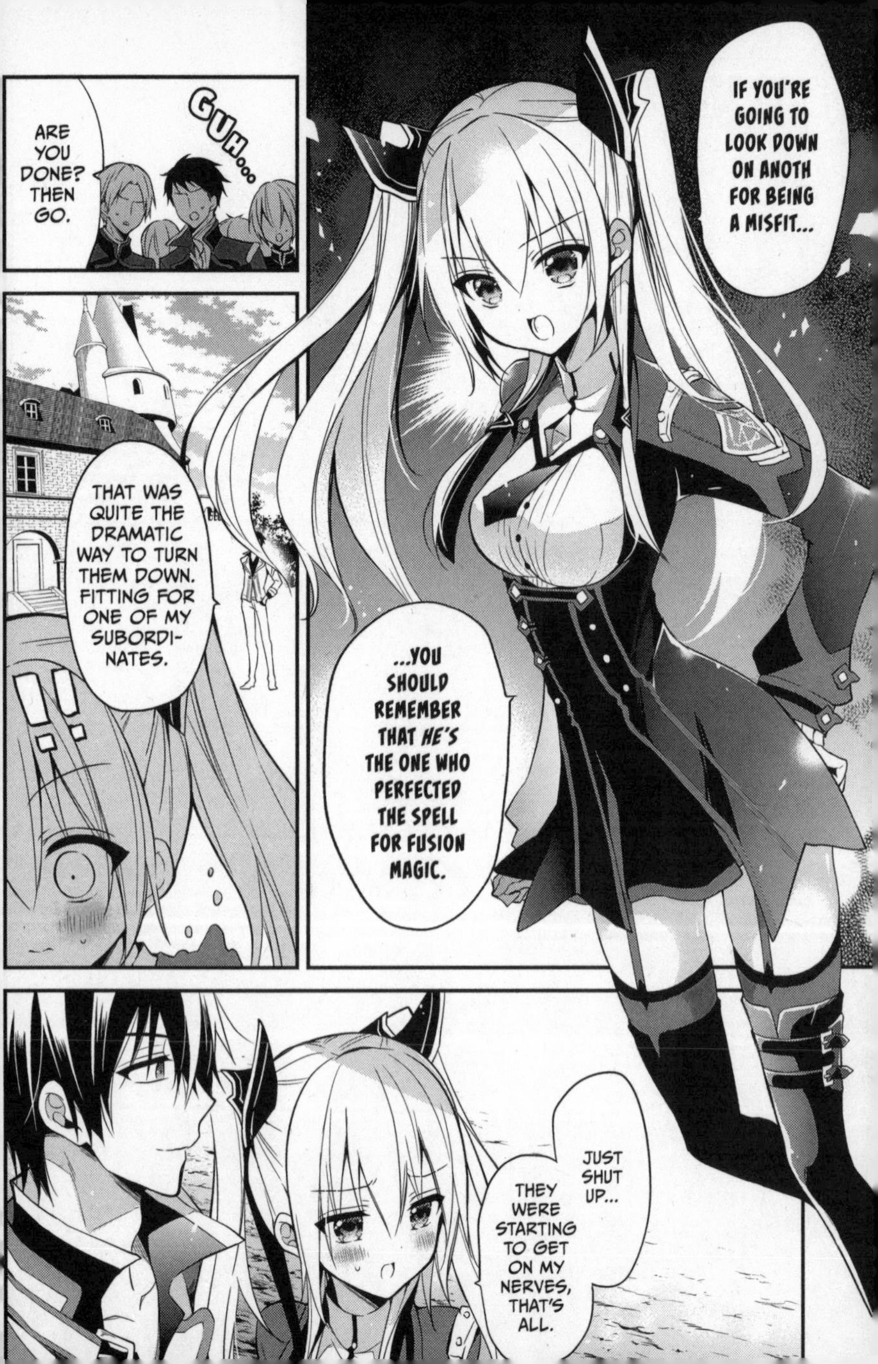
IF YOU'RE GOING TO LOOK DOWN ON ANOTH FOR BEING A MISFIT...
...YOU SHOULD REMEMBER THAT *HE'S* THE ONE WHO PERFECTED THE SPELL FOR FUSION MAGIC.
GUH...
ARE YOU DONE? THEN GO.
THAT WAS QUITE THE DRAMATIC WAY TO TURN THEM DOWN. FITTING FOR ONE OF MY SUBORDI-NATES.
!!
JUST SHUT UP...
THEY WERE STARTING TO GET ON MY NERVES, THAT'S ALL.

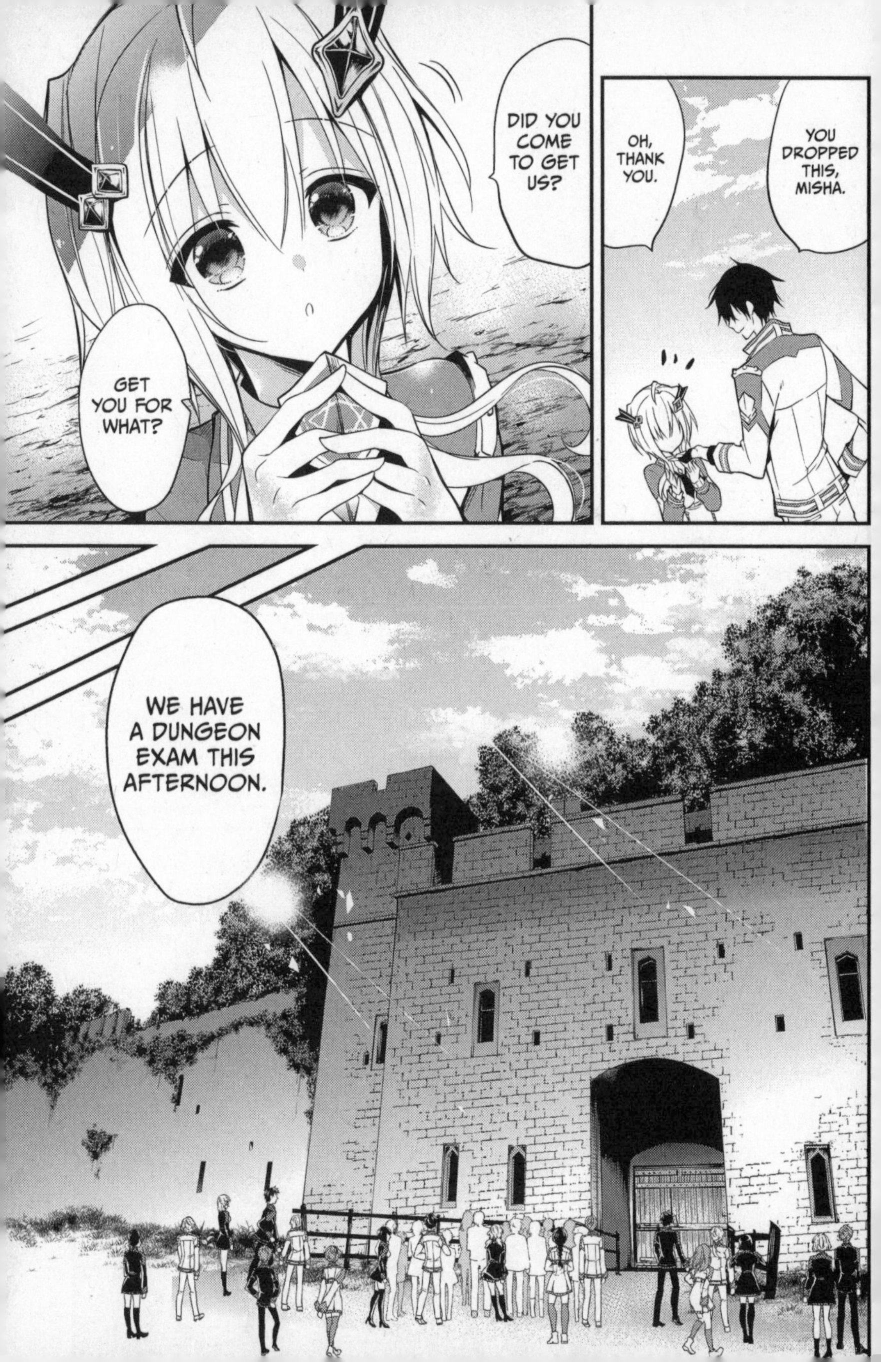
YOU DROPPED THIS, MISHA.
OH, THANK YOU.
DID YOU COME TO GET US?
GET YOU FOR WHAT?
WE HAVE A DUNGEON EXAM THIS AFTERNOON.

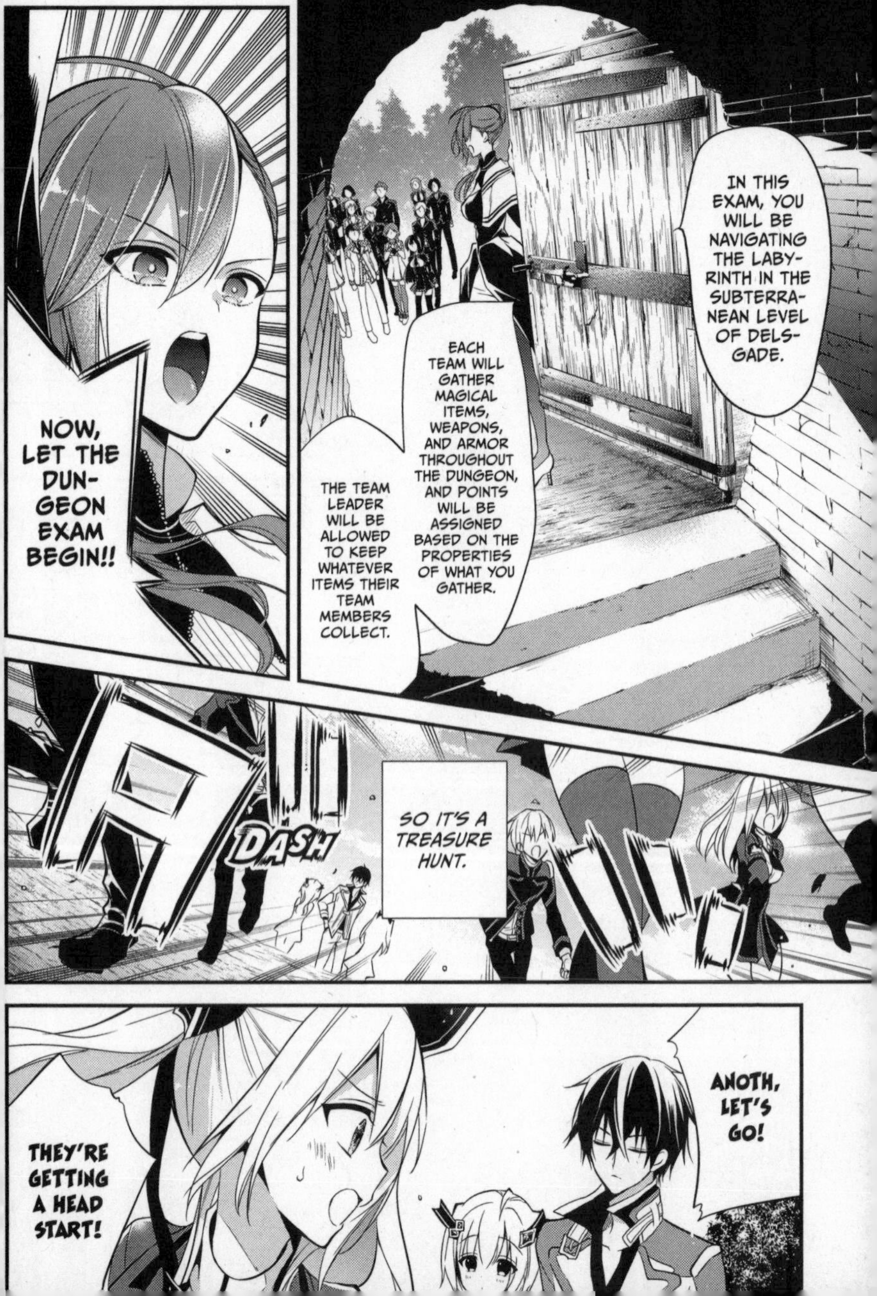
IN THIS EXAM, YOU WILL BE NAVIGATING THE LABY-RINTH IN THE SUBTERRA-NEAN LEVEL OF DELS-GADE.
EACH TEAM WILL GATHER MAGICAL ITEMS, WEAPONS, AND ARMOR THROUGHOUT THE DUNGEON, AND POINTS WILL BE ASSIGNED BASED ON THE PROPERTIES OF WHAT YOU GATHER.
THE TEAM LEADER WILL BE ALLOWED TO KEEP WHATEVER ITEMS THEIR TEAM MEMBERS COLLECT.
NOW, LET THE DUN-GEON EXAM BEGIN!!
SO IT'S A TREASURE HUNT.
DASH
ANOTH, LET'S GO!
THEY'RE GETTING A HEAD START!

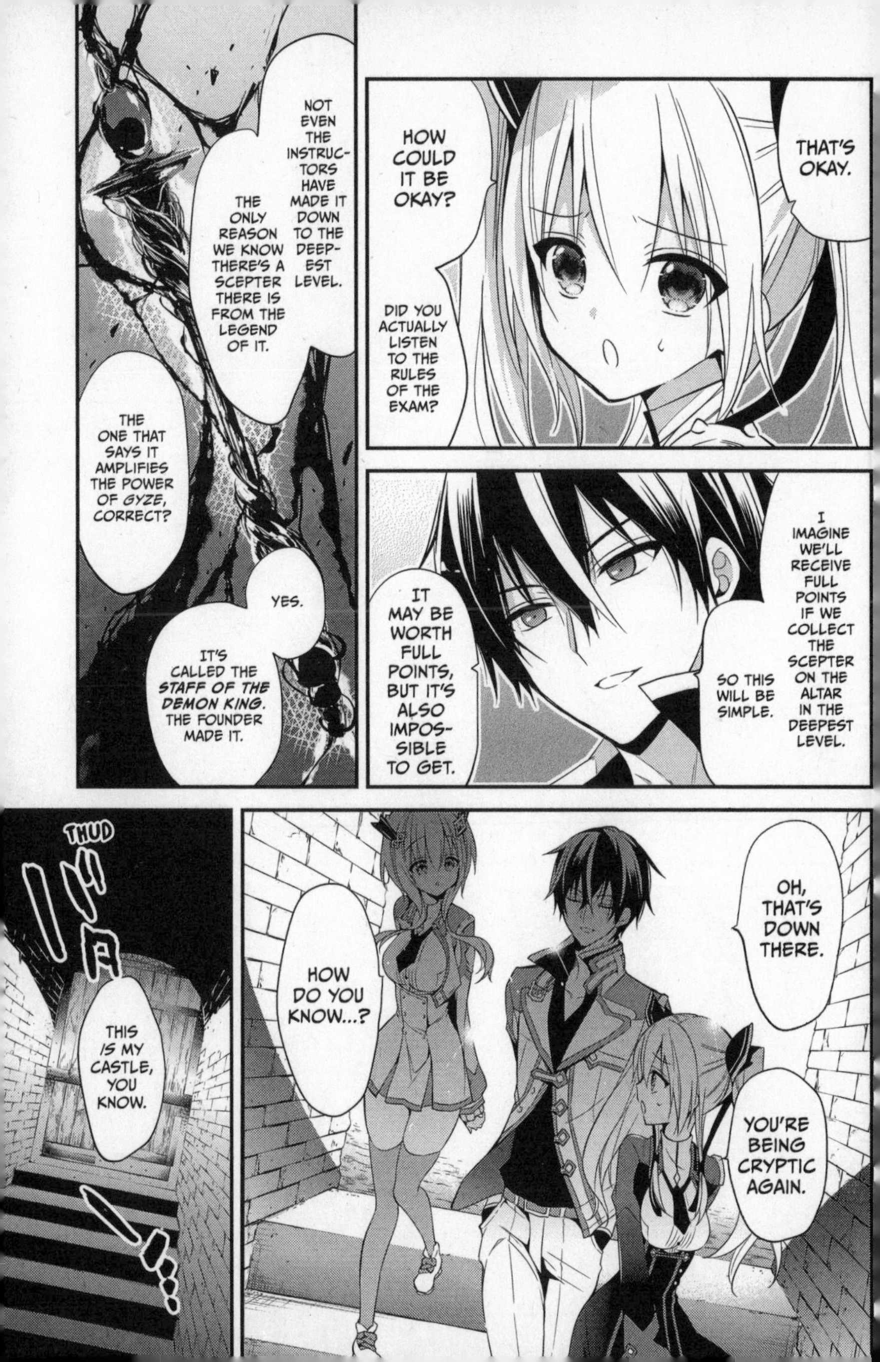
THAT'S OKAY.
HOW COULD IT BE OKAY?
DID YOU ACTUALLY LISTEN TO THE RULES OF THE EXAM?
I IMAGINE WE'LL RECEIVE FULL POINTS IF WE COLLECT THE SCEPTER ON THE ALTAR IN THE DEEPEST LEVEL.
SO THIS WILL BE SIMPLE.
IT MAY BE WORTH FULL POINTS, BUT IT'S ALSO IMPOSSIBLE TO GET.
NOT EVEN THE INSTRUCTORS HAVE MADE IT DOWN TO THE DEEPEST LEVEL.
THE ONLY REASON WE KNOW THERE'S A SCEPTER THERE IS FROM THE LEGEND OF IT.
THE ONE THAT SAYS IT AMPLIFIES THE POWER OF *GYZE*, CORRECT?
YES.
IT'S CALLED THE ***STAFF OF THE DEMON KING***. THE FOUNDER MADE IT.
OH, THAT'S DOWN THERE.
YOU'RE BEING CRYPTIC AGAIN.
HOW DO YOU KNOW...?
THUD
THIS *IS* MY CASTLE, YOU KNOW.

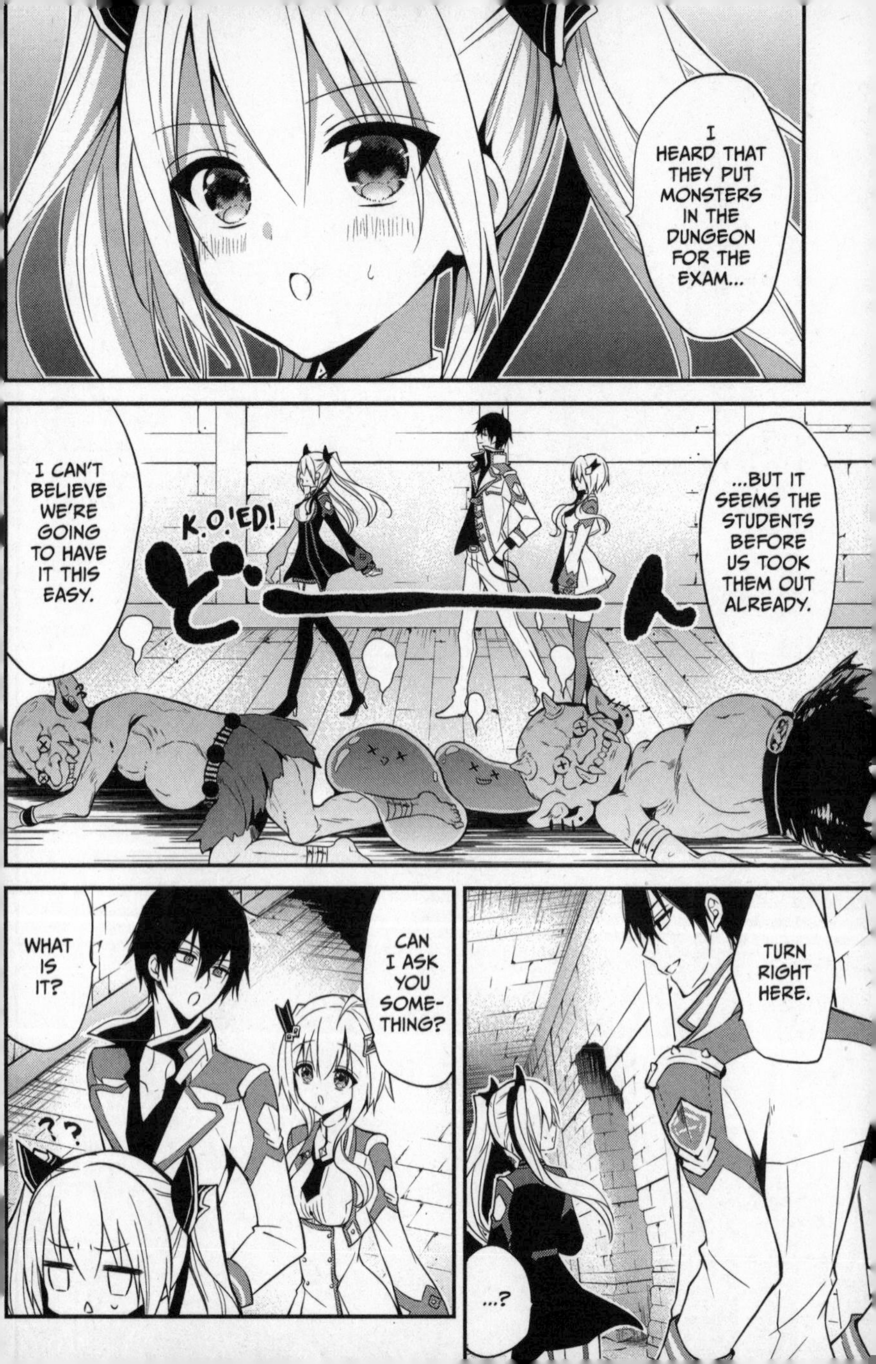
I HEARD THAT THEY PUT MONSTERS IN THE DUNGEON FOR THE EXAM...
...BUT IT SEEMS THE STUDENTS BEFORE US TOOK THEM OUT ALREADY.
どーん
K.O.'ED!
I CAN'T BELIEVE WE'RE GOING TO HAVE IT THIS EASY.
TURN RIGHT HERE.
...?
CAN I ASK YOU SOME-THING?
WHAT IS IT?
??

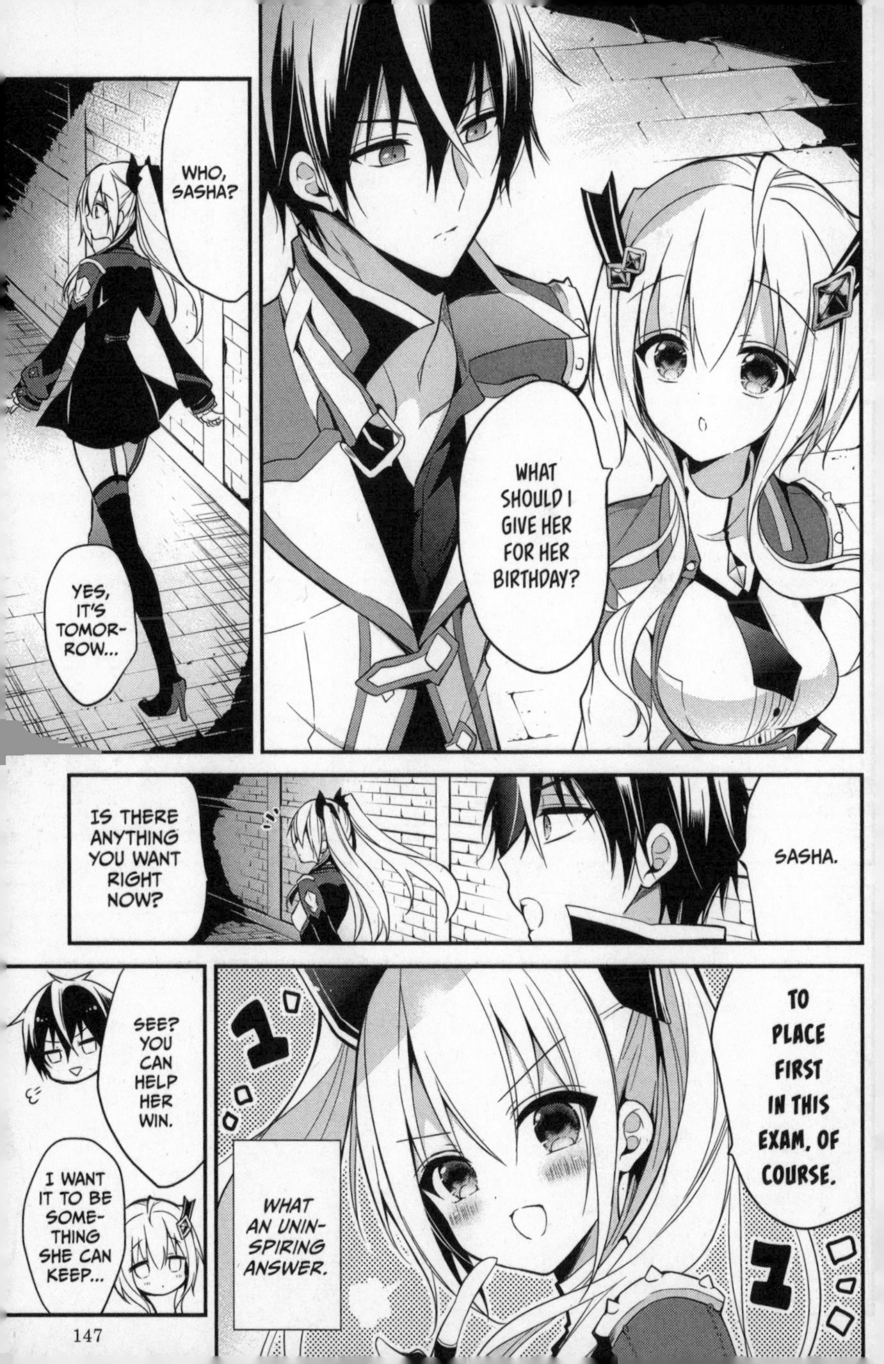
WHAT SHOULD I GIVE HER FOR HER BIRTHDAY?
WHO, SASHA?
YES, IT'S TOMOR-ROW...
SASHA.
IS THERE ANYTHING YOU WANT RIGHT NOW?
TO PLACE FIRST IN THIS EXAM, OF COURSE.
WHAT AN UNIN-SPIRING ANSWER.
SEE? YOU CAN HELP HER WIN.
I WANT IT TO BE SOME-THING SHE CAN KEEP...

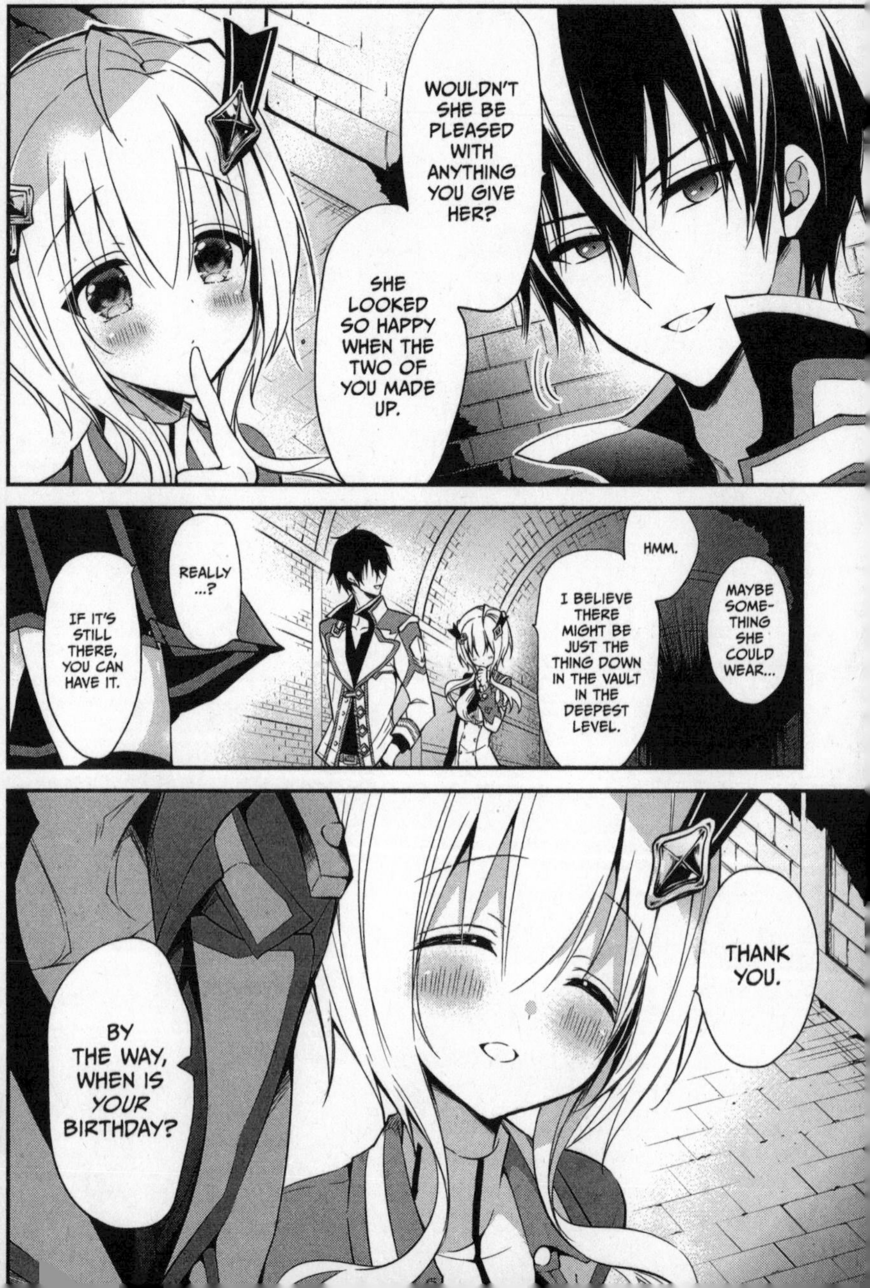
WOULDN'T SHE BE PLEASED WITH ANYTHING YOU GIVE HER?
SHE LOOKED SO HAPPY WHEN THE TWO OF YOU MADE UP.
HMM.
MAYBE SOME-THING SHE COULD WEAR...
I BELIEVE THERE MIGHT BE JUST THE THING DOWN IN THE VAULT IN THE DEEPEST LEVEL.
REALLY ...?
IF IT'S STILL THERE, YOU CAN HAVE IT.
THANK YOU.
BY THE WAY, WHEN IS *YOUR* BIRTHDAY?

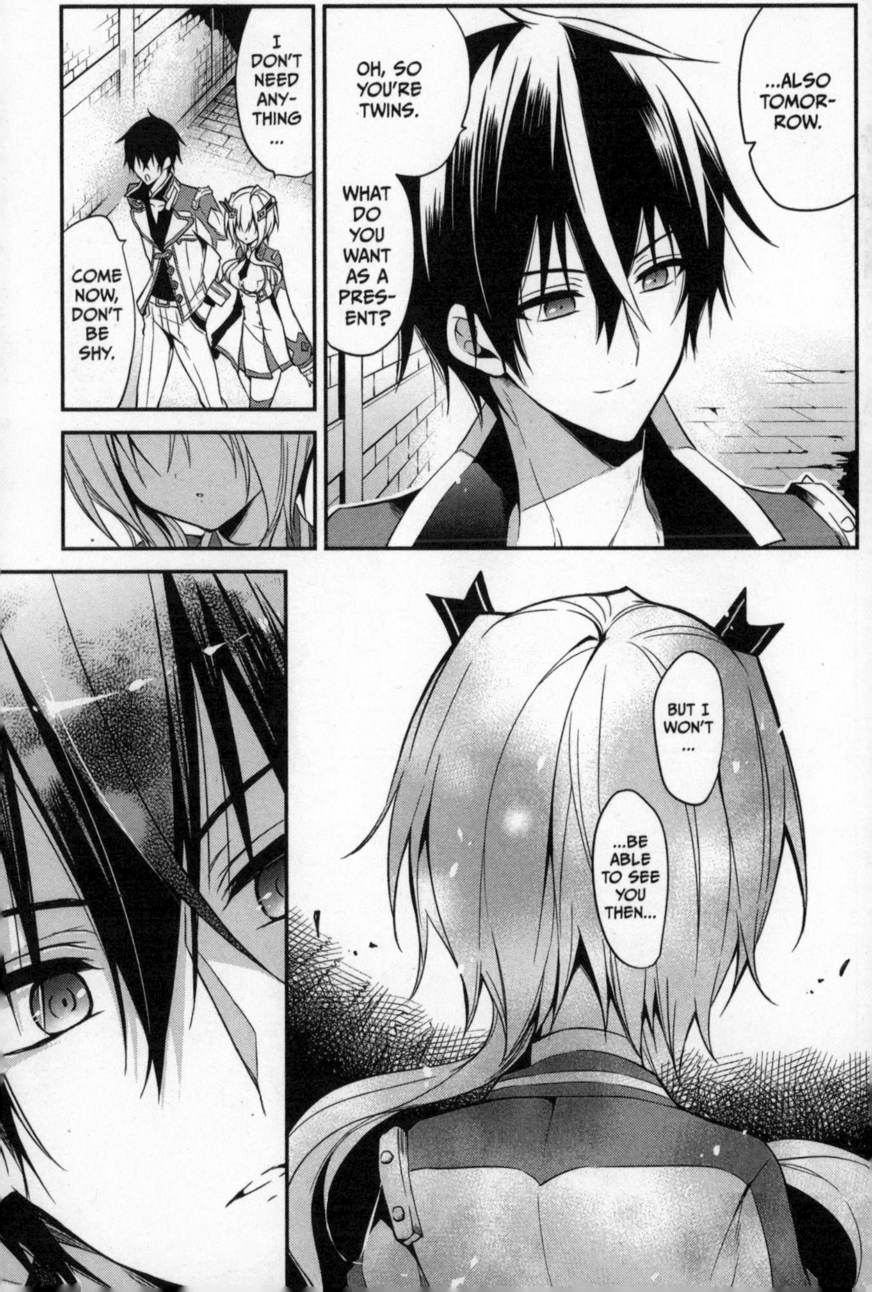
...ALSO TOMORROW.
OH, SO YOU'RE TWINS.
WHAT DO YOU WANT AS A PRESENT?
I DON'T NEED ANYTHING...
COME NOW, DON'T BE SHY.
BUT I WON'T...
...BE ABLE TO SEE YOU THEN...

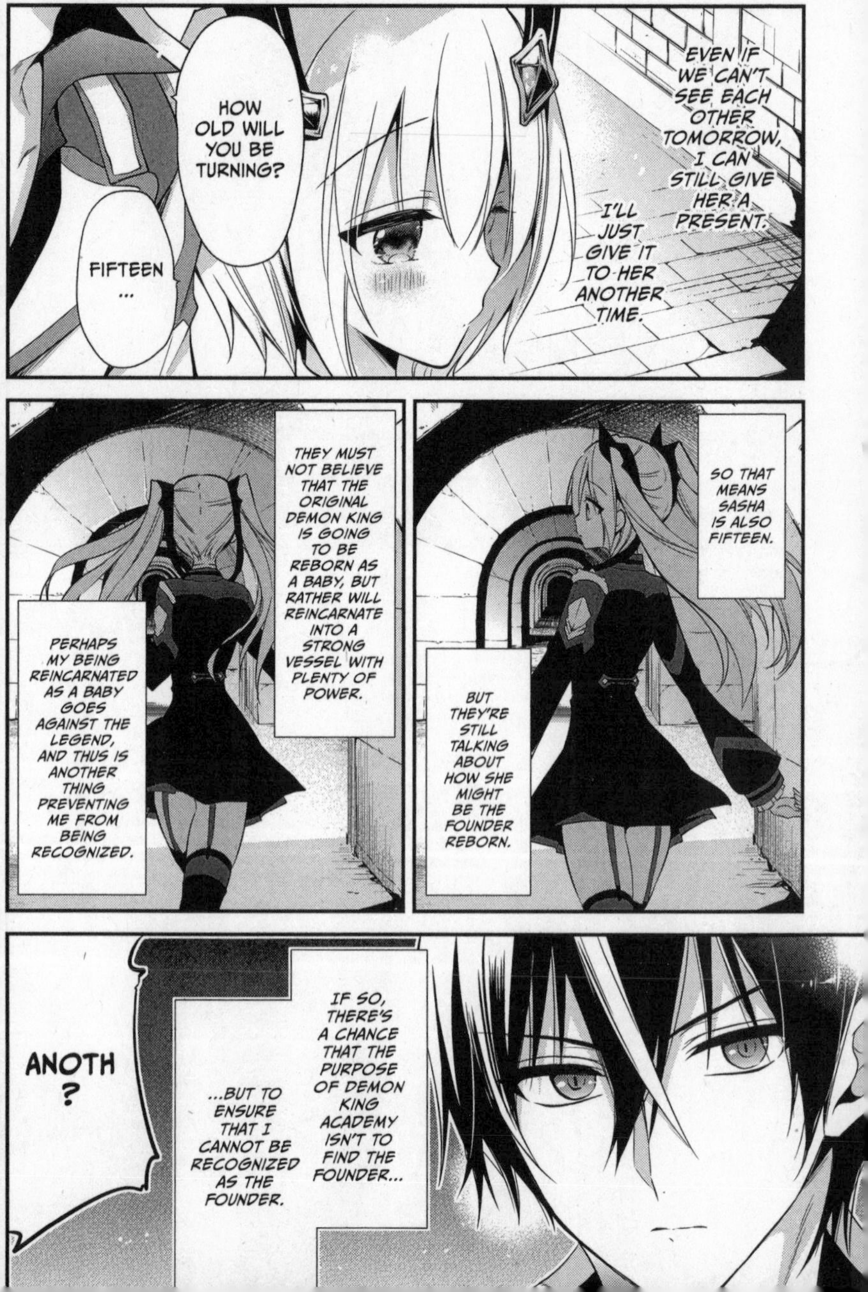
EVEN IF WE CAN'T SEE EACH OTHER TOMORROW, I CAN STILL GIVE HER A PRESENT.
I'LL JUST GIVE IT TO HER ANOTHER TIME.
HOW OLD WILL YOU BE TURNING?
FIFTEEN ...
SO THAT MEANS SASHA IS ALSO FIFTEEN.
BUT THEY'RE STILL TALKING ABOUT HOW SHE MIGHT BE THE FOUNDER REBORN.
THEY MUST NOT BELIEVE THAT THE ORIGINAL DEMON KING IS GOING TO BE REBORN AS A BABY, BUT RATHER WILL REINCARNATE INTO A STRONG VESSEL WITH PLENTY OF POWER.
PERHAPS MY BEING REINCARNATED AS A BABY GOES AGAINST THE LEGEND, AND THUS IS ANOTHER THING PREVENTING ME FROM BEING RECOGNIZED.
IF SO, THERE'S A CHANCE THAT THE PURPOSE OF DEMON KING ACADEMY ISN'T TO FIND THE FOUNDER...
...BUT TO ENSURE THAT I CANNOT BE RECOGNIZED AS THE FOUNDER.
ANOTH ?

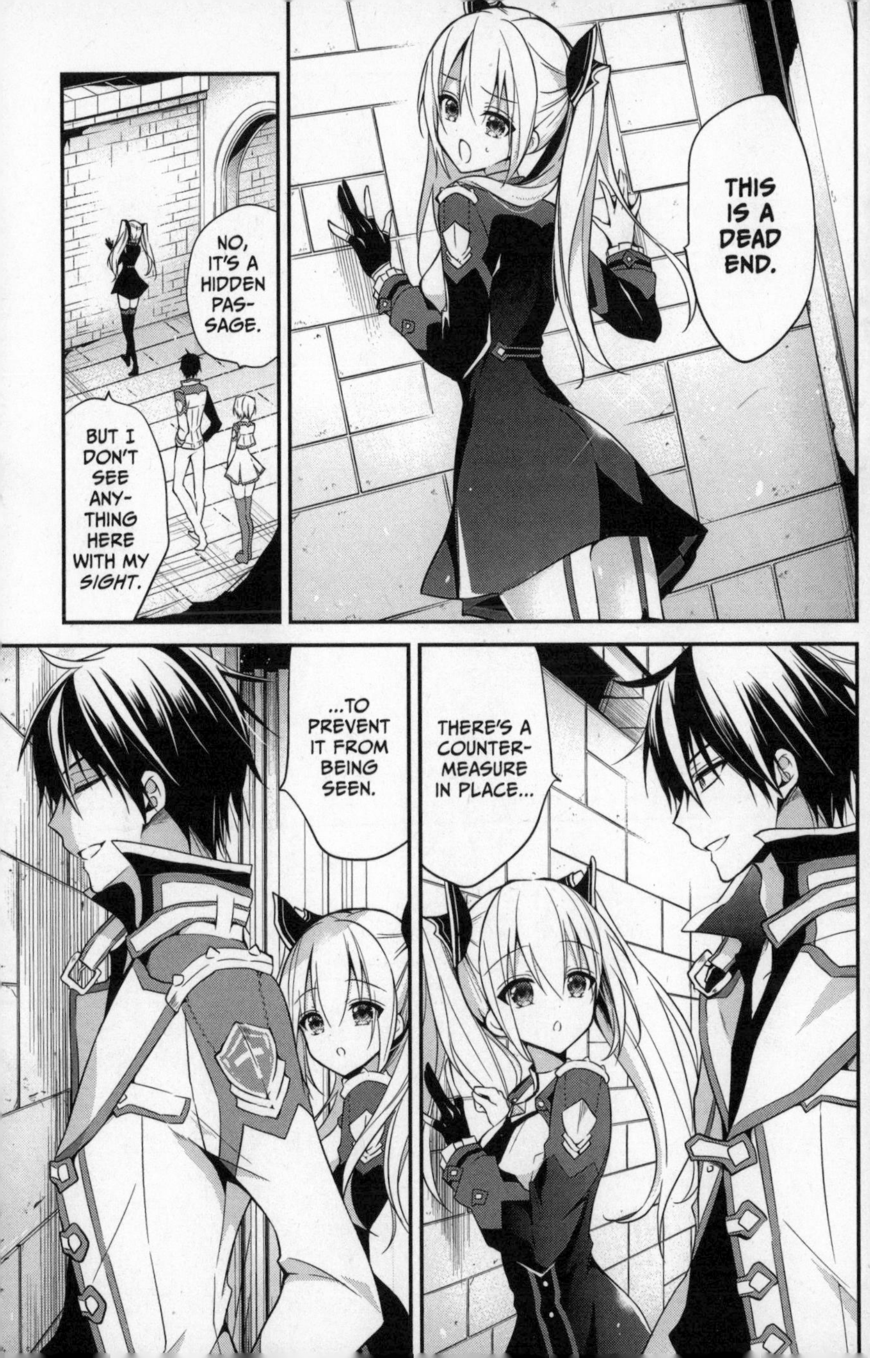
THIS IS A DEAD END.
NO, IT'S A HIDDEN PASSAGE.
BUT I DON'T SEE ANYTHING HERE WITH MY *SIGHT*.
THERE'S A COUNTERMEASURE IN PLACE...
...TO PREVENT IT FROM BEING SEEN.

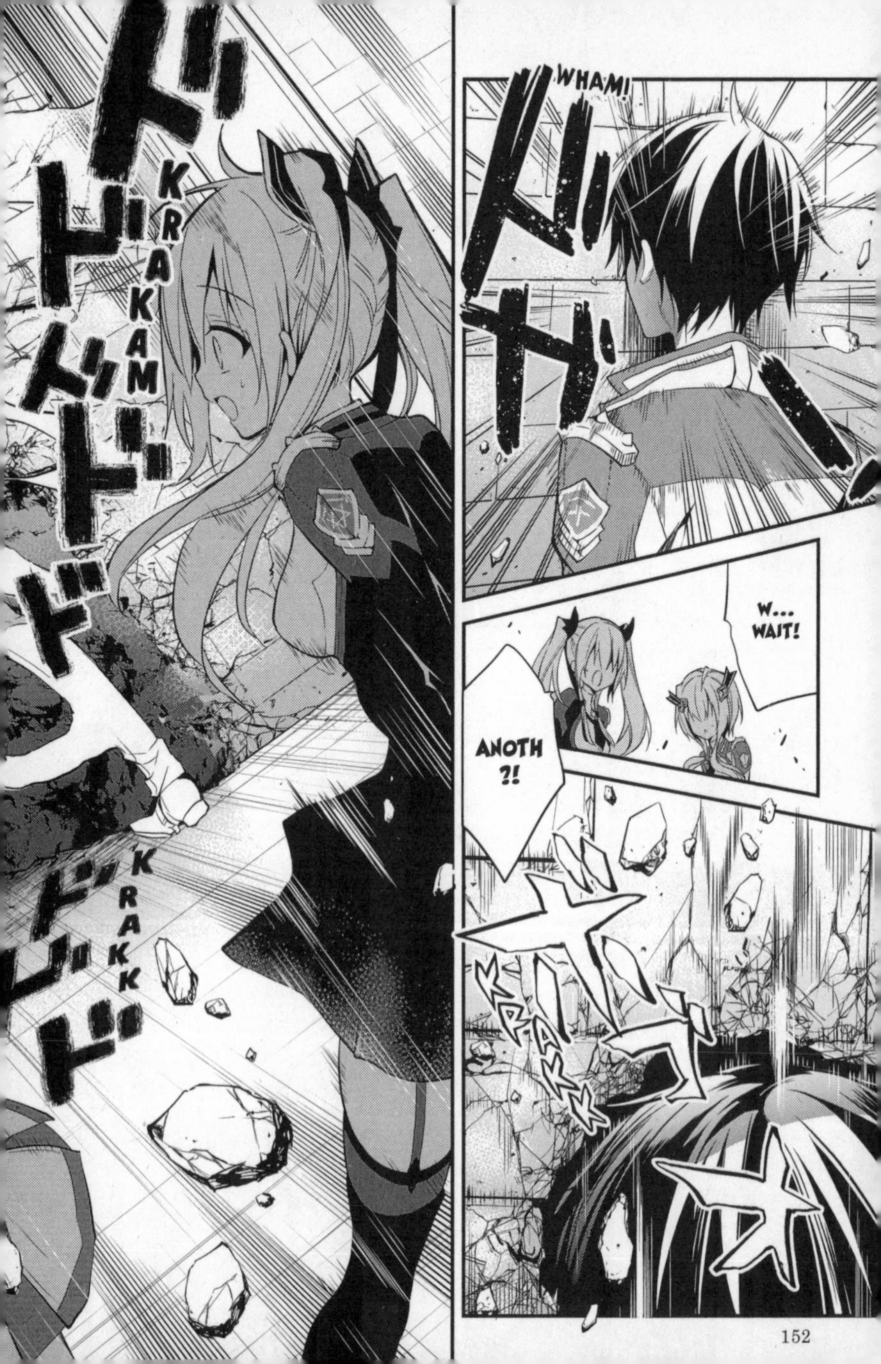
WHAM!
W... WAIT!
ANOTH ?!
KRAKK
KRAKAM
KRAKK

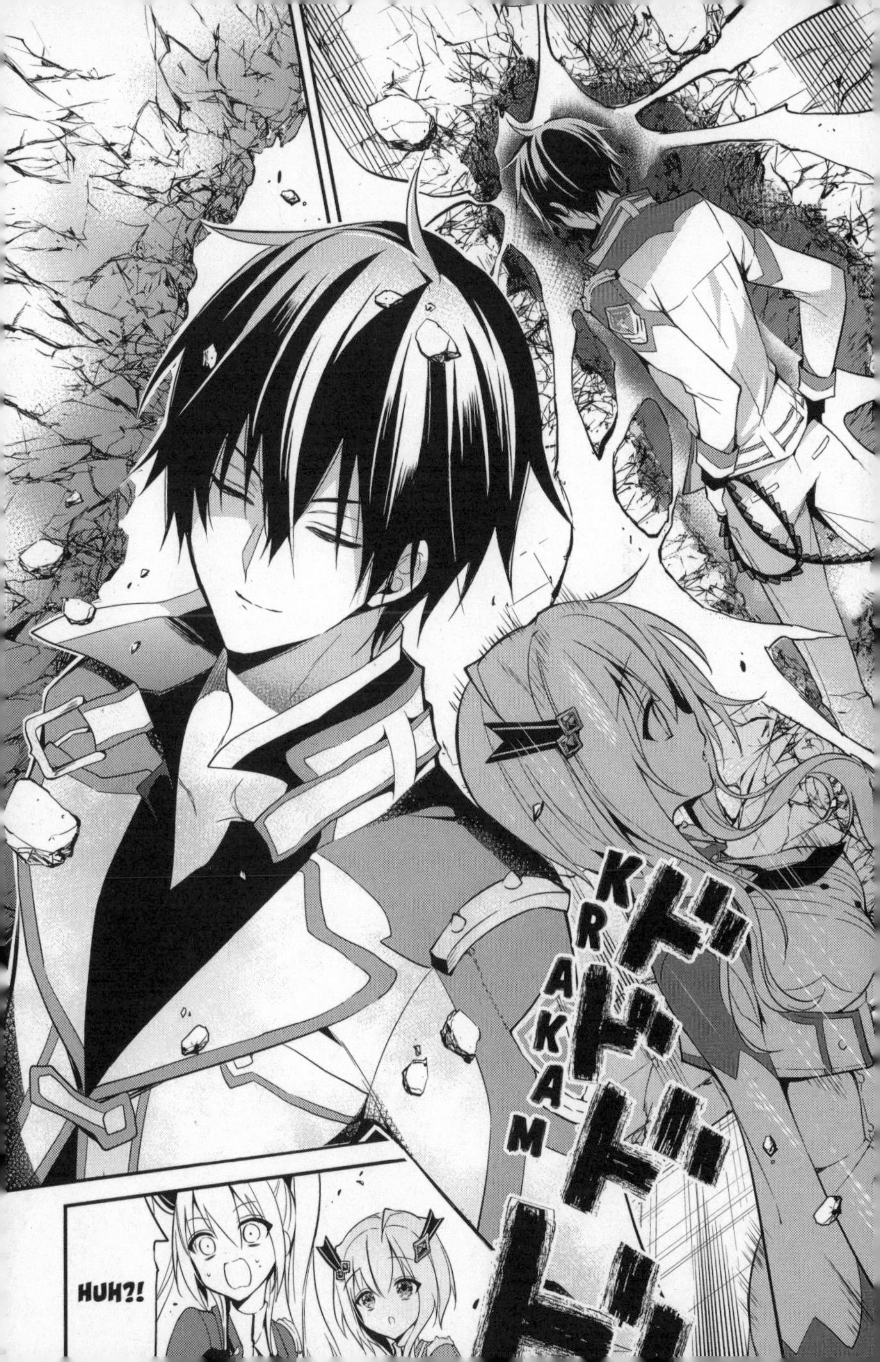
KRAKAM
HUH?!

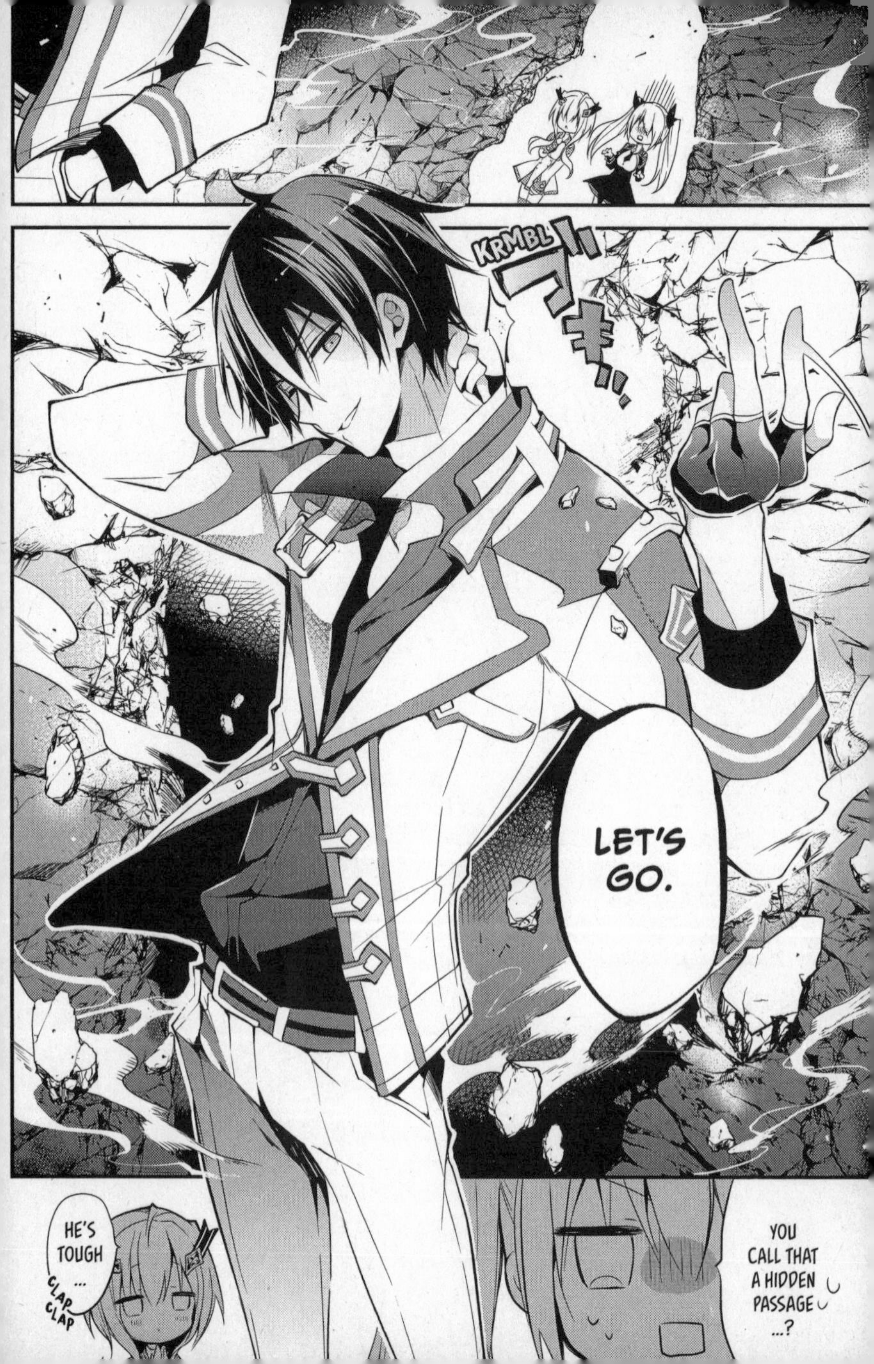
KRMBL
LET'S GO.
YOU CALL THAT A HIDDEN PASSAGE ...?
HE'S TOUGH ...
CLAP CLAP

The Misfit of Demon King Academy

HISTORY'S STRONGEST DEMON KING REINCARNATES
AND GOES TO SCHOOL WITH HIS DESCENDANTS

The Misfit of Demon King Academy

HISTORY'S STRONGEST DEMON KING REINCARNATES AND GOES TO SCHOOL WITH HIS DESCENDANTS

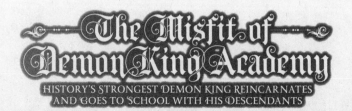

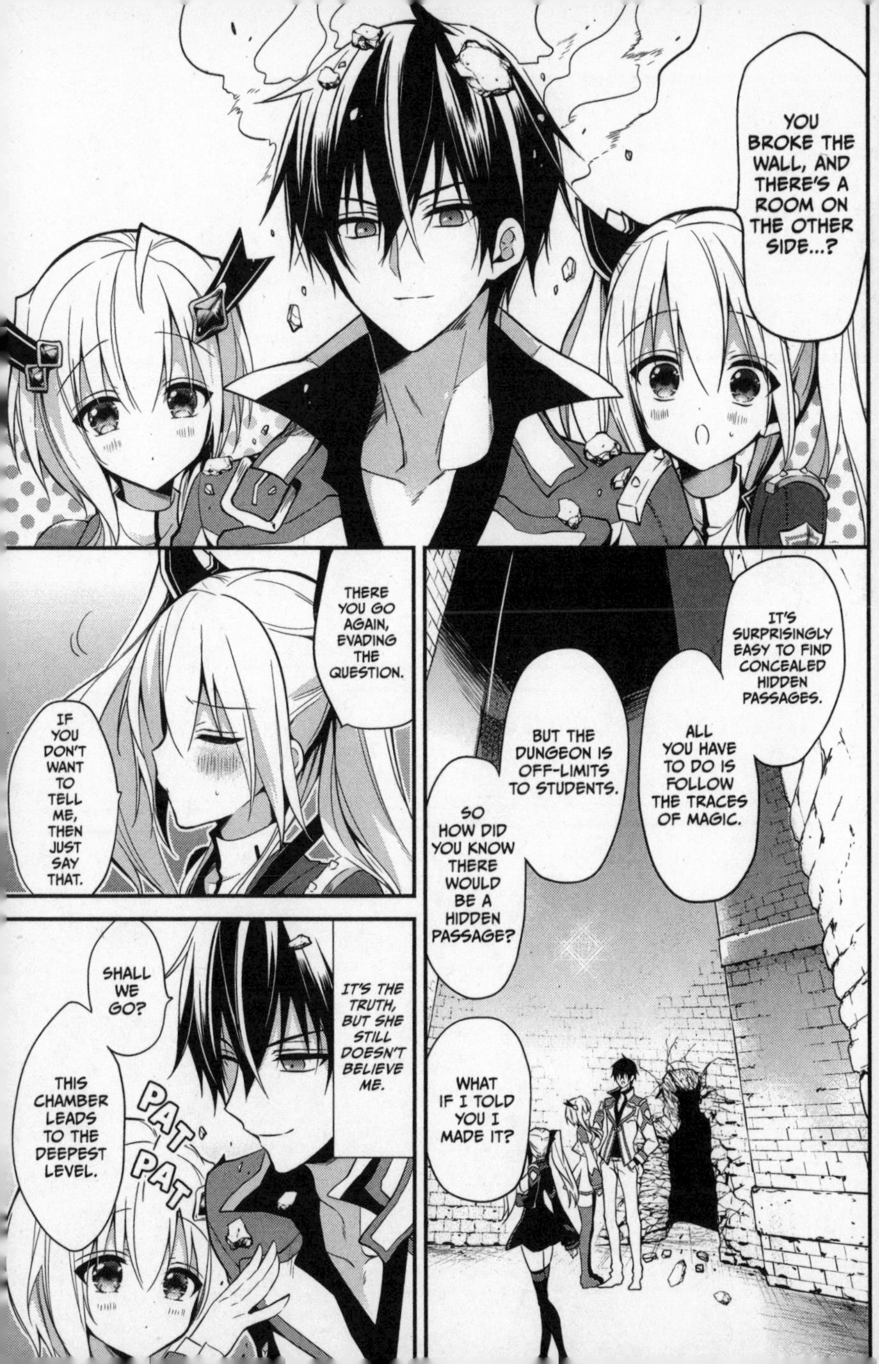
YOU BROKE THE WALL, AND THERE'S A ROOM ON THE OTHER SIDE...?
IT'S SURPRISINGLY EASY TO FIND CONCEALED HIDDEN PASSAGES.
ALL YOU HAVE TO DO IS FOLLOW THE TRACES OF MAGIC.
BUT THE DUNGEON IS OFF-LIMITS TO STUDENTS.
SO HOW DID YOU KNOW THERE WOULD BE A HIDDEN PASSAGE?
WHAT IF I TOLD YOU I MADE IT?
THERE YOU GO AGAIN, EVADING THE QUESTION.
IF YOU DON'T WANT TO TELL ME, THEN JUST SAY THAT.
IT'S THE TRUTH, BUT SHE STILL DOESN'T BELIEVE ME.
SHALL WE GO?
PAT PAT
THIS CHAMBER LEADS TO THE DEEPEST LEVEL.

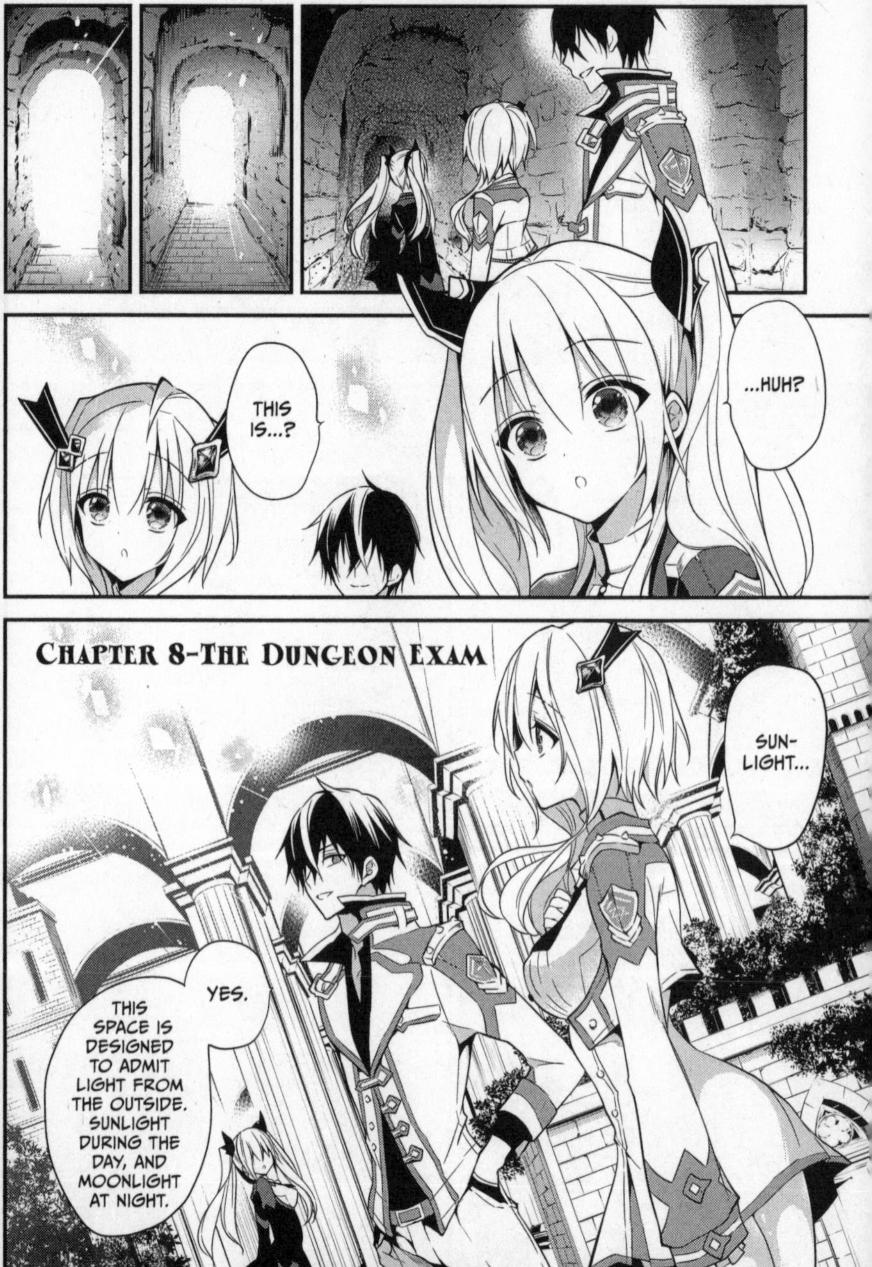
...HUH?
THIS IS...?
CHAPTER 8–THE DUNGEON EXAM
SUN-LIGHT...
YES.
THIS SPACE IS DESIGNED TO ADMIT LIGHT FROM THE OUTSIDE. SUNLIGHT DURING THE DAY, AND MOONLIGHT AT NIGHT.

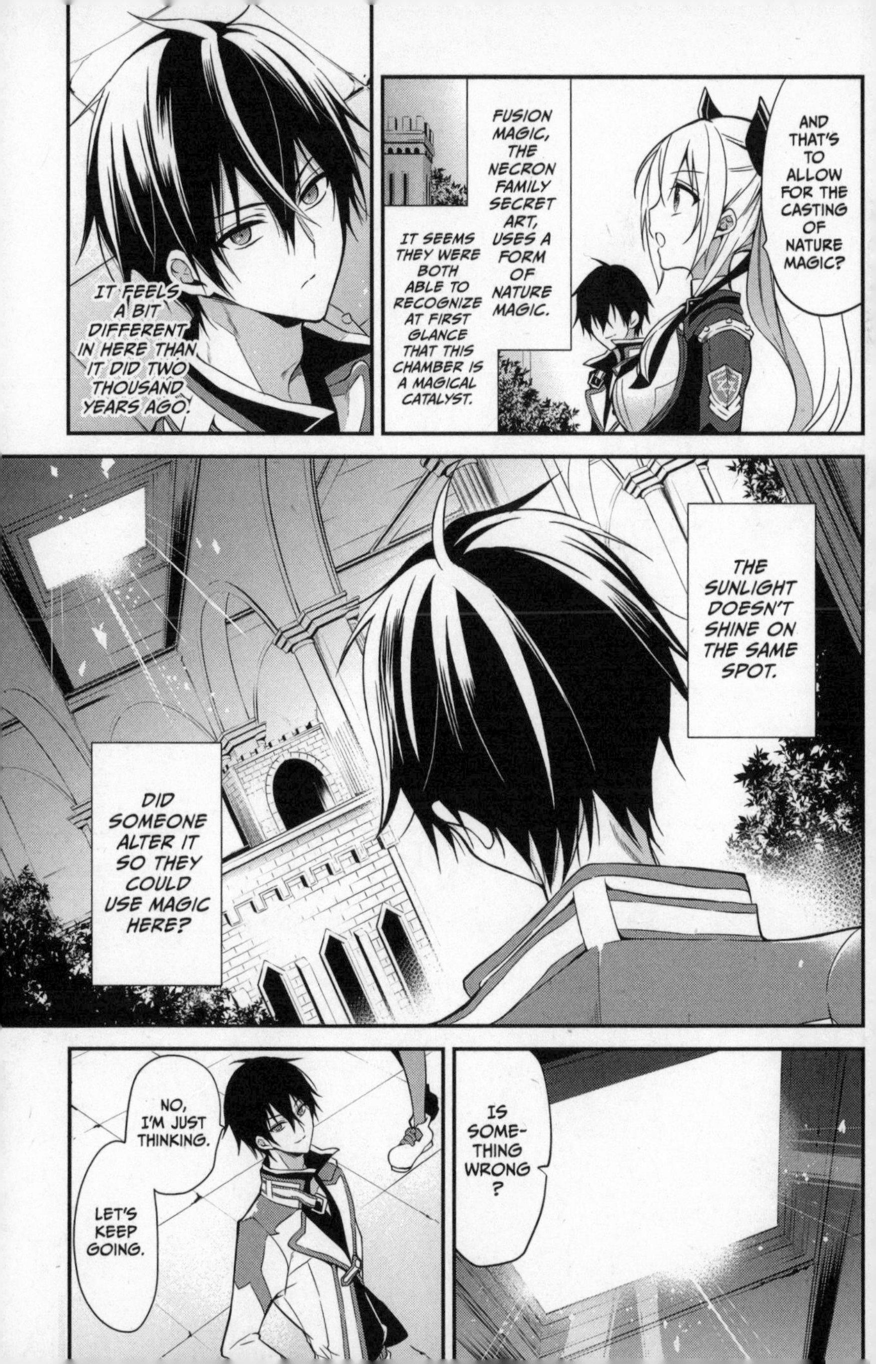
AND THAT'S TO ALLOW FOR THE CASTING OF NATURE MAGIC?
FUSION MAGIC, THE NECRON FAMILY SECRET ART, USES A FORM OF NATURE MAGIC.
IT SEEMS THEY WERE BOTH ABLE TO RECOGNIZE AT FIRST GLANCE THAT THIS CHAMBER IS A MAGICAL CATALYST.
IT FEELS A BIT DIFFERENT IN HERE THAN IT DID TWO THOUSAND YEARS AGO.
THE SUNLIGHT DOESN'T SHINE ON THE SAME SPOT.
DID SOMEONE ALTER IT SO THEY COULD USE MAGIC HERE?
IS SOME-THING WRONG?
NO, I'M JUST THINKING.
LET'S KEEP GOING.

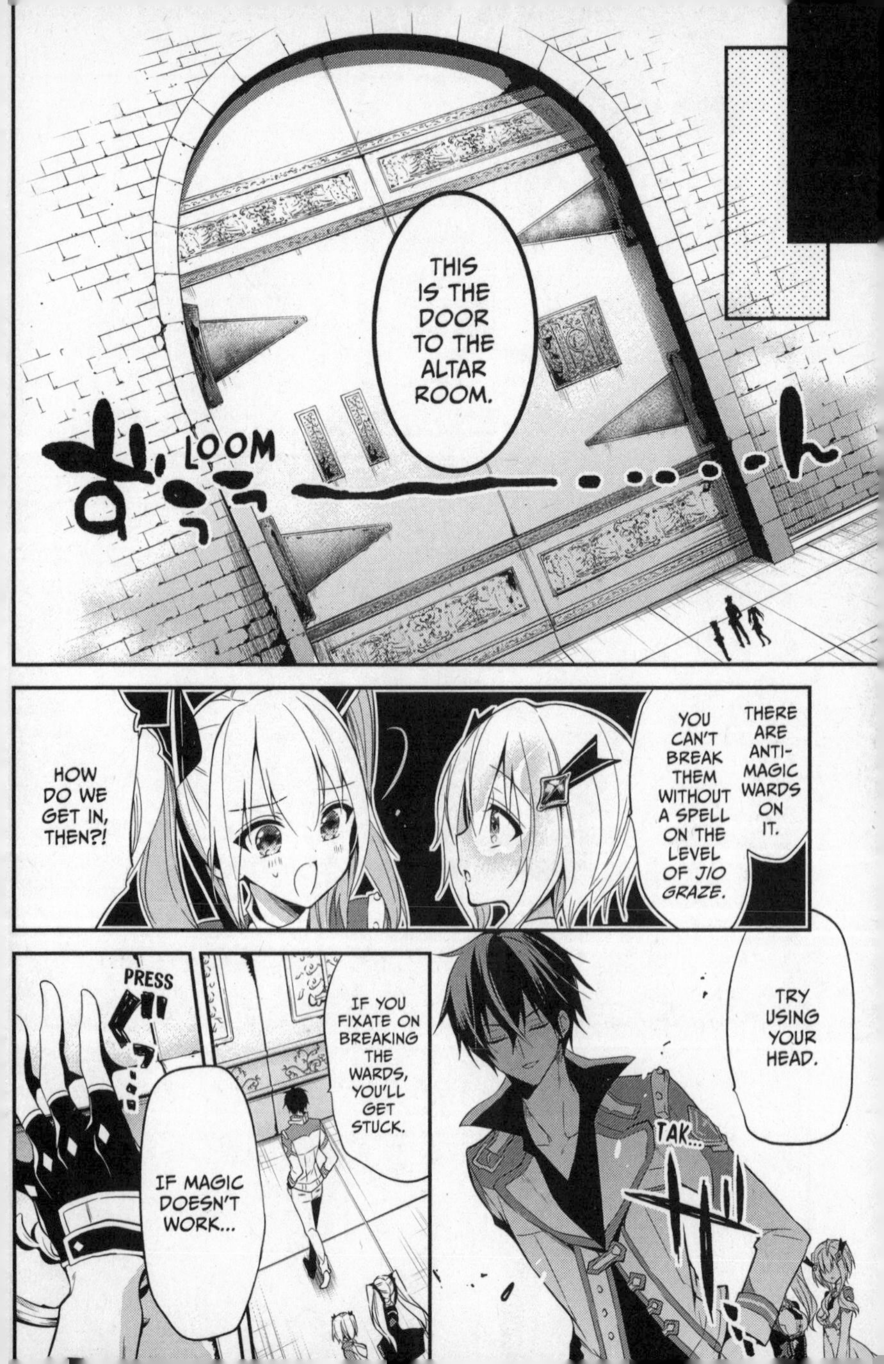
THIS IS THE DOOR TO THE ALTAR ROOM.
LOOM
THERE ARE ANTI-MAGIC WARDS ON IT.
YOU CAN'T BREAK THEM WITHOUT A SPELL ON THE LEVEL OF JIO GRAZE.
HOW DO WE GET IN, THEN?!
TRY USING YOUR HEAD.
TAK...
IF YOU FIXATE ON BREAKING THE WARDS, YOU'LL GET STUCK.
IF MAGIC DOESN'T WORK...
PRESS

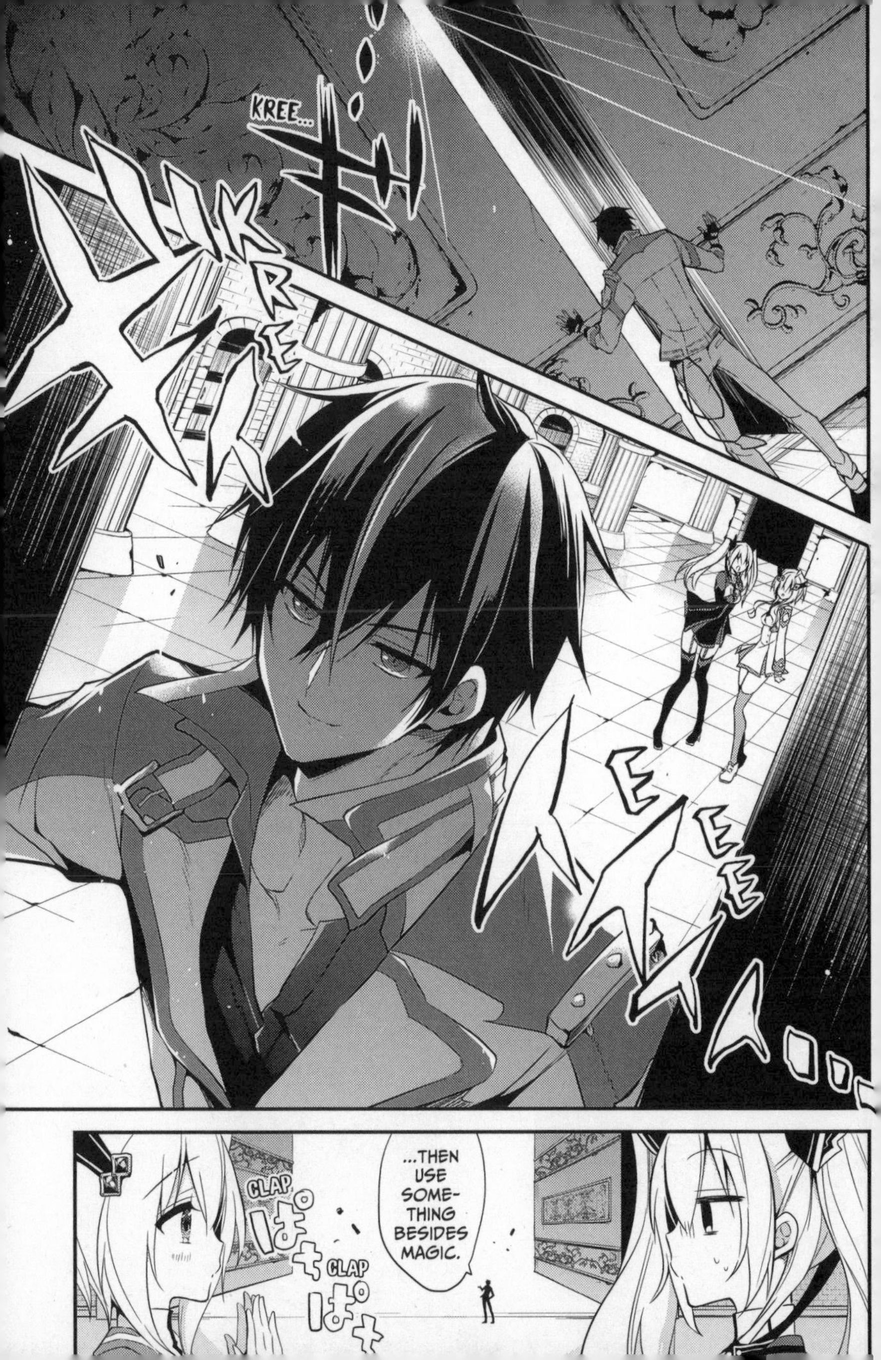
KREE...
ギィ
SKREEEEEEE...
...THEN USE SOME-THING BESIDES MAGIC.
CLAP
ぱち
CLAP
ぱち

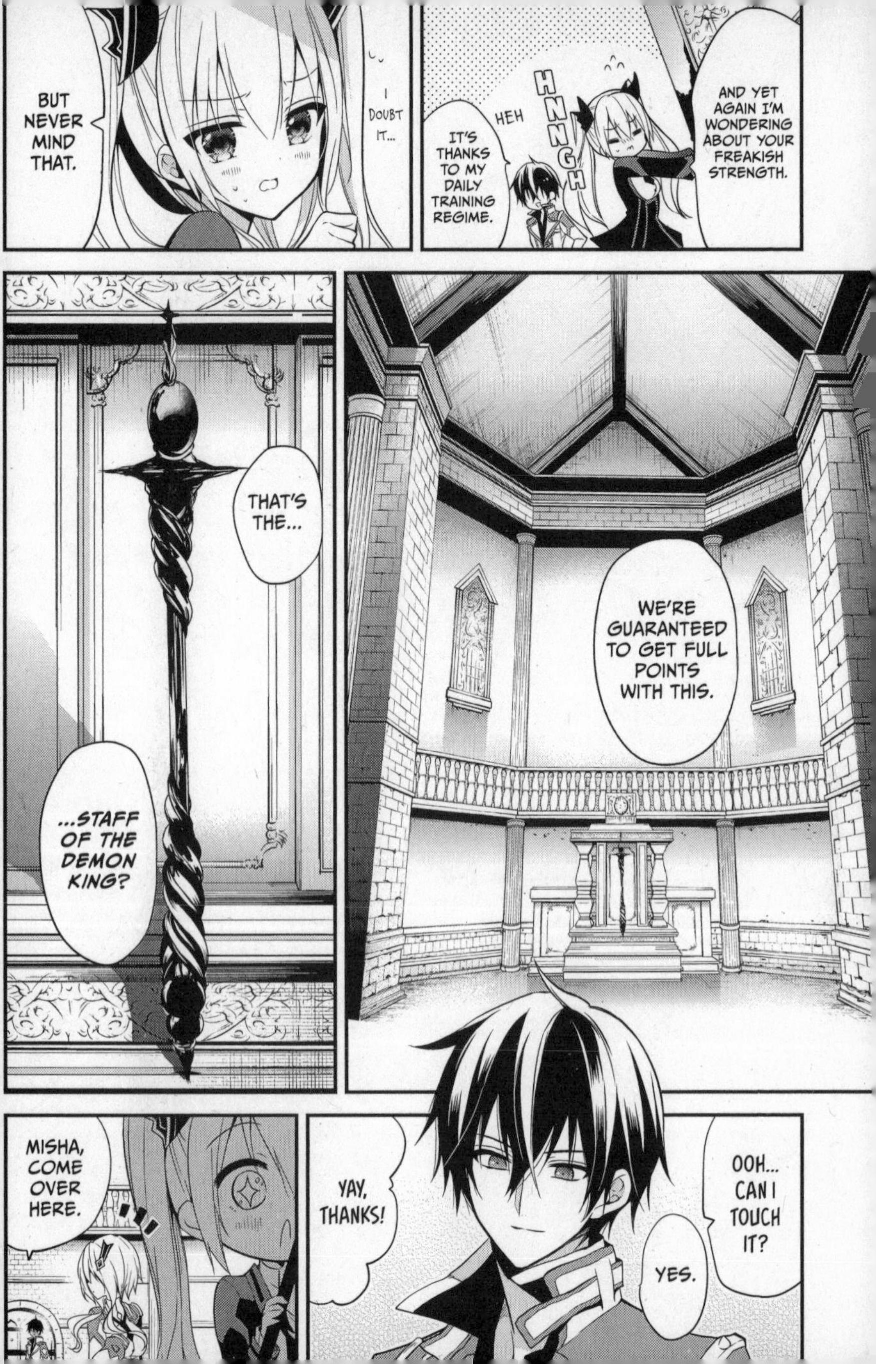
AND YET AGAIN I'M WONDERING ABOUT YOUR FREAKISH STRENGTH.
HNNGH
HEH
IT'S THANKS TO MY DAILY TRAINING REGIME.
I DOUBT IT...
BUT NEVER MIND THAT.
WE'RE GUARANTEED TO GET FULL POINTS WITH THIS.
THAT'S THE...
...STAFF OF THE DEMON KING?
OOH... CAN I TOUCH IT?
YES.
YAY, THANKS!
MISHA, COME OVER HERE.

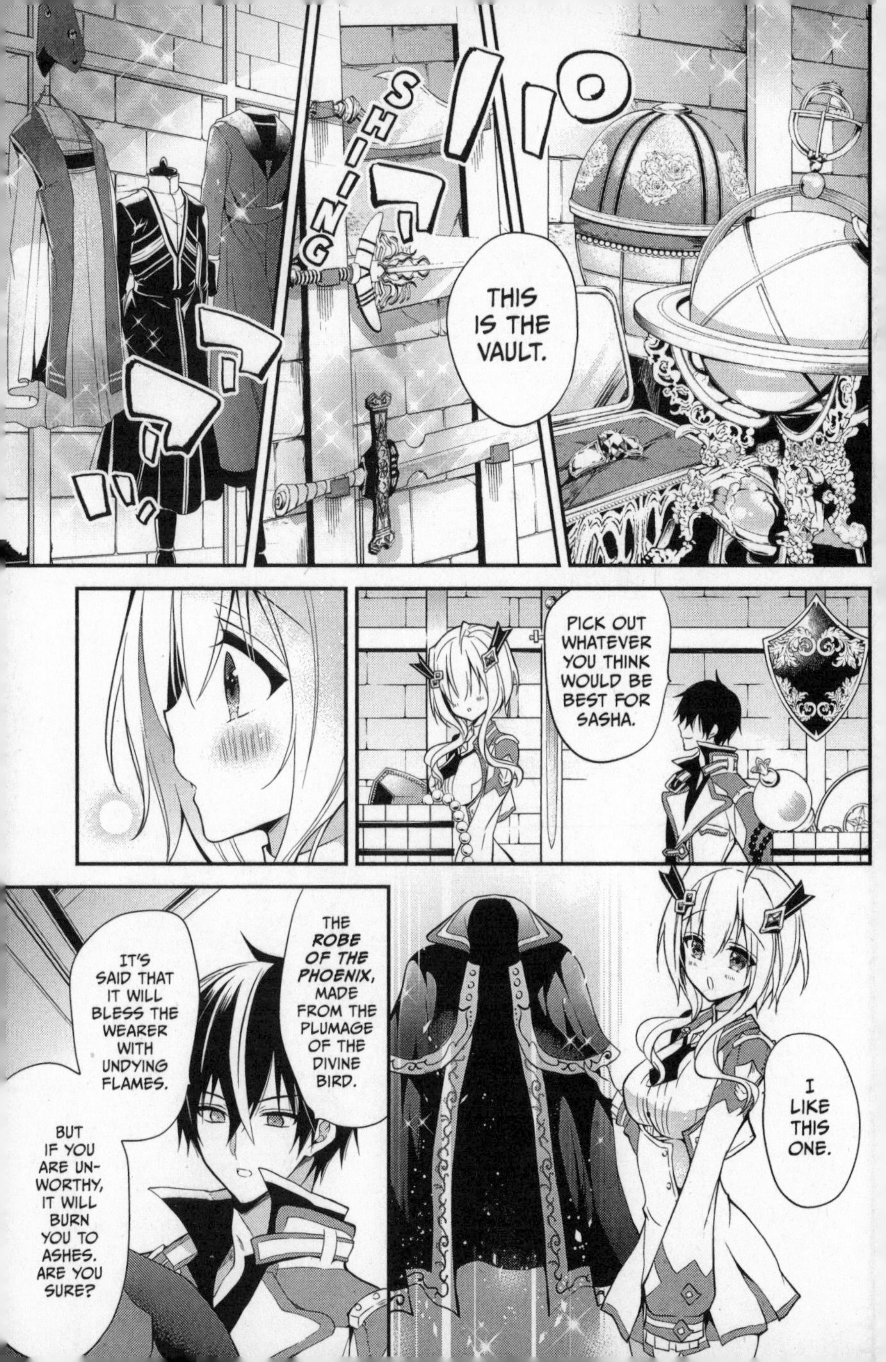
SHIIING
THIS IS THE VAULT.
PICK OUT WHATEVER YOU THINK WOULD BE BEST FOR SASHA.
I LIKE THIS ONE.
THE *ROBE OF THE PHOENIX*, MADE FROM THE PLUMAGE OF THE DIVINE BIRD.
IT'S SAID THAT IT WILL BLESS THE WEARER WITH UNDYING FLAMES.
BUT IF YOU ARE UNWORTHY, IT WILL BURN YOU TO ASHES. ARE YOU SURE?

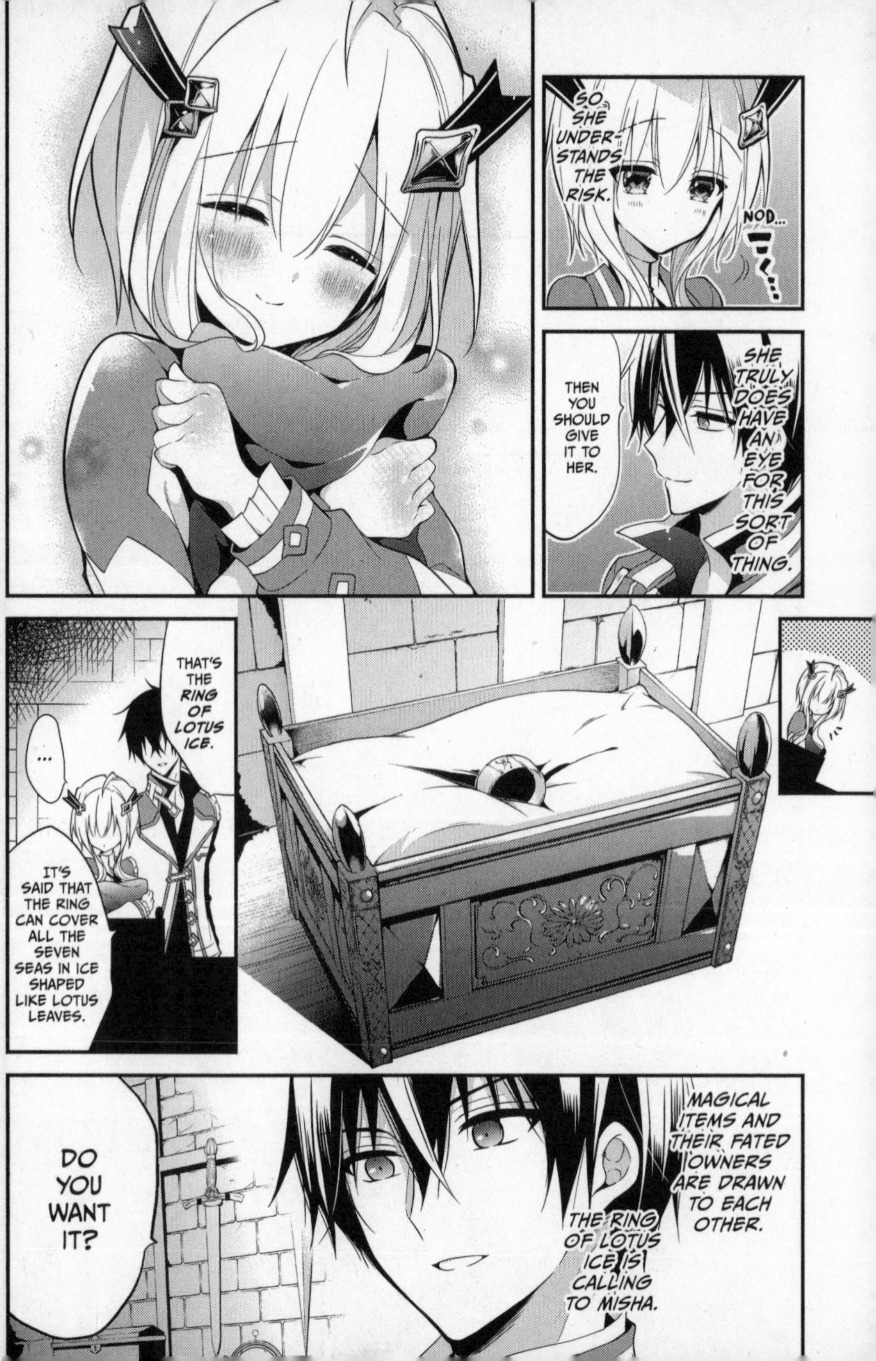
SO SHE UNDERSTANDS THE RISK.
NOD...
SHE TRULY DOES HAVE AN EYE FOR THIS SORT OF THING.
THEN YOU SHOULD GIVE IT TO HER.
THAT'S THE RING OF LOTUS ICE.
...
IT'S SAID THAT THE RING CAN COVER ALL THE SEVEN SEAS IN ICE SHAPED LIKE LOTUS LEAVES.
MAGICAL ITEMS AND THEIR FATED OWNERS ARE DRAWN TO EACH OTHER.
THE RING OF LOTUS ICE IS CALLING TO MISHA.
DO YOU WANT IT?

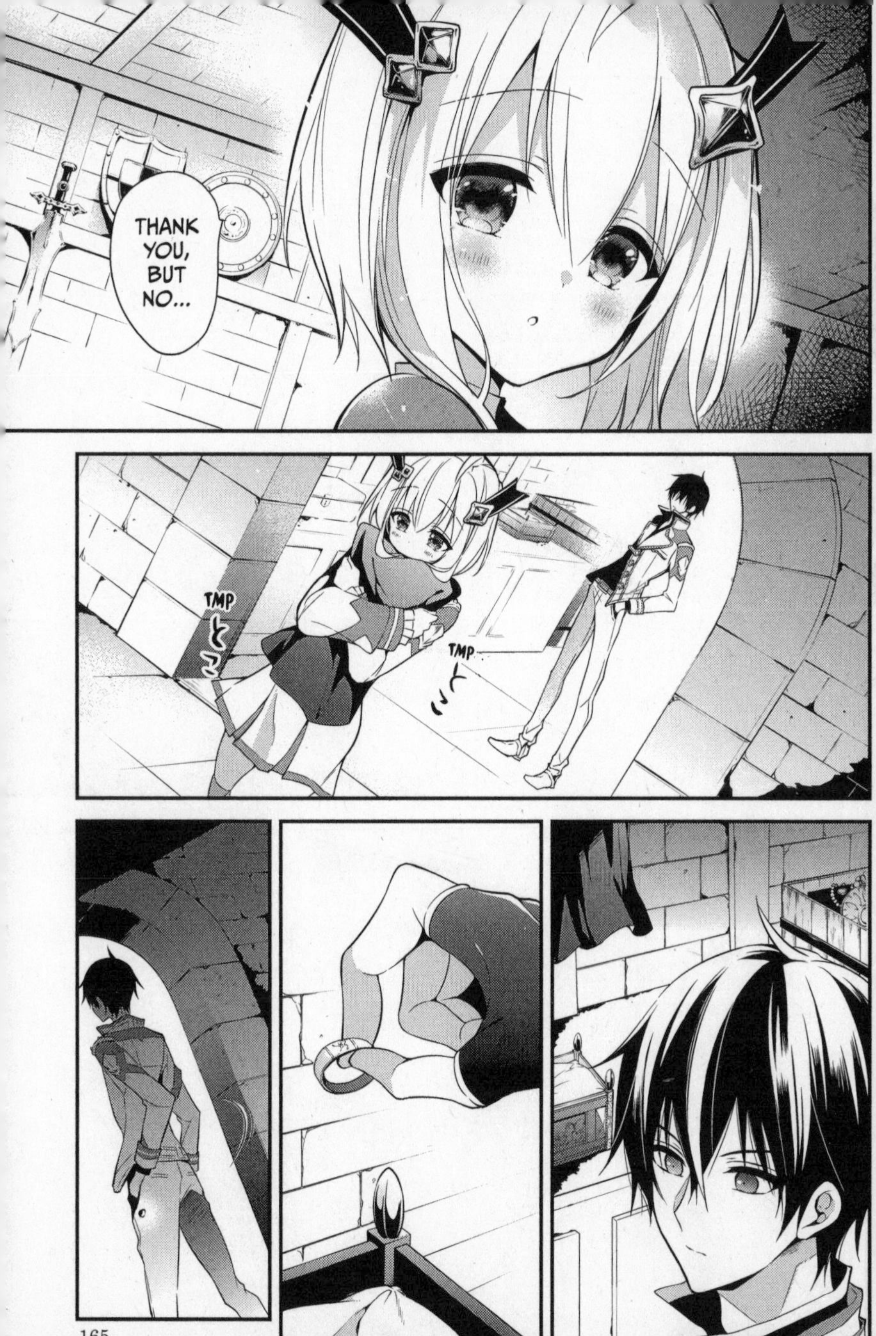
THANK YOU, BUT NO...
TMP
とこ
TMP
とこ

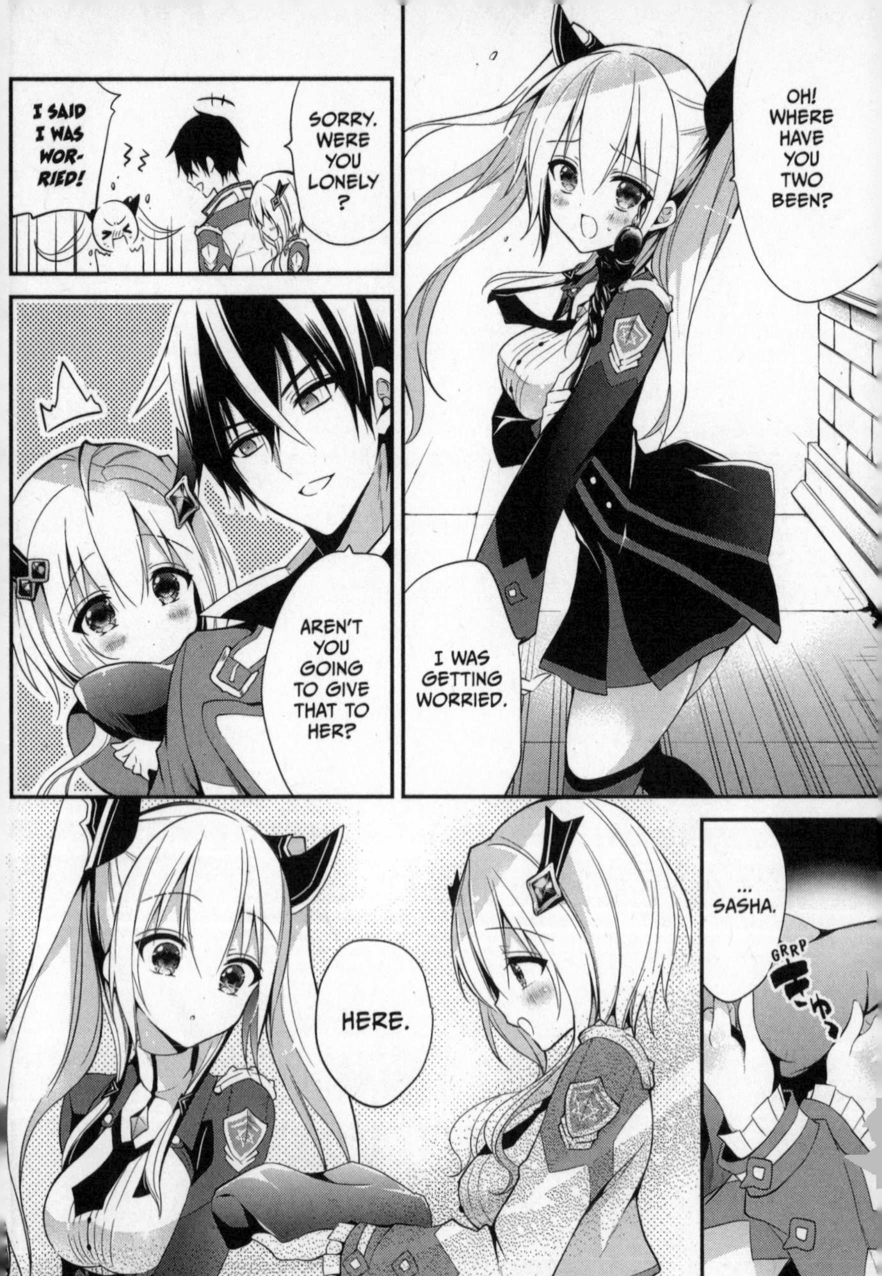
OH! WHERE HAVE YOU TWO BEEN?
I WAS GETTING WORRIED.
SORRY. WERE YOU LONELY?
I SAID I WAS WOR-RIED!
AREN'T YOU GOING TO GIVE THAT TO HER?
... SASHA.
GRRP
HERE.

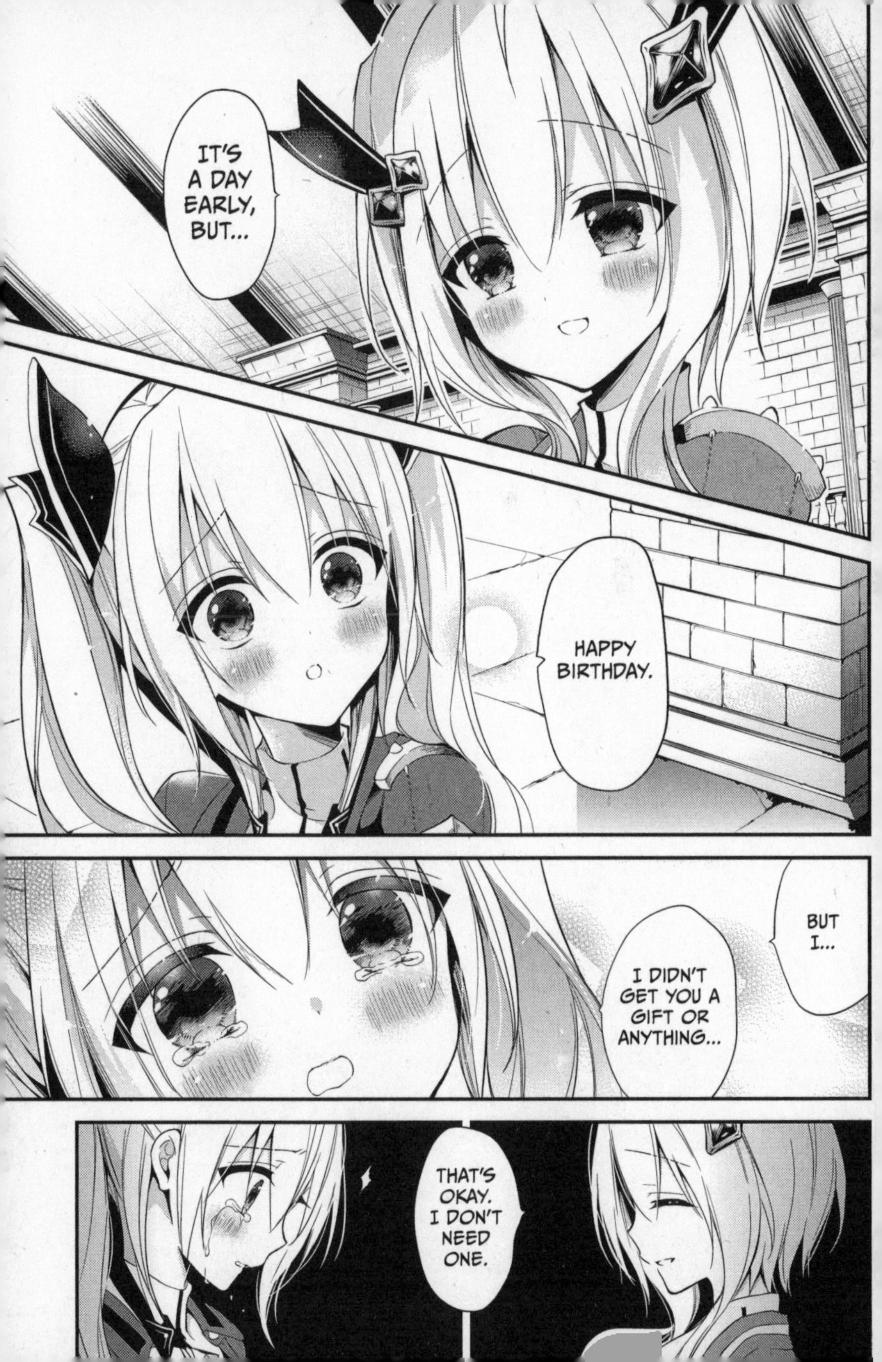
IT'S A DAY EARLY, BUT...
HAPPY BIRTHDAY.
BUT I...
I DIDN'T GET YOU A GIFT OR ANYTHING...
THAT'S OKAY. I DON'T NEED ONE.

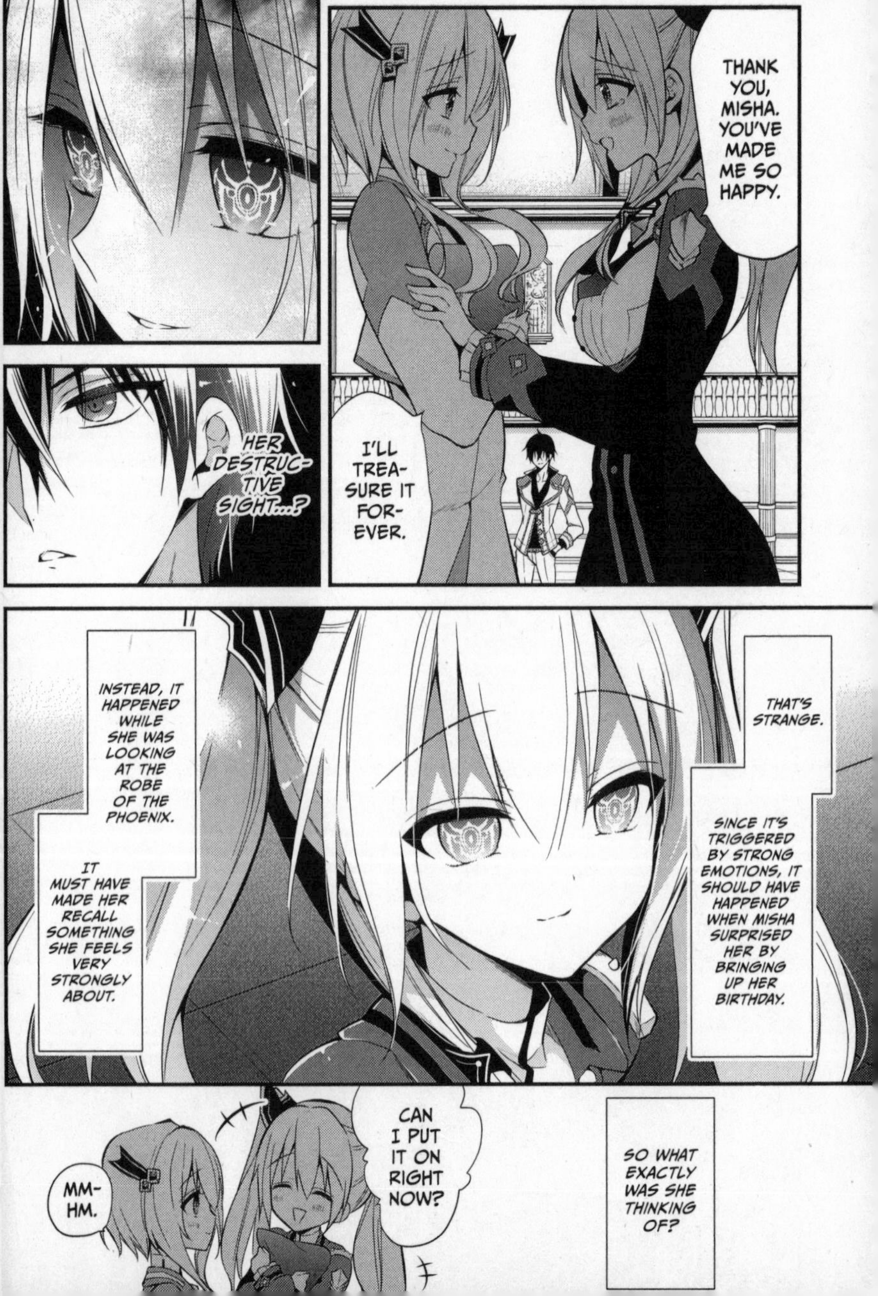
THANK YOU, MISHA. YOU'VE MADE ME SO HAPPY.
I'LL TREASURE IT FOREVER.
HER DESTRUCTIVE SIGHT...?
THAT'S STRANGE.
SINCE IT'S TRIGGERED BY STRONG EMOTIONS, IT SHOULD HAVE HAPPENED WHEN MISHA SURPRISED HER BY BRINGING UP HER BIRTHDAY.
INSTEAD, IT HAPPENED WHILE SHE WAS LOOKING AT THE ROBE OF THE PHOENIX.
IT MUST HAVE MADE HER RECALL SOMETHING SHE FEELS VERY STRONGLY ABOUT.
SO WHAT EXACTLY WAS SHE THINKING OF?
CAN I PUT IT ON RIGHT NOW?
MM-HM.

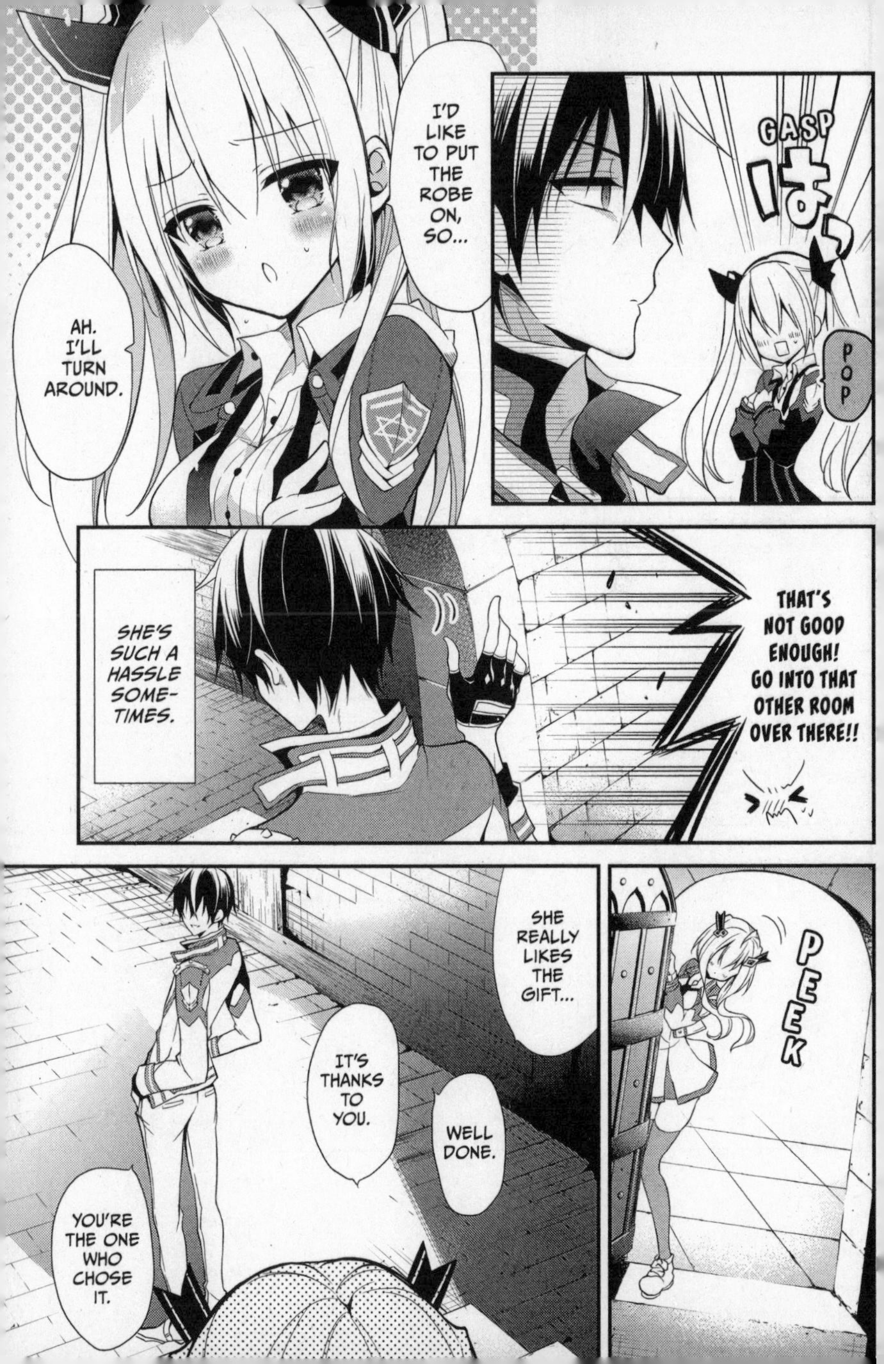
GASP
はっ
POP
I'D LIKE TO PUT THE ROBE ON, SO...
AH. I'LL TURN AROUND.
THAT'S NOT GOOD ENOUGH! GO INTO THAT OTHER ROOM OVER THERE!!
SHE'S SUCH A HASSLE SOMETIMES.
PEEK
SHE REALLY LIKES THE GIFT...
WELL DONE.
IT'S THANKS TO YOU.
YOU'RE THE ONE WHO CHOSE IT.

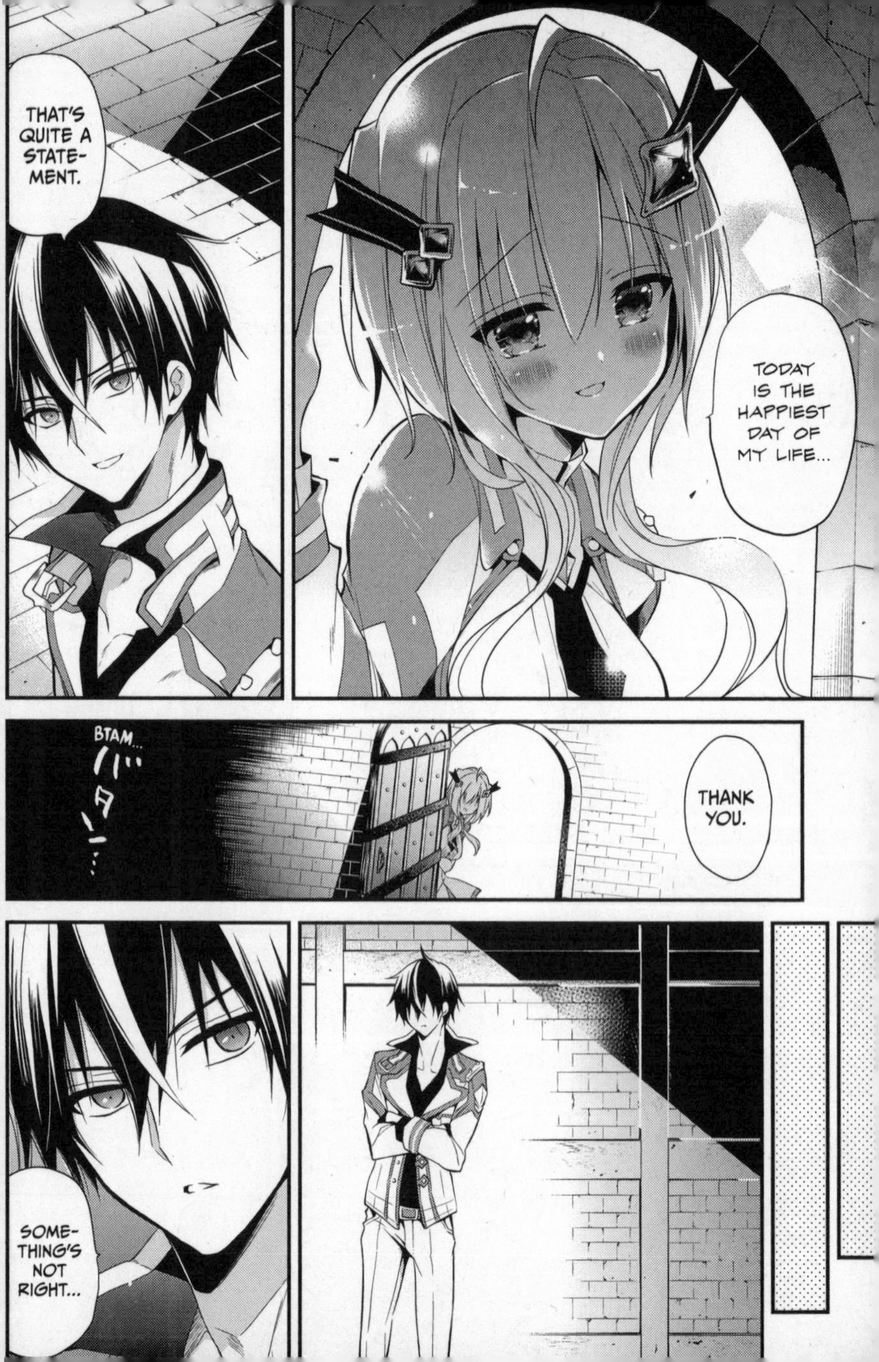
TODAY IS THE HAPPIEST DAY OF MY LIFE...
THAT'S QUITE A STATE-MENT.
THANK YOU.
BTAM...
バタン…
SOME-THING'S NOT RIGHT...

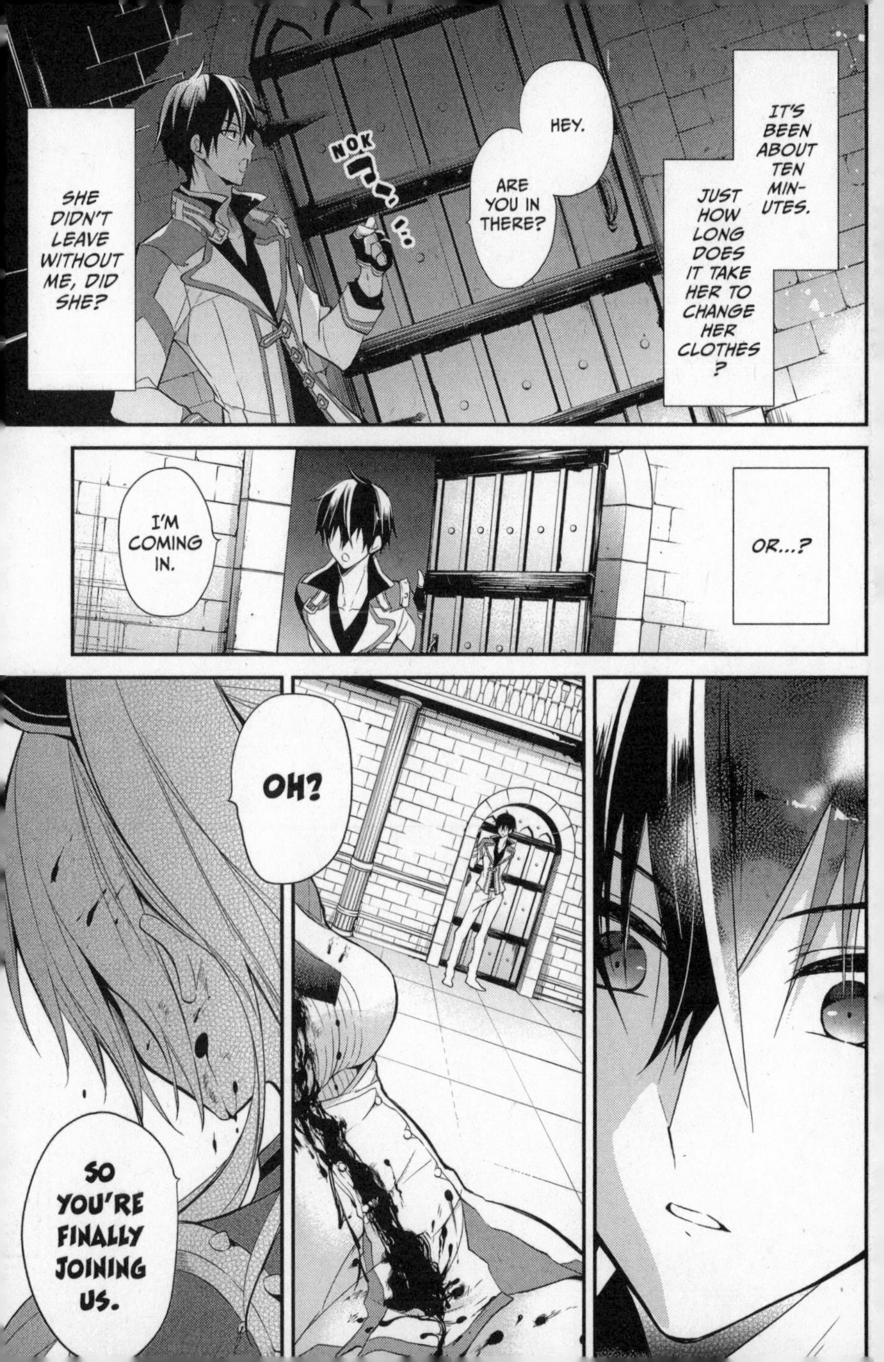
IT'S BEEN ABOUT TEN MIN-UTES.
JUST HOW LONG DOES IT TAKE HER TO CHANGE HER CLOTHES?
HEY.
ARE YOU IN THERE?
NOK
SHE DIDN'T LEAVE WITHOUT ME, DID SHE?
OR...?
I'M COMING IN.
OH?
SO YOU'RE FINALLY JOINING US.

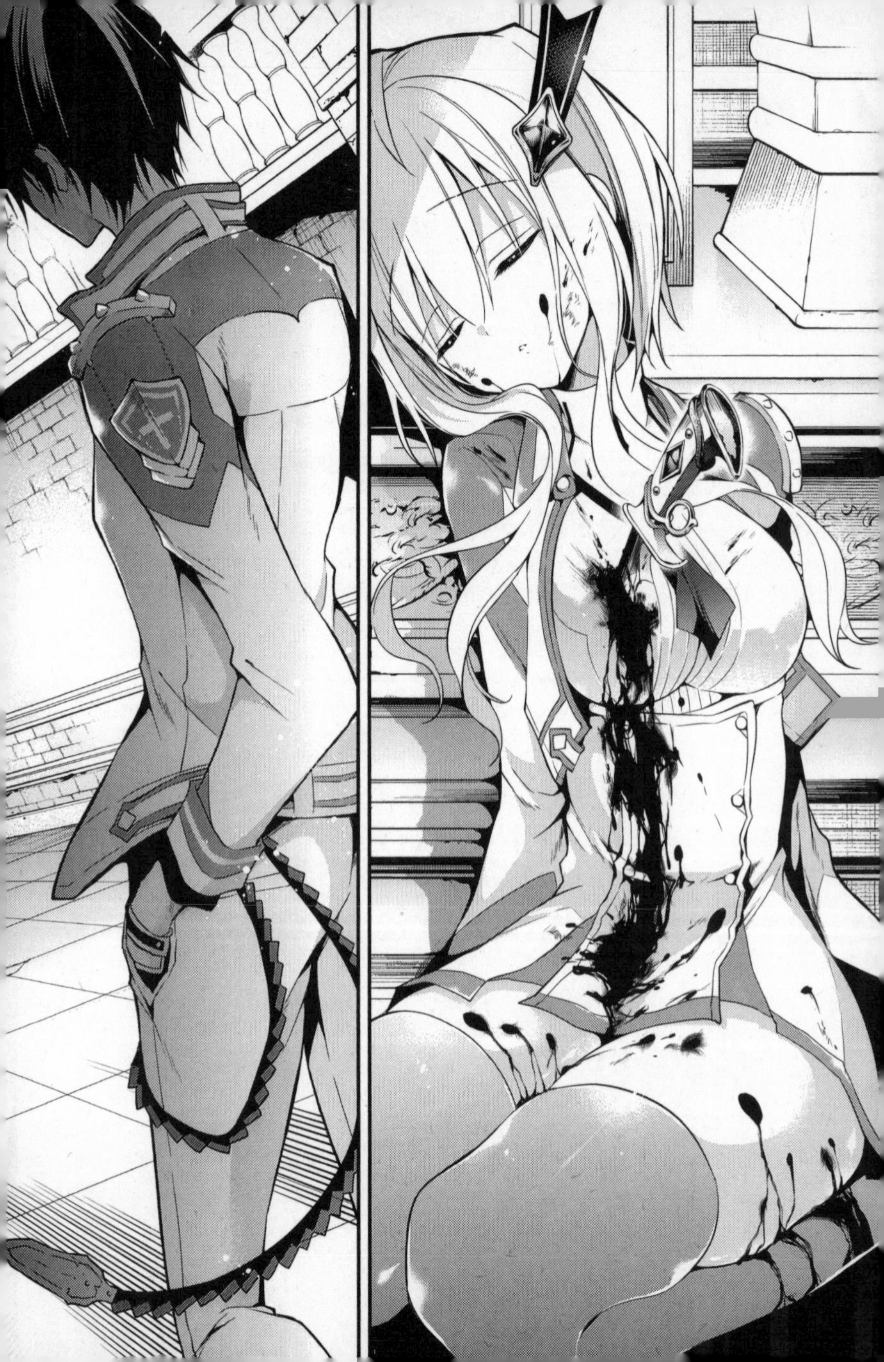

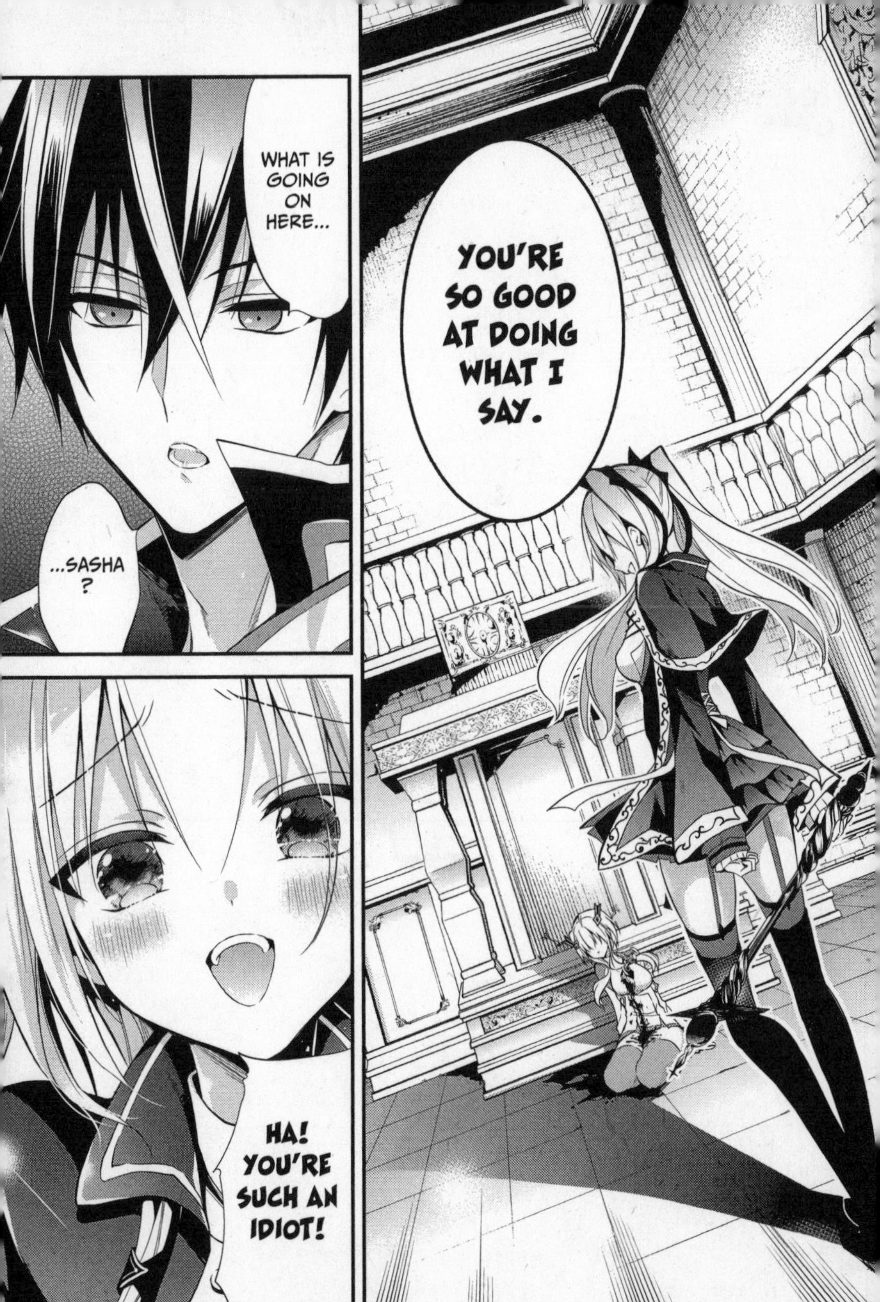
YOU'RE SO GOOD AT DOING WHAT I SAY.
WHAT IS GOING ON HERE...
...SASHA?
HA! YOU'RE SUCH AN IDIOT!

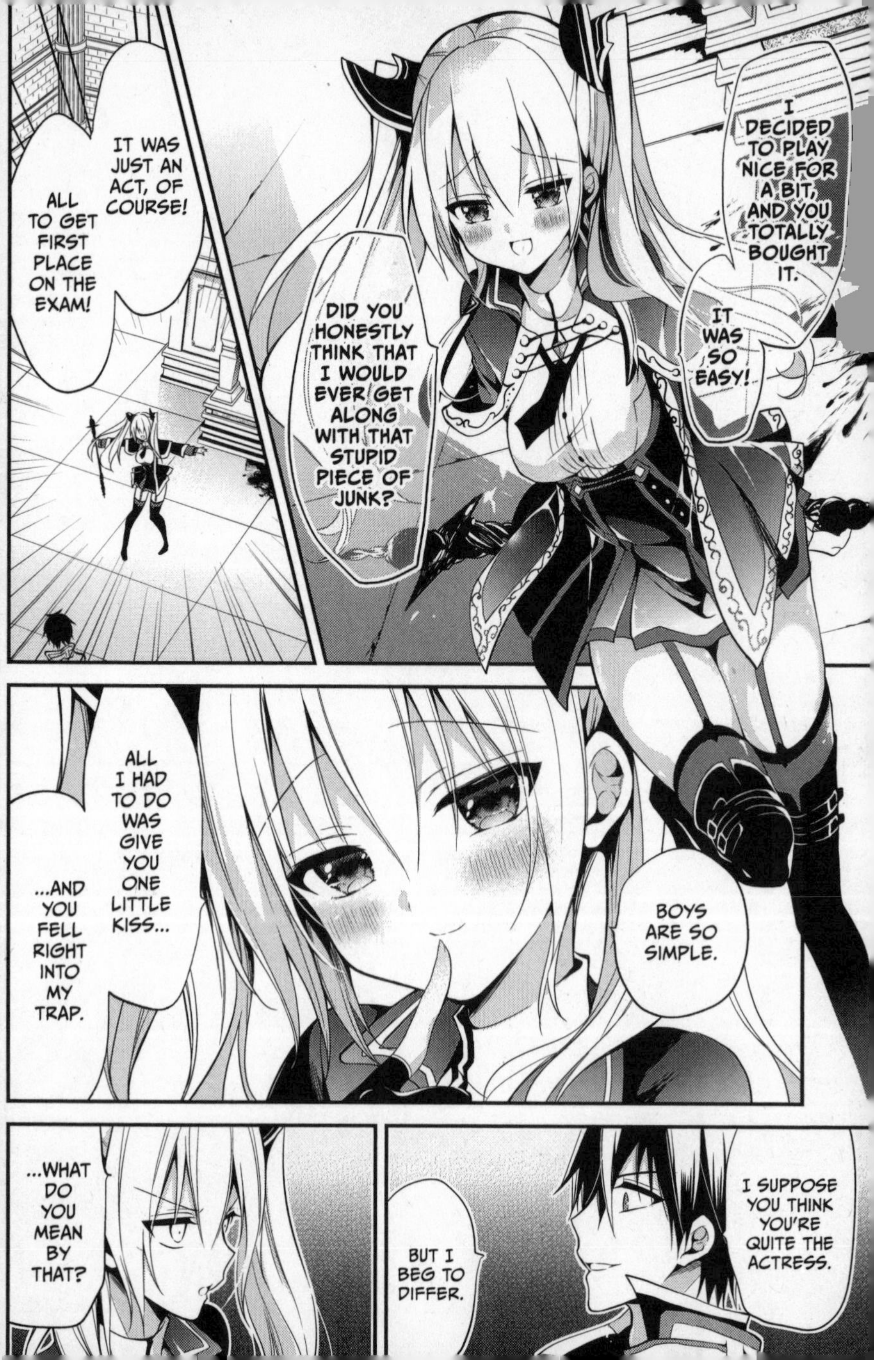
I DECIDED TO PLAY NICE FOR A BIT, AND YOU TOTALLY BOUGHT IT.
IT WAS SO EASY!
DID YOU HONESTLY THINK THAT I WOULD EVER GET ALONG WITH THAT STUPID PIECE OF JUNK?
IT WAS JUST AN ACT, OF COURSE!
ALL TO GET FIRST PLACE ON THE EXAM!
BOYS ARE SO SIMPLE.
ALL I HAD TO DO WAS GIVE YOU ONE LITTLE KISS...
...AND YOU FELL RIGHT INTO MY TRAP.
I SUPPOSE YOU THINK YOU'RE QUITE THE ACTRESS.
BUT I BEG TO DIFFER.
...WHAT DO YOU MEAN BY THAT?

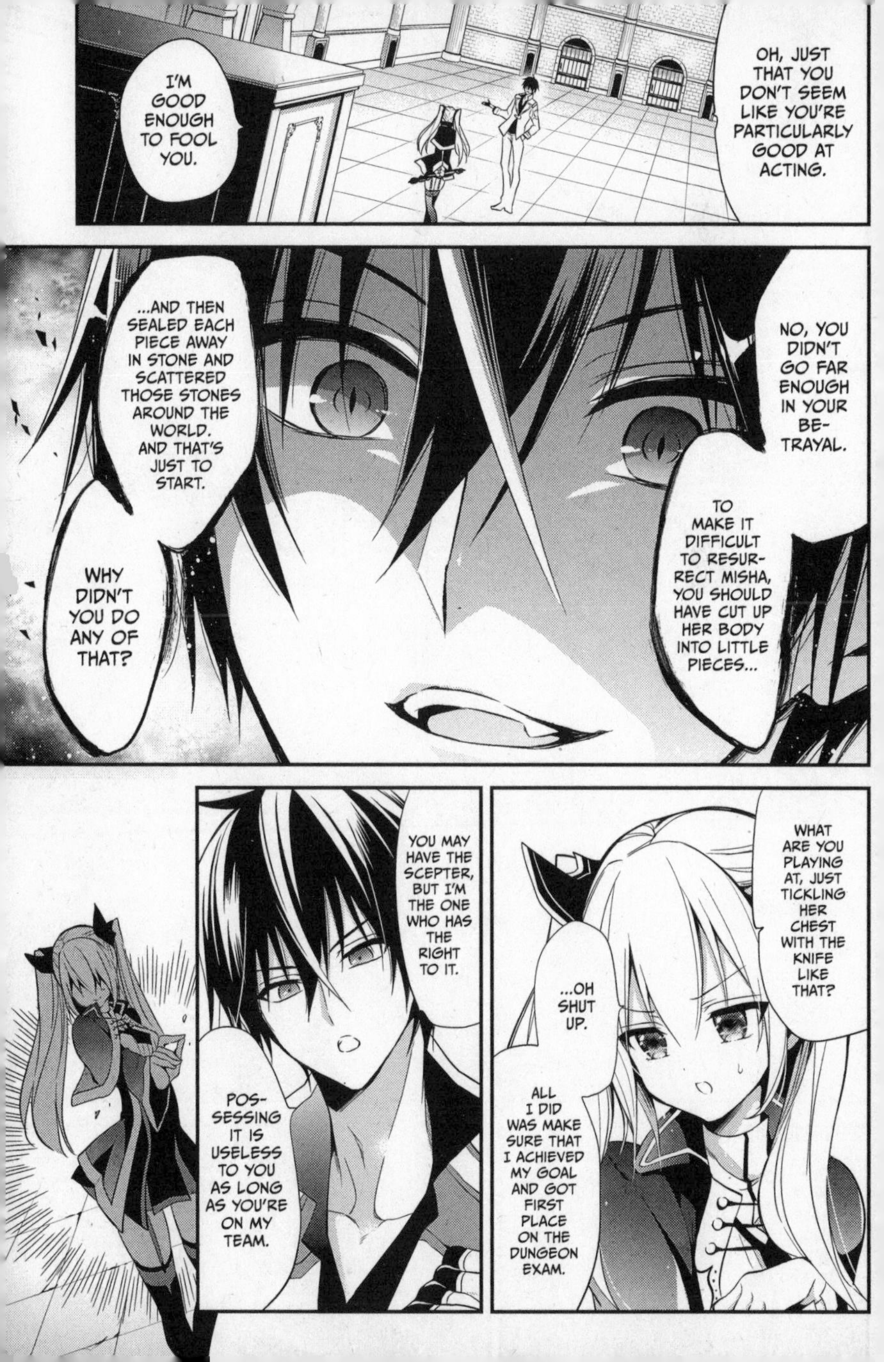
OH, JUST THAT YOU DON'T SEEM LIKE YOU'RE PARTICULARLY GOOD AT ACTING.
I'M GOOD ENOUGH TO FOOL YOU.
NO, YOU DIDN'T GO FAR ENOUGH IN YOUR BE-TRAYAL.
TO MAKE IT DIFFICULT TO RESUR-RECT MISHA, YOU SHOULD HAVE CUT UP HER BODY INTO LITTLE PIECES...
...AND THEN SEALED EACH PIECE AWAY IN STONE AND SCATTERED THOSE STONES AROUND THE WORLD. AND THAT'S JUST TO START.
WHY DIDN'T YOU DO ANY OF THAT?
WHAT ARE YOU PLAYING AT, JUST TICKLING HER CHEST WITH THE KNIFE LIKE THAT?
...OH SHUT UP.
ALL I DID WAS MAKE SURE THAT I ACHIEVED MY GOAL AND GOT FIRST PLACE ON THE DUNGEON EXAM.
YOU MAY HAVE THE SCEPTER, BUT I'M THE ONE WHO HAS THE RIGHT TO IT.
POS-SESSING IT IS USELESS TO YOU AS LONG AS YOU'RE ON MY TEAM.

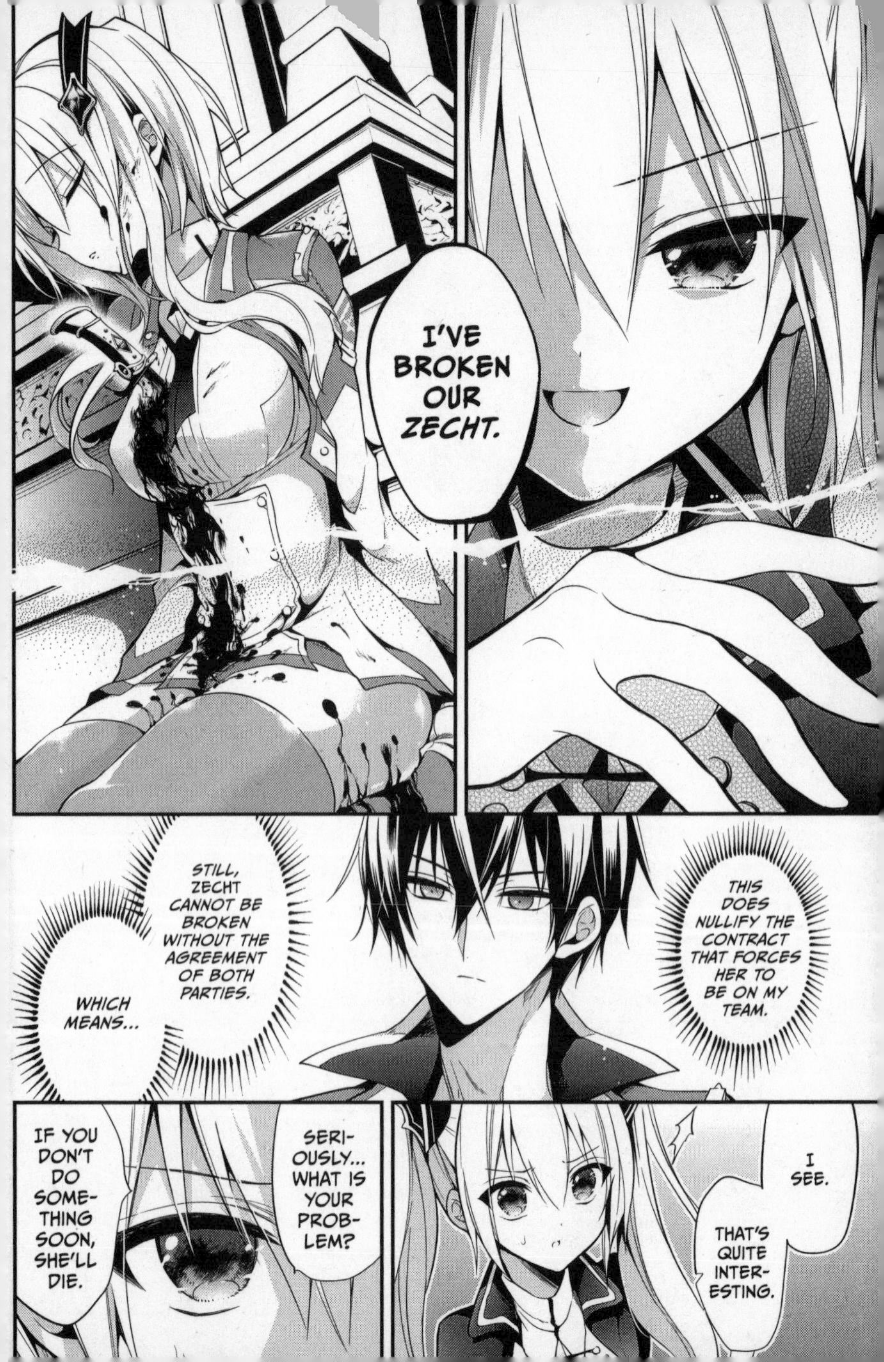
I'VE BROKEN OUR ZECHT.
THIS DOES NULLIFY THE CONTRACT THAT FORCES HER TO BE ON MY TEAM.
STILL, ZECHT CANNOT BE BROKEN WITHOUT THE AGREEMENT OF BOTH PARTIES.
WHICH MEANS...
I SEE.
THAT'S QUITE INTER-ESTING.
SERI-OUSLY... WHAT IS YOUR PROB-LEM?
IF YOU DON'T DO SOME-THING SOON, SHE'LL DIE.

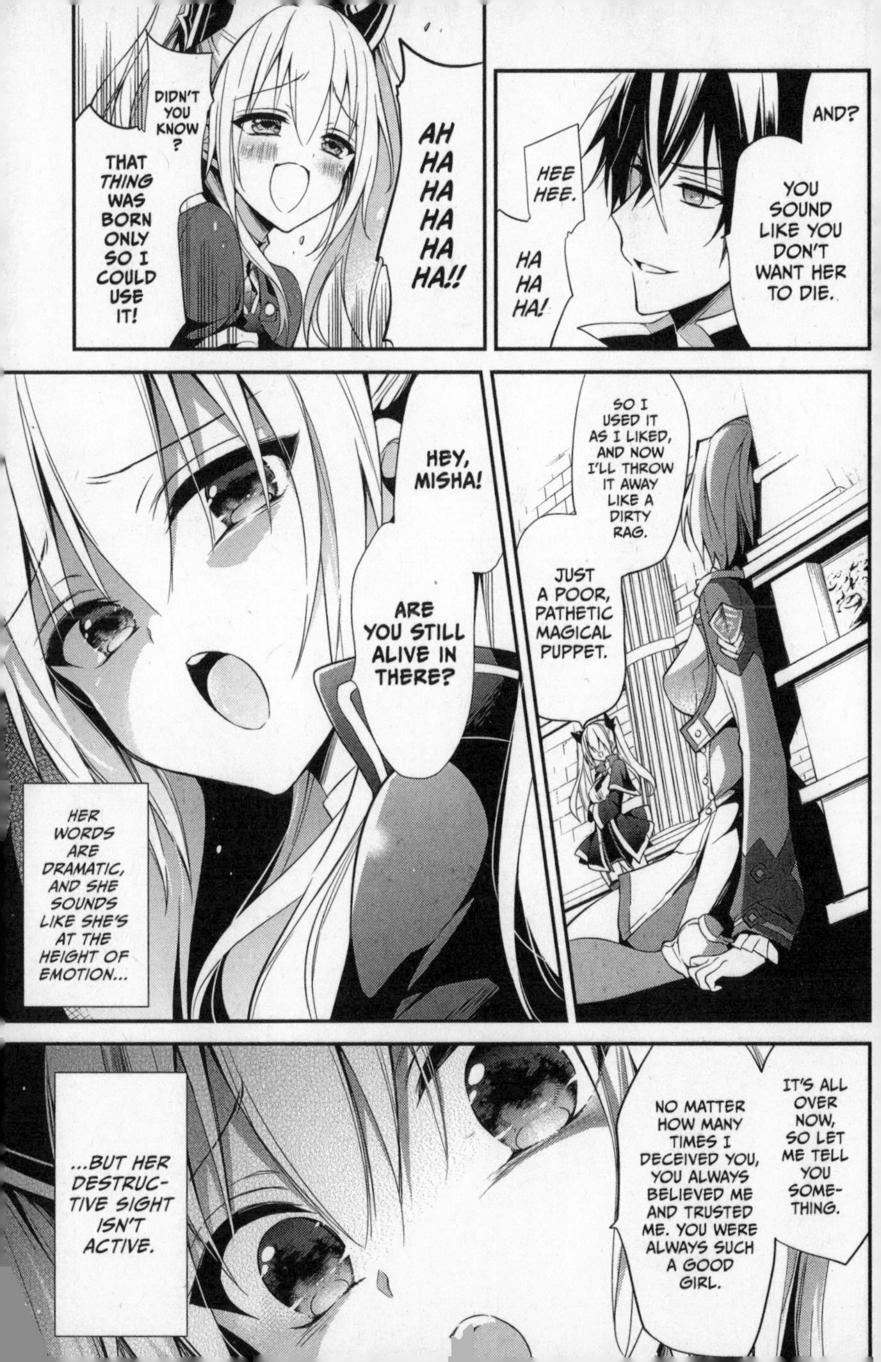
AND?
YOU SOUND LIKE YOU DON'T WANT HER TO DIE.
HEE HEE.
HA HA HA!
AH HA HA HA HA HA!!
DIDN'T YOU KNOW?
THAT THING WAS BORN ONLY SO I COULD USE IT!
SO I USED IT AS I LIKED, AND NOW I'LL THROW IT AWAY LIKE A DIRTY RAG.
JUST A POOR, PATHETIC MAGICAL PUPPET.
HEY, MISHA!
ARE YOU STILL ALIVE IN THERE?
HER WORDS ARE DRAMATIC, AND SHE SOUNDS LIKE SHE'S AT THE HEIGHT OF EMOTION...
IT'S ALL OVER NOW, SO LET ME TELL YOU SOME-THING.
NO MATTER HOW MANY TIMES I DECEIVED YOU, YOU ALWAYS BELIEVED ME AND TRUSTED ME. YOU WERE ALWAYS SUCH A GOOD GIRL.
...BUT HER DESTRUC-TIVE SIGHT ISN'T ACTIVE.

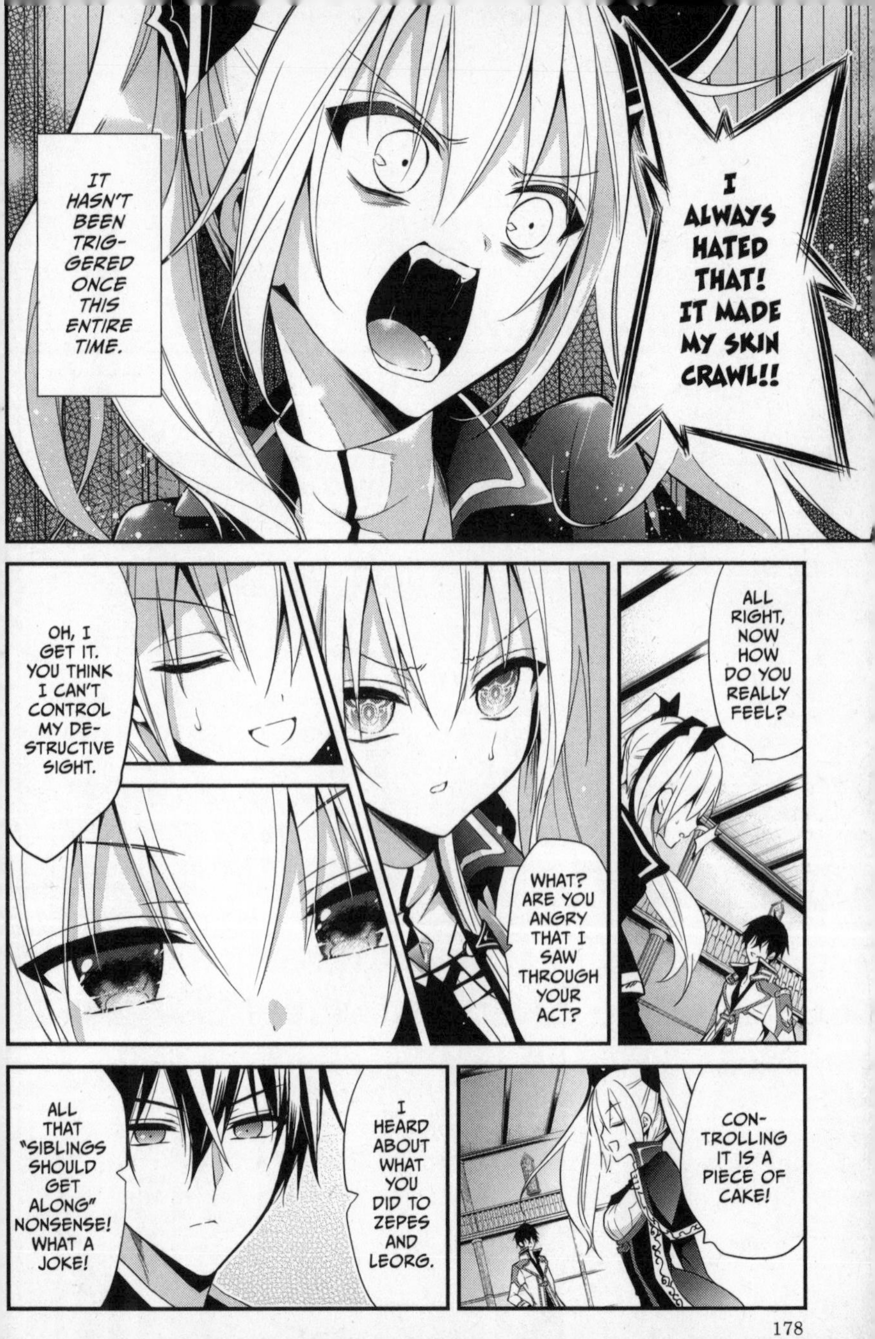
I ALWAYS HATED THAT! IT MADE MY SKIN CRAWL!!
IT HASN'T BEEN TRIGGERED ONCE THIS ENTIRE TIME.
ALL RIGHT, NOW HOW DO YOU REALLY FEEL?
WHAT? ARE YOU ANGRY THAT I SAW THROUGH YOUR ACT?
OH, I GET IT. YOU THINK I CAN'T CONTROL MY DESTRUCTIVE SIGHT.
CONTROLLING IT IS A PIECE OF CAKE!
I HEARD ABOUT WHAT YOU DID TO ZEPES AND LEORG.
ALL THAT "SIBLINGS SHOULD GET ALONG" NONSENSE! WHAT A JOKE!

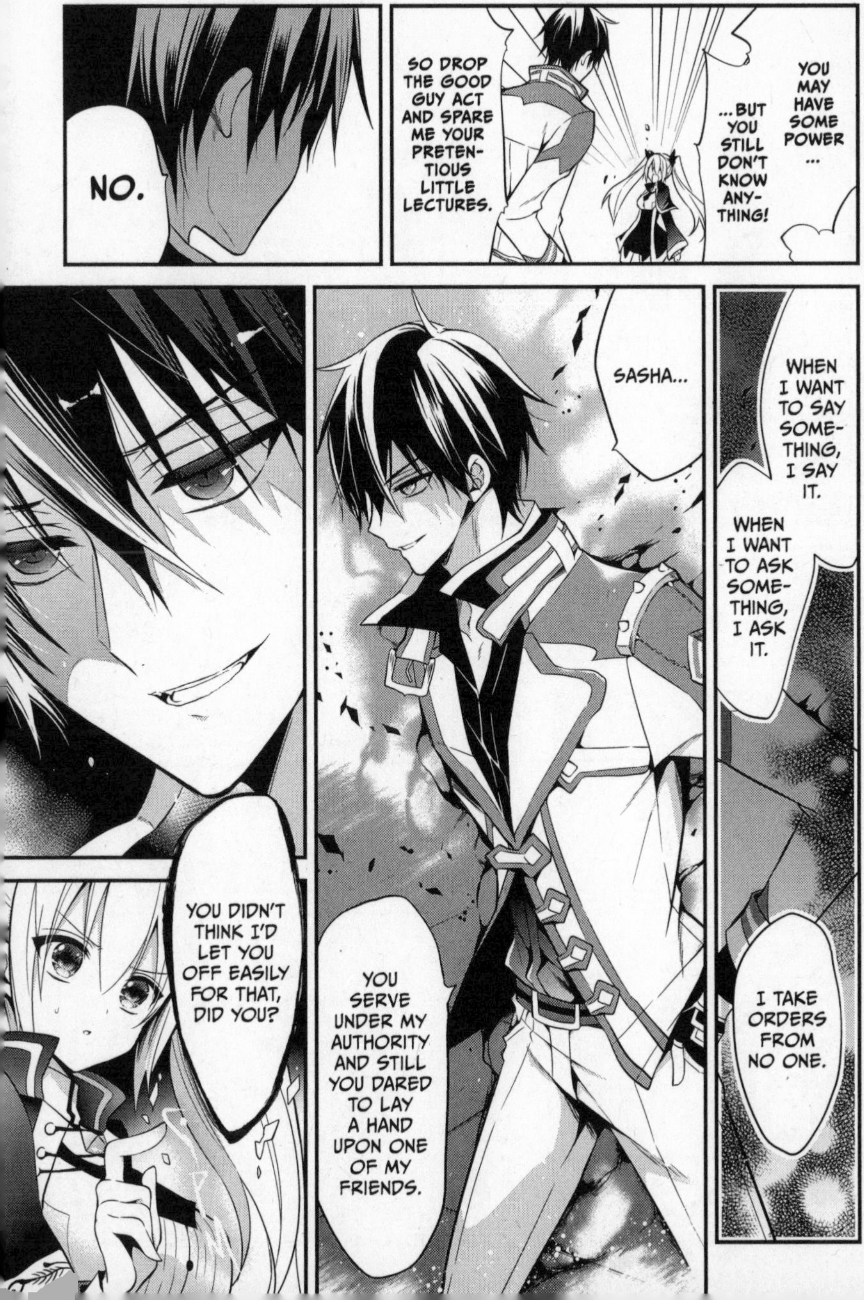
YOU MAY HAVE SOME POWER ...
...BUT YOU STILL DON'T KNOW ANYTHING!
SO DROP THE GOOD GUY ACT AND SPARE ME YOUR PRETENTIOUS LITTLE LECTURES.
NO.
WHEN I WANT TO SAY SOMETHING, I SAY IT.
WHEN I WANT TO ASK SOMETHING, I ASK IT.
I TAKE ORDERS FROM NO ONE.
SASHA...
YOU SERVE UNDER MY AUTHORITY AND STILL YOU DARED TO LAY A HAND UPON ONE OF MY FRIENDS.
YOU DIDN'T THINK I'D LET YOU OFF EASILY FOR THAT, DID YOU?

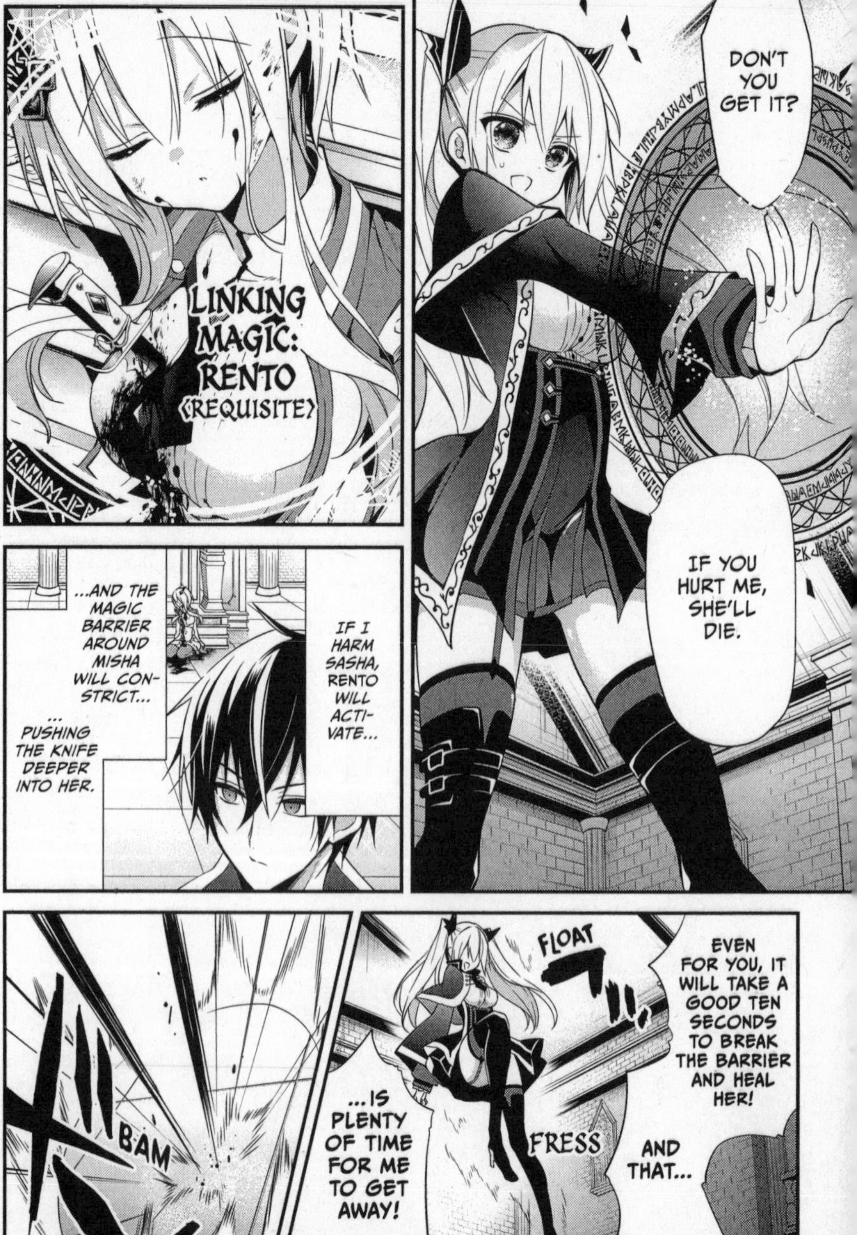
DON'T YOU GET IT?
IF YOU HURT ME, SHE'LL DIE.
LINKING MAGIC: RENTO 《REQUISITE》
IF I HARM SASHA, RENTO WILL ACTIVATE...
...AND THE MAGIC BARRIER AROUND MISHA WILL CONSTRICT...
...PUSHING THE KNIFE DEEPER INTO HER.
EVEN FOR YOU, IT WILL TAKE A GOOD TEN SECONDS TO BREAK THE BARRIER AND HEAL HER!
FLOAT
AND THAT...
FRESS
...IS PLENTY OF TIME FOR ME TO GET AWAY!
BAM

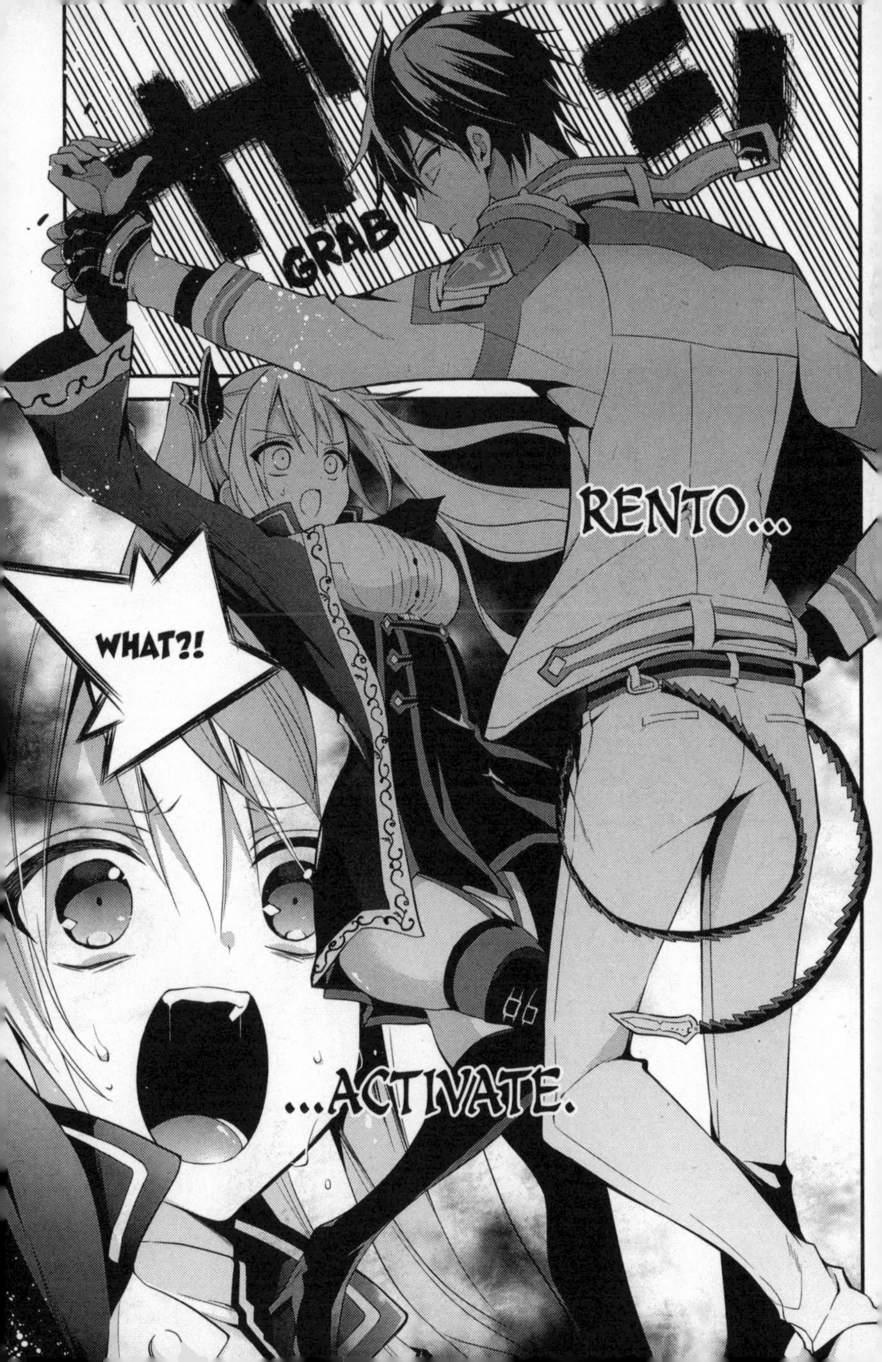
GRAB
RENTO...
WHAT?!
...ACTIVATE.

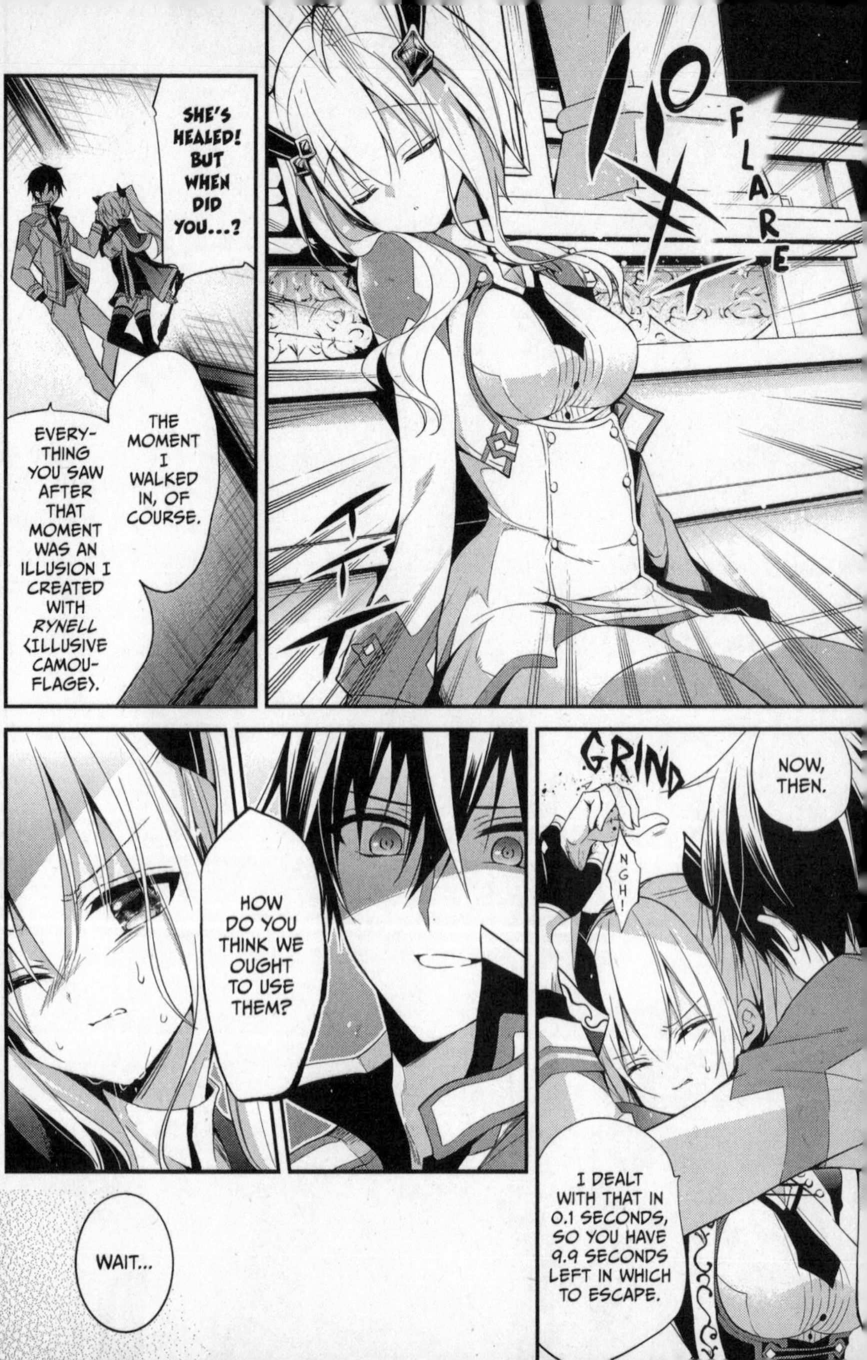
FLARE
SHE'S HEALED! BUT WHEN DID YOU...?
THE MOMENT I WALKED IN, OF COURSE.
EVERYTHING YOU SAW AFTER THAT MOMENT WAS AN ILLUSION I CREATED WITH *RYNELL* <ILLUSIVE CAMOUFLAGE>.
GRIND
NOW, THEN.
NGH!
I DEALT WITH THAT IN 0.1 SECONDS, SO YOU HAVE 9.9 SECONDS LEFT IN WHICH TO ESCAPE.
HOW DO YOU THINK WE OUGHT TO USE THEM?
WAIT...

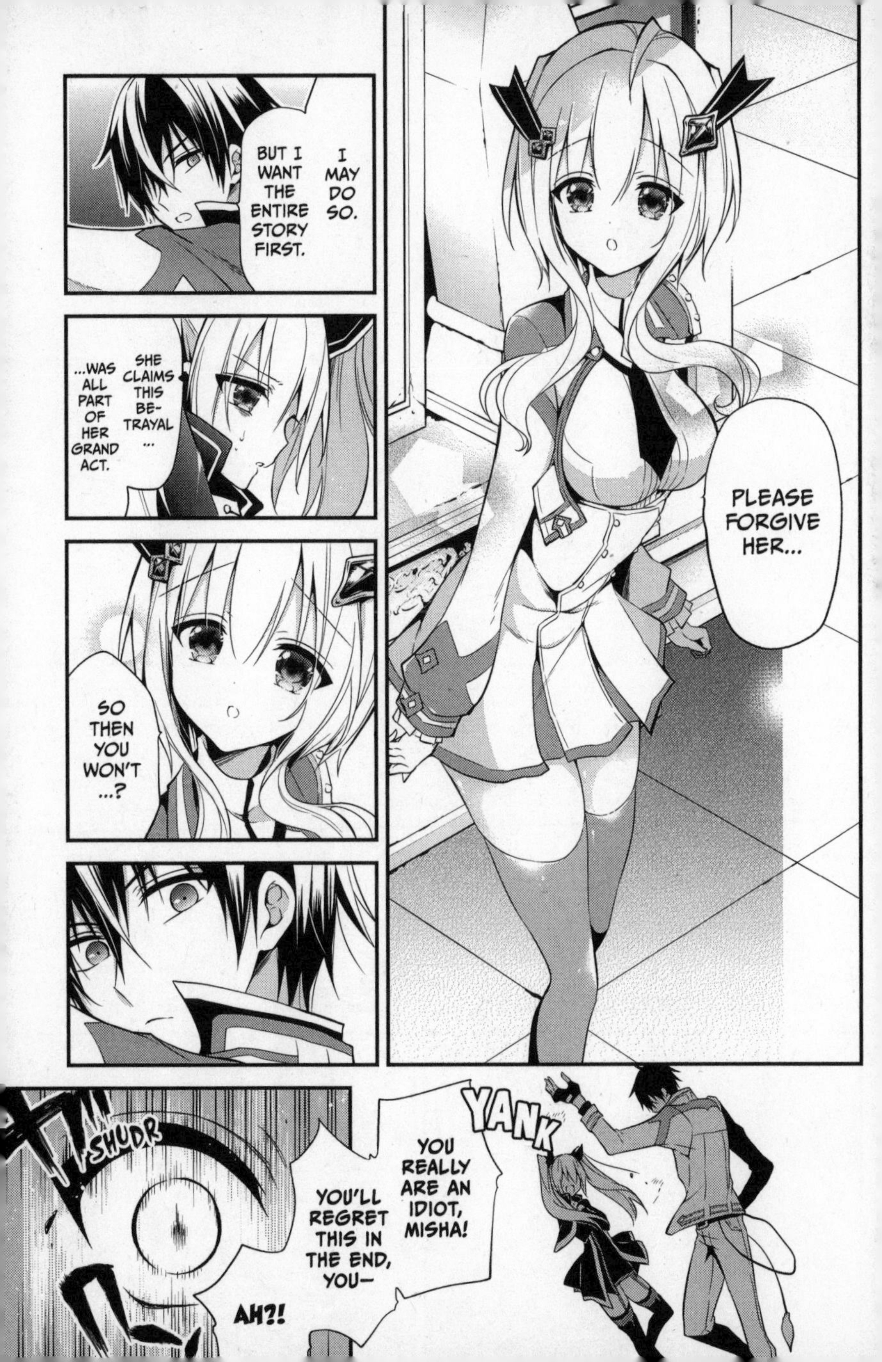
PLEASE FORGIVE HER...
I MAY DO SO.
BUT I WANT THE ENTIRE STORY FIRST.
SHE CLAIMS THIS BE-TRAYAL...
...WAS ALL PART OF HER GRAND ACT.
SO THEN YOU WON'T ...?
YANK
YOU REALLY ARE AN IDIOT, MISHA!
YOU'LL REGRET THIS IN THE END, YOU—
SHUDR
AH?!

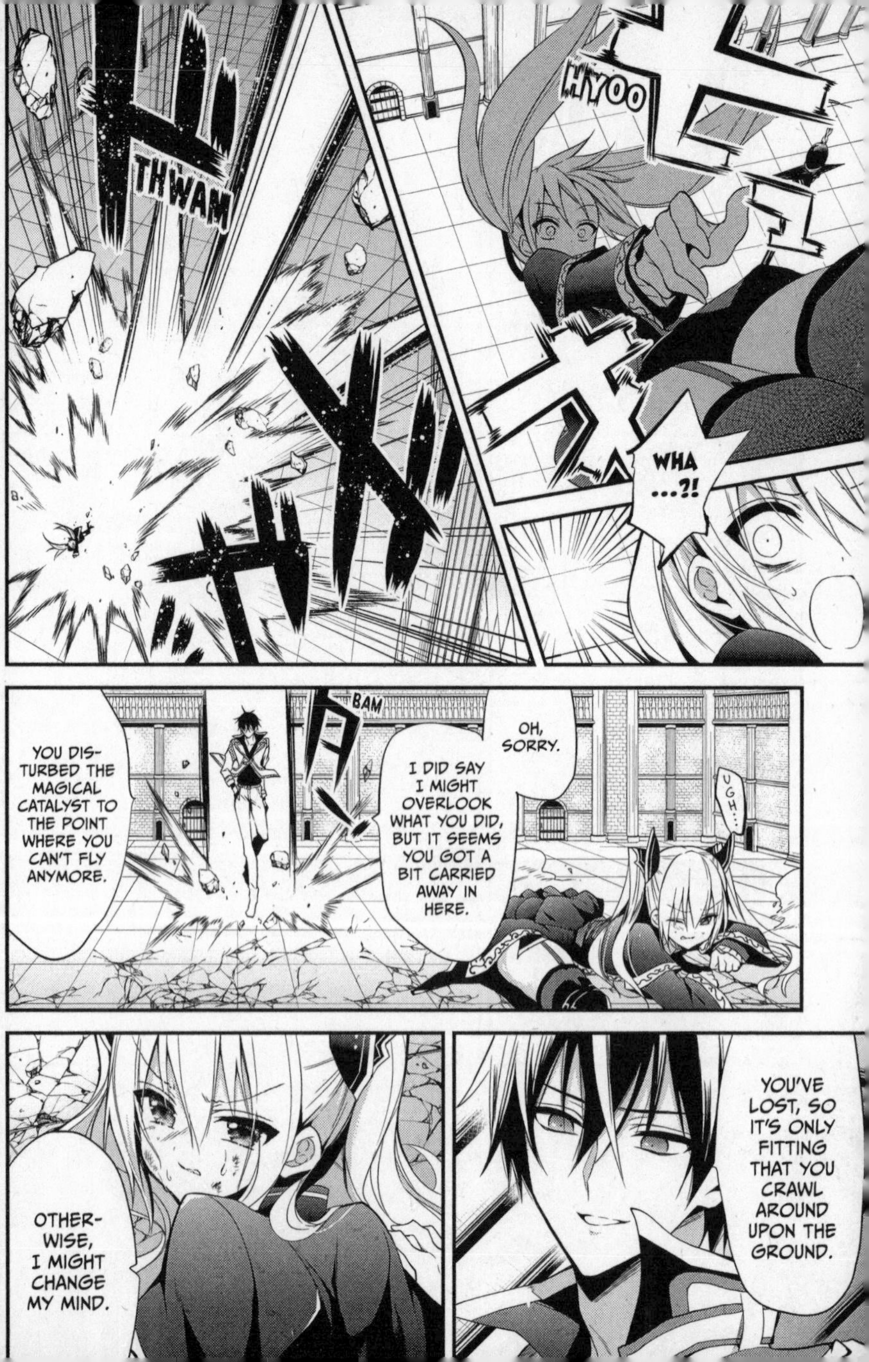
HYOO
WHA ...?!
THWAM
BAM
OH, SORRY.
I DID SAY I MIGHT OVERLOOK WHAT YOU DID, BUT IT SEEMS YOU GOT A BIT CARRIED AWAY IN HERE.
UGH...
YOU DIS-TURBED THE MAGICAL CATALYST TO THE POINT WHERE YOU CAN'T FLY ANYMORE.
YOU'VE LOST, SO IT'S ONLY FITTING THAT YOU CRAWL AROUND UPON THE GROUND.
OTHER-WISE, I MIGHT CHANGE MY MIND.

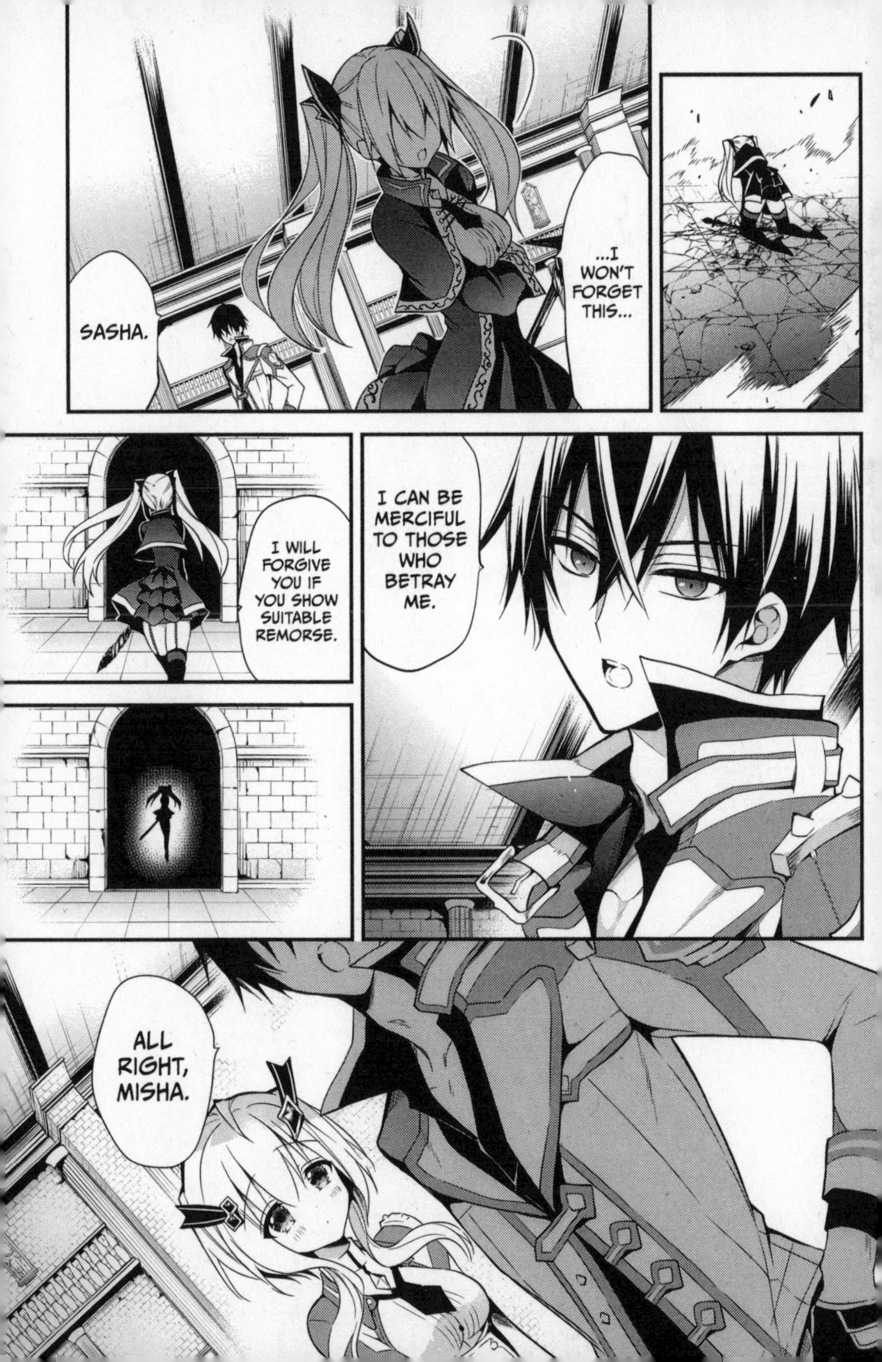
...I WON'T FORGET THIS...
SASHA.
I CAN BE MERCIFUL TO THOSE WHO BETRAY ME.
I WILL FORGIVE YOU IF YOU SHOW SUITABLE REMORSE.
ALL RIGHT, MISHA.

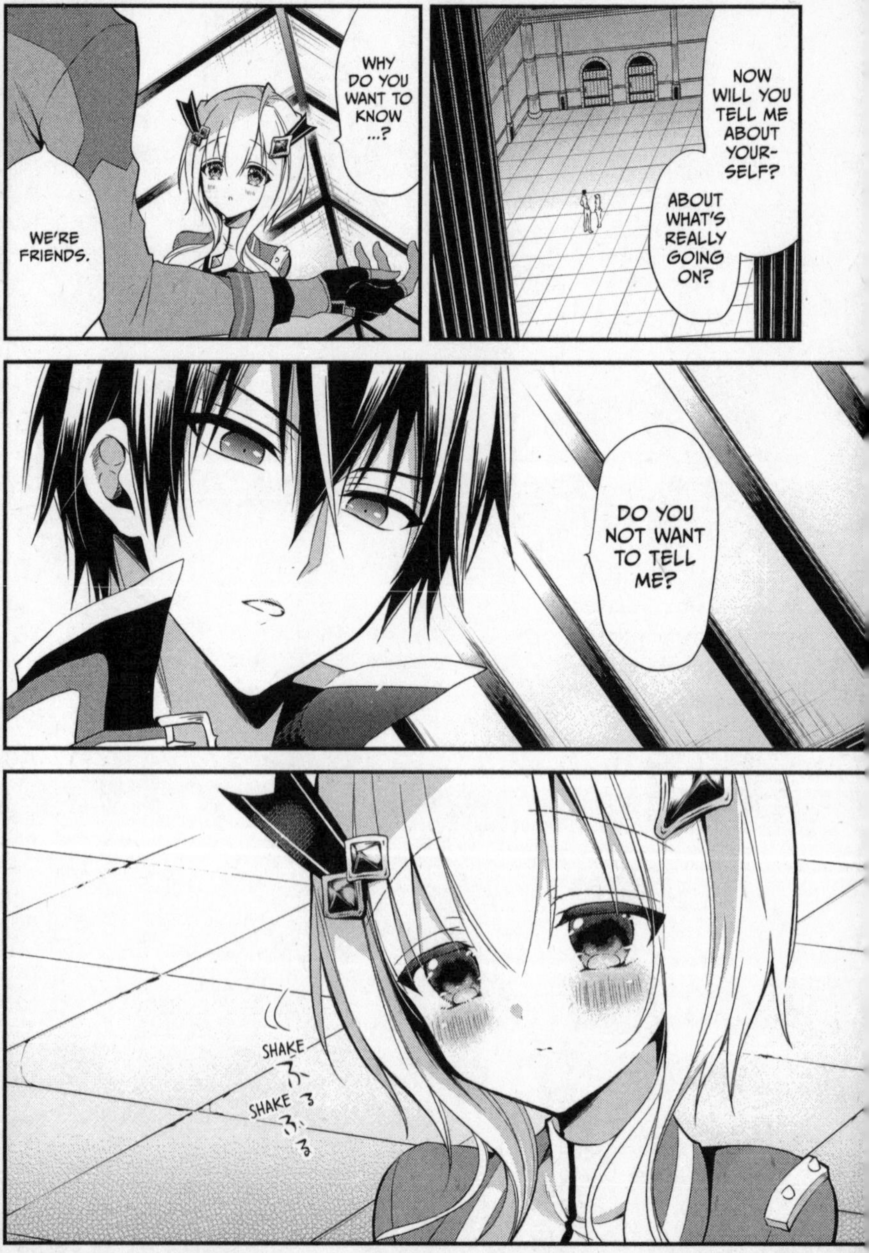
NOW WILL YOU TELL ME ABOUT YOUR-SELF?
ABOUT WHAT'S REALLY GOING ON?
WHY DO YOU WANT TO KNOW ...?
WE'RE FRIENDS.
DO YOU NOT WANT TO TELL ME?
SHAKE
SHAKE

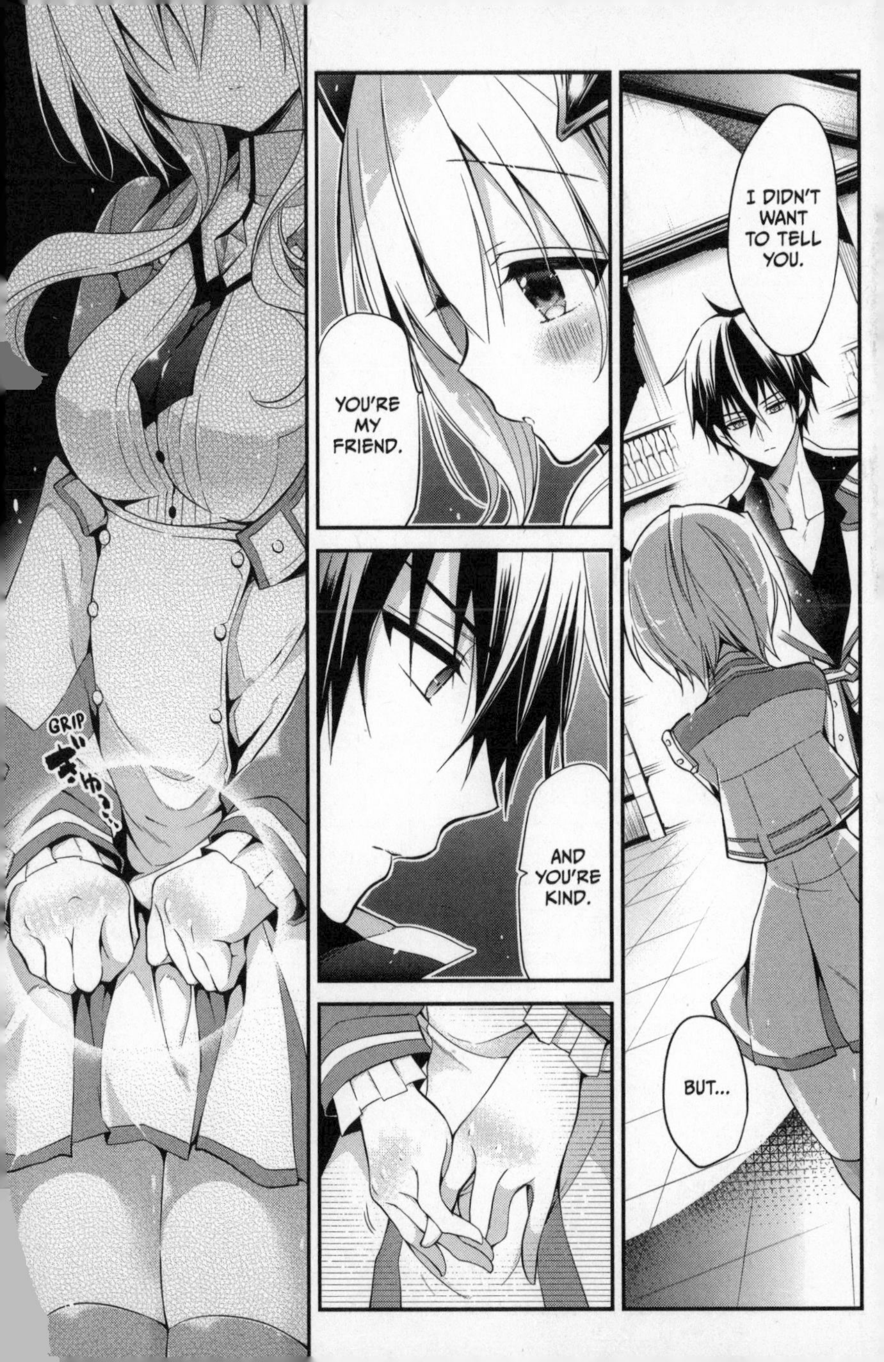
I DIDN'T WANT TO TELL YOU.
BUT...
YOU'RE MY FRIEND.
AND YOU'RE KIND.
GRIP

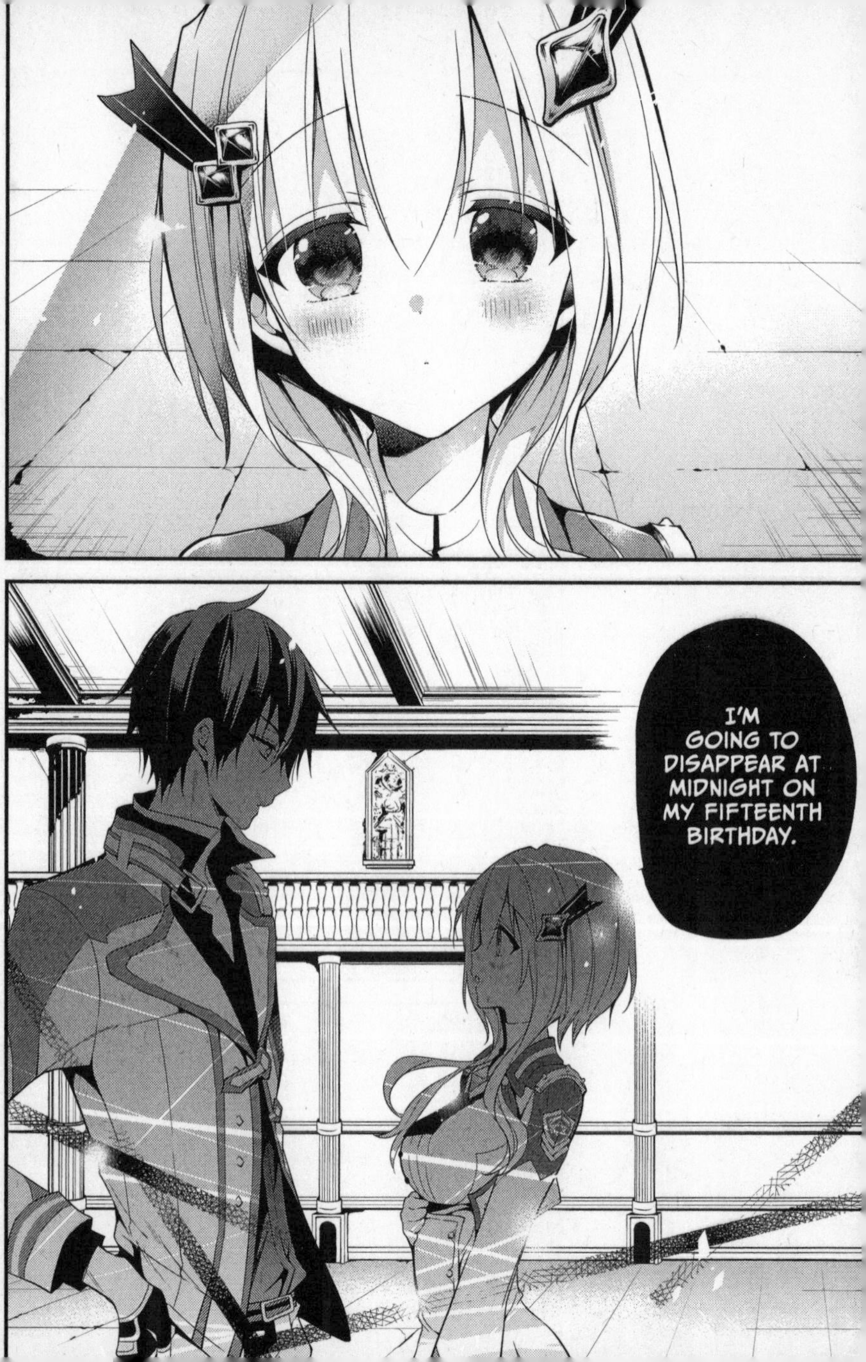
I'M GOING TO DISAPPEAR AT MIDNIGHT ON MY FIFTEENTH BIRTHDAY.

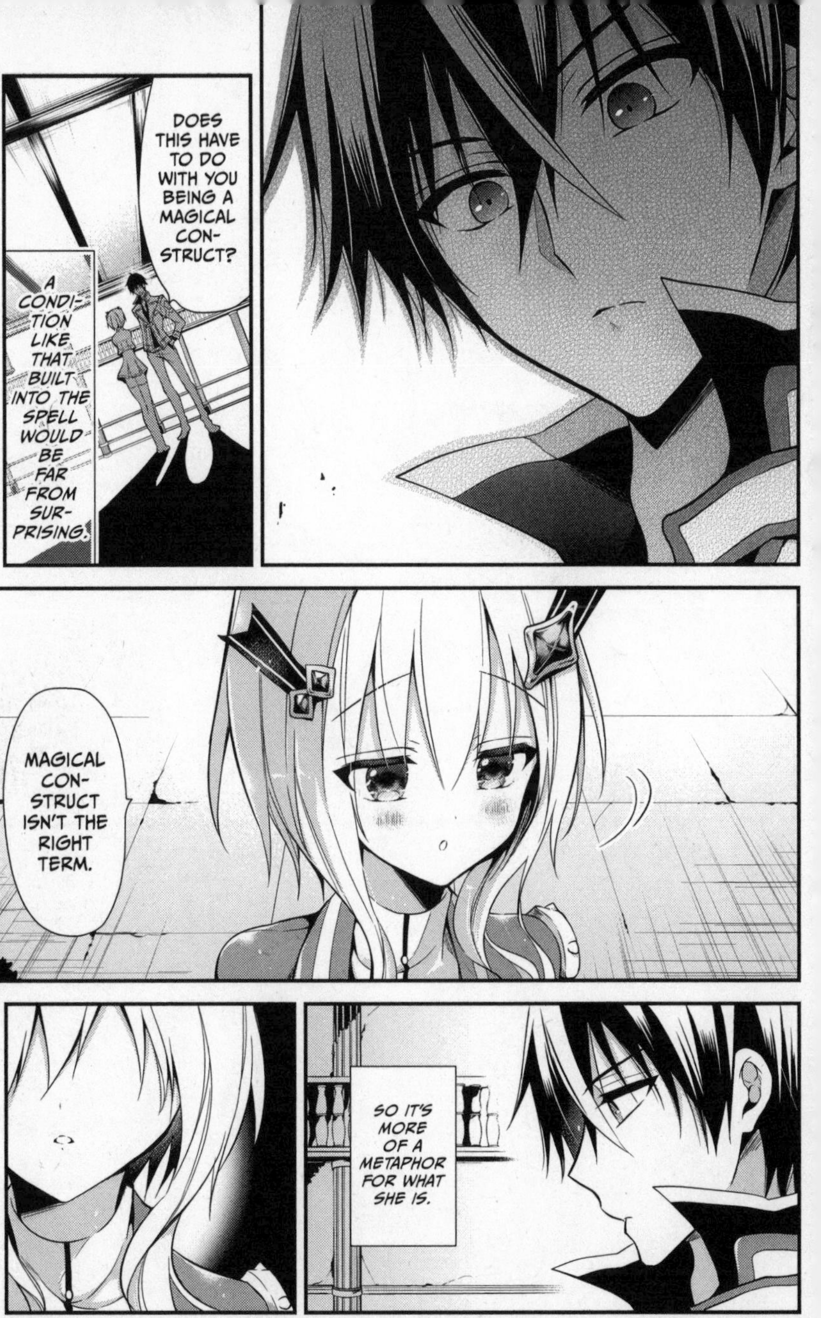
DOES THIS HAVE TO DO WITH YOU BEING A MAGICAL CON-STRUCT?
A CONDI-TION LIKE THAT BUILT INTO THE SPELL WOULD BE FAR FROM SUR-PRISING.
MAGICAL CON-STRUCT ISN'T THE RIGHT TERM.
SO IT'S MORE OF A METAPHOR FOR WHAT SHE IS.

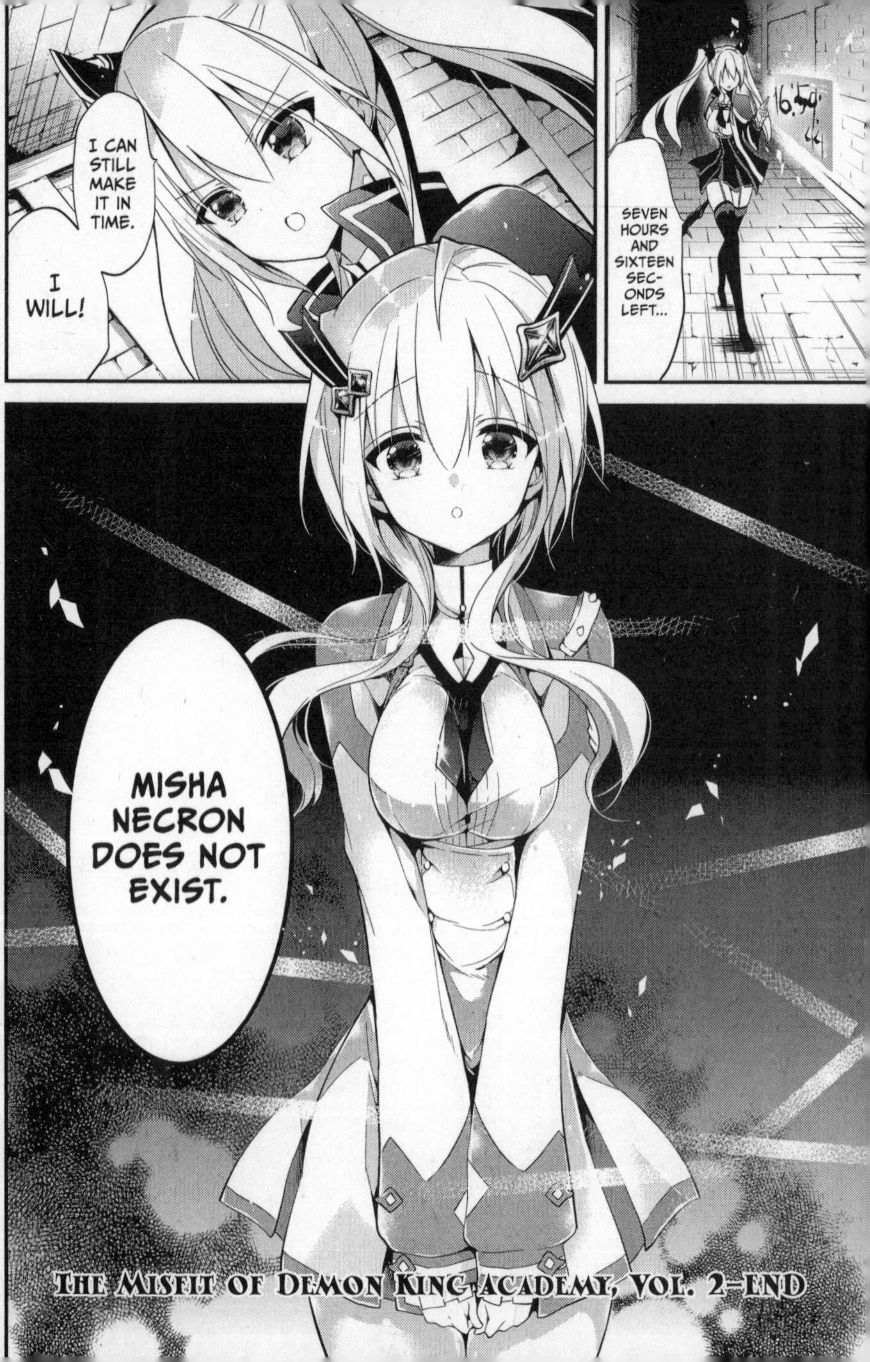
SEVEN HOURS AND SIXTEEN SEC- ONDS LEFT...
I CAN STILL MAKE IT IN TIME.
I WILL!
MISHA NECRON DOES NOT EXIST.
THE MISFIT OF DEMON KING ACADEMY, VOL. 2—END

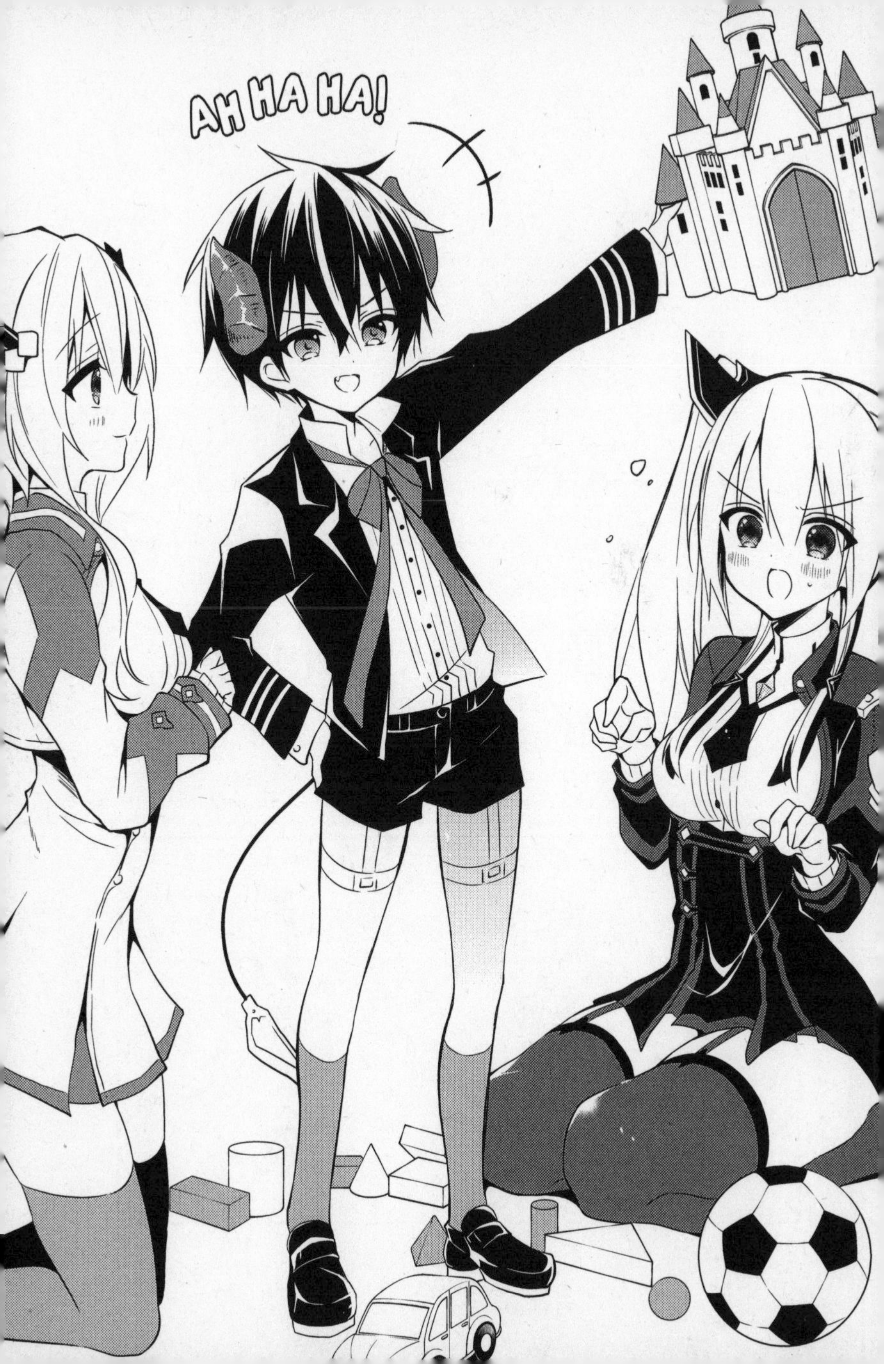
AH HA HA!

The Misfit of Demon King Academy

HISTORY'S STRONGEST DEMON KING REINCARNATES AND GOES TO SCHOOL WITH HIS DESCENDANTS

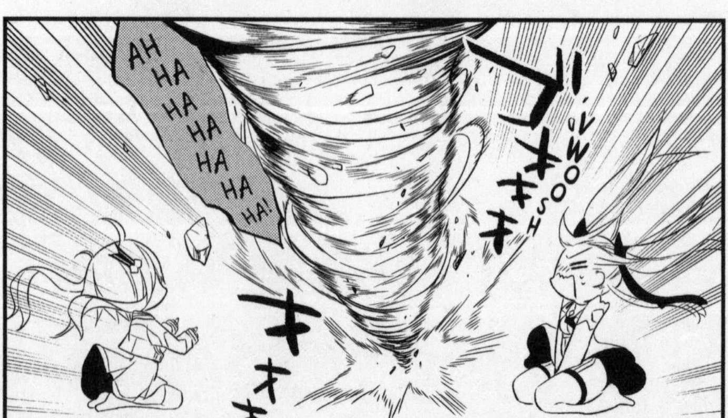

AH HA HA HA HA HA HA!
WOOSH

SHU (Story)

Since the scope of a manga is smaller than that of a novel,
I had to trim down the original text and figure out how to set
the scenes properly on a different scale. In this second volume,
that gave me a lot of headaches. Another difference between
manga and novels is that while you're in the drafting phase for
manga you have to think about the paneling too, not just the
writing. So as with first volume, I had my work cut out for me.
The story starts to pick up in this volume, so I hope you
enjoy both the plot advancement and Kaya sensei's incredible
portrayals of Anoth and the other characters.

KAYAHARUKA (Art)

I'm thrilled that I get to draw Anoth as part of my work. I have
a huge amount of respect for SHU sensei! The characters'
backstories and Anoth's magnetic appeal are just so well made.
It's clear Anoth really is the Demon King!

The Misfit of Demon King Academy

2

ORIGINAL STORY BY SHU
ART BY KAYAHARUKA
CHARACTER DESIGN BY YOSHINORI SHIZUMA

Translation: Leighann Harvey
Lettering: Phil Christie
Cover Design: Andrea Miller
Editor: Leyla Aker

THE MISFIT OF DEMON KING ACADEMY Volume 2
© SHU 2019
© 2019 Kayaharuka/SQUARE ENIX CO., LTD.
Licensed by KADOKAWA CORPORATION
First published in Japan in 2019 by SQUARE ENIX CO., LTD.
English translation rights arranged with SQUARE ENIX CO., LTD. and SQUARE ENIX INC.
English translation © 2020 by SQUARE ENIX CO., LTD.

ISBN: 978-1-64609-043-3

Library of Congress Cataloging-in-Publication data is on file with the publisher.

Printed in the U.S.A.
First printing, August 2020
10 9 8 7 6 5 4 3 2 1

SQUARE ENIX
MANGA & BOOKS

www.square-enix-books.com